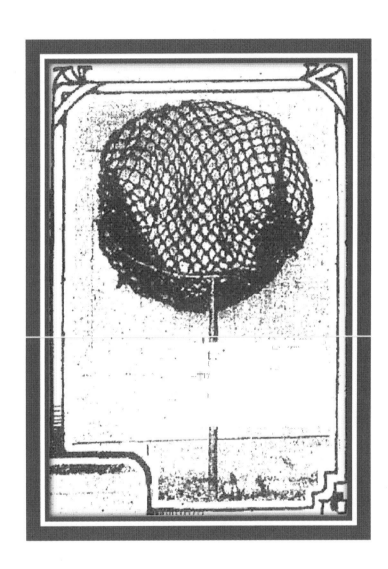

MANGY CURS AND STONED HORSES:

ANIMAL CONTROL IN THE DISTRICT OF COLUMBIA FROM THE BEGINNINGS TO ABOUT 1940

HAYDEN M. WETZEL

INTRODUCTION BY DR. BERNARD UNTI

WITH DRAWINGS BY LAURA FRIEND SMYTHE

2019

Complete Copy

This work is licensed under the Creative Commons Attribution-NonCommercial 4.0 International License.

TABLE OF CONTENTS

Foreword i

Introduction iii

Part One: The Corporations of Washington and Georgetown (1791-1871) 1

    Chapter 1   Farm Animals 3

                    Summary of laws (Colonial-era – Georgetown – City of Washington) – Narrative

    Chapter 2   Dogs 11

                    Summary of laws (Georgetown – City of Washington – Country of Washington) – Narrative

    Chapter 3   The Corporation Pound 17

                    William M. Simaker – A proposed dog-pound

    Chapter 4   Cruelty to Animals 21

                    Summary of laws (City of Washington – Georgetown)

    Chapter 5   Summary 23

    Chapter 6   Dead Animals 25

                    Georgetown – City of Washington – County of Washington

    Illustrations: One Hundred Years of Advertising Found Animals
                    Early Legal Notices

Part Two: The Territorial and Early Commissioner Period (1871-1912) 31

    Chapter 7   The Contractor Pound 33

                    Poundmasters T. Zell Hoover – M. M. Wheelock and Von Essen Essex – J. H. Smith and A. L. G. Mason – Henry Young – A proposed County pound

    Chapter 8   Samuel Einstein 41

    Chapter 9   Legalities of the Pound Operations 45

                    Farm animals – Dogs – Jurisdiction – Things the pound didn't do

    Chapter 10   Corralling the Population of Farm Animals 49

                    Early trials – Success – Chickens

    Chapter 11   The Dog War 55

                    A typical expedition – Dog tax/tags – Muzzles/Rabies – The mad-dog scare of 1899 – Dog-Owners' Association of DC – George W. Evans – T. Edward Clark – Muzzling becomes quasi-permanent (orders of 1908, 1910) – Cecil French – Types of muzzles – "At Large"/Leashing – Washington Kennel Club – Bringing the dog population to heel – Private legal actions

Chapter 12   Cats 79

> *Washington Cat Club – Voluntary impounding of cats – Mrs. Henry L. West – Cats taken from the streets*

Chapter 13   Pound Operations and Miscellany 85

> *Poundmaster – Staff – Equipment/Uniforms – Facilities – Conditions – Redemption/ Purchase of animals – Killing animals – Finances – Record-keeping – Jurisdiction – Relationship with MPDC – Legal challenges – Pound mascots and escapees*

Chapter 14   Einstein's Last Years: The Pound as an Institution 109

> *The pound's work widely accepted – Einstein honored*

Chapter 15   Amazing Adventures of the District Poundmen 113

Chapter 16   Theodore Gatchel and the Establishment of the SPCA 117

> *Theodore F. Gatchel – Early history of the Society*

Chapter 17   SPCA and WHS 121

> *New Initiatives (paid agents – abused children) – SPCA becomes WHS – General organization/ operations – The Cruelty Act of 1892 – Operations "on the street" – Relationship with MPDC/ with the city's population – Makeup of membership/of abusers – Horses vs. dogs/cats vs. autos – Attempt to take over the pound – Horse Owners' Mutual Protective Association – District Team Owners' Association*

Chapter 18   Summary 141

Chapter 19   Dead Animals 143

> *Board of Health – F. M. Draney – Patrick Mann – Legalities – Washington Fertilizer Company – Miscellany*

Illustrations: The Poundmasters
               The Poundmen
               Scenes from the Dog War
               Boys vs. Dog-Catchers
               Pet Paraphernalia
               The Old Pound
               The New Pound
               Einstein at Rest
               WHS Notices
               WHS Graphics and Shelter
               The 1895 Municipal Trash Incinerator

Part Three: The Later Commissioner Period (1913-40) 163

Chapter 20   The Pound Under Later Poundmasters 165

> *Poundmasters Emil Kuhn – George W. Rae – Edgar R. Sando – Walter R. Smith – Frank B. Mark – The 1939 review of animal laws – Farm animals/chickens/homing pigeons/others – Dogs (rabies/muzzling – leashing – act of 1945 – neighboring jurisdictions – licensing) – Cats – Operations – Portraits of the poundmaster's duties in 1930/in 1941 – The pound in a new era*

| Chapter 21 | The Washington Humane Society (Continued) | 181 |

Funding/Membership – Finding new issues – John P. Heap – WHS's Time of Troubles

| Chapter 22 | The Early Shelter Movement | 185 |

Shelter vs. pound – Legalities – Cat shelters (Barber Refuge for Animals – Mr. and Mrs. Frank J. Buckley – WHS's replacement shelter – Sarah L. Beckley – Mrs. Beckley's cat shelter – The Friendly Hand Society) – Dog shelters (Society for Friendless Dogs)

| Chapter 23 | The Washington Animal Rescue League | 191 |

Establishment – Relationship with WHS – Goals and plans – The first three shelters and their procedures – Killing animals – Abandonment of pets for vacations – Christmas Feast for Horses and other projects – Finances – Governance – Tales from the WARL Shelter *– The O Street shelter – WARL/WHS compared – Three adjunct organizations (Washington Herald/ Times-Herald Animal Rescue Service – Maryland-Virginia Animal Rescue League – Tail-Waggers' Club)*

| Chapter 24 | Later Humane Organizations | 209 |

Humane Education Society – James P. Briggs – Virginia W. Sargent – Church Humane Education League/Animal Relief and Humane Education League/Animal Protective Association – Times Free Animal Clinic – Animal Defense Society – Other humane organizations (suburban – coordinating – ancillary)

| Chapter 25 | Summary | 219 |
| Chapter 26 | Dead Animals | 221 |

The District takes over the service

Illustrations: Cat Shelters
WARL in the News
The WARL Shelter
Personages
Secondary Shelters

Afterword: What Happened to Them All 231

The Pound (legalities/procedures – Animal Allocation Board – Poundmaster John R. King, Jr. – moving the pound – public criticism – Poundmaster Ingrid Newkirk – WHS takes over) – WHS – WARL – HES/NHES – Other humane organizations – Dead animals

Illustrations: The Facilities Today

Appendix A: Basics of District of Columbia History 241

A1: Chronology of District Governance
A2: Maps of the District, 1854 and 1891
A3: Population of the District

Appendix B: Laws Relating to Animal Control..245

Appendix C: Statistical Complications 263

    C1: Farms and Farm Animals in the District of Columbia
    C2: Complaints Regarding Hogs, Cows and Fowl
    C3: Animal Capture Statistics
    C4: Dog Tax Receipts, Pound Income ("Pound Fees"), and Pound Expenses
    C5: Animal-Related Arrests/Prosecutions
    C6: Cases of/Deaths from Rabies
    C7: Animal Cruelty Statistics
    C8: Animals in Shelters
    C9: Collection of Dead Animals

Appendix D: Textual and Other Materials 301

    D1: Board of Health Minutes Regarding Animals and the Pound, 1822-78
    D2: Good Newspaper Profiles of the Pound and Its Operations/of WHS Operations/of the WARL Shelter/of the HES Shelter
    D3: Pictures of the Dog Hunt (The Epic of the Raid – Boys vs. Dog-Catchers – Chatter Among the Poundmen)
    D4: The District Pound Compared with Those of Other Cities
    D5: Citizens Write MPDC About Dogs
    D6: The Mythical Origin of Washington's Stray Animals
    D7: Mark Twain Lampoons the Animal Problem in Washington
    D8: Washington Cats Immortalized (?) in Poetry
    D9: Samples of Cases Handled by SPCA/WHS Agents
    D10: Mrs. Beckley and Her Cat Shelter
    D11: The WARL Shelter Compared with the Pound
    D12: U.S. Capitol Police Deal with Critters (and Humans)
    D13: Tangential Notes on Animals in the District (Dog names and breeds, common and presidential – Buying pets – U.S. Government cats – Rats and cats flee Center Market – Starlings! Pigeons! Squirrels! – In-town hunting – Protecting animals in wartime)
    D14: Miscellaneous Notes for Further Research

Bibliography 337

Notes on Sources 345

Foreword

When people consider urban development many issues come to mind: sewage, finances, policing, transportation, administration . . . Seldom do we think of animal control. The reason for this is that in most cities – certainly in the U.S. – this is one urban problem that has been solved. Virtually none of us have experience with wandering cattle and pigs, or packs of unhoused dogs in our streets and parks. And yet this success did not grow by itself like a weed, but had to be planned and nurtured; it was the result of conscious effort and supportive trends – urbanization, mechanization, our evolving view of animals as pets rather than work-animals – in society.

The present study follows the development of animal control in the specific case of the nation's capital, Washington, D.C. It grew from a request of the Southwest Neighborhood Assembly, a community group in Southwest Washington, for me to research a modest brick building in its neighborhood for nomination as a city landmark site (which would give it protection from demolition); it turned out to be the old District pound. Entering this virgin topic, I ran into the annual Poundmaster Reports and was soon swept down a current of fascinating and highly entertaining information into an unexplored world of . . . well, the reader will see this world himself. I will say only that I soon had enough information to write the history of the building and then needed to decide what to do with the rest – throw it away, or go on and write up the whole thing. Here is the result.

This is, as far as I can find, the sole general case study of the history of animal control in an American city. In only a few important instances (the establishment of our pound, for example) did I make an attempt to learn what was happening in other places. "Animal Control" here means animals in public places: streets and parks, markets, uninvited in peoples' front yards – treatment of animals in farms, slaughterhouses, stables, zoos, and other private places is left for someone else to research.

Other topics bypassed are: the role of animals in the local economy; protection of wild animals in the larger parks; such humane concerns as vivisection, treatment of animals in transshipment through the city, and other issues that were essentially lobbying projects; conditions and regulation of veterinarians; racing; circuses and exhibitions; farm regulations; extermination of rodents, insects and other pests; regulation of pet stores; disposal of fish offal from wharves and carcasses from butcher shops and other commercial places; city- and federally-owned animals such as Fire Department horses and police dogs; and hunting regulations. In a few cases these are touched on, usually in footnotes, when I had some information to record. A few notes toward further study of these subjects are given in the Appendix.

I have tried to pay special attention to the popular and legal aspects of leashing dogs in public places, inasmuch as this is such a standard part of our current etiquette.

This study led me a long and enjoyable chase through many local archives and libraries, gratefully acknowledged in the footnotes, bibliography and the related Notes on Sources. Three promising sources are unhappily absent: the records of the Health Officer beyond the published annual reports (including, alas! that office's ordinances), and records (including opinions) of the Police Court, both of which seem not to have survived; and complaints of early travelers about the city's unseemly quadrupeds, which would have required thumbing through many, many volumes for the chance observation.

Believing that few would care to re-trace my steps through so much primary material I have been as thorough as reasonably possible with this study; hence the larding of the footnotes. To make further research convenient I have organized all copied material (including texts of all laws and regulations that I found, and a full set of Poundmaster Annual Reports) for deposit in the Washingtoniana Division of the Martin Luther King Library here in the city, where I found so much useful information.

If I am the father of this work then Mr. Bernard Unti of the Humane Society of the United States is its midwife. He oversaw its final trimester, arranged the hospital (publishing venue) and oversaw the actual procedure, all with sympathy and graciousness; I cannot thank him enough. His colleague, Mr. Erich Yahner, patiently formatted the text and illustrations preparatory to uploading and this was an onerous and much-appreciated effort.

Regarding the illustrations: Most of the graphic material seen here comes from contemporary newspapers, often now only available on microfilm, which does not scan or copy well; drawings come through all right but not photographs. Ms. Laura Friend Smythe (https://www.laurafriendart.com/), a professional artist (and attorney), has reproduced a number of these graphics with great fidelity and to very good effect. All of these drawings are copyright Laura Friend Smythe.

All materials taken from the Evening Star after 1923 are under copyright held now by the Washington Post (which bought the defunct Star holdings); permission to use these items is controlled by the D. C. Public Library system, Washingtoniana Division/Evening Star Collection, which generously allowed me to use them without the usual fee. I also thank the Humane Rescue Alliance which has been most kind in giving me access to both the WHS and WARL archives and permission to reproduce this material.

And finally, a sort of apologia: I came into this study without the need so frequently felt by academic writers to demonstrate some great cosmic thesis, or the goal seen in chroniclers of the humane movement to advocate a cause – this is simply a straight-forward history with occasional and obvious conclusions noted. In this modest ambition I have followed the historian's charge as stated by one of my favorite practitioners, William Prescott, namely that of "advancing the interests of humanity by the diffusion of useful truth."

(This "complete copy" corrects various small spelling and format errors and most importantly restores one page of material on the early career of Virginia Sargent which had dropped out of the initial uploaded document. I thank my long-time colleague Mr. Valentin Vucea for his generous editing work.)

Hayden M. Wetzel
haydenwetzel@hotmail.com

I take this opportunity to honor Mr. Kael Anderson, resident of southwest Washington and past president of the Southwest Neighborhood Assembly, who has worked with great diligence to save the history of his community, including the old District pound.

INTRODUCTION

Hayden Wetzel's monograph on animal control in the District of Columbia is a remarkable achievement. To my knowledge, no one else has carried out a community-level study of comparable depth and scope for any other town or city, making this a wonderful example for other researchers and scholars to follow. It was a prodigious undertaking to locate, examine, and evaluate the suite of municipal laws and statutes involved, to gather popular references and images from the nineteenth century press, and to make gainful use of the limited sources available in organizational archives. It is a richly sourced work, and a well-interpreted one.

As a kind of microhistory, Wetzel's work contains many insights about the transition from the traditional domestic animal economy to the era of modern pet-keeping. It traces this evolution through social practices, law, and administrative regimes. It is at once a history of municipal government, of public health, of social practices, and of animal protection. The story Wetzel relates is also overlaid with the history of class and race in the city, and of Washington's status as the nation's capital.

As a contribution to the history of animal protection, Wetzel's scholarship helps to situate American's nineteenth and early twentieth century humane societies as public health institutions, with duties and responsibilities similar to those of a municipal services agency.

But their first charge was to end cruelty. Animal protection was one of the most vital of social reforms in the post-Civil War period, as the first societies for the prevention of cruelty to animals took on cruelty to horses used for conveyance and transportation, the suffering of farm animals transported to slaughter via railroad, animal fighting, inhumane methods of euthanasia, and other problems. A rapidly urbanizing and industrializing society produced more visible and severe cruelty that reformers recognized as a substantial evil. Animal cruelty was also a problem because of its connections to social disorder and domestic violence. For that reason, animal protection had strong ties to the temperance and child protection movements which shared its concerns about the social threats associated with male violence – against animals, against women, against children.

The movement spread rapidly throughout the United States in the period 1866-1900, with independent humane societies forming in both large and small communities. They worked, sometimes at close quarters with municipal authorities and agencies, to address a wide range of issues tied to the presence of animals. By the 1880s, more and more humane societies concentrated their focus on municipal animal control, promoting reforms or taking charge of the dog pounds in their communities. In time, they constructed and operated their own shelter facilities to carry out such work, picking up strays, investigating cruelty, educating the public, and eventually, becoming centers of animal adoption.

As Wetzel demonstrates, in Washington at least, private societies did not always get on well with municipal agencies, or with one another. But they shared a common burden, of ensuring that their community brought a measure of kindness to its dealings with animals, while safeguarding human and animal health. Over time, the evolution of their work and duties came to reflect the growing shift from purely utilitarian attitudes to more affectionate views of animals.

Today, Washington, DC is home to local, regional, and national animal protection societies of great distinction and reach. Wetzel's monograph grounds their origins and history, too, and stands as a kind of prehistory of present and future developments of which most of the individuals he writes about here could never have imagined.

Dr. Bernard Unti
The Humane Society of the United States

PART ONE

The Corporations of Washington and Georgetown
(1791-1871)

The hotel in which we live is a long row of small houses fronting on the street, and opening at the back upon a common yard . . . Two great dogs are playing upon a mound of loose bricks in the centre of the little square; a pig is turning up his stomach to the sun, and grunting "that's comfortable!" (Charles Dickens, <u>American Notes for General Circulation</u>. 1842, pp. 279-80)

A bachelor correspondent . . . writes us from 12th Street between F and H: . . . "a locality undisturbed by the sacrilegious tread of the policeman, . . . where rank weeds overgrow the pavement, and where cows, hogs, ducks and goats revel in . . . unrestricted freedom, and where alleys swelter in filth and reek in rottenness; where night is made hideous by the shouts and yells of boys who nightly congregate there, and to which, when added the barking of dogs, the mewing of cats, and the screams of . . . unattended babies, there is furnished a scene outrivaling Pandemonium and Bedlam combined. . . From whence cometh relief?" (Evening Star, 4 Sept 1868, p.4)

Animal control in the nation's capital before 1871 developed along two general tracks:

- Horses, livestock, geese and other domestic animals (referred to here as "farm animals") generally constituted a nuisance only when they strayed into city streets and private property. Although these animals required more trouble to house than dogs, they represented less of a financial burden for the city because their owners were likely to redeem them and if not then they could generally be sold to the public;

- Dogs, on the other hand, were always far more plentiful on the streets, were less likely to be redeemed, and had less of a market (mostly as pets, guard dogs and hunting use). Not only were they a nuisance and sometimes aggressive but they carried rabies. For the city government stray dogs were mostly a problem and financial drain.

Under the separate Corporations of Washington and Georgetown (1791-1871) animals came under city purview only because they were a nuisance – strays, abandoned, or dangerous. Broad protection of animals out of concern for their own welfare—"cruelty to animals"—did not enter into municipal regulations until 1871, although some earlier laws imposed fines for specific mistreatment.

Sources: With fewer newspaper articles than in the later periods and almost no government reports available, animal control efforts in the District of Columbia for this early time are mostly documented through the laws of the two Corporations. These generally will be referenced in text by their year of approval but are listed more specifically in the list of Laws Relating to Animal Control in Appendix B. (A diligent search turned up no Congressional statutes relating to animals in the District from this period.)

CHAPTER ONE

Farm Animals

Cows had the run of the town from Georgetown to Anacostia Creek, grazing on the pavements, breaking into front yards, disturbing the slumbers of the citizens by their incessant lowing, and making themselves generally obnoxious. (Reminiscences of a retired policeman, Wash. Post, 7 Sept 1902, p. 22)

When we lived on 4th Street, opposite Judiciary Square, every evening we watched the cows passing along the street and over the common at the side of our house, to their home in Swampoodle for their milking. (From the account of an early resident; Kelly, "Memories")

Some Quixotic citizens of Georgetown are laboring to prevent swine from running at large in the streets. Useless effort – the owners of the hogs have votes. (Evening Star, 1 May 1869, p. 2)

Stray farm animals were the most obvious problem for early Washingtonians. We will first summarize the legal trail; if this is too tedious the reader might skim it and go to the Narrative below.

Summary of Laws

The earliest (**colonial-era**) laws[1] relating to animals in the area of Washington dealt with farm animals, and this is natural since there were no sizeable towns where stray dogs could congregate but certainly many farms from which valuable stock could wander. A 1715 statute of Maryland penalized those killing strays ("estrays") and then removing ownership marks, and another of the same year permitted finders to shoot any stray horse after twice notifying the animal's owner.[2] Numerous acts of the State from the 1790s dealt with loose swine and geese in various towns, such as that of 1799 prohibiting hogs in Montgomery County "within three miles of Georgetown" and allowing anyone finding strays there to sell the animals.[3] The 1748 act of incorporation for Alexandria, Virginia,[4] prohibited the keeping of unenclosed swine within the city

---

[1] The District continued to recognize colonial and early State laws if no Congressional or District act specifically dealt with a particular issue, and these early laws formed the background of later D.C. regulations. For a brief resume of District governance and development see Appendix A.

[2] "Md., 1715, ch. 26, sec. 5 and 6", summarized in Thompson, M., An Analytical Digest . . ., 1863, p. 414 (see also ch. 31, sec.1 of the same year, cited in Compiled Statutes . . . 1887-'98), full text of both in Kilty, The Laws of Maryland. The latter law ("to prevent. . . the great evil [of] the multiplicity of useless horses, mares and colts that run in the woods") was referred to, curiously, in a legal case of 1876 (Evening Star, 3 May 1876, p. 4, "The Horse Shooting Case").

[3] Davis, William A., The Acts of Congress . . ., pp. 497-498. Kilty, The Laws of Maryland, includes all of these, which I have copied and deposited with the other materials from this research.

[4] Davis, p. 535.

limits and allowed "any person whatsoever to kill or destroy the same," but they must then inform the owner.

The 1819 Code of Laws for the District of Columbia (which gathered all laws then in force, though many passed at an earlier time) included comprehensive rules and penalties regarding enclosures of property and trespass of animals onto legally fenced land. This act "Regarding Enclosures and Certain Trespasses" allowed "any person" (there was no mention of constables) to hold horses or "any beast" found on their property "in any open pound" until the owners paid a fine and expenses to the finder. The same law similarly regulated boats found adrift.

Georgetown's earliest ordinance regarding nuisance farm animals (1791) allowed "all person or persons" to kill stray geese or swine (later the word "hog" was more commonly used) on sight. The finder must then inform the authorities and deliver the carcass to the town market; if the owner did not claim it within four hours the finder could take possession and sell it himself. It was "the particular duty of the Constables to attend to the carrying of this law into effect." An act of 1795 limited the capture of swine to whites, who could keep the animal "for his own use." An officer finding stray swine was to immediately sell the carcass at the market and "for his trouble" split the proceeds with the Corporation. This process was extended to goats the following year. In October 1796 owners of strays were fined $2 and responsibility for the animal's removal "in any means they may judge proper" specifically given to the constabulary. "Stoned horses" (those having stones, or testicles, i.e., stallions) came under penalty of $20 per day if untended on the street in 1799, the fine shared by the finder ("informer") and Corporation. Restrictions on horses[5] tightened in 1814.

The Corporation greatly restricted the raising of swine within city limits in 1827 (strengthening these regulations in 1858 and 1862), and cows in 1865.

In 1837 custody of stray animals was given to the Corporation's Poor House, which sold them. Owners could redeem their stock for a fine (which, of course, increased over the years). Anyone attempting to "rescue" animals from the Poor House "may be seized" and fined ($1-10).[6] Further acts (1845, 1858) required the Poor House to pay the constables for each delivery.[7] By 1859 the Corporation had to demand that the recalcitrant Poor House return all hogs to their owners if they showed up to claim the animals, a law which needed to be stated again in 1867.

Apparently the police resisted this task, since the 1837 and later ordinances specified that they were required to perform their duty under penalty of fine. Payment to the police for the expense of rounding up and holding stray swine became a city line-item in 1862.

Statutes for the City of **Washington** largely followed the trends in Georgetown, if enacted somewhat later. A March 1809 act[8] outlawed stray swine and allowed "any citizen or constable" to butcher an unmarked (lacking "iron rings in their snouts") stray and divide the resulting proceeds with "the poor of the Corporation." Later that year the keeping of unenclosed swine was prohibited south of Massachusetts Avenue. 1836 and 1838 acts specified the nature of legal enclosures and clearly gave responsibility of enforcement to the constables. The city's half of sales proceeds bobbled from the Asylum to the Corporation coffers (Oct 1809), to the Asylum (1817), to the Corporation (1820), and back to the Asylum (1841). The Asylum Intendent was required to release animals to their legitimate owners by an 1868 act

---

[5] "Any horse, mare or gelding" was considered distinct from "stoned horses" (stallions) in these laws.
[6] For a ground-level view of this operation see Evening Star, 24 Sept 1866, p. 2, relating to captured goats.
[7] An article of 1858 refers to two other hog-related acts (1855 and a later one) but which could not be found in the official compilations (Evening Star, 6 Mar 1858, p. 3).
[8] "To Prevent Swine from Rooting or Otherwise Destroying the Pastures of the City of Washington".

and keep the payment for the institution.⁹ Regulations in force in 1833, but perhaps passed much earlier (they refer to "marshals" rather than "constables"), specified the sum allotted for feeding slaves and livestock seized in legal proceedings and awaiting sale.¹⁰

Geese received the same treatment in 1815; they were taken to the Trustees of the Poor and the finder received 25 cents for each. Goats came under restrictions in 1819 but the officer was to simply bury the carcass, for which he was paid a fixed amount. Although a proposed act of 1868 would have kept them confined to yards, goats were not finally controlled until the Board of Health issued a prohibition four years later.¹¹ The same provisions came into force in 1828 for sick ("affected with the glanders or any other contagious or infectious disease") or blind horses set loose by their owners, and for stallions at large in 1835 and '53. These regulations were all re-stated in a comprehensive ordinance of 1853¹² and again in 1856, which latter act also required owners to kill and bury diseased horses.¹³ Responsibility for stray horses was given to the Justices of the peace by 1855 and fines to owners raised from $5 to $20. Cows saw some regulation in 1863, as in Georgetown.¹⁴

Narrative

Generally, ordinances of both corporations moved from protecting the ownership of stray animals to attempting to get them off the public streets, first offering incentives to the general population and then gradually passing this task off to the constabulary, a remedy only somewhat effective. The Corporations also increasingly restricted the areas allowed for keeping such animals.

As the number of animals and animal-related complaints grew, enforcement of regulations grew increasingly confused, a result of the clashing views of: annoyed Citizens/animals' Owners/both parties' Elected Representatives/a reluctant Police Force. Records of Corporation Council meetings from the 1840s through '60s are spangled with petitions and proposed bills to allow swine and other animals to run loose (often in one ward only) for some specified time, generally in the summer. Most of these were referred to the Committee on Police; some were rejected but others clearly passed, since we find notices of such

---

⁹ As with the police, the poorhouses of both corporations seem to have been uncertain partners in this business.
¹⁰ These interesting figures are: slaves – 20 cents/day; horses and mules – 17 cents; cattle and hogs – 9 cents; sheep and goats – 6 cents, to be paid by the plaintiff. A System of Civil and Criminal Law..., 1833, Ch. XXII "Executions", sec. 17. The proposed Washington County pound of 1874 specified daily boarding charges as: bulls -- $1; horses, mules and asses – 75 cents; cows and hogs – 50 cents; goats and sheep – 25 cents (see below, "The Contractor Pound," for a discussion of this law).
¹¹ Evening Star, 5 May 1868, p. 4; 16 Nov 1872, p. 2.
¹² Cf. comprehensive regulations of 1849 regarding raising of swine and outlawing all hogs and goats at large, as well as detailed redemption and enforcement procedures, which apparently were not approved (Daily Nat. Intelligencer, 12 Sept 1849, p. 1). A similar act was passed in Alexandria in 1858 (Evening Star, 20 May 1858, p. 3). Constables received $4 for burial of a horse according to the 1857 Code, ch. 40, sect 1.
The 1853 and 1856 Board of Health acts included these provisions, thus tying the stray animal problem to that body.
¹³ "With the hide on," according to the 1855 regulations.
¹⁴ "An Act Relating to the Keeping of Beef Cattle or Other Animals Intended for Slaughter" of 1852 kept such animals at least 75 feet from any residence. Police officers not enforcing this regulation faced a fine of $5 for the first offense and dismissal thereafter. An act of 24 May 1866 (see Webb, The Laws of the Corporation . . ., p. 120) allowed residents to keep two cows "for their immediate use."

allowed periods in newspaper accounts.[15] For example, hogs were allowed at large June-September by 1867, in which year September was lopped off. Georgetown allowed similar periods for free-range porkers.[16]

That the city suffered from a loose-animal problem was universally acknowledged. "The greatest cause of complaint now existing . . . is the large number of hogs and dogs running at large contrary to law," reported the Chief of Police in 1858. Complaints about the nuisance added spice to local newspapers throughout this period. "Go through almost any street in the city, and you will see one or more Washington pets reclining cosily in some refreshing mud hole, with a squad of geese standing guard close by," ran a typical witticism. Washingtonians were convinced (correctly or not) that no other city in the U.S. or Europe tolerated such unpleasantness: "There is not another city in the country where such a nuisance is permitted; and I, for one, am becoming tired of it." Furthermore, what did our visitors think?[17]

The general public (at least those complaining of the nuisance) wondered why owners risked losing their animals – the loss of income and of meat, the possibility of theft, the fines.[18] Much of this problem derived from the long-established habit of turning animals loose overnight to graze in city parks and commons, a result of the simple tradition of common pasturage and limited available private land. Horses ("belonging to the poorer classes as a rule") were frequently draft animals. Cows found their way into streets when boys hired to supervise "neglect them to play ball." Hogs and sheep often belonged to local butchers.[19] The most common complaint about strays was that they ravaged the city's parks and householders' gardens, and broke or fouled fences,[20] although aggressive or simply wandering animals also presented health and safety problems.[21]

The loose animals also had their defenders. A surprisingly consistent argument was that they served as effective trash-collectors (or –eaters) in a city ill-served by its paid Scavengers. Baltimore used them

---

[15] I have not found any of these acts in the official published annual compilations, and wonder if they were simply issued as lesser-grade ordinances of some kind. For examples of these proposals, see: (hogs) Daily Nat. Intelligencer, 25 July 1849, p. 1; (geese) 19 Aug 1867, p. 1.

[16] (Hogs) Evening Star, 24 Apr 1867, p. 2; 19 Aug 1867, p. 3; (G'town) 15 Nov 1858, p. 3 ("The law forbids them being penned until after the 1st of November").

[17] (Police) Evening Star, 7 Sept 1858, p. 3; (complaint) 13 Aug 1870, p. 1; (tired) 31 Aug 1861, p. 3; (visitors) 5 June 1868, p. 2.

[18] "It is surprising that the owners of hogs . . . will subject themselves to the loss of so much good pork" (Daily Nat. Intelligencer, 30 Nov 1838, p. 3); "they are liable to be stolen by loafers" (16 Nov 1838, p. 3).

[19] See Nat. Republican, 15 June 1874, p. 4; Evening Star, 30 Aug 1890, p. 12; Poundmaster Ann Rpt, 1878; Wash. Post, 10 Apr 1904, p. B6. Daily Nat. Republican, 28 Aug 1874, p. 1 gives a lurid picture of a large hog pen just where Union Station is today ("When the evening appears the filthy, noxious vapors from the pen spread over the entire neighborhood. And . . . the yells, groans and shrieks of the hogs frequently keep the residents . . . awake during the . . . night").

[20] E.g., "The first crop of grass has made its appearance on the K-Street park. The hogs, cows and goats have also made their appearance, and this morning were vigorously making the earth bare again" (Evening Star, 13 Oct 1870, p. 2); "Not a gate can be left unhinged or a door unlatched but in walks one of these Egyptian plagues" (10 Mar 1868, p. 2); "Not a yard, flower garden, or bit of grass can be secured from their depredations" (13 Aug, 1870, p. 1). And the problem continued: "Complaints are frequent, and irate citizens often call me to witness the ravages wrought upon a lawn or flower-garden" (Poundmaster Ann Rpt, 1877); "In protecting trees and parks we are certainly contributing to the beauty and probably . . . to no small degree the healthfulness of the District" (Poundmaster Ann Rpt, 1880). The south lawn of the White House received a wooden fence and ditch in 1801 to protect the gardens from grazing intruders. In 1821 newly-created Lafayette Park, across from the White House, was enclosed with a fence, the Capitol grounds in 1826, and the largely unused National Mall in the early 1830s, all for similar purpose.

[21] (Health) Evening Star, 13 July 1854, p. 2; (safety): (hogs) Daily Nat. Intelligencer, 24 Mar 1839, p. 3; (horses) 5 Aug 1839, p. 3.

for this purpose.²² The other point frequently made was simply that many poor people depended on these beasts: "He [Council member Hines, in debate] advocated at length the cause of the poor people who were compelled to keep cows and geese."²³ The writer "H" made the most thorough and reasoned defense of hogs in a letter of 1839: they help keep the streets clean; they dry up stagnant pools by their wallowing; they clean out water conduits of debris; they discourage contagion by "turning over the accumulations in the street"; and, in answer to critics: they do not harm or attack the public; they have no specially offensive smell, as do goats; they present no danger to vehicles on the street. No mention was made of their feces. He unrealistically advocated allowing them at large but only on streets.²⁴

Washington seems to have experienced the same resistance to these duties from its police as did Georgetown. An 1817 act specifies "that it shall not only be lawful, but the duty of the police constables . . . to seize and carry any animal of the hog kind . . . remaining at large in this City." Shirking this duty resulted in a fine of $5-20, repeated in 1838. The same law also imposed a fine of $1-5 on "any person [found to] molest or disturb a police constable while employed in seizing any hog". An act of 1841 lowered the penalty on obdurate officers ($5-10), and raised it on recalcitrant owners ($2-10).

One of the earliest newspaper articles (1845) describing animal control practices warns hog-owners to keep their animals "securely penned, especially on Sundays, as the police constables are in the habit of rising quite early on Monday morning, and coming down upon the swinish multitude, and carting them out to Buttsville." The article reminds "those who censure the . . . constables for seizing hogs" that officers are threatened with a fine for avoiding their responsibility and that they also capture goats and shoot mad dogs.²⁵ These sporadic raids, preceded by stern warnings in the local papers, began in the 1830s and continued until the pound crew took over the job in 1872. Dogs helped the officers in this work.²⁶ We find no reports of the large-scale community resistance met later by Poundmaster Einstein during his grander and more thorough operations, but they occasionally produced the usual humorous incidents: in 1859 one hog-catcher found his own animal in the take (for which he had to pay); and in the same year a Capitol Hill resident, complaining of the animal-nuisance in his neighborhood, saw the resulting raiding party capture his prize porker ("he cursed and swore and committed numerous indiscretions" but ultimately paid the fine). Captures from these exercises lay in the 15-30-hog range, probably representing just one of the Corporation's seven wards. An 1859 sweep of Capitol Hill brought in 140 geese.²⁷

In the wake of such raids the public saw temporary improvement: "There are no hogs running at large now," reported the Evening Star's Georgetown correspondent in 1857. More realistically a second writer observed: "But of course this was too happy a state of things to last long, and when the police were fairly out of sight . . . the streets began to resume their familiar look with hogs rooting, wallowing and grunting as usual."²⁸

---

²² "Mr. Bayly and other gentlemen [members of the Common Council speaking during debate] thought the hogs were good scavengers, particularly in the neighborhood of camps, and ought to be allowed to run at large this warm weather" (Evening Star, 6 Aug 1861, p. 3); (Baltimore) Daily Nat. Intelligencer, 24 May 1839, p. 3.
²³ Evening Star, 30 Aug 1870, p. 4.
²⁴ Daily Nat. Intelligencer, 22 July 1839, p. 3.
²⁵ Daily National Intelligencer, 29 Sept 1845, p. 3. Buttsville was a local term for the Washington Asylum, a work and almshouse so named after its intendent, Richard Butts. (Thanks to Ryan Shepard and Mark Herlong for this information.)
²⁶ However, "dogs fit for that purpose are rarely to be met with" (Daily Nat. Intelligencer, 18 Sept 1840, p. 3).
²⁷ (Anecdotes) Evening Star, 11 July 1859, p. 3; 21 July 1859, p. 3; (geese) Evening Star, 15 July 1859, p. 3, which describes the procedure.
²⁸ (Georgetown) 14 July 1857, p. 3; (aftermath) 16 July 1968, p. 2.

Owners redeemed their pigs from the Asylum for $1.25 after application to the Council, something frequently seen in that body's minutes. There was no specified holding period. Goats were simply shot, and we have no information on cows. The Asylum sold the swine and (reportedly) cooked the geese.[29]

Complaints about animals and their owners were mirrored by those about the police – why were they not more effective? The usual answer was that they didn't like the work – "It would spoil their good clothes" (especially after the re-organized force got smart new uniforms). Pushback from owners was also cited. Confusing and regularly changing regulations made enforcement difficult. One observer made a perceptive conclusion: "This is the most unpleasant of all duties . . . because the hogs generally belong to persons not able to lose them or recover them after [being] taken to the Asylum."[30] In the end, it is likely the police saw this duty as too unpopular and too tangential to their real work to deserve regular attention, rather like the non-enforcement of jaywalking laws today.

The increasing legal confusion (or stand-off?) came to a head in the ever-pressing question of hogs. The 1853 legislation banned them from running at large – period, though as noted this seems to have been loosened for certain periods and in certain wards. The 1863 law establishing Simaker's short-lived contractor pound (below) also prohibited all farm animals from city streets; as is common with legislation, it routinely repealed all earlier conflicting laws. This bill was, in its turn, repealed in 1866.

Now began a grand battle between the Corporation and its own police force: since the 1853 law banning animals at large had been repealed by its 1863 successor, and now with that law removed, did the Corporation have any regulation still in force regarding the menace? The Corporation held that the earlier bill returned to force; the police rejoined that now all cards were off the table and that although they sincerely wanted to take up hogs they had no legal authority to do so. Anthony Bell, in 1868, demanded the return of his pig on this latter basis and the Corporation Council agreed on a 6-5 vote.[31]

The whole question was perfectly summarized by a writer of 1868: "The City regulates the hogs, makes laws prohibiting them from running at large, makes other laws amendatory to the laws prohibiting them from running at large, and makes yet other laws abolishing the laws amendatory of the laws prohibiting them from running at large . . . [Police] Superintendent Richards asked the Councils to amend the law or to declare what they meant to mean: but the hog-owners have votes, and so the Democratic Councilmen and the Radical Councilmen and the Republican Councilmen, and all the other councilmen, thought it best not to agitate the question. Now that the election is over, perhaps the City Fathers will take courage and deal with the hogs, [but] probably . . . next year . . . will find the hogs still rooting."[32]

The 1853 act was revived in 1868.[33]

In their frustration, citizens offered creative suggestions (beyond higher fines and stricter enforcement). "The Provost Guard and other of our soldiers who desire to practice at a target might . . . be allowed to provide the troops with a little fresh pork in this way. Seriously, I am in earnest." And we cannot pooh-

---

[29] (Redemption) Evening Star, 24 Apr 1867, p. 2; (charge) 21 July 1859, p. 3; (goats) 27 June 1867, p. 2.

[30] (Uniforms, resistance) Evening Star, 10 Mar 1868, p. 2. This clever article describes "the colored virago, Mary Ann Burke" who "rescued her porker from a lightweight policeman" and then "not content with this tossed both officer and pig into the muddy sty." It also tells us that a Corporation Alderman theorized "pig-blindness" – an inability of certain officers to see pigs. (Regs) Evening Star, 5 June 1868, p. 2 ("The police say they can't make head or tail of the law as it stands"); (unpleasant duty) 24 July 1857, p. 3. For a sympathetic analysis of the problem see Daily Nat. Intelligencer, 18 Sept 1840, p. 3.

[31] These shenanigans are perfectly laid out in: Evening Star, 16 Mar 1868, p. 2; 17 Mar 1868, p. 4; (Bell) 10 Mar 1868, p. 4.

[32] Evening Star, 5 June 1868, p. 2.

[33] Or so it would seem; although reported so in the newspapers it does not appear in the Acts of that year and perhaps passed only one chamber.

pooh the suggestion that local boys receive the 25 cents for catching geese ("and be diverted from other less lawful pursuits") when we learn that the son of Jackson Pumphrey of Southwest actually cleared $120 (= 480 geese) <u>in one day</u> by just this method. A writer wondered why no citizen brought a civil suit against the Corporation for non-enforcement.[34]

The most efficient of the Corporation's overlapping remedies was the handling of horses by a Justice of the Peace.[35] The Justice had the animal appraised (for $1), recorded by a Corporation clerk ($1), and then advertised the find and its description in a local newspaper (also $1). A verifiable owner could redeem his horse, paying these expenses and a fine,[36] with a longer period of claim for particularly valuable stock. An unclaimed animal became the property of the finder (the "taker-up"), who had in the meanwhile been holding and perhaps using it anyway. This law treated lost boats with the same procedure.

Recourse to this system was frequent, judging from the number of newspaper ads placed by Justices. These were often headed "Washington County" but gave locations throughout the District. About an equal number of similar notices appeared placed by landowners holding strays and advertising them on their own initiative. Owners sometimes advertised for lost animals.

Congressional fiat replaced the inefficient and politicized dual day- and night-constabulary of the Corporations with a unified Department of Metropolitan Police in 1861[37] and the following year considerably amended MPDC's charge to include creation of a Property Clerk to hold stolen property, including "horses and other animals taken by the police," which could be sold after twenty days. This procedure was refined four years later. Public notices then appeared under the authority of the Metropolitan Police (and claims by owners were to be made to the Property Clerk) rather than the Justices of the Peace. Since these ads always referred to horses, we can guess that disposition of other animals continued as before. The newly appointed poundmaster (briefly) placed his own advertisements, as will be discussed below.

After establishment of the new Police Department we have annual reports giving the number of stray animals (always horses and cattle) recovered: in the 60-80 range for 1864-67 (and separately about 20-35 "horses and vehicles"), and closer to 200 for the two categories combined in 1868-71. Appendixes C1 and C2 give such statistics as are available for the number of farm animals and nuisance hog pens in the city in the late Corporation period.

Emergency situations were handled ad hoc. Occasional newspaper articles of this period describe animals (sometimes with their owners) rescued from floods, fires, falls into sewers/wells, or other mishaps. This rescue was accomplished by the police, fire department, nearby soldiers or bystanders.[38] Stable fires were sadly common as long as there were stables in the District.

---

[34] (Shooting) Evening Star, 31 Aug 1861, p. 3; (geese) 21 Sept 1855, p. 3; 17 Oct 1861, p. 3; (suit) 13 Oct 1870, p. 2.
[35] The law describing this process is included in the 1819 Code of Laws of DC and reiterated in the 1855 code, but I don't know when it was passed. The earliest newspaper advertisement placed by a Justice I have found is from 1816. Although it refers to the District of Columbia, one wonders if much of the procedure and wording was taken from a colonial statute.
[36] The proposed regulations for a Washington County pound of 1874 (see below, "The Contractor Pound") would have allowed the county poundmaster to charge 25 cents for each animal redeemed, 12 cents for a copy of the legal certificate, plus 4 cents for each mile travelled to take the animal.
[37] 6 Aug 1861; the force is referred to here conventionally as MPDC.
[38] For a few examples, see Evening Star, 23 Feb 1856, p. 3 (mule team in an icy river); 22 May 1857, p. 3 (horse in canal); 11 Apr 1864, p. 2 (cow in a sewer); Nat. Republican, 28 Aug 1861, p. 3 (horses in burning railroad cars).

CHAPTER TWO

Dogs

A gentleman [living in "the Island", i.e., Southwest DC] assures us that on a fine moonlit night lately he counted no less than 93 dogs trotting past his door, in single file, apparently on some foray. (Evening Star, 15 July 1857, p. 3)

It has been sometimes thought that functionaries holding office by the people's suffrage dislike to . . . make themselves unpopular with the voters by killing their pets [dogs]; no such excuse should be now received, as the election is just over. (Evening Star, 15 June 1854, p. 3)

There seem to have also been plenty of noisome dogs in the new city. As before, we start with a legal summary and then a more entertaining Narrative.

Summary of Laws

The first laws of the Corporation of **Georgetown** relating to taxes (licenses, in modern parlance)[1] on dogs – 1792, 1798, 1803, 1805 – all carried the title "An Ordinance to Diminish the Number of Dogs" and in no case could the text be discovered because each successive act was superseded by its successor, the 1807 act being the earliest available.

"Whereas the great number of dogs kept in this town have become a public nuisance," the Corporation replaced its "inadequate" earlier ordinances with new measures "for preventing the evil." The 1807 law levied an annual tax on each dog ("animals of the dog kind," as it was always put): $1 for a male, $2 for a female, and higher amounts for each above that number. The city issued a receipt upon payment of this tax, and owners were instructed "to place a collar round the neck of such animal with the owner's name." Failure to comply brought a fine of $10, split between the informer and the Corporation. Unlicensed dogs found at large could be killed "by any person whomsoever." The only role of the Corporation constables was to report scoff-laws and to advise new-comers of the regulation.

A resolution of 1808 banning stray dogs related to an outbreak of rabies and expired after one month – the first such pronouncement.

Police were given "the special duty . . . to kill any animal of the dog kind going at large" in 1811 and bury it outside city limits, receiving $1 for each. As with larger animals, the text noted that this duty must be undertaken by the police, and protected them somewhat by fining $20 to "any and every person who shall assault or in any wise obstruct them . . . in the discharge of their duty." Another source of annoyance for the constables was indicated when, in 1828, the city had to formally define "owner" as "persons who shall, directly or indirectly permit or suffer any . . . dog . . . to remain on or about their

---

[1] The latter word, however, was commonly used in official and unofficial parlance.

premises." On the other hand, proposed revision of this ordinance in 1846 would have prohibited officers from employing substitutes or using shot "the size of double B" or larger, revealing complaints with the constables' work.[2]

The Corporation continued to struggle with its unwanted canine population. The dog tax was raised in 1815, and again in 1822 to $5 for each male and $20 for each female. This apparently pushed things too far, since two years later the tax returned to $1.50 for the first male and $5 for the first female (it rose with further animals), while increasing various other fines. In 1824 constables were required to actually check dog ownership of each household against the Corporation Clerk's registration list and to report offenders. After 1829 those not registered were to be killed and buried by the constables (who received 50 cents for each).

In 1819 the Corporation revised these regulations, prohibiting wandering dogs in the summer months only, and fining their owners the very high sum of $20. Georgetown allowed dogs to run at large from 1855 on but only if muzzled. This innovation did not satisfy the dog-annoyed public, who continued to hunt them down, and the local papers were "requested" to publicize the policy again "for the benefit of our fellow citizens and the police" two years later. The 1819 ordinance on strays was revived in 1836.

A law of 1804 "To Prevent the Evils Arising from the Multiplicity of Dogs in and about the Market House" set a fine ($1) for bringing dogs into that building. It called out butchers in particular for this practice.[3] The Corporation revived this ordinance in 1829.[4]

Georgetown's dog regulations were comprehensively restated in 1859. This act continued the earlier fines, fees and special provisions (no dogs in markets, restrictions when the mayor declares a rabies-emergency) with slight revisions. A further ordinance of 1860 created uniquely numbered brass tags ("checks") for dogs' collars to accompany the licenses. It was declared "lawful, and . . . is hereby made the duty" of police to check each household and collect the fee for unregistered dogs (keeping the 25 cent fee for himself); recalcitrant citizens would see their dogs seized and killed in the same way as strays. As before, police faced a fine for avoiding this duty ($2). This law explicitly condemned "fierce or dangerous dogs" that were allowed to run loose, and fined their owners both for the offense and also $1 if the animal had bitten someone.

The last law of independent Georgetown regarding dogs largely followed its immediate predecessors but also made the first mention of spayed females, which were taxed as males. These last ordinances envisioned the income from licenses and fines covering any expenses associated with administration and enforcement.

The Corporation of **Washington's** first dog-related act (1803) also was a tax, lumping tax on dogs with taxes on property in general, including slaves. All dogs required payment of $1 annually.[5] Perhaps collection proved difficult, because the following year the Corporation repealed the fine for non-payment, and replaced it with a system of house-to-house registration (by the Corporation treasurer) of both dogs and slaves, with a stiff $10 fine for hiding animals. The informer and city split this money.

---

[2] Georgetown Advocate, 7 May 1846, p. 1, which contains much similar interesting discussion.

[3] Butchers and farmers brought dogs to guard their goods. "These are generally of the bull-terrier breed and as fierce as lions" (Evening Star, 1 Apr 1874, p. 4).

[4] Meaning that it had somehow lapsed, although there is no indication that it had been withdrawn.

[5] We might note here that while dogs were generally treated as nuisances by authorities and therefore females were taxed at a higher rate than males, the reverse was true for slaves, who were in this act taxed at 50 cents per female and $1 per male. Farm animals, except those "necessary for the use and consumption of the persons to whom the same shall belong," were apparently included in "real and personal property" taxed 25 cent/$100 in value.

An act of 1807 separated dogs from property and laid out more extensive regulations: besides restating the tax provisions, dogs needed to wear collars marked "City of W" or "Washington"[6] and the owner's name, and outlawed unlicensed strays, which the city constables or "any other person" would kill and bury ("constables only" receiving 20 cents for each). Already the Corporation felt the need to threaten a fine ($10) for constables avoiding this duty. Dogs accompanying non-residents into the city were exempted from these regulations.[7] As the dog population increased, the tax on females ($10, later reduced to $5) and the amount paid constables for eliminating strays (50 cents) also rose.

The Corporation government in 1817 empowered its mayor to impose a curfew on dogs when an outbreak of rabies occurred, keeping them confined until he saw fit to lift the emergency regulations. Constables received $1 for killing strays during these periods. The first such proclamation was made in November of the same year[8] and they appeared with depressing regularity (two or three a year) into the 1860s.

Stray dogs were banned throughout the city in the summer months only, and all dogs from markets at any time, in 1819. Those found in the constables' weekly inspections were killed and buried[9] (the constable receiving $1, paid by the owner), the penalty rising to $3 in 1844. Dogs accompanying their master on the street had to be leashed, and escaped dogs given one hour to be recovered. Free blacks only received permission to own dogs in 1838.[10]

A comprehensive act about dogs, gathering all these provisions and tweaking the details, passed in 1820. This law banned strays throughout the year. Dogs "viciously disposed or in any way dangerous" and let to run at large "at anytime of the year" were addressed in 1826.[11] Another comprehensive act of 1829 raised fines and repeated the warning and fine for delinquent constables.

We have little information relating specifically to the **County of Washington**. An ordinance of 1864[12] mandated that all unlicensed dogs there would be killed by the police. An act of the County Levy Court, undated but coming into effect in April 1867, established a dog tax of $1 annually for males and $2 for females, described the "brass checks" ("stamped with the numbers 1, 2, 3, and upwards"), provided a fine of $2-5 for failure to pay the tax ($5-10 for counterfeiting a tag), and generally laid out a procedure similar to that of the Corporations, to be handled by the Clerk of the Levy Court.[13]

---

[6] This wording changed regularly over the years.
[7] The Washington Hunt was given special permission to keep a pack of 52 hounds for a flat tax of $40 annually if properly enclosed and supervised (Acts, 6 Aug 1834).
[8] Daily Nat. Intelligencer, 27 Nov 1817, p. 2. The writer "T" pleaded for such a proclamation in the same newspaper on 18 Nov 1817, p. 2. The proclamations will be found in the Corporations' Ordinances and Acts.
[9] "In some remote place," according to the 1820 act, four-feet deep according to the 1857 Code, ch. 40, sect 1.
[10] A publication "New Era", 19 July 1855, p. 114 (sic), apparently an abolitionist journal, included this right among those granted freedmen by a law of October 1836 but I could not find this ordinance.
[11] This law was enforced: Cranch (Reports, p. 391) reports a case "United States v. Henry McDuell" of 1838 in which "a certain large dog of a very fierce and furious nature" almost killed a neighbor's cow, resulting in the owner being fined $20.
[12] Apparently local, but I can't find the original source. It was included in a US statute of 1873. The Corporation Council had requested the military governor (through the Levy Court) to prohibit farm animals and dogs at large throughout the County by military order in 1863 (Evening Star, 26 May 1863, p. 3).
[13] Callan, pp. 15-16

Narrative

Laws relating to dogs in both corporations mostly aimed at controlling them, and perhaps making a little money on the side. Both towns instituted a tax regimen and both gave responsibility for their control to the police, as unsuccessful here as with larger animals. Over time more specific concerns such as vicious animals were addressed directly.

While the drumbeat of increasing restrictions and taxes indicate a general concern about the city's canine population, some citizens resisted these moves. "I much doubt that our Corporation, or any other body of that kind, has the authority of ordering Dogs to be constantly confined. This would establish a tyranny of which even Europe does not furnish a precedent," wrote "A Butcher" to the local newspaper in 1818. "Of what use would the dog be to the Butcher, or the pointer to the Sportsman?" "Humanitas" pleaded the cause in two lengthy missives the following year, arguing that whisky was a greater danger than dogs.[14] Nonetheless, the Council reiterated its prohibition on dogs in markets in 1824.

All of these careful regulations and procedures depended on the cooperation of the Corporation constabulary.[15] (We have no way to know how frequently ordinary citizens captured loose dogs but certainly it was less remunerative than taking farm animals, which was commonly done.) We have already encountered acts back to 1807 fining officers who failed to enforce the laws on stray dogs. The 1820 and 1829 acts set this fine at $10. Mayor Gales issued an official directive in 1827 reminding "Police Officers of the several Wards" that "the laws concerning Dogs must be rigidly enforced, and that the said Police Officers will be held responsible for every instance of neglect, . . . this measure being rendered necessary by a regard to the comfort, if not to the safety, of the people of this city, and called for by urgent representations from heads of families therein." Perhaps this agitation had some effect, for in 1848 a correspondent to the Semi-Weekly Union reported "the dogs having been nearly all killed off by the unsparing slaughter waged against them," for which "the boys" were paid 50 cents a head.[16]

Beginning about this time we begin to find short news items giving the public's views of matters. Complaints about lax police attention equal those about the canines themselves: "The police officers of this ward take no notice whatever of the dogs daily infesting our streets"; city laws prohibited dogs in the markets, but "this wholesome law is frequently evaded"; and so forth.[17] These complaints increased in the 1850s, not only citing safety and nuisance problems, but also loss of tax revenue and even outside investment (dogs chased away visiting businessmen), attacks on domestic animals, and of course chasing horses and carriages.[18]

---

[14] Washington Gazette, 7 Nov 1818, p. 3. He was complaining about a law passed "last night" by the Lower House of the city's bicameral council, but apparently not the Board of Aldermen, since it does not appear in the printed Acts of that year. The same newspaper (12 November 1818, p. 2) carried a longer broadside in the same vein, and "Canis" made this essentially libertarian argument in Daily Nat. Intelligencer, 6 Aug 1838, p. 3 ("To what extent may not this assumption or extortion be carried? May not every article of property be subjected . . . to a similar demand?"). (Humanitas) National Messenger, 4 Aug 1819, p. 2; 9 Aug 1918, p. 2; and many flowery rebuttals in the same publication.

[15] "A war of extermination is again commenced against the poor dogs. It is to be hoped no negroes will be employed by our police officers to entice and whistle these faithful animals from their masters' yards, . . . that they may be shot and the fee obtained" (City of Wash. Gazette, 20 Sept 1821, p.2).

[16] Op cit., 25 July 1848, p. 3.

[17] Daily Nat. Intelligencer, 11 Jan 1842, p. 3; and 3 July 1837, p. 3 respectively; 18 Aug 1821, p. 2 provides another good example.

[18] How sad that we don't have a fuller account of the 1856 Board of Aldermen meeting which considered a comprehensive dog bill: "A somewhat rambling discussion ensued, in the course of which much curious information was elicited in regard to dogs and their habits – especially Seventh Ward dogs" (Evening Star, 16 Dec 1856, p. 3).

The Washington police and Council tried to deal with the rising dog problem. A proposed act from 1853 would have required "a strong and safe muzzle of iron wire . . . not armed with spikes or other dangerous weapons" on each dog allowed at large.[19] Notices placed by the police warning citizens to license their dogs also began to appear. An 1855 act relating to Justices of the Peace felt the necessity of fining owners $20 for hiding their (aggressive?) dogs from the police.

In 1854 newspapers reported a push by the Council for a wholesale shooting of stray dogs,[20] the discussion centering on the necessity of a cash incentive for the officers (shooting animals is "dirty business"; as opposed to "It is the duty of the police officers, who are salaried, to kill dogs without additional compensation") and whether the animals should be shot ("There is a universal horror of shooting. It is dangerous, inhuman, and revolting to the feelings of the present day") or poisoned. ("A voice [from the rear]: 'A stout club would do as well.'".) With the specific means of execution left unspecified "the resolution . . . passed, while not a few dogs were sporting and barking outside." The police tried sausages laced with strychnine, to mixed success.[21]

At that time there were an estimated 8,000 dogs in the city. "The large number serve but to terrify our citizens by day and <u>serenade</u> them by night!" Police reported that just one ward (Two) held 2,000-3,000. A lower estimate in 1857 – 3,500 for the whole city – contrasted that figure with 2,000 in 1850.[22] The number of <u>licensed</u> dogs during the 1850s stayed in the 900-1,500 range (at $1/dog; Appendix C4).

The Seventh Ward (South Washington) was always described as the center of the canine population: "We are told that Seventh Warders, moving into neighborhoods more sparsely populated with dogs, have so missed the familiar yelpings as to pass sleepless nights, and have been compelled either to return or to colonize large numbers of dogs on their premises." Observers complained of "six, eight, or ten, and sometimes as high as fifteen dogs attached to the premises of some poverty-stricken white or colored man."[23]

Confusion continued in the Corporation's canine-control project after passage of the nebulous 1854 orders. Use of strychnine-laced meat ("luscious morsels prepared by order of the authorities") continued until 1864, when shooting returned to use. Citizens enthusiastically joined the effort, some "exacting vengeance" on unfriendly mutts and others preparatory to planned burglary. When officers picked up their firearms again (fowling rifles, two men per ward), they took to the challenge con brio: in the first day police of the Fourth Ward killed 25 dogs; Officer Gordon took three with one shot and then two with his next ("Tall Shooting" the newspaper article headlined it); five wards reported a total of 136 dogs (in one week?) dispatched.[24]

---

[19] Daily Nat. Intelligencer, 27 July 1853, p. 1.
[20] See the Wash. Sentinel, 8 June 1854, p. 3 for a complete and entertaining account, as well as other local newspapers of the time. The Corporation had neglected to supply officers with the required ammunition, remedied later in the year (Evening Star, 30 May 1854, p. 3; 11 July 1854, p. 3). A much later account tells us that the constables were provided with shotguns for the purpose. "Whether the policemen winged some of the citizens in their efforts to fulfill this task is not on record" (Wash. Times, 7 Aug 1904, p. 4; see Evening Star, 15 Oct 1860, p. 3, for a contemporary statement of this fear).
[21] Wash. Sentinel, 11 July 1854, p.3. The Evening Star, 13 July 1854, p. 3, reported unsatisfactory results and speculated that the strychnine was adulterated. On the other hand: "Dogs are falling and dying in all directions; and the streets are nearly clean of them" (Wash. Sentinel, 14 July 1854, p. 3). In New York they were drowned (Baltimore Sun, 15 July 1858, p. 4). A gruesome description of the methods of "dog killers" in Philadelphia will be found in Portland (ME) Advertiser, 23 Aug 1859, p. 2.
[22] Wash. Sentinel, 11 July 1854, p.3; Evening Star, 15 July 1857, p. 3; 24 July 1857, p. 3.
[23] Evening Star, 15 July 1857, p.3.
[24] (Shooting reinstated) Evening Star, 6 Aug 1864, p. 3; (citizens) 24 June 1857, p. 2; 23 July 1859, p. 3; (bags) 6 Aug 1864, p. 3; 12 Aug 1864, p. 2; 17 July 1866, p. 3.

And yet citizens angrily demanding disposal of all unhoused canines continued uncomfortable with any public method of their extinction. "It is a difficult matter to decide how the animals shall be killed with the least disgust to human beings," opined the Daily Union; poisoning, shooting, "a fatal crack over the skull" all were unacceptable. The paper suggested that "some enterprising and industrious gentleman" would undertake to "remove them from the city, and deprive them of existence in some secret mode, into which inquiry should not be made."[25]

The city restated all of its dog regulations once again in an act of 1858, much like its predecessors but with increased fines, a provision for muzzling, and a special fine ($10) for allowing females in heat to run at large. Two new items are suggestive: the specification that "dog" applies to female as well as male animals (necessitated by clever lawyers?), and a new fine ($5-20) for any constable or other person killing "any . . . dog . . . properly licensed, collared, etc.," including removing the collar or luring the animal onto the streets (indicating that the fee paid by the city attracted at least some takers). The Council demanded muzzling in 1869, to no effect.[26]

---

[25] (Killing methods) Daily Union, 16 July 1857, p. 3 ("Leave the pistol and bludgeon for those bipeds whose sentiment is not such as philanthropists especially admire"). Poisoning resulted in the death of many licensed (and valuable) animals (Evening Star, 23 July 1859, p. 3).

[26] Journal of the 67th Council (16 Aug 1869), p. 306.

CHAPTER THREE

The Corporation Pound

Before 1863 stray or abandoned animals in the City of Washington were: kept with their finder or the Justice of the Peace (horses, mules), or taken to the Asylum (hogs) until redeemed or forfeited; donated directly to the Asylum (geese); shot and buried outside city limits (goats, dogs). There was no provision for redeeming the latter two categories.

In 1863 the Corporation established the city's first pound – a place to hold unwanted animals, and with a manager (the poundmaster) and staff to capture and handle them. This law was printed in the Daily National Intelligencer, the city's publication of record, on 27 Mar 1863, p. 1,[1] but not included in the annual compilation of acts for that year, nor is there any mention of it in the Council Journal for that week. Indeed, it would be easy to think that the law was never actually effectuated except that one advertisement of captured animals appeared in the local newspaper, signed by the poundmaster.

In taking this step Washington was following a national movement: New York City had established a pound by 1845 which was described admiringly as a new type of institution by the correspondents of other cities' newspapers ("One of the institutions in New York worth the visit of the curious," according to the Baltimore Sun).[2]

The ordinance prohibited any farm animals (including "neat cattle" – a general term for common bovines, but not dairy cows) from being loose anywhere within city limits, which could be redeemed for a fine of $2. An appointed poundmaster furnished, "without expense or charge to the city, proper and sufficient enclosed yards for a pound" at least 200 yards from any dwelling but his own. The appointee deposited a bond of $500 for this position. Any citizen finding a stray farm animal could take it to the pound and receive 50 cents (12 cents for each goose). Owners redeemed their stock for $1 per head (13 cents for geese) plus a boarding charge. After five days, and three days' advertisements, the poundmaster sold the animals, kept the sum of the redemption and expenses and passed the remainder to the Corporation treasury. The poundmaster was to make an annual report of his activities.

---

[1] See also the same, 17 Feb 1863, p. 3, reporting Council discussion on establishment of a pound.

[2] Op. cit, 2 July 1857, p. 1, so described after its 1856 re-organization to handle specifically dogs; New York Herald, 8 July 1845, p. 2; see also Daily Nat. Intelligencer, 15 Aug 1854, p. 2. An electronic search of early American newspapers for the word "poundmaster" shows the office present in a good number of New York State and New England towns as early as 1810. The first appearance of "poundmaster" or "dog pound" beyond these smaller towns occur for: New Orleans LA 1842, Jackson MI 1851, Chicago IL 1855, Newark NJ and Baton Rouge LA 1857, Stockton CA 1858, Newark NJ and Philadelphia PA 1859, Sacramento CA 1860, Madison WI and Cincinnati OH 1861, San Francisco CA 1862, Charleston SC 1865, Springfield IL 1866, St. Louis MO and Jersey City NJ 1867, Cleveland OH 1868, Hoboken NJ and San Antonio TX 1869, Rockford IL and Columbus GA 1870. When the District's later pound was established in 1871 The Evening Star (14 June 1871, p. 2) expressed the "gloomy satisfaction of knowing that Washington is the last city in America, or the civilized world to make this concession to the march of improvement." Constantinople was the international horror-case of dog-infestation usually cited at the time.

The pound also took in dogs (paying 25 cents bounty for each), which could be redeemed for $2. Unclaimed dogs were killed and buried by the poundmaster, who received 25 cents per animal. The ordinance penalized anyone stealing animals from the pound or obstructing the work of the pound's men, and also anyone stealing animals to bring them to the pound for the reward.

The new poundmaster was **William M. Simaker**, who established his pound at the corner of 11th and K Streets NW. Simaker is an elusive man who does not appear in any search of newspapers beyond an advertisement in 1861 for a horse lost from the Northern Liberties Market and one in 1863 for a horse lost from the pound.[3] The City Directory of 1864 listed him as "huckster" (peddler) in the Central Market. Four years later he had a letter in the city's dead-letter office.[4] With these few notices Simaker's short-lived pound disappeared from our record, as did the poundmaster himself.

Between 1864 and 1871 Washington had no functioning pound. Shooting returned to the streets, but after a short-lived period of sympathy for the poor mutts and the accidental wounding of a bystander (by a ricocheting bullet) MPDC Superintendent Richards suspended the extermination campaign in July 1866, only to start it again by the fall. In the meanwhile bills were introduced to the council in 1866 and 1867 "to prevent cruelty to dogs" – police shooting them – and instead putting them in a pound, as did Baltimore.[5]

An act of 1867 mandated a "**Dog-Pound**",[6] built by the city, the appointed poundmaster to keep all "rewards" (fines) taken in. The general outline of this planned operation reflected the earlier act with only a few differences: the period of redemption was lengthened to six days; the poundmaster was admonished to "take proper care of the dogs, [and] give them sufficient food and water while in his custody"; children under 15 could not bring in animals;[7] stray dogs were prohibited only in the summer months; penalties for vicious dogs were stiffened. Muzzled dogs were not considered strays.

The city dog pound never materialized and the dog problem festered. Animal control returned to the District police. A police sweep in 1869 killed 84 street curs in one day. Here are three entries from a precinct log-book of 1869: "Tell Wm. Oppenheimer on 4½ street that the Lieutenant knows where his Two cattle is. Tell him to go to Georgetown"; "Strayed: an Iron Grey horse, 17 hands high, seven years

---

[3] (Market) Evening Star, 8 Oct 1861, p. 3; (pound) Evening Star, 15 Aug 1863, p. 3. The MPDC Ann Rpt for 1864 lists the arrest of "pound-master" among its achievements, apparently an opaque reference to the gentleman.

[4] Evening Star, 18 Sept 1868, p. 1.

[5] (Sympathy): Evening Union, 16 July 1866, p. 2 ("The heat of . . . last night . . . was made more distressingly annoying by the constant discharge of firearms, followed by the howling and yelping of the unfortunate quadrupeds that fell by hands of the vigilant officers of the law"), et al.; (bystander): Evening Star, 23 July 1866, p. 2; 24 July 1866, p. 3; (suspended): 24 July 1866, p. 2; 27 July 1866, p. 3; (bills) Evening Star, 11 July 1854, p. 3; 24 July 1866, p. 1; 31 July 1866, p. 3; 2 July 1867, p. 4; Daily Nat. Intelligencer, 2 July 1867, p. 3.

Shooting dangerous dogs continued a police duty and became an oft-cited incentive to modernize MPDC weapons and training: "[I commend the officer who] displayed good judgment when he used his baton to kill a dog rather than fire a ball with 15 grains of powder back of it, at short range," and thus endangering bystanders (MPDC Ann Rpt, 1899).

[6] Besides the law itself, found in the annual Acts, see also the Journal of the 65th Council (19 Aug 1867), p. 172. An appropriation of $500 was approved on 4 October.

[7] This was to prevent the unhealthy practice of poor children capturing animals for the fee. When children were prohibited from so doing in New York in 1859 they continued the habit and passed them on to adults ("dog brokers"), who turned them over to the pound and split the reward. (Evening Post, New York City, 8 June 1859, p. 1; see also Daily Nat. Intelligencer, 29 June 1857, p. 3 for a curious instance of this business – the broker died from hydrophobia!)

old, white halter and blanket on. Ans: We have a Bay here taken up astray"; and "The ammunition for shooting dogs is ready at Tysons on 7th street."[8]

---

[8] (Shooting) Evening Star, 2 July 1869, p. 4; (log) 11 Jan 1959, p. A1.

CHAPTER FOUR

Cruelty to Animals

Summary of Laws

The statutes cited above all consider animals only in their relationship with people – as valuable commodities (farm animals), nuisances (dogs and decrepit horses), possibly a source of tax revenue, and certainly as an administrative and financial headache. None see animals as creatures in their own right. Humane laws, spotty before the Civil war, only took root in the U.S. after the Civil War, led (as usual) by New York State with its landmark statutes of 1866 and 1867.[1]

Early residents of **Washington** showed some sensitivity to the lives of their fellow creatures – we can recall the objections made in 1854 to shooting dogs as "inhuman".[2] The few laws passed before 1871 ameliorating their conditions generally related to public situations. Most of the acts concerning animals in sports[3] -- horse racing, dog fights – dealt only with the event and not the animals used. Concerns of a later period – welfare of circus animals, vivisection, animals in transit through the city – did not appear in pre-1871 laws.

In the City of Washington, a comprehensive law in effect in 1819 "Regarding Gaming" not only forbid any sort of animal fighting "for profit or sport" but continued to a much wider field: "nor shall any person for profit or sport, or in anger, cruelly, wantonly or inhumanly, unreasonably beat, vex, wound or otherwise abuse or torment or cruelly treat any animal whatsoever; nor shall any person unreasonably overload any beast of draught or burden; nor shall any person suffer his or her dog or dogs unreasonably to chase, worry, tear, wound, mangle or torment any other animal whatever." Offenders were liable to fines up to $1,000 and one year imprisonment (!).[4]

Horses received special protection in an 1821 act. Adults "who . . . wantonly abuse or cruelly beat the same" faced a $5-10 fine, minors $5 (paid by their parents, of course), and slaves five to ten lashes (all fines reduced to $3 in 1853). A letter to the Evening Star of 1854 mentions the police enforcing this law.[5] Thompson's <u>Abstract of Laws</u> of 1855 added "cut[ting] off the hair of the tail or mane of a horse, when

---

[1] The texts of these (and many, many other animal-related statutes and court rulings) will be found in Michigan State University's Animal Legal and Historical Center (https://www.animallaw.info).

[2] Was shooting the dog more painful to the animal than poisoning it? Or was the objection actually to the public noise of the discharge? Note poundmaster Einstein's concerns about the "brutalizing" effects on his staff of shooting, below.

[3] (Racing, Wash) 9 Dec 1809; (dog fights): (Wash) 3 June 1853, Sheahan, p. 150; cock fights: (G'town) 10 Oct 1796; ("exhibiting wild beasts . . . of a ferocious or dangerous character" without a license, G'town) 4 Nov 1835.

[4] It would be interesting to know if such an extraordinary punishment was ever ordered. Could it have been a misprint?

[5] And wonders why they didn't instead enforce laws against dogs; op. cit., 24 June 1854, p. 3.

done maliciously," "wanton cruelty to animals in general," and poisoning animals to this list.[6] Protection was extended to all domestic animals in 1867.

Cruelty-prevention laws did not reappear among subsequent statutes in the District of Columbia until 1860. In that year calves accompanying their mothers ("milch cows") into the city must have their mouths left ungagged so that they could feed. The treatment of animals in city markets received attention two years later: they were no longer allowed to be bound and left on the market floor "for many hours in sunshine and in storm, in cold weather and in hot, unrelieved," which was "cruel, inhuman and offensive to passers by." For each offense the market clerk collected $1 and the same for every half-hour the animal remained so.

Trespass of these laws was actually prosecuted. Cranch's digest of legal rulings by the Washington circuit court lists two such cases, one regarding cruelty to a horse (1821) and the other a cow (1834).[7] Arrests for cruelty to animals (considered a crime against property) reported annually after the 1861 organization of the Police Department (Appendix C5) range from 6 to 33 each year between 1862 and 1869; in 1870 there were 40 such cases.

The Corporation of **Georgetown** passed similar legislation protecting market animals (1868) and horses "or any other domestic animal" (1869) – much later than Washington.

---

[6] Op. cit., pp. 31-32.

[7] Op. cit., U.S. v. Logan, II, 259, and U.S. v. Jackson, IV, 483 respectively. The latter involved the brutal beating and killing of a cow "in view of the . . . streets and dwellings [of the] citizens . . . to the terror and disturbance . . . and the common nuisance . . ., to the evil example of all others, and against the peace and government of the United States." The defendant's attorney argued (unsuccessfully) that Maryland law acknowledged no such crime, and that Virginia law only punished cruelty to slaves.

CHAPTER FIVE

Summary

A review of the laws and reports of the two Corporations' efforts to control animals in the pre-1871 era shows that:

- Farm animals were treated as property which would generally be redeemed by their owners or profitably sold, and were secondarily (though far too often) nuisances when they strayed or were turned loose to pasture. Taxes on these formed a source of income for the Corporations. Sheep were only mentioned in passing, and chickens seem to have been too minor (and perhaps too common) to create concern;

- Dogs had practical use for their owners, who tried to protect them from capture, but the numerous unclaimed dogs living in the streets were a nuisance from the earliest days. Justified fear of rabies added to the constant complaints. Taxes on dogs largely were intended to control their number.[1] While most stray farm animals were held for return, stray dogs were taken to destroy. Note that the other common domestic pet – cats – never appear in these regulations, probably for the same reason as the absence of chickens;

- Financing animal control was a regular conundrum for the Corporations. While farm animals largely paid for themselves, dogs were an expense for the city. Regularly changing combinations of financing through fines/license fees/Corporation funds show that no scheme worked when the number of unwanted dogs requiring rounding up, execution and burial so greatly overwhelmed those owners willing to pay for a license or redeem their lost animals;

- And finally, the Corporations never found a really workable plan to capture dogs. Ineffective incentives for citizens to take them gradually disappeared from the regulations as the duty fell more and more on the official constabulary, but the need to both regularly raise the special payment for carrying out this assigned duty and the fines for avoiding it tell the story. Whether this hesitancy on the part of the police originated from distaste for the work or from citizen opposition is not clear. (Note the increasing penalties for those hindering the police from taking dogs; this resistance will be seen to increase in the near future.);

- The city markets were a regular target for dog laws, probably because farmers and butchers brought in dogs to protect their wares, and the close aisles prevented the public from avoiding the animals. Note also that the few (though seemingly fervent) cruelty laws of the period center on the market and on horses working the street – publicly visible sites.

---

[1] In spite of this belief, dog taxes were useful to Corporation finances: the $300 collected by Washington in 1820 would have paid over half the $432 spent that year for support of "the poor, aged and infirm."

CHAPTER SIX

Dead Animals

An evil exists in this city of a most serious and alarming description: . . . putrid offals of fish, dead cats, dogs, etc. are to be found in every nook, common, highway, in their most putrescent and disgusting state. This is . . . obvious to every one who has perambulated the city. (Nat. Intelligencer, 26 May 1814, p. 1)

Whose business is it to attend to the removal of that dead dog in the street . . . near Judiciary Square? It is a disgusting object, and pollutes the air in that vicinity. (Evening Star, 28 Aug 1861, p. 3)

A word might be said here about a tangential issue: removal of dead animals from city streets. The Corporation of **Georgetown** in 1795 prohibited "any carrion, stinking fish, dead creatures, or other offensive filth to be, remain, or continue above ground for the space of eighteen hours" or to be thrown onto other property under pain of fine.

The 1809 **City of Washington** act prohibiting swine at large also required owners "of every horse, cow, ox or other animal . . . found dead in any of the streets or on any open unenclosed ground" to bury the carcass,[1] any resulting fine shared by the informer and the city. This provision was repeated in 1820; if the owner balked (for a $5-20 fine) or no owner could be found the task fell to the Ward Commissioners.

An act of 1803 created the position of Superintendent of Police and gave that official responsibility for clearing and prosecuting accumulations of construction debris and other "nuisances." The newly-created (1819) District Health Officer took a general oversight of "all nuisances coming under his observation . . . which . . . endanger the health of the citizens" but not otherwise defined, and this vague responsibility passed to the successor Board of Health three years later. Further acts (1823, 1832) enabled the Board to use government resources to remove nuisances but a specific list of what constituted nuisances – including dead animals – and the Board's procedures for their removal waited until an 1848 comprehensive act "Relating to the Appointment, Powers, and Duties of the Board of Health," and its 1853 and 1856 iterations. The Board declared "dead carcasses" a nuisance in an 1843 ordinance.[2] The 1853 act specified that owners of diseased or dead animals should destroy and bury them; failing this, the owner faced a $5-20 fine and the Board would remove the body.

Washington instituted the position of Scavenger in 1820 (Georgetown already had a smaller crew), and collecting animal carcasses fell to this crew. City scavengers received $1 for each dog buried.[3] A

---

[1] "At least two feet below the surface of the earth," according to the 1820 and 1853 ordinances.

[2] It published an annual list of outlawed substances for public notice "during the summer season". This is the earliest I have found. Oddly, carcasses did not appear in the omnibus Nuisance act of 1853. The Board of Health acts of 1848 and later copied the language of the 1809 legislation.

[3] As reported in the discussion cited above regarding shooting or poisoning strays (Wash. Sentinel, 8 June 1854, p. 3). The Register's Ann Rpt, 1847, lists every expenditure of that fiscal year and so names the several men

Corporation act of 4 Feb 1856 gave collection of "fluid and solid offal" to contractors; the Board commended their work in its 1858 annual report and recommended the same for street cleaning. As a result the following year (1859) "the contractors for the removal of dead animals, etc." removed a great quantity of dead dogs "which were seen lying about in the streets and alleys of the city."[4]

Citizens certainly had legitimate complaints about the nuisance. As early as 1814 "Y" complained in the National Intelligencer of the city's annoying "infernal effluvia" and its deleterious effect on health and business. "If you will go there [the Georgetown waterfront]" reported a Government study of 1872 "you will find ever so many dead cats and dogs, and there comes out such a stench that people have to pass over the other side of the street." Scavengers removed four cartloads of dead hogs from the Seventh Ward alone on one day of 1861. The Evening Star reported a dead horse left at the intersection of K and 17th Streets NW for three days in 1867.[5]

The hated Washington Canal held cats, dogs "and some horses' legs." "We undertook to count them," wrote an intrepid citizen. "It was a very warm day, and I think we rather enjoyed other parts of our ride better than we did that." "It appears to be a common practice for persons to send dead dogs, cats and hogs from their premises to be thrown into the canal." The District Commissioner of the Canal had responsibility for clearing it of carrion and other debris.[6]

The 1862 Congressional act expanding the scope of the new Department of Metropolitan Police created a Sanitary Company (or Office, commonly the Sanitary Police). This Company's duties as specified in the legislation extended only to private property – "ferry-boat, manufactory, slaughter-house, tenement-house or edifice" – and covered any complaints related to safety or health; in this work it received assignments from and reported to the Board of Health. Its work included removal of dead animals. Probably the police retained the contractor, for "Mr. Drifus" had a contract to "remove the defunct animals beyond the city's limits for their bones, hides and tallow" in 1869.[7] Annual reports of MPDC first show removal of dead animals (usually described as horses) in 1864 totaling 285, rising to 861 "horses, cows, etc." and 786 "hogs, dogs, cats, etc." in 1867. Reportage ceased in 1871.[8]

---

remunerated for taking up carcasses. They were paid in increments of $2 (per animal? per haul?) and all worked as scavengers or laborers. G. T. McGlue collected $15.50 – could he have been the father of George T. McGlue, the MPDC officer assigned to WHS duty in 1901?

[4] Evening Star, 23 July 1859, p. 3.

[5] "Affairs . . .", pp. 433, 622; Nat. Intelligencer, 26 May 1814, p. 1; Evening Star, 15 Feb 1861, p. 3; 17 June 1867, p. 3. These complaints continued: the District's Superintendent of the Free Bathing Beach, then on the Potomac, argued for creation of today's Tidal Basin reasoning that improvements to the Potomac Flats would eliminate the "dead animals, weeds, logs, and trash [that have] floated onto our beach" (Beach Supt's Ann Rpt, 1895).

[6] "That useless, nasty, stinking mantrap, the Washington Canal" (Evening Star, 25 June 1863, p. 2). Evening Star, 28 Oct 1861, p. 3; unfortunately I have lost the citation for the citizen's comment.

The problem extended to other District waterways. Stated a report of 1895: "All slops and filth of every kind, dead animals, manure from stables are thrown into the [C&O] canal [in Georgetown] by boatmen, and the people living along it certainly use it for very much the same purpose" (Health Off Ann Rpt, 1895). Tiber Creek was similarly polluted (Wash. Sentinel, 12 Apr 1854, p. 3; Evening Star, 30 May 1872, p. 4, "The Grand Avenue of Pestilence").

[7] (Drifus); Evening Star, 22 July 1869, p. 4. "The duties [of] the sanitary police, although of a very disagreeable character, are still of an inestimable value, and are probably rarely properly appreciated except by those acquainted with their daily experiences" (MPDC Ann Rpt, 1867, p. 507). On the other hand, the force was "composed mainly of illiterate men, a majority of whom could hardly write their names" – ten men and two officers, with no attached physician – "and these were the guardians of the health of the city of Washington" (Anonymous, "Affairs . . .", p. 727).

[8] Besides the original act, see also Bd of Health minutes, 21 Jan 1869. It is sad to note 18 dead and abandoned infants reported in 1869 and 29 the following year; the number reached 75 in 1885 and nearly 100 in 1888!

The **County of Washington** government (the Levy Court) in 1863 outlawed putting carcasses and other offal "into any river, creek, pond, road, street, canal, lot, field, meadow or common, or any other place whatever" under penalty of $5-20 and to 30 days imprisonment.[9]

---

[9] Callan, p. 1.

One Hundred Years of Advertising Found Animals

ESTRAY

Horatio Trumdel, of Georgetown, has this day brought to my view, a *Bay Gelding*; about fourteen and a half hands high, nine years old, with hanging mane and switch tail: which he stated has been tresspassing on him, for several days last past—that he has reason to believe said gelding belongs to some person in Georgetown, and that he has taken him up as an estray at large.

DANIEL REINTZEL,
Justice of the peace.

The owner of said Gelding is desired to call, prove his property, pay charges, and take him away.

HORATIA TRUNDEL.

March 12—3t†

Federal Republican, 12 March 1816, p. 3

STRAY COW.—Come to the farm of the subscriber, about one mile north of the Capitol, on or about the 16th of December last, a small red and white spotted Cow, with one horn broke off. The owner of said Cow is requested to call immediately, prove property, pay charges, and take her away.

feb 3—3t
DAVID MOORE.

Daily Nat. Republican, 7 February 1837, p. 1

SALE OF HOGS.—Will be sold at the Washington Asylum, on Saturday, the 1st of June next, at public auction, a lot of Hogs, the same having been carried there by the police officers, as provided for by an act of the Corporation of Washington, to prevent hogs from running at large in said Corporation.

Sale to commence at 12 o'clock M.
Terms of sale, cash.
may 31—
RICHARD BUTT,
I. W. A.

Daily Nat. Intelligencer, 1 Jun 1839, p. 3

TAKEN ESTRAY BY THE METROPOLITAN POLICE—On the 9th ultimo, a Sorrel Horse, having white face and left hind foot, with a saddle, were found estray. The owner is requested to prove property to the satisfaction of the Property Clerk of the District at his office, No. 483 Tenth street west, prior to 1st o'clock A M. Thursday, March 11th, 1864, or the same will be then sold for cash to the highest bidder, at the bazaar of W. L. Wall & Co, No. 98 Louisiana avenue.

By order.
GEO. R HERRICK, Property Clerk.
mar 1—1,5,10
W L WALL & CO, Auctioneers

Daily Nat. Intelligencer, 1 March 1864, p. 3

HOGS SOLD AT POUND SATURDAY AT 12 o'clock.
M. M. WHEELOCK,
1t*
Poundmaster.

Evening Star, 26 Oct 1871, p. 2

FOR SALE, AT THE WESTERN POUND, corner of 23d street and New York avenue northwest, SATURDAY, October 5, proximo, at 1 o'clock p. m. one white Horse, one light bay Mare, one black Colt, about eighteen months old, one sorrel Colt, about three years old, and twelve Geese. The horses above named were seized in the northwestern section of this city and impounded on the 24th instant, at 8 o'clock p. m., and if not redeemed prior to day of sale will be sold in accordance with an act of the Board of Health, dated December 5, 1871.

By order of Superintendent Board of Health.
se28&oc4
HENRY YOUNG, Pound Master.

Evening Star, 4 October 1872, p. 3

POUND SALE—There will be sold at the Pound, corner of 23d street and New York avenue, at 11 o'clock MONDAY MORNING, the 2d day of June, 1873, if not redeemed on or before that date—

One DARK BAY MULE taken (and impounded by the Board of Health) up in the northwestern section of the City.

m27-2t* SAMUEL EINSTEIN, Pound-Master.

Evening Star, 27 May 1873, p. 3

THERE WILL BE SOLD AT THE POUND, South Capitol and F streets southwest, at HALF-PAST TEN O'CLOCK A.M., ON FRIDAY, OCTOBER SIXTH, 1916, one bay horse, taken up in the vicinity of 15th and H streets northeast. By order of the health officer.

GEORGE RAE, Poundmaster.

Evening Star, 5 October 1916, p. 21

Early Legal Notices

SALE OF HOGS.—Will be sold at the Washington Asylum, on Saturday, the 1st of June next, at public auction, a lot of Hogs, the same having been carried there by the police officers, as provided for by an act of the Corporation of Washington, to prevent hogs from running at large in said Corporation.
Sale to commence at 12 o'clock M.
Terms of sale, cash. RICHARD BUTT,
may 31— I. W. A.

Daily National Intelligencer, 31 March 1830, p. 32

DOGS! DOGS! DOGS!—REGISTER'S OFFICE, *December 21, 1859.*—Notice is hereby given, that Licenses issued to owners of Dogs, will expire on the 31st instant, and that said Licenses must be renewed, in compliance with law, at this office within ten days after that time.
de21-dtJ1 WILLIAM MORGAN, Register.
[Intel. & Con.]

Evening Star, 31 December 1859, p. 2

MAYOR'S OFFICE, CITY HALL,
WASHINGTON, D. C., July 7, 1868.
All persons are hereby notified that the ordinances of the Corporation to prevent Hogs and Geese from running at large within the city limits will be rigidly enforced on and after the 10th instant, and that every Hog and Goose so found running at large on and after that date, will be taken up by the police, carried to the Workhouse, and be disposed of according to law.
No exceptions will be made in any case, but all will be dealt with alike.
The law also imposes a penalty on the owners of Goats found at large, which penalty will be strictly enforced on and after the 10th instant.
jy 8-10t S. J. BOWEN, Mayor.

Evening Star, 14 July 1868, p. 2

CITY REGISTER'S OFFICE.
WASHINGTON, D. C., Dec. 31, 1870.
Notice is hereby given that on MONDAY, January 2d, 1871, will expire all licenses given by the corporation of the City of Washington to Hucksters, Pawnbrokers, Bill Posters, Butchers of the several markets, Keepers of Dogs, Insurance Agents, Auctioneers, &c.
All said corporation licenses expiring on said date must be promptly renewed.
Deposits for licenses to this corporation are now by law made with the City Collector, by whom a certificate will be given, which must be countersigned by the City Comptroller, and then presented to the City Register, who will issue the license.
JOHN F. COOK, City Register.
dec23-eo10t [Star Pat & Chron]

Daily National Republican, 7 Jan 1871, p. 2

Pound Report. Animals impounded 141, redeemed 28, killed 113 Amt realized $29.00.

Pound Report. Animals impounded 247. Redeemed 55. Killed 192. Amt realized $59.

The Health Officer submitted an adverse report on the petition of Alex Dodge, Edward B. Hughes, and others asking return of $4.00 to Mrs. Catharine Lynch, paid by her for redemption of 2 cows from Pound Master, Mrs. Lynch having resisted the officers in the discharge of their duties etc. The report was approved.

Bd of Health minutes, 31 May and 20 June 1876

PART TWO

The Territorial and Early Commissioner Governments (1871-1912)

Going up into the town [we passed] by private homes where green benches invited to a dreary rest, by dogs pursuing pigs in sheer maliciousness, and brutal roosters crowing at the sport, and by negro kitchens in the rear of every dwelling. (George Alfred "Gath" Townsend, <u>Washington, Outside and Inside</u>. James Betts & Co., Hartford CN. c. 1873, p. 303)

Mary had a little lamb,/And it went straying round,/Till Wheelock's fellows gobbled it,/And put it in the pound. (Evening Star, 24 July 1871, p. 4)

In former years . . . the men employed were paid a fee for each animal impounded, which led to great abuses . . . The pound men were called thieves and robbers, and often richly deserved the name. (Nat. Republican, 15 June 1874, p. 4)

In 1871 Congress consolidated the two municipal Corporations and one County government into the Territorial government of the District of Columbia. This new entity famously began an ambitious building and upgrade program that created the modern city of Washington and also swamped the government itself in a flood of corruption and debt, leading to imposition of the Commissioner government in 1874.

In this period animal control continued to follow two somewhat separate tracks, as before, but these had now changed focus:

- Concerns relating to farm animals gradually disappeared as the animals themselves disappeared from the city. Although the pound handled cases of these larger beasts, they did not figure greatly in city concerns both because of their decreasing numbers and because, as before, being valuable they were likely to be redeemed by their owners;

- Control of nuisance animals – primarily dogs – became a much more organized and efficient operation and completely under the control of the District government, i.e., the pound and its staff;

- A new area of concern – the humane treatment of animals – came to the fore but with enforcement undertaken not by the pound but by SPCA, leading to something like parallel though not really competing agents of animal control.

Sources: For this later period there is a wonderful body of documentary material. Besides the rather dry trail of legal materials (now better preserved in the records of the U.S. Congress, which passed the laws, and the orders of the Commissioners), we have annual reports (Commissioners, Poundmaster, SPCA/WHS), Congressional hearing transcripts, and also newspaper articles so numerous that no researcher can read them all. The subject lent itself to clever and memorable writing (including that of Poundmaster Einstein) and one could write at least three narratives all covering the same ground for this period and not duplicate the quoted material.

CHAPTER SEVEN

The Contractor Pound

Among the famous works of improvement to the District of Columbia by the Territorial government, the establishment of an effective pound operation can easily be overlooked, but to the city's population it (in time) made a distinct improvement in the quality of urban life.

Previous measures having failed to curb animal-nuisances in Washington, the Corporation Council in 1870 re-organized the Board of Health and gave it responsibility for solving the problem.[1] The clearest-eyed account of this action was given in a newspaper article of the following year:[2]

> The Corporation act of 1870 gave the Board [of Health] certain powers 'to determine what it may regard as nuisances or sources of disease in the city and to direct the abatement thereof.' The act also required the Police Department to co-operate in the abatement of nuisances.
>
> Under the provisions of this act, the Board, previously a mere nullity for want of power, entered upon the work of correcting various evils that have given our city a bad name throughout the country. They found poudrette [fertilizer] factories within city limits;[3] hogs, goats, cows and geese roaming the streets; and many other nuisances tolerated in no well-regulated community and they proceeded, with more or less opposition from interested parties, to correct these abuses. Among the most troublesome they found the strongly entrenched animal nuisance.
>
> The Board of Health undertook to do what the Corporation authorities had failed to do, and resolutely set about the abatement of the nuisance. The result was a great hubbub amongst the pig-owners, thus disturbed in their vested right of free pasturage, and the Board extended the time for enforcement of the order [from June] until January [1871] to give opportunity for 'killing and curing' the animals.[4]
>
> The following January, 1871] these parties immediately hurried to the councils [and had the Board's powers rescinded.[5] The Star saw] no remedy for this disgraceful state of things but through the establishment of a

---

[1] The Board's minutes seldom mentioned stray animals, although stray animals fell under its purview after 1819 (see Appendix D1). Clearly the Police did this work. The Board's earlier organizational history is briefly sketched in the preceding section Dead Animals. The following narrative depends greatly on contemporary news accounts, the Board minutes being either unhelpful or non-existent for most of this period.

[2] Evening Star, 14 Jan 1871, p. 2, abridged here. See also Evening Star, 4 Jan 1871, p. 2, amusingly describing an earlier (apparently recent) campaign by the police ("The police . . . taking precious good care not to get very near the animals lest they . . . dirty their good clothes") and recounting the lobbying of the pig-men.

[3] For an interesting profile of the poudrette industry, see a detailed report in the Board minutes of 27 Oct 1855.

[4] See Bd of Health minutes, 13 Sept 1870.

[5] A notice of January 1871 from the Secretary of the Board ordered all owners of cows to enclose their animals (Evening Star, 7 Jan 1871, p. 2); a separate announcement on the same page by the City Manager reminded the public that a variety of licenses, including those for dogs, needed to be renewed. The outcome of this activity was summarized by Sen. George Edmunds two weeks later in debate: "The other day the Board of Health voted to abolish the nuisance, and the Councils abolished the Board of Health" (Evening Star, 24 Jan 1871, p. 4).

Metropolitan Board of Health by Congress, outside the control and influence of local politicians.[6] [After all,] the members [of Congress] are all interested in the health of the city, and many have property here detrimentally affected by [these] nuisances.[7]

And that is exactly what happened – the Congressional act creating the Territorial Government of February 1871 specifically assigned responsibility "to make and enforce regulations to prevent domestic animals from running at large in the cities of Washington and Georgetown" to the re-established Board of Health.[8] In early May the Board adopted a comprehensive code regarding Nuisances in the District, which included restrictions on strays and dogs. As anticipated, the Territorial Council challenged the Board's authority; the newly constituted House of Delegates (the lower chamber) officially inquired of the Board in May under what authority it had begun construction of a municipal pound,[9] but the Federal Government supported the Board.

"The Board of Health held a meeting last evening [May 1871] and . . . the secretary was authorized to . . . have distributed a poster warning all persons that they must enclose all domestic animals in and after June 15, 1871." This order anticipated a Board ordinance: "An Ordinance to Prevent Domestic Animals from Running at Large within the Cities of Washington and Georgetown" of 19 May 1871.[10] The May announcement, generally banning all types of farm animals from running at large in the two municipalities, made the first mention of "the public pound in Washington and Georgetown."

The new pound, as the old one, operated as a private, contractor service, judging from newspaper accounts of the arrangements and from its actual operations. The operative ordinance envisioned two pounds but we learn very little of the one in Georgetown. It was "on the corner of Washington Street [30th Street] and the canal" and was physically similar to the one in Washington. That more famous establishment stood at 1st and Q Streets NW, "consisting of a palisade covering a space of ground fifty yards square" with enclosures for horses, cattle, geese and dogs, as well as a house for the night watchman. The law required "that no suffering is occasioned" to impounded animals.[11]

---

[6] This account is confirmed by the anonymous "Affairs in the District of Columbia," p. 727: "The Board of Health we had was without authority and without means."

[7] See Evening Star, 15 June 1871, p. 1, which notes that "some . . . senators, wrathful about the manner in which their premises have been overrun by Washington's sacred porkers and bovines," specified the animal-clause in the Territory legislation.

[8] Sen. Edmunds declared during the debate that "one feature . . . in the present municipal government was infamous, and that was the abominable nuisance of cows, sheep, goats, and pigs running at large. There were not two trees in the city that did not show marks of injury from animals." He feared the deplorable state of the city would lead "Western men" to propose moving the Capital (Evening Star, 24 Jan 1871, p. 4).

[9] See the House's journal of 23 May 1871 (the first page for that day – the pages are unnumbered here). The response forwarded by the Governor was received on 15 June (p. 177) but unfortunately not copied into the book; it is probably the official opinion of Assistant Attorney-General Hill printed in the Evening Star, 17 June 1871, p. 1. The same entry records receipt of a request from President Gatchel of SPCA for erection of public drinking fountains "for the use of man and beast."

[10] Evening Star, 12 May 1871, p. 4; 7 June 1871, p. 1. The text is lost but we have the revised version of 1872; I summarize the 1872 ordinance in the later section "Legalities". Congress "legalized" this ordinance, and a number of other earlier Board ordinances, on 24 April 1880, and again on 7 Aug 1894. Some vestige of the 1871 ordinance might be found in the comprehensive "nuisance" ordinance of 19 Nov 1875, sec. 25, which consolidated earlier Bd of Health regulations. When Emil Kuhn was appointed poundmaster in 1911 the Commissioners order cited the 1871 ordinance as its authority.

[11] Evening Star, 8 June 1871, p. 4 gives a very detailed description of the facility.

Provisions for redemption – public advertisement, a holding period of six days, payment of a fine and charges – and for sale of unclaimed animals were similar to earlier ordinances.[12] As with the 1863 attempt, the poundmaster built and maintained the facility (and presumably expenses of his staff) himself, receiving a daily boarding-stipend from the city[13] and keeping half of all fines and charges. Unclaimed animals (except dogs) were sold after five days and those proceeds taken by the city. The poundmaster was bonded. His contract required that operations be ready to start on 15 June 1871.

As first poundmaster the Board made the mistake of appointing **T. Zell Hoover**,[14] "who has an unsavory police record here"; "who has been before the courts so often on charges of swindling," fired as poundmaster "because of his notoriously bad character"[15] – a type of dishonest and incompetent contractor common then and now. Hoover was listed in the 1869 and '71 City Directories as a "provisions-broker". He seems to have lived on the edges of municipal contracts: in 1868 he ran for the Board of the Washington Asylum; in 1869 he bid for contracts to transport "paupers to the alms-house" and convicts to labor sites.[16] He had worked as a broker and real estate agent, and he published the short-lived Daily Evening Dispatch in 1867.[17]

As the stated 15 June round-up of animals approached excitement grew. The joy of the Evening Star[18] was too delicious to let pass:

> Blessed Hope and Relief! From and after tomorrow the cities of Washington and Georgetown will cease to be common pasturage and browsing ground for vagrant animals. Roaming droves of porkers will no longer be permitted to ravage our yards, root up our grass-plats, and carry destruction to our flower and kitchen gardens. No longer will they be allowed to make a hog-wash of every gutter, and afterwards to paint our palings with mud. No longer will the exuberant cows have the run of our shrubberies and parked streets. No longer will the musical geese contest with pigs for the possession of the puddles and the sidewalks. No longer will the frisky goats carry on their pugnacious frays on the footways, or make lively butting raids on juveniles. Thus pass away time-honored institutions under the ruthless hand of modern innovation.

Like many successful frauds, Hoover began his tenure impressively – crack at 12:01 AM, 15 June, Hoover, "eager to make hay while the sun shines," "promptly entered on the work of capturing and impounding all stray animals."[19] His catch totaled 45 cows, over 15 hogs and several dogs. "As may be imagined, the precincts of Swampoodle, Goose Level, et al. were in a blaze of excitement" – so much so that a mob of 300-400 gathered at the new pound "some threatening to tear down the . . . building, and others imploring the inexorable poundmaster to deliver up their property." Police held off the mob until,

---

[12] The financial arrangements were a complicated matter, to say the least: the Critic-Record (7 June 1871, p. 2) complained that the Board had decided for the poundmaster's remuneration to equate with the pound's fines ("This does not 'enrich the State,' which, by the way, is not exactly in the condition of the Rothchilds or the Bank of England"), and on the very day of opening a judge ordered seizure of the entire building "and things appertaining thereto . . . unless the Board comes to the rescue" (Critic-Record, 15 June 1871, p. 3). The following summary of pound regulations is taken from: Evening Star, 20 May 1871, p. 4; 8 June 1871, p. 4; Daily Nat. Republican, 20 May 1871, p. 4.

[13] Horses, mules, cows – 75 cents/day; sheep, goats, hogs – 50 cents, according to the Republican (above), but 50 and 25 cents respectively to the Star.

[14] Often also seen as "T. Z. Hoover"; the T stood for Thomas.

[15] Respectively: Evening Star, 14 Oct 1895, p. 2; Critic-Record, 23 Feb 1884, p. 2; Evening Star, 6 Feb 1873, p. 1.

[16] (Asylum) Nat. Republican, 18 July 1868, p. 3; (paupers) 9 Feb 1869, p. 4; (convicts) 2 Feb 1869, p. 4.

[17] For exactly two weeks; see Bryan, "Bibliography"; Evening Star, 6 Feb 1873, p. 1 for the other two professions.

[18] Op. cit., 14 June 1871, p. 2 (abridged here).

[19] This account taken from Evening Star, 15 June 1871, p. 4; and Critic-Record, 16 June 1871, p. 3.

at 10 AM, word came from the Board of Health that the ban began at midnight of that evening. "The animals were promptly released, and to those who had paid the fees the money was returned, and in a short time all became quiet." Not only had Hoover jumped the gun, but his contract had not yet been signed nor his bonding approved.

The next morning Hoover made his next foray, "out with a wagon and several assistants," netting cows, hogs, goats, one horse and mule, and dogs. The animals were mostly redeemed except the "mean 'yaller dogs'," which would "doubtless at the end of 24 hours . . . have forfeited their lives." Again, the pound crew "did not have a very agreeable time," smuggling eleven geese past an angry crowd in 14th Street NW only "by fast driving." This day Dr. Verdi,[20] Secretary of the Board, visited the pound and informed all pleaders that Hoover's actions were lawful and they would in fact have to pay the redemption fine. "In consequence . . . Goose Level, Swampoodle, and Cow Town are in commotion . . . and on the commons there are numbers of boys and girls watching the cows."[21]

In spite of this apparently strong start, Hoover was soon in hot water. Some of the complaints against him no doubt stem from the predicted resistance of lax owners, but the persistence of the complaints and his disreputable later career point to (at the least) an imperious and impolitic nature.[22] Just two days later[23] the Board felt the need to lay out specific procedures for pound operations, including some protections for legal horses (giving the idea that Hoover had been taking them willy-nilly). Others of these instructions imply that Hoover had been padding his charges.

Further "armed resistance" met the poundmen that week, when a mob of 40, including several Marines, sought to block capture of some sheep outside the Navy Yard, again necessitating police intervention. The Board debate on this matter "showed anything but unanimity upon the pound-question." The adopted resolution tightened Hoover's scope of animal-capture (he now needed a written permit <u>signed by the President and Secretary of the Board for each animal</u>), but also touched on police protection of pound employees and the question of very young children claiming to supervise cattle.[24] The following week the Board continued this desultory discussion, generally tending favorable to the injured animal owners.[25]

Hoover's end came quickly. The Board of Health, meeting on 3 July 1871, heard a report that the poundmaster's bonding was not sufficient. "Mr. Langston offered resolutions which were adopted, that T. Z. Hoover has failed to keep his contract with the Board . . . and that said contract be annulled.[26] **Von**

---

[20] Tullio S. Verdi, later President of the Board. He joined the reconstituted SPCA in 1884. The Secretary, successor to the Commissioner of Health established by the 1856 act, was the only full-time employee of the Board; he handled all administrative affairs and made most on-the-ground decisions.

[21] Evening Star, 16 June 1871, p. 4. See also 17 June 1871, p. 8 for a brief account of the next day's haul and specifics of pound procedures.

[22] The press made much of "The Goose War", in which Hoover and his men roughed up a lady while impounding her goose. He "told his men to knock the cat down, tie her legs, and throw her in the wagon with the dogs" (Evening Star, 23 June 1871, p. 4).

[23] Evening Star, 20 June 1871, p. 1.

[24] Evening Star, 22 June 1871, p. 1; Critic-Record, 23 June 1871, p. 3 (two articles).

[25] Critic-Record, 27 June 1871, p. 3, demanding prosecution of "parties who had attempted to interfere with the Poundmaster"; Evening Star, 3 July 1871, p. 4, recounting the Board's discussion, generally unfavorable to Hoover.

[26] Hoover sued the Board for damages "on account of his removal from . . . office" (Daily Nat. Republican, 28 Sept 1872, p. 4).

Essen Essex was then elected poundmaster of Georgetown, and **M. M. Wheelock** poundmaster of Washington."[27]

We cannot overlook Hoover's later career, sordid as it was. That very November (1871) he was convicted of defrauding female employees of the Treasury Department, and two years later was caught up in the Credit Mobilier scandal. In 1875 he was passing himself off as a kind of lobbyist-for-hire ("Special Attention given to any Bills or Claims that may need legislation by Congress. No Commission until Claim or Bill has passed."). The only notice of him in the next decade related to his conviction for "false pretenses," promising to procure government jobs for dupes. Hoover hit his ludicrous bottom in 1895, when he claimed to have learned of a plot to dynamite the British embassy. Predictably "T. Zell Hoover was the only man who could frustrate the plot." The conclusion of this farce was too ridiculous to copy here, but the article boldly reported: "Hoover claims he has reformed."[28]

The Board's next choice of poundmaster was M. M. Wheelock. Unlike Hoover, Wheelock was not hopelessly dishonest, but simply the wrong man for the job. He has left less record. The 1864 City Directory listed him as "Huckster, Cent. Mkt."[29] In the 1871 directory he was a patent agent. After his stint as poundmaster news items indicate he served as a notary and had various business dealings, including managing the Lenox Hotel. He died in 1891.[30]

Wheelock also started his duties with a bang. He left Hoover's pound at 1st Street for a new one at 17th and Massachusetts Avenue NW, in a former cavalry stable. "The building is about 40 feet wide, 175 long and 16 high, . . . and is furnished with large doors and windows, making quite a comfortable place." Separate compartments housed horses, cows (these two "provided with stables"), goats, geese and dogs. "With a plentiful supply of water at hand, and attentive assistants, the animals will fare well."[31] He also planned a facility near the Capitol but nothing came of this. "It will be well for owners to look out for their cows, horses, goats, hogs and geese."[32]

By late July the new poundmaster and his crew were in full operation. The Evening Star announced a few livestock available at the pound, but "most of [the stock] has been redeemed. He has no end of dogs, however, but will not have so many tomorrow morning. Nothing but stamps [?] will save them from destruction."[33] The following month Wheelock "gobbled" three of President Grant's escaped horses, which a presidential staffer properly redeemed the next day.[34]

Wheelock's problems to some degree mirrored Hoover's – the active resentment of owners, invariably those of swine, and an uncontrolled crew. Within a month of starting operations, the new poundmaster was accused of "following the ways of the old one who had been dismissed." His employees were "a set of ruffians and cut-throats" who "brought disgrace upon the Board by their outrageous behavior."[35] Through

---

[27] Evening Star, 5 July 1871, p. 1; Critic-Record, 5 July 1871, p. 3. This is the only reference I find either to Essex or the Georgetown pound except for that establishment's abolition soon after this. For a clue to Essex, who seems to have come from a wealthy family, see the Evening Star, 14 July 1866, p. 2 (perhaps relating to his father); 25 Sept 1893, p. 9.

[28] Critic-Record, 13 Dec 1875, p. 1; Daily Critic, 8 July 1884, p. 4; Evening Star, 15 Nov 1871, p. 1; 6 Feb 1873, p. 1; 23 Feb 1884, p. 2; 14 Oct 1895, p. 2.

[29] He was the "Marcus M. Wheelock, provisions" of the 1862 directory. See also Evening Star, 19 May 1863, p. 1.

[30] Evening Star, 28 Jan 1891, p. 8.

[31] Evening Star, 14 July 1871, p. 4. It was a frame building earlier used by the 5th U.S. Cavalry, and after its pound use a local man stored lumber there, according to an account of its accidental burning in 1873 (Nat. Republican, 18 Oct 1873, p. 5).

[32] Critic-Record, 12 July 1871, p. 3.

[33] Op. cit., 29 July 1871, p. 4.

[34] Critic-Record, 25 Aug 1871, p. 3.

outrageous behavior."³⁵ Through 1872 newspaper accounts of assaults on the pound's staff mounted – and also of them attacking citizens.³⁶ The irrepressible President Gatchel of SPCA (see below) once arrested pound driver Henry Harris for "overloading and cruelly beating his horse."³⁷ Poundmen became so identified with aggressive behavior that in October 1871 several "well-known thieves" (including Jerry Wormley and "Tom Cat" Mokin) posed as agents of the pound and began rounding up domestic animals in southwest Washington. Angry residents beat off the raid but a number of warriors had to visit the local hospital.³⁸

During this period the Board of Health took some steps to support its poundmaster. In July 1871 the Board discussed improved regulations for both redemption and disposal of stray dogs,³⁹ and in March 1872 authorized the poundmaster to take all animals "running at large." The re-organized Board of the Territorial period, which the Evening Star approvingly noted was independent of "the hog vote" (in contrast to the old Corporation Council), again outlawed hogs running at large in August 1871.⁴⁰ Several articles refer to a prohibition against unmuzzled dogs.⁴¹ Furthermore, in August 1871 the Board united pound operations of Washington and Georgetown under Wheelock. "Our citizens are rejoiced . . . His advent will be hailed with delight."⁴²

In less than a year Wheelock followed Hoover into private life. "At the meeting of the Board of Health last evening, Dr. [D. W.] Bliss . . . reported [that] the poundmaster does not devote that personal attention to his duties which is necessary, and that he had employed irresponsible boys to take up animals at so much per head, [so that] these parties have invaded private property for the purpose of seizing animals, and then obtaining a fee, [while] some sections are overrun by animals at large."⁴³

Bliss recommended that Wheelock's contractor pound be replaced with "a public pound" – or actually two: eastern (Washington) and western (Georgetown). The new poundmasters would be salaried city employees, receiving $1,000 per annum (the same as inspectors), and the city would build the new facilities. The Board approved this plan by revising the 1871 ordinance (in March 1872) and hired **A. L. G. Mason** as the eastern and **J. H. Smith** as the western poundmasters.⁴⁴ This new approach marked the

---

³⁵ Critic-Record, 15 Aug 1871, p. 3; Evening Star, 8 June 1872, p. 4. The latter comment came during a Council debate; replied another member: "It is impossible to get gentlemen with kid gloves to attend to the business of hog and cow catching." The police arrested the "pound-master" in 1871, according to their annual report of that year, whether Hoover, Wheelock or one of their men we do not know.
³⁶ For example, see: (attacking the poundmen) Evening Star, 9 Sept 1871, p. 4 "Assault on a Dog-Catcher"; 8 May 1872, p. 4; 2 June 1873, p. 4 "A Pound Man Shot Yesterday"; (they attack owners) Critic-Record, 30 June 1871, p. 3; Evening Star, 28 May 1872, p. 4. (This last, in an echo of the Goose War, involved a poundman who "threw his lasso at [the owner], saying he would take her too." She lost two teeth. For a much-later replay of this sort of kerfuffle, see Wash. Post, 16 Oct 1936, p. X19.)
³⁷ Daily Critic, 23 Aug 1871, p.3.
³⁸ Evening Star, 16 Oct 1871, p. 4. Local criminal Bill Burke "was arrested some days ago upon the charge of representing himself as a poundmaster"; Evening Star, 20 July 1872, p. 4.
³⁹ Evening Star, 6 July 1871, p. 4. This article only reports the proposal, which presumably was voted on at a later meeting. "Mr. Marbury said the law against dogs had not been enforced because there was no law providing compensation for killing them" (suggested here at 25 cents each).
⁴⁰ Critic-Record, 13 Mar 1872, p. 3; Evening Star, 18 Aug 1871, p. 4; 13 Nov 1871, p. 2.
⁴¹ E.g., Evening Star, 17 Aug 1871, p. 4.
⁴² Evening Star, 2 Aug 1871, p. 4.
⁴³ Evening Star, 2 Mar 1872, p. 4; Daily Nat. Republican, 2 Mar 1872, p. 5. For Bliss, see Daily Nat. Republican, 13 July 1871, p. 1.
⁴⁴ Evening Star, 2 Mar 1872, p. 4; see Evening Star, 13 Mar 1872, p. 4 for further discussion of the new policies. Daily Critic, 15 June 1872, p. 3 mentions a fresh Board report on the duties of the poundmaster, which we fain

beginning of the city-operation that characterized Washington's animal control efforts for the next hundred years.⁴⁵

Once again citizens waited for new management to bring improvement to their animal-harried lives. A facility was planned at 4ᵗʰ and Massachusetts Avenue NW ("a fence 8 feet high of boards, enclosing a space 40 feet square, covered with a suitable roof, which would not cost over $200"), but "not a single dog or hog had been taken up for the last month [February-March] and it was folly to be paying the poundmasters . . . for doing nothing."⁴⁶ Mason advertised a few animal sales – on the grounds of the Washington Asylum – in May and July,⁴⁷ but of Smith's work not a word remains. Wrote a frustrated resident in late March: "Hurry Up the Georgetown Pound . . . West Georgetown is overrun with an army of half-starved and mangy curs, and the citizens are praying for relief."⁴⁸

Pound operations continued under regular criticism. In one meeting (May 1872) the Board heard "innumerable complaints" about animals wrongly taken. "Mr. [John] Marbury . . . did not blame the poundmaster, but thought his employees were unfit for business." Some blamed imprecise laws for the problems and others unfriendly courts: "Dr. Verdi said as the law was now the poundmen would be convicted every time they were arraigned." In August several Board members explicitly stated that the U. S. Attorney was hostile to its employees, proven by the number of prosecutions.⁴⁹

In October of that year an advertisement for an animal sale was signed by "**Henry Young**, Poundmaster" of the western pound. The address given – 23ʳᵈ Street and New York Avenue – is the first indication of the new facility which would (unhappily) continue in use for forty years.⁵⁰

Amid these woes the Board of Health fought back, issuing a report by the omnipresent "T. F. Gatchell [sic; also the SPCA president], esq., the present superintendent of pounds." Gatchel found that the pounds presented a "successful operation, [in spite of] no little opposition on the part of interested persons . . . arraigned against the poundmaster and his agents." He concluded that "under all the disadvantages and obstructions interposed to prevent the proper execution of the law, the pound could not have been more economically conducted," an assessment repeated in the Board's first annual report (1872). Mr. Langston, of the Board, reported the same early the following year.⁵¹

In spite of these rosy encomiums, the pound and Board continued under attack. A writer of January 1873 suggested turning over Board functions to the Metropolitan Police, which handled things more

---

would have. Smith was active in the local Republican party (Daily Nat. Republican, 8 Apr 1872, p. 4, et al.); of Mason I find no information.

⁴⁵ Mr. Marbury: "If the Board was to run this pound business they should first annul the law which makes it obligatory on the poundmaster to do all this work himself"; Evening Star, 13 Mar 1872, p. 4.

⁴⁶ Ibid.

⁴⁷ Daily Nat. Republican, 9 May 1872, p. 2 was the earliest.

⁴⁸ Evening Star, 20 Mar 1872, p. 4.

⁴⁹ (Laws) Evening Star, 15 May 1872, p. 4; (hostile) 10 Aug 1872, p. 4; 16 Nov 1872, p.4, gives the Attorney's response.

⁵⁰ Evening Star, 4 Oct 1872, p. 3. With such a common name it is impossible to identify this poundmaster among the Henry Youngs in newspaper articles of the period – the lawyer? the party activist? the drunken thief? The only other notice I find of him is a very early profile of the pound (Critic-Record, 24 July 1873, p. 1), in which he toured a reporter around the new operation, describing himself as "in charge of the pound," but a list of Board employees of May 1873 shows him making the same $2/day as the other five (all named) poundmen (Daily Nat. Republican, 9 May 1873, p. 4). Interestingly, the Board of Health Ann Rpt for that year (Evening Star, 1 Dec 1873, p. 5) says nothing about either a pound or dead animal removal.

⁵¹ (Gatchel) Evening Star, 18 Dec 1872, p. 1; Nat. Republican, 18 Dec 1872, p. 1. Unfortunately we have only these summaries of Gatchel's report. He was described as "Superintendent" at a Board meeting of the previous week (Evening Star, 13 Dec 1872, p. 4); (Langston) 14 Apr 1873, p. 4.

efficiently. A bill introduced that May in the House of Delegates proposed exactly the same thing.[52] At just this time we find the first reference to "Samuel Einstein, Poundmaster", and as of his first day – 23 March 1873 – a new era had begun for pound operations.

(A wonderfully detailed act of the fourth session of the Territorial Legislature, 1874, bound into the official compilation of acts but marked: "Passed by the legislature but did not become law," proposed to ban all farm animals from running at large in **the County** and to **establish one or more pounds there**. The general outline of procedures follows that of the City pound above but allowed the poundmaster to keep all pound fees – which are specified individually --, pay certain sums to the animal's finder, and turn over the remainder to the District treasury. No further remuneration for the poundmaster was described, nor whether he was a direct County employee or contractor. Redemption and other pound fees, and fines would have been somewhat higher than in the City. Although this law did not take effect, at 28 sections over eight ms. pages, its many details fill in specifics of procedure and policy otherwise lost.)[53]

---

[52] Evening Star, 22 Jan 1873, p. 4 (two pound-related articles on the page; the other reports that citizen complaints were "referred to the sanitary police committee," a name familiar from many Board meetings); 9 May 1873, p. 4.

[53] It is the last item in the second volume; a copy is deposited in the Washingtoniana Division. No exact date is given. A bit of preliminary debate is preserved in Evening Star, 19 May 1874, p. 4, where we learn that the chief concern of legislators was whether to make a new, independent institution to take up county animals or give the responsibility to the established Board of Health, which some feared would be more costly. Perhaps there was also some territoriality at work: "The county desired to keep aloof from the Board . . . and the city as much as possible. . . People there had much rather have the cattle run at large than the Board of Health." Their chief complaint related to cows.

CHAPTER EIGHT

Samuel Einstein[1]

Socially I am fond of dogs, but in my official capacity I am their sworn enemy – that is, if they don't abide by the law. (Wash. Times, 13 Apr 1902, Ed/Drama p. 17)

Although the poundmaster's name probably appeared over a thousand times in Washington newspapers we have only a sketchy history of his personal life. He was born in 1848[2] in Buttenhausen, Germany and moved to Alexandria, Virginia at age 18. He was active in that city's business and social life.[3] Perhaps he met his future wife Jennie there (born in 1859, also of a German family though hailing from Indiana), since she had an unclaimed letter in the Alexandria post office in 1874. They married in 1876.[4] His brother, Ferdinand J. Einstein (1861-1946) and his daughter Lillie (Boswell) received regular notice from the newspapers, the former for his business dealings and the latter for her social engagements. He also had two sisters – "all of Washington."[5]

Einstein moved to Washington in 1873 to assume his pound duties and died still serving. After a period on New Jersey Avenue NW, the family settled in Georgetown. In an age of pervasive social/service organizations, Einstein showed the usual "joining" enthusiasm, particularly for organizations related to Germany and Judaism: the Schuetzen Verein, B'nai B'rith, Sons of Benjamin, B'rith Abraham, Scottish Rite, Eastern Star, Knights of Labor. He belonged to the Washington Hebrew Congregation and was on the board of Hebrew Charities.[6] He was at least somewhat active in local politics and civic events.[7] Mrs. Einstein's activities mirrored those of her husband.[8]

---

[1] Spelled Einstine in a few early accounts
   For pictures of Einstein, see: Wash. Times, 13 Apr 1902, Ed/Drama p. 17; Evening Star, 20 Sept 1908, pt. 4 p. 4 (both at the pound); 21 Mar 1909, pt. 7 p. 6; and 10 July 1911, p. 3 (the same image); a nice drawing of a somewhat younger Einstein is in 30 Aug 1890, p. 12.

[2] Both birth dates taken from their gravestones. His death certificate showed him as 63 years, two months and one day old on 9 July 1911. I thank Mr. Ali Rahmann of the D.C. Archives for this document. The 1900 census entry is clearly in error.

[3] We don't know his business but he helped organize the 1871 Eintracht ball (Alex Gazette, 31 June 1871, p. 2) and the Concordia L. A. (Ladies Association?) masquerade ball (29 Nov 1871, p. 3).

[4] Alex Gazette, 5 Sept 1874, p. 2 for the letter. The other information comes from the 1900 census, Einstein's obituary, and an account of the couple's twelfth anniversary party (Evening Star, 16 Oct 1888, p. 6; see also 10 Apr 1900, p. 5; 16 Oct 1901, p. 5), which mentions friends coming from Philadelphia and Newark for the event.

[5] Lillie is identified in the Evening Star's and Wash. Post's obituaries and mentioned in the papers, but the Wash. Herald said the couple was childless. For one of his sisters see Nat. Republican, 25 Dec 1885, p. 4. The two brothers and their wives are buried together in the Washington Hebrew Congregation Cemetery as is Einstein's niece Fannie (1879-1903), also born in Germany and clearly very close to the couple (she is buried in the same gravesite).

[6] (Schuetzen) Daily Critic, 30 July 1877, p. 4; (B'nai B'rith) Evening Star, 9 July 1883, p. 3; (Benjamin) 5 Jan 1891, p. 3 – he frequently served as an officer; (Abraham) 14 Aug 1893, p. 8; (Scottish Rite) 24 Oct 1895, p. 13 – he apparently achieved the 33rd degree; (Eastern Star) 10 July 1911, p. 3; (Knights) 18 July 1896, p. 11.

Although holding a position "which [as his obituary commented] does not tend to increase the popularity of those engaged in it," Einstein seems to have been personally and professionally popular all of his long life. The near total absence of newspaper items describing any sort of personal or professional dispute (except with recalcitrant dog owners) says much.[9] He regularly showed concern for the welfare of his pound staff, of the animals under his care, and of the community. "He performed the duties of his office with conspicuous tact and fairness. I shall always recall his genial personality with pleasure and regret," eulogized a city official at his funeral.[10]

He once stopped a man from committing suicide, and served as pallbearer for a friend who died in that way. When smallpox struck the city he organized the quarantine efforts, personally moving stricken persons and disinfecting their quarters. He helped evaluate the sanitary conditions of public schools, and the quality of river water, and donated to the relief of C&O Canal flood victims. "During the big blizzard a number of years ago the poundmaster had to engage in a severe struggle in the southeast section in an effort to furnish food to several poor families." Summarized the Washington Bee: "Mr. Einstein is always on the alert for the good of the city."[11]

Although conscientious and somewhat strict in his professional duties, Einstein infused his work with the tact and humanity noted at his funeral. A few anecdotes (abridged) among the many must suffice:

- The animal was playing with a little child on the steps of a modest house. "Hold!" [Einstein] cried, "Don't throw the nets, men! I won't have it said that Samuel Einstein destroyed the happiness of an innocent child. I'll get that dog some day next week when the kid's asleep." All of which goes to show Samuel Einstein's kindness of heart and inflexible devotion to duty. *(Wash. Times, 13 Apr 1902, p. 17)*[12]
- Sixty-five dogs, apparently of sixty-five different breeds, were howling the crescendo strains of the damned in chorus yesterday afternoon. "Poor Fido!" said Mr. Einstein to a little red dog with a sacrificial blue ribbon around his neck. This little dog was shedding tears as he peered longingly through the iron grating. "Poor Fido," repeated Mr. Einstein, but Fido could not be cajoled into taking his watery eyes off the butcher's post. He fell back on his haunches and howled like [a] pipe organ. *(Wash. Times, 11 Aug 1897, p. 8)*

Records of the Washington Hebrew Congregation indicate that he held no position of responsibility there. In 1896 the congregation formally thanked the Einsteins for their "valuable assistance and self-sacrificing display of spirit" in the recent fund-raising fair; the president, H. King, added his personal tribute: "I shall ever hold you in grateful remembrance for your kindness and friendship to me." Such displays were unusual in the normally staid financial reports of the synagogue. (My thanks to Dr. Michael Goldstein of the Congregation's Archives Committee for his research into Einstein's documentation.)

[7] He attended the Congressional nominating convention (in Alexandria) of the Conservative Party (Nat. Republican, 30 Aug 1878, p. 1). For more general civic work see, inter al., Evening Star, 15 Jan 1897, p. 7; 23 Nov 1899, p. 16; 16 Jan 1902, p. 5.

[8] A member of ladies' branch of the Sons of Abraham (Evening Star, 11 Nov 1901, p. 6); at a society function (31 Dec 1892, p. 3; Evening Critic, 15 Feb 1882, p. 4).

[9] For one amusing example see Evening Star, 12 Nov 1884, p. 3. The National Archives holds a multi-volume index of every letter received by the Commissioners from 1874 to 1897 including a one-line summary of the contents; in reviewing all entries 1874-95 I found only four that distinctly complained about the poundmaster or poundmen.

[10] Evening Star, 10 July 1911, p. 3.

[11] (Stopping suicide) Critic-Record, 7 Aug 1877, p. 4; Evening Star, 29 May 1883, p. 3; (pallbearer) Evening Star, 19 Apr 1894, p. 8; (smallpox) 21 Nov 1894, p. 11; (schools) 22 Sept 1891, p. 8; (river) Wash. Critic, 13 June 1889, p. 1; (flood) Wash. Post, 11 June 1889, p.1; (blizzard) Evening Star, 21 Mar 1909, pt. 7 p. 6; (quotation) Wash. Bee, 3 Oct 1891, p. 2.

[12] "That morning there was a near mistake: . . . one of [the poundmen] told us that the dog they'd been chasing belonged to a little girl. He nodded toward a golden-skinned child nearby, holding onto a large black retriever. Her brown eyes were afraid. Later, one of the . . . dog-baggers told me that they never took a dog from a kid if the kid had control over it" (Evening Star, 16 Nov 1969, Sunday Magazine p. 22).

- While on the way to the pound an owner of one of the dogs hailed the poundmaster and demanded her dog. As a matter of course the request was not complied with unless the money to redeem the animal was brought forth. A good tongue lashing was given the poundmaster, all of which he bore like a veteran, and finding she would be obliged to bow to the will of the poundmaster, she produced the necessary amount and the dog was released. *(Nat. Republican, 18 June 1874, p. 4)*
- General Eynestyne [sic] came smilingly to the front and explained to the lady how it would have been impossible for the festive goats to have made their way [out of her yard legally]. "Och, it's a lie, sure," exclaimed the Emerald Islander, "Ye are all a lot of thieves together, and –" "Madam," gravely broke in the philosopher, "you are past the time of life for using such language in such a reckless manner." *(Nat. Republican, 14 May 1875, p. 4)*
- As we journeyed through the outskirts of the city, "General" Einstein observed a horse grazing on a vacant lot. For a moment it seemed as if he were almost to turn and go after the beast, but he pushed resolutely forward, glancing back now and then with regret and bewailing the fact that he was unable to take [it] up. "If I put the horse in the wagon with the dogs," he said, "there would be an awful row and probably everything would be smashed to pieces. Too bad, too bad," he muttered ruefully with another farewell glance at the grazing horse. *(Wash. Times, 13 Apr 1902, p. 17)*
- Poundmaster Einstein is frequently asked what becomes of the dogs that are so unfortunate as to fall into the hands of the "dog-catchers," to which he invariably replies: "Oh, we just get rid of them." *(Wash. Post, 22 July 1906, p. F9)*

The great pleasure of his life was fishing, and he served many years as an officer of the Old Anglers' Association.[13] Einstein died in 1911 from tubercular meningitis, and was buried in the Washington Hebrew Congregation Cemetery in Anacostia. One year later appeared in the Evening Star his wife's memorial: "In sad but loving tribute to my dear devoted husband, Samuel Einstein, who died one year ago, July 9, 1911. By his devoted lonely wife, Jennie Einstein." Mrs. Einstein moved from the N Street house soon after his death. She died in 1923, struck by an automobile.[14]

---

[13] Which he joined in 1882. Evening Star, 26 June 1886, p. 2; 20 Mar 1890, p. 5; 11 May 1895, p. 18. Notes on his fishing expeditions appeared regularly. See 18 Mar 1895, p. 10 for his opinion on flies. He also belonged to the Washington Angling Association – perhaps the same organization? (Evening Star, 14 Jan 1891, p. 6); and was a founding member of the Anglers' Association (Wash. Times, 25 Oct 1895, p. 2).
[14] (Death/obituary) Evening Star, 10 July 1911, p. 3; Wash. Post, 10 July 1911, p. 2; Wash. Herald, 10 July 1911, p. 10; (tribute) 9 July 1912, p. 7; (moving) 23 Sept 1911, p. 9; (J's death) records of the Washington Hebrew Congregation.

CHAPTER NINE

Legalities of the Pound Operations

The immediate importance of the mad-dog problem has encouraged some citizens to traverse the confusing labyrinth of Congressional statutes regarding dogs, as found in the District of Columbia Code of Laws. (Evening Star, 31 Oct 1943, p. 42)

Before describing Einstein's pound and its operations it will be good to sketch the laws under which he worked. After the abolition of the bankrupt Territorial government in 1874 Congress imposed the temporary administration of three presidentially-appointed commissioners. This system was made permanent in 1878.[1] While dismantling the free-spending Board of Public Works in 1874, Congress continued the Board of Health. That ineffectual body was replaced in 1878 with a single Health Officer.[2] Under the Commissioner government, legislated laws emanated only from Congress. Congressional act of 1879 gave the appointed Commissioners authority "to prescribe rules for . . . animals found running at large in the District of Columbia."[3] The Board (or Health Officer), however, effectuated most mundane procedures of animal control through its ordinances, which we must hunt up singly in the Commissioners minutes, police regulations, and in news reports.

The District pound service was under the oversight of the Health Officer's Office of the Chief Clerk, who otherwise supervised such operations as record-keeping and finances.[4]

The poundmaster was bonded both by the DC government (to protect the city from neglect of duties) and the federal government (as a notary, a necessity for sales and other pound transactions). He was not allowed to charge for notarizations, and furthermore had to pay for both bonds himself.[5]

In 1872 the Territorial Board of Health replaced the former contractor-operated pound with an operation financed and administered by the District government. This 1872 ordinance gives a good idea of the basic procedures under which Einstein operated. It relates only to farm animals.

---

[1] Acts of: (Territorial govt) 21 Feb 1871; (temp Commissioner) 20 June 1874; (perm Commissioner) 11 June 1878.

[2] This was after years of complaining that it got no respect, no cooperation and no appropriations, and after regular re-organizations. In fact, the well-meaning but clueless Board (it only met twice in some years) would remind modern Washingtonians of the recently neutered Board of Education. It was changed to the Health Department in 1903, though still headed by the Health Officer.

[3] This act is titled "An Act Authorizing the Commissioners . . . to Extend the Area for the Taking Up and Impounding of Domestic Animals", and so it seems to both place the Commissioners above the Health Officer and to specifically allow them to take animal control into the county.

[4] At least in its early years the responsibility was not welcomed by the Board: "By some accident, or strange association of ideas, the 'prevention of animals running at large . . .' was enacted by Congress to be the duty of the Board of Health" (Bd of Health Ann Rpt, 1875). Later reports indicate considerable pride in the pound's success.

[5] This, at least, was true in a later period (Senate Comm on DC, "Giving Police Power"). The bond was set at $1,000 by the Board (Bd of Health minutes, 19 May 1876).

No **farm animals** (horses, mules, bulls, steers, cows, calves, heifers, sheep, goats, hogs, geese) were to roam free in the cities of Washington or Georgetown; those that did would be impounded. Animals not claimed and paid for would be sold after 48 hours, with proper advertising beforehand. The poundmaster acted as auctioneer. All money from the sale went to the District government. Verifiable owners could collect this sale price from the city within one year, less applicable boarding expenses (carefully listed by species) and fines.

The ordinance seems to assume one facility and one poundmaster. Although it does not directly address responsibility for building, staffing, etc., the poundmaster and the pound are both spoken of as employees/property of the city rather than outside contractors. The poundmaster turned all received money over to the Health Officer and had no provision for keeping any part of it as was the case with the earlier contractors. He had to be bonded.

Specific provisions prohibited "breaking open [the] pound [to] take or let any animal out of said pound" or interfering with pound staff "engaged in . . . carrying to such pound any animal" (fine: $5-25). The poundmaster was enjoined against turning over animals without adequate proof of ownership, perhaps fearing potential corruption.

Hogs and diseased animals of any sort were banned from the two municipalities and their "more densely populated suburbs" in an omnibus ordinance of 1875 relating to all kinds of nuisances.[6]

The Territorial Legislature prohibited all animals from public parks in 1873, attaching a fine of $5-20 to the owners. Life for farmers and dealers was restricted further in 1875 when the Commissioners prohibited driving "cattle and other livestock" through the city "to protect the trees, shrubbery and parking [public space] along the streets." An 1887 order enlarged the prohibition to other farm animals and specified times allowed, number of animals per herd and other details (including that drivers must be at least 16 years old). This order was extended to paved suburban streets in 1891, and again in 1910 (this last time from a concern for traffic).[7]

Dogs represented a more complicated legal challenge to District leaders because of their ambiguous love/hate place in the community. In 1873 the District's Supreme Court heard the appeal in the case of *Mayor of Washington v. Meigs*, relating to the 1869 arrest of Return J. Meigs for keeping an unlicensed dog. Meigs argued his own plea (he later served as clerk of the court), claiming property rights over the animal. The court agreed (after a long discourse about the role of dogs in history) and voided the 1858 licensing act.[8] This decision surely explains the lacuna in revenue reported from the dog tax in 1872-78 by the District government (Appendix C4).

Perhaps in view of this case, the Territorial legislature in 1872 made a basic change in the status of dogs in the District: "From and after the passage of this act dogs shall be deemed and held to be personal property." Specifically, properly licensed and restrained canines were protected, and could be recovered

---

[6] This ordinance perhaps incorporates earlier declarations.

[7] Einstein discussed this problem in his 1878 report and again in 1883. The 1875 order was "revived" in 1881, which supplies the original text; see also Evening Star, 22 Sept 1875, p. 4. The 1891 order listed approved routes, hours, number of animals allowed and other specifics; later police regulations extended the list of acceptable routes. The 1910 order prohibited lame or diseased animals on the road. See also the police regulations of 1894 and 1906, Section 6.

[8] Mayor of Washington v. Meigs (MacArthur, pp. 53-60). This was confirmed by the Corporation Counsel in 1911 (Counsel Opinions, 25 Sept 1911; Vol. 22, p. 43).

by their owners (by application to the Police Court – there was still some confusion about MPDC/pound responsibilities and jurisdiction), and theft of a dog carried a fine of $5-50. It also opened owners to liability if their animal harmed a person or property. This law eliminated the earlier distinction between "useful" farm animals and "nuisance" dogs, which we will now speak of as one. It reflects a growing shift in urbanizing Washington society away from the keeping of farm and work animals and toward the view of dogs as valued pets. This provision was repeated in the 1878 Congressional act.

Dog-related laws as of the Territorial period are well summarized in the D.C. Assembly Commission's 1872 compilation Laws of the District of Columbia.[9]

The District's (federal) animal control laws were assembled in the Compiled Statutes . . . 1887-'89[10] (supplemented by the 1887 Police regulations[11]) and will bear summarizing here. They deal only with dogs and are mostly directly copied from the landmark Congressional act of 1878.

All dogs required tax tags worn on collars; tagged animals could run at large.

Dogs running at large were to be muzzled during the summer for fear of rabies (discussed at length later). The Commissioners could declare a rabies emergency and prohibit all unmuzzled dogs from the streets for that period. Uncontrolled and dangerous dogs brought a fine of $10 for the first offense and would be killed after the third. "Barking, biting, howling" or other annoying dogs were prohibited, and dangerous ones had to be leashed on the streets.

Removing tags from licensed dogs for the purpose of taking up the animal was fined up to $20. This seems to have been directed at those – including bad poundmen? – who wanted to claim a finder's fee, though the act does not authorize such a payment. Directly stealing another's dog was fined at $5-50.

Another legality to note is that of **jurisdiction**: the 1871 pound law specified its effectiveness only within the two municipalities, and the 1874 attempt to create a pound for the County proved abortive. The Attorney for the District (the legal office of the local government) issued an opinion in the 1874 or '75 summarized in its index: "Cattle, Swine and Geese – Running at large in the county – There is no remedy to prevent this." Benjamin P. Davis, county school trustee, complained in 1878 that "the school children are frightened by the cows, the grass [is] uprooted by the swine and the geese make it particularly disagreeable."[12] The index of orders of the Temporary Commissioners lists two undated orders prohibiting "Animals Running at Large in the County" and declaring that they will be impounded, but the second volume of orders is missing and we cannot recover the text.

---

[9] It is not easy to find, residing on a microfilm roll with other Territorial government documents, including the Legislative Journal, in the Washingtoniana Division of the ML King Library. A copy is deposited with other papers from this project.

[10] Op. cit., ch. 3 "Animals", and ch. 66 "Washington Humane Society", with all relevant acts and court decisions carefully cited. Some colonial-era laws relevant to farmsteads are included after this, hardly applicable by the 1880s. WHS and animal cruelty laws will be discussed in a later section.

[11] The first year of such regulations, per a Congressional act of 26 Jan 1887.

[12] Listed in the Index of Counsel Opinions as in Vol. 1, p. 56 ½, but that earliest volume (beginning with 1874) is missing and so we cannot read the report. See also Evening Star, 10 Apr 1878, p. 4; Critic-Record, 11 Apr 1878, p. 2.

A Commissioners order of 1879 (following the Congressional act "to Extend the Area for Taking Up Domestic Animals")[13] took the regulation on stray animals to certain areas in the county: "the villages of Mount Pleasant and Anacostia," areas north of Columbia, Brown's and Gleason's Roads, west of Seventh Street Road (now Georgia Ave), and "any point in the County of Washington within one mile of the cities of Washington and Georgetown." This was further extended in 1891 to "all improved subdivisions within the District," and two years later to the entire District.[14] The prime target of this expansion was farm animals, which "were running at large on several of the new subdivisions and destroying the sodding."[15]

Neither the pound crew nor police intervened in tangential animal-related situations that today would be called in to the District shelter, viz.:

- They did not take cats from trees or other such minor services;
- They did not rescue larger animals from emergencies such as fires or falls into wells, which continued to be dealt with by whoever was at hand – police, firemen, owners, bystanders (discussed also in the Corporations section);
- They did not take intruding or even dangerous wild animals (e.g., snakes, foxes) from private property.

These problems in time became the province of WHS agents and thence passed to the current shelter workers. Furthermore:

- Diseased farm animals fell under the authority of the Board of Health's inspector of animals after 1868. The Commissioners gave this responsibility to the Bureau of Animal Industry in 1887. In earlier years the actual killing seems to have been done by contractor, but passed to approved abattoirs after 1896, when the District's Health Department re-established its inspection service.[16]
- District- and federally-owned animals were the exclusive charge of their various government owners. The city employed a Municipal Veterinarian.

---

[13] According to Health Officer Smith Townshend: "Since the enactment of the [1870] law the suburbs have become very thickly populated, and the people throughout the county of Washington, . . . suffering from the depredations of domestic animals, are calling [for] protection" (Congressional Record, 46th Cong/1st Sess, Senate, 24 June 1879). Discussed in Bd of Health minutes, 29 Jan 1878.

[14] According to Evening Star, 9 Jan 1891, p. 3; I could not find the 1891 order in the Comm Minutes/Orders. The authority of the Commissioners to issue the 1893 extension was undergirded by the Corporation Counsel (Counsel Opinions, 15 Aug 1893; Vol. 2, p. 833). Ordinances of the earlier Board of Health, and thus effective only in the Corporation of Washington, were legalized by Congressional resolution on 24 Aug 1880 and extended throughout the District in the appropriations bill of 7 Aug 1894.

[15] Evening Star, 9 Jan 1891, p. 3.

[16] Comm Minutes/Orders, 21 Aug 1888; 5 Sept 1893; Evening Star, 17 Mar 1868, p. 4; 16 Nov 1894, p. 2; 6 May 1896, p. 13; 17 June 1907, p. 8; Daily Nat. Republican, 26 Feb 1876, p. 1. The District and federal agencies' efforts were intertwined beyond the scope of this study (see, e.g., Evening Star, 18 Jan 1884, p. 1); the Health Officer Ann Rpts, with regular reportage of the inspectors, tell the story.

CHAPTER TEN

Corralling the Population of Farm Animals

We have many complaints from citizens respecting cows coming close to their dwellings, dropping their filth, and frightening children. (Poundmaster Report, 1882)

Our Poundmaster and his men have pursued their calling with a doggedness of purpose worthy of the cause . . . The only . . . arguments brought by the people . . . in their visits to the outskirts of the city have been sticks and stones, and other missiles propelled by the indignant mob, . . . but our representatives . . . were neither cowed nor rendered hors de combat. (Bd of Health Annual Report, 1875)

When Einstein commenced his duties he rode astride a tremendous public cry against the stray dog population; only the occasional aggrieved owner dared stand against his forces. The same was hardly true of his efforts to clear the public ways of more-valuable farm animals: "At the time the pound service was established . . . the city was overrun with animals of all kinds . . . When Poundmaster Einstein and his . . . assistants started upon their crusade they found **their task was a troublesome one**. Clubs, brickbats and stones greeted them daily, the appearance of the pound wagons never resulting in anything but trouble, more especially in the sections known as 'Foggy Bottom' and 'Swampoodle' . . . No owner of a goat was ever known to surrender his . . . animal without a fight, and assistance was never lacking."[1]

Here is a typical account of such a fracas, in this case on Sherman Avenue NW in 1882, somewhat abridged: "General Einstein and his gallant men no sooner approach the neighborhood than the news of their arrival spread in every direction, and an immense crowd, principally Irish women with a sprinkling of negroes of both sexes, gather to resist the intruders and protect their pigs, sheep, etc. from the inroads of the poundmaster. Between 5 and 6 o'clock this morning the dog-catchers visited this section when they were overtaken by the mob, and stones and clubs and missiles of every kind began to fly thick and fast, and a very spirited battle began, which raged for several minutes during which Albert Fortune, one of the poundmaster's colored assistants, was struck with some stones and severely bruised. The poundmaster was stabbed [by] a drunken Irish woman but escaped with a slight scratch and a long rent in his coat and shirt." Several rioters were arrested and fined.[2]

In 1874 the poundmen were surrounded by an angry mob (claimed to number 400-500) in Swampoodle and had to take cover in their wagon while Einstein hurried to secure police protection; a similar attack near Lincoln Park (memorialized as "The Battle of Lincoln Park") resulted in the wagon's

---

[1] Evening Star, 10 July 1911, p. 3. Blue-collar Swampoodle, north of Union Station and long destroyed (now site of the glitzy NoMa neighborhood), was a particular bête noire for Einstein, as it was the police: "In the delectable region called Swampoodle," begins a complaint in his 1877 report; and two years later he named it "the goatland of the District" (Einstein hated goats).
[2] Evening Critic, 19 Aug 1882, p. 4. The most fruitful runs were made at night, when many animals were left out to graze (Wash. Post, 10 Apr 1904, p. B6). See also Evening Star, 28 Jan 1951 [sic], p. 47 for another detailed account.

complete destruction; in 1882, a horse-owner shot Einstein in the shoulder.[3] Rioters usually received fines in the $5-10 range for "assault and interfering with the poundmaster."[4] Citizens took the poundmen to court, charging them with use of profane language, unnecessary roughness, cruelty to animals, trespassing, or (in one case) carrying a concealed weapon – all unsuccessfully.[5] Einstein held a special commission from MPDC allowing him to arrest miscreants, which he did regularly.[6]

Impounded farm animals could be claimed only at the pound or, if not, then sold at auction, as described below. Very seldom was a larger animal destroyed.

An obvious question presents itself: how was Einstein able to succeed in ultimately taming the city's farm animal population when his predecessors could not? Five factors come to mind:

- The Commissioners were less susceptible to influence by the animal owners than had been the Corporation or Territorial assemblies, which was, after all, the hope of Congress in creating the Commissioner government in the first place;
- Pound operations remained free from political manipulation and patronage appointment. The long-serving Einstein and his hand-picked men were none of them political hacks, their appointments resting on the next election results; the Commissioners were non-political;[7]
- Poundmaster Einstein enjoyed the solid and continuous support of the re-organized Metropolitan Police Department, something his predecessors could not claim;
- Einstein showed a careful balance of tact and determination lacking in his predecessors. His professional yet sympathetic approach contrasted strongly with the hot-headed Hoover or Wheelock (as far as we know him); the later poundmasters seem to have hardly tried;
- Most importantly, by the 1880s the city was clearly moving past the time when such animals roaming the streets and uprooting trees and shrubs in yards and the new public squares was considered a normal if somewhat inconvenient aspect of urban life. The keeping of farm animals gradually became associated with blue-collar communities (so frequently described as representing "all colors of people, white, black and Irish")[8] as Swampoodle and the eastern edges of Capitol Hill near the city jail and Asylum.

As early as 1874 the Health Officer's annual report claimed: "The comparative freedom of the two cities from animals running at large marks how well the work [of the pound service] is done."[9] Violent resistance to the poundmaster's forays largely ended by the late 1880s. (Remember that this was a full fifteen years after Einstein took up his job) "It was almost as much as a man's life was worth to go to

---

[3] (Swampoodle) Nat. Republican, 10 Aug 1874, p. 1; Evening Star, 10 Aug 1874, p. 4; (Lincoln Park – a favorite story of Einstein's) Wash. Times, 7 Aug 1904, p. 4; Evening Star, 16 July 1905, pt. 4 p. 1; 10 July 1911, p. 3; (shooting) Evening Star, 10 July 1911, p. 3.

[4] E. g., Daily Critic, 6 June 1881, p. 4; Wash. Critic, 22 Sept 1888, p. 4.

[5] (Profanity) Evening Critic, 31 Mar 1882, p. 4; (roughness) Evening Star, 21 May 1873, p. 4; (cruelty) Evening Critic, 16 Oct 1882, p. 2; (trespassing) Wash. Critic, 7 July 1885, p. 4; (weapon) Evening Star, 10 Aug 1874, p. 4. See also Evening Star, 28 May 1873, p. 4, in which the Chairman of the Sanitary Police Committee stated that Einstein was justified in all complaints made against him – welcome support, no doubt!

[6] Renewed regularly; see, e.g., Wash. Post, 30 Mar 1897, p. 10.

[7] This observation comes from a reading of Jessica Wang's monograph "Dogs and the Making of the American State", cited in the appendix D14, which I gratefully acknowledge.

[8] Wash. Critic, 22 Sept 1888, p. 4.

[9] Quoted in Nat. Republican, 15 June 1874, p. 4.

some sections and pick up a goat or horse," he recalled at the end of his career. "It has been only during the past few years that my assistants have experienced practically no trouble."[10]

Of course, the chief cause of the decline of farm animals in the District was the decline in the number of farms; the Bureau of Census figures given in Appendix C1 demonstrate this, and indeed, one is surprised how much acreage remained in this use into the early twentieth century.[11] The annual statistics of animals impounded by type tell the same story: the number of larger animals impounded held at 350-500/year in the 1870s to the mid-1880s, when the number drifted to a lower 150-250/year. At the end of the 19th century farm animals totaled 100 or fewer each year, and with so many dogs occupying pound space Einstein regularly (regretfully) passed by lone strays if they were not making trouble.[12]

As the city increased in density the number of singly-owned animals must have also declined. The Commissioners in 1897 prohibited the keeping of cow-yards and stables within 200 feet of a neighbor's residence, exempting "persons keeping one or two cows for their own use [or] the selling of milk" by their owners; this restriction was elaborated by an order of 1902.

"Hog-pens have disappeared entirely from the city; cow-stables are fast following."[13] "The capture of goats and cows is falling off annually [Poundmaster Report, 1884]. The march of improvements forces these animals from their former feeding grounds, the 'commons' and open squares, to the fenced pasture ground beyond the city limits." "Goats are seldom taken now, and the poundmaster says there are not many of them in the city.[14] Cows were caught in great number years ago, but the city is comparatively free of them now [1899]."[15] And in 1913 the poundmaster noted: "The impounding of the larger domestic animals now forms an inconsequential part of the pound work." Concluded Einstein correctly: "The growth of the city is responsible for the change. There is no more pasture to be found in the streets."[16] Most of the city ordinances restricting pasturing, raising and transitting of farm animals in the District (Appendix B) had been anticipated by the poundmaster as early as his 1875 annual report.

By 1890 the public had become so accustomed to its new peace free of strolling pigs and goats that citizens could turn their attention to another annoyance hitherto considered too minor and common to merit notice: roving **chickens**.[17] Police regulations of 1887 prohibited at-large fowl in the two former Corporations and directed the poundmaster to seize such free-wheeling miscreants and redeem them for 50 cents each or sell them; offending owners were fined $2-5 for each animal. The regulations also

---

[10] Evening Star, 10 July 1911, p. 3.
[11] Institutions such as St. Elizabeths Hospital, the Industrial Home School (the reform school), the Asylum (poorhouse), the Home for the Aged and Infirm, the District Workhouse at Occoquan, the Reformatory at Lorton (both in Virginia), and the Soldiers Home kept horses, hogs and cattle for commercial purposes.
[12] Wash. Times, 13 Apr 1902, Ed/Drama p. 17. Einstein, citing applications for permits to keep dairy farms, stated that the District held 1,356 cows in 1897; "no estimate of the number of other domestic animals can be made" (Poundmaster Ann Rpt, 1897).
[13] Health Officer Ann Rpt, 1884.
[14] Einstein's 1878 Ann Rpt gave his opinion of goats: "pestiferous animals" which "will positively hesitate at nothing which they can masticate." Nat. Republican, 14 May 1875, p. 4 includes a humorous account of his encounter with an Irish goat-owner
[15] Evening Star, 13 Oct 1899, p. 16; "Poundmaster Einstein expresses the opinion that in all of Washington there are not two dozen goats at the present time. Occasionally a horse, having broken loose from some country pasture, starts for its city home." Cows and geese had disappeared (Wash, Post, 8 July 1901, p. 10).
[16] Poundmaster Ann Rpt, 1884; Evening Star, 13 Oct 1899, p. 16; Poundmaster Ann Rpt, 1913; (quote) Wash. Times, 7 Aug 1904, p. 4.
[17] I have found one earlier complaint: "Old Tax-Payer" wrote the Board of Health in 1874: "I like chickens and eggs, especially about Christmas, but I say . . . they that have chickens should keep them in their yards" (Evening Star, 11 Apr 1874, p. 4).

outlawed "crowing, cackling" or otherwise annoying fowl, which could be killed by the police on sight. Einstein lamented the new regulations in his report for that year and baldly stated that he could not comply for lack of resources.[18]

In spite of such (largely ignored) regulations, the Rev. Dr. Chester of the Stanton Square neighborhood complained: "The chickens have torn up my grass and flowers and dropped litter on the pavement which is tracked into the house. The question . . . is whether we are to be permitted to keep our parks and flower beds in order and to beautify the city or whether the chickens are . . . permitted to dig up such places and make them eye-sores." Protested Charles Neurath, a boy charged with failing to supervise his flock: "I ain't the only one who owns chickens that go in the park, but lots of other people have got them too." Poundmaster Einstein continued his refusal to collect chickens, saying the pound had no area for them.[19]

Raising chickens and pigeons in any square over 75% improved without a permit was banned in 1906,[20] and two years later no fowl allowed to roam the streets at all and other regulations strengthened (no fowl to be kept within 100 feet of any dwelling or building of assembly) by order of the Commissioners. The law exempted grocers and public marketers keeping fowl in coops for 24 hours, and allowed homing pigeons. Later orders further tightened these restrictions, which were all entered as Police regulations. Negligent owners faced a fine of $2-5, and on the second offense the bird was killed.[21] On the other hand, an 1898 revision to the police regulations required that complaints about crowing roosters come not from one person but "the neighborhood" (i. e., at least two).[22]

A Commissioners order of 1909 laid out specific conditions for raising "any kind of domestic fowl or pigeons": houses (coops) had to be "dry, well ventilated, . . . with window . . . to admit sunlight," and cleaned weekly in the winter and biweekly in the summer; perches and nests also had to be kept "cleaned, aired and sunned," and the birds required fresh water at all times.

The testimony preceding the 1906 order sounds wonderfully contemporary and demands to be summarized: Anti-chicken – they are unsanitary and a nuisance, especially the crowing roosters; Pro-chicken – they are educational, good pets, can be kept cleanly, represent a bastion of property rights (including as a source of income), can be of distinguished breed (this from the Homing Pigeon Club), are of better nutritional quality if raised at home (i.e., they're organic), and raised in more natural conditions (i.e., free-range, this from the Retail Grocers' Protective Association). Huffed one chicken-raiser: "The insanitary condition in this city comes more from the people than from chickens." And an ever-true observation responding to the rooster complaint: "Unfortunately . . . we have a great many chronic

---

[18] And repeated this the following year. A MPDC precinct log-book of 1869 refers to police capturing chickens (Evening Star, 11 Jan 1959, p. A1). The Washington Humane Society, attempting to prosecute a case of cruelty to a chicken in 1891, was refused on the grounds that the law did not recognize chickens as animals – they had never been listed in relevant ordinances (WHS Ann Rpt, 1891).

[19] Evening Star, 13 Mar 1890, p. 3. See also Poundmaster Ann Rpt, 1888, where he makes the same statement. The animals were killed on the second complaint, "but few arrests have been made" (Evening Star, 23 Apr 1909, p. 24).

[20] The troublesome Police Court voided this law the following year (D.C. v. Albert M. Keen, #306,679; found in National Archives, RG 351, Item 21, file 1-113a "Fowls") on the basis that it unfairly favored merchants (who did not face such restrictions) over householders, leading to the 1909 re-write.

[21] Evening Star, 23 Apr 1909, p. 24. The article points out that the law did not specify who got the carcass. The problem persisted: in 1915 a US Representative requested an investigation into illegal chicken farms in the District (H Resolution 648, 62nd Cong).

[22] Counsel Opinions, 16 Dec 1898 (Vol. 9, p. 269).

kickers who complain against the ringing of church bells and the laughter and frolic of the child on the street."[23]

Not only chickens attracted complaints: the National Republican in 1874 published a series of frantic complaints regarding a noisy pet mocking bird living on the 1300 block of F Street NW, eliciting report of a similar guinea hen on Corcoran Street NW ("The question is for how long? – Oh, for how long? – one of those aforesaid guinea-hens, that is at it all night, all day, all the next night . . .").[24]

As the number of impounded farm animals shrank, so did a parasitic type of human whose living depended on these animals: the con man. It will be recalled that in the 1860s and '70s hooligans stole domestic animals claiming to be poundmen. Now, with a better organized and recognizable force, accounts of these frauds disappeared. Only one such made the papers in Einstein's time: James Foley, arrested in 1884 for "playing the confidence game on a credulous community [including an MPDC officer] by representing that General Einstein had impounded several of his cows and he needed fifty cents . . . to get his cows out of hock." A clever lawyer got him off the charge.[25]

---

[23] Comm Minutes/Orders, 9 Nov 1906.
[24] (Mocking birds) Daily Nat. Republican, 20 Aug 1874, p. 4; 21 Aug 1874, p. 4; (guinea hens) 26 Aug 1874, p. 4.
[25] Critic-Record, 5 Sept 1884, p. 1.

CHAPTER ELEVEN

The Dog War

General Einstein begins on Monday to wage war upon the Washington dogs. He will make his headquarters as usual under the shadow of the Observatory. This is not a notice of Einstein. This is a notice to dogs. (Nat. Republican, 12 May 1876, p. 4)

About this time of year the mad-dog scare begins, and continues throughout the summer. (Evening Star, 18 May 1899, p. 2)

Few efforts could bring Einstein's pound (and the Board of Health) more good will from the citizenry than control of the stray dog population. Although hardly free of risks ("Being shot at, knocked down, hit with stones and bricks are but a few ways . . . enraged dog owners have of showing their disapproval"),[1] the poundmen taking stray, unclaimed dogs did not meet the aggressive community resistance that protected goats and hogs, which were always owned by someone.

Preparatory to sending the poundmen out to engage the canine population in battle the Territorial Council had a legal question to resolve, one reminiscent of the absurd issue of the 1860s whether or not it had active laws allowing it to take up swine: in this case, did the local government have the power to collect dogs at all?[2] The crux of this matter lay with the undoubted authority conferred by Congress on the newly-reconstituted Board of Health in 1871 to "make and enforce regulations to prevent domestic animals from running at large" – simply put, were dogs "domestic animals"? If there was some question about this (a problem "in consequence of the defective laws on the subject"), couldn't the Council or the Board simply issue a clarification and take them up at its pleasure?

The Board's Committee on Ordinances reported "that it was unwise and impracticable . . . either to amend the ordinances or to engraft a new one in regard to the matter," whether from practical restraints ("the poundmaster would have a nice time of it rushing about after the dogs") or legal ones ("the Board had not the power to go further at this time") was not reported. Dr. Verdi favored using existing legislation to extend muzzling year-round. This desultory debate continued through the spring of 1874. The issue was somehow resolved by July when the Board authorized the campaign. During this entire period, the poundmen continued to pick up stray dogs.[3]

---

[1] Wash. Post, 24 Mar 1908, p. 16.
[2] There had perhaps been a harbinger of this question: the first draft bill to establish a Corporation pound (Simaker's operation; Daily Nat. Intelligencer, 28 Aug 1862, p. 1) included an explicit clause (sect. 12) requiring impounding of dogs, which was dropped from the final version. A similar question arose the following year (1875) in regard to the Board's authority to regulate cattle herded through city streets (Evening Star, 22 Sept 1875, p. 4). In both cases Congressional legislation ultimately authorized the restrictions but also served to cripple the District's own decision-making power.
[3] "Continued to pick up" but perhaps at decreased rates – the newspapers from exactly this time carried numerous complaints about lax attention to dogs ("Pretty soon the poundmen paid no attention to dogs, but were zealous in

A Board of Health ordinance passed in 1871 required all dogs running at large to be muzzled from 15 June to 15 September, and set the redemption period at 24 hours and the fee at $1. The period of muzzling was extended in 1874 and again in 1875.[4] This regulation was made in response to fear of rabies, which is discussed below. Einstein's maneuvers in the Dog War originally occurred only during the summer when the city required dogs at large to be muzzled. Following the passage of the Congressional dog-tax law in 1878, which re-instated the levy, the campaign extended throughout the year.[5] In its earliest years the first foray began precisely on 15 June and became something of an annual event for newspaper reporters.

Here is a **picture of an expedition** in Einstein's Dog War (as it was regularly called), pieced together from newspaper accounts of the 1870-90s:[6]

> Dog runs (one or two daily, depending on the season) began at 4 AM and commonly ended at 8 AM, although in the earliest years they could continue to mid-evening. The National Republican (1875) explained that the pound crew started so early "chiefly to avoid the inconvenience of a crowd of officious and zealous followers," (it was also when the dogs were most active, looking for breakfast)[7] but all accounts describe the pound wagon surrounded by "a crowd of boys, white and black" shouting "Dog-catcher! dog-catcher!" and chasing away their canine friends. After the hunting season was extended, in cooler weather the run began about 9 AM, since the dogs came out later and the annoying boys were then in school.[8]
>
> Einstein rode first, in a buggy, followed by the "iron-caged wagon," equipment – mostly nets – secured under the vehicle, and three or four poundmen. After 1878 a police officer was assigned to accompany the crew.[9] Einstein himself seldom engaged in the actual work of capturing animals – he had an eagle eye for dogs with no or expired tags, and also dealt with angry owners. "Whether it carries a tag or not, no dog that appears to be following an owner is seized." The wagon on these rounds looked exclusively for dogs and took up other animals separately.[10]

---

gobbling up horses and cows"; Evening Star, 18 Mar 1874, p. 2). This legal tale can be followed in: Evening Star, 18 Mar 1874, p. 4; 1 Apr 1874, p. 4; 8 Apr 1874, p. 4; 1 July 1874, p.4.

[4] The specifics will be discussed in the section on Muzzling/Rabies.

[5] The Wash. Post's 1897 report (see sources below) explained that the busy season for catches was April-June, and that the crew made no rounds in July so that owners could procure new annual tags.

[6] Nat. Republican, 15 June 1874, p. 4; 18 June 1874, p. 4; 19 May 1875, p. 4; 7 July 1876, p. 4; 25 June 1877, p. 4; Evening Star, 19 Sept 1885, p. 2; 30 Aug 1890, p. 12; Wash. Post, 30 Aug 1891, p. 9; 9 May 1897, p. 21; 18 Dec 1899, p 12; Morning Times, 28 July 1895, pt. 2, p. 9; Wash. Times, 27 Sept 1916, p. 5. In-text citations refer to these accounts. A brief but useful overview of the pound will be found in the 1883 annual report of the Washington Humane Society – useful because this source could well have been antagonistic to the operation but was not.

[7] Einstein himself claimed that at this time "the dog went to sleep in the barrel in the back yard, after howling himself hoarse and scratching half the night at the back door" (Nat. Republican, 1875). He regularly claimed that dogs could not be caught at night but began a night run for the big sweep of 1908 and it was quite successful (Wash. Times, 4 July 1908, p. 12). Runs occurred on rainy days but were unproductive; for one thing, the cotton nets became wet and therefore too stiff to use (Wash. Post, 1899).

[8] See Appendix D3 for some account of the boys. The Evening Star, 17 July 1922, p. 6 printed an idyllic editorial on this eternal relationship and included some interesting information on practices of dog-catching in other cities.

[9] Poundmaster Ann Rpt, 1878.

[10] Wash. Post, 1897. One of the chief responsibilities of both the poundmaster and police attendant was to ensure that all catches were made correctly, and thus to protect the dog-catchers from later legal complaints; see Wash. Post, 1897; Hearings . . . 1907 (House), 7 Mar 1906, pp. 734-736.

Reporters delighted in detailing the techniques of capture: "The hunter's net is attached to a long and heavy pole. It requires not only good judgment, but considerable strength to throw it effectively . . . A man born to the business handles the net from the start with peculiar dexterity. It is almost useless for a young man to adopt dog-catching as a means of livelihood unless he displays this aptitude and feels some enthusiasm" (Evening Star, 1885). A gentle, deceptively reassuring voice,[11] a good back-up man to handle the net, quick legs and the spirit of the chase characterized Einstein's men. His best man (unnamed) spurned the net and took his prey by hand. "He has been bitten time without number . . . without . . . suffering any after consequences from such bites. The mere lacerations of the bites he does not mind" (Wash. Post, 1897).[12]

The wagon returned to the pound when it had captured its capacity – a typical take could run to two dozen, but one article counted 37. Each new animal was recorded by breed and color and a dated tab put around its neck "to know when his time for death comes."[13] Dogs were also delivered to the pound by owners or frustrated citizens, and the wagon picked up unwanted animals from homes, receiving 20-50 (telephone) calls each day for such service.[14]

All accounts agree both on the inherent melancholy of the place (or occasionally joy when a child or elderly owner recovered his pet) and on the thoughtful care Einstein gave his condemned guests. "Mr. Einstein . . . is very kind to the animals while in his charge, and during the period of grace . . . allows the dogs, before shooting them, . . . every comfort" (Nat. Republic, 18 June 1874).

Needless to say, owners of all classes badgered, argued or pleaded with, and sometimes attacked or sued the poundmaster and his men if they caught him taking their guard dog or pet. Citizens had to visit Foggy Bottom to claim their dogs. "There is a small, unpretending inclosure just outside the . . . Observatory grounds containing an office, a stall for horses and a shed or two. This is the pound. The poundmaster, Mr. Einstein, will welcome you, thinking you have come to reclaim some unfortunate" (Nat. Republican, 1875). If not redeemed within the specified 48 hours the dogs were sold or destroyed, as described below.

(Details of the pound and its equipment, staff and – yes – methods of destroying unredeemed animals will be treated separately.)

---

[11] "He puts out his hand, calls softy, 'Doggy, doggy; come yer, doggy.' . . . After a little more coaxing [the dog] advances with a playful bound and looks into the man's face. He don't [sic] find the same cheery smile after he has once come within reach. Smiles are precious and the dog-catcher can't waste any on a dog after he is once captured" (Nat. Republican, 1875).

[12] In 1921 veteran dog-catcher Joe Burrell described in detail the techniques of throwing the net and bringing in the captives to a Washington Post reporter (op. cit., 25 Sept 1921, p. 10). In 1915 poundman Washington Jones was held liable for injuring a dog: "It appears that the net and handle were thrown at the dog and not dropped over him" (Counsel Opinions, 29 July 1915; Vol. 26, p. 27).

[13] The tab was blue (Wash. Times, 11 Aug 1897, p. 8).

[14] Einstein: "These [dogs] are brought here at the request of their owners, who for some reason wish to be rid of them" (Morning Times, 1895). Sometimes they were sick, but more frequently the owner couldn't afford the tax. See a touching example in Wash. Times, 11 Aug 1897, p. 8 ("The boy pushed his only friend in [the enclosure], not, however, before the only friend had licked him on the cheek."). (Pick-up) Wash. Times, 7 Aug 1904, p. 4.

The city's policies toward dogs revolved around three issues: dog licenses/tags; muzzling; and fear of rabies.

It will be remembered that both Washington and Georgetown had from very early days a **dog tax**, requiring payment to the Corporation treasurer annually in exchange for a receipt and, in time, a **tax-tag** (as it was called) for the animal's collar. My own guess is that this tax was originally imposed as much to control the number of dogs as to raise revenue, something that did not work because the Corporations had no effective way to take up unlicensed curs. The 1873 Mayor v. Meigs decision voided this tax until the Congressional act of 1878. Let Einstein speak, looking back from 1904: "There was no tax in those days . . . The only law regarding dogs was that they must wear a muzzle during June, July, and August, months when they are likely to go mad. The fine for the violation of this was $1. Later, this restriction was extended to May and September. This condition remained until 1878, when the present laws were enacted."[15]

Congress's act of 1878 was named "An Act to Create a Revenue in the District of Columbia by Levying a Tax upon All Dogs Therein . . . " and (re-)created an annual tax procedure for all dogs in the District.[16] "Formerly, unmuzzled dogs were hunted as a matter of precaution against biting . . . and hydrophobia. Now [1885] dogs are hunted for revenue only."[17] The pound (as specified in the 1878 act) paid all of its proceeds – fines, boarding charges – to the city treasurer. Owners paid their $2 dog tax (now for both males and females) to the Collector of Taxes, Dog License and Tag Branch (although statistics on sales of licenses were generally released by the Health Officer).[18]

In the early Commissioner period citizens could pro rate their dog tax on the claim of having moved into the District or acquired a dog part way into a fiscal year, and the Index to Letters Received by the Commissioners shows numerous such requests to 1881, when the procedure was presumably shifted to the Collector of Taxes. How common such a practice remained we do not know, but the Corporation Counsel wrote in 1897 that it remained legal (but not for dogs planned to be moved <u>out</u> of the city later in the year). In 1906 the Counsel reversed itself and declared the pro rata dog tax invalid.[19]

However, as Einstein stated in his annual report of 1878 (the year of the act): "There is one defect in this law which demands a remedy . . . Why is the dog law not enforced? is a question asked me daily. . . The defect . . . is that it is frequently impossible to collect the fine imposed, and there is no other penalty attached to the keeping of an unlicensed dog excepting possible capture by the poundmen." He asked permission to hunt unlicensed dogs on private land.[20]

In 1893, "with a firm conviction that there were many who escaped the tax, and with a desire to increase the coffers of the District," Einstein obtained aid from the city police in canvassing for illegal mutts. "The result was astonishing to everyone save the poundmaster. . . Suspected houses were visited by the blue coats and the owners of dogs warned to take out a license. Several arrests followed. The next

---

[15] Wash. Post, 10 Apr 1904, p. B6. His assertion of a June-August muzzling seems an example of Einstein's faulty memory, something seen in his later interviews.

[16] It generally followed the procedures of an 1874 Maryland state law (Evening Star, 8 Apr 1874, p. 2).

[17] Evening Star, 19 Sept 1885, p. 2. Reported the District Treasurer in 1877: "The old Corporation law in relation to dogs, if revived by . . . Congress, would bring considerable revenue to the District government, besides relieving the community from the surplus of worthless and dangerous animals" (Evening Star, 17 Nov 1877, p. 4). This echoes the current debate over the purpose of parking meters and traffic cameras.

[18] Wash. Post, 9 July 1909, p. 16. The original Congressional proposal had suggested $1.50 (Evening Star, 14 Mar 1878, p. 1).

[19] Counsel Opinions 2 Aug 1897 (Vol. 8, p. 78); 30 Apr 1906 (Vol. 16, p. 256).

[20] This is discussed in detail in Counsel Opinions, 9 Oct 1897 (Vol. 8, p. 164). For an earlier discussion see Evening Star, 10 Aug 1878, p. 4.

day Dr. Clark, the dog-tax clerk, was confronted by a small army of dog owners." The city took in $6,000 the first day – "clear profit to the District."[21]

In 1897 another snag developed. "Attention is invited to the diminution in the amount of pound fees, and probably in the amount of receipts for dog licenses, through the ruling of the attorney for the District that the requirement . . . that the poundmaster seize all dogs . . . without the tax tag . . . is void" (Poundmaster Report, 1897).[22] As Einstein reported, his men regularly collected dogs without tags that owners reclaimed with their tax receipt but without paying the fee. Furthermore, many owners paid for one dog and used the receipt to rescue others. And indeed, on 25 March 1897 the Commissioners ordered that the $2 redemption charge be suspended pending legal review.

Not until 1899 was the charge re-instated. Einstein made a special report on the improved situation: "Up to December 11, 1899 . . . the purchasing of dog tags was almost at a standstill . . .. but after December 11, when four dog wagons made their appearance in all parts of the District, . . . the demand for tags commenced anew and continued until we had . . . more than ever issued in any license year since 1878."[23] There was a similar disruption of licensing in 1912 when the Police Court inexplicably ruled that a restrained dog did not require tags.[24]

Owners renewed dog tags every July and they expired promptly on 30 June. During the entire month of July the pound crew refrained from taking tagless animals – "a month of grace"[25] – and police canvassed residents to remind them of their obligation.[26] The tags themselves were made of aluminum or, after 1902, of German silver (nickel).[27] The shape changed each year and was decided by a committee. The tag carried a number corresponding to the entry number in the tax clerk's register; in 1893 one man's dog still had the number issued it (or its predecessor) in 1878. The largest number licensed to one owner was eight. With a self-addressed, stamped envelope it would be mailed, and one could request a specific number. Replacement tags cost 25 cents and required an affidavit that the original had in fact been "absolutely lost."[28]

---

[21] Evening Star, 9 Oct 1893, p. 8. The District's bill for new tags jumped from $91 in 1884 to $433 the following year as a result. For an amusing account of a later run on the tax office see Evening Star, 15 Aug 1936, p. 7: "Lots of folk arrive . . . with excited pets in tow . . . Dog fights enliven the corridors . . . Trick dogs sometimes approach the tag windows with the $2 . . . in their mouths, their fond masters bursting with pride."

[22] Unhappily I could not find this among the Corporation Counsel's papers.

[23] Commissions order, 16 Dec 1899; Evening Star, 15 Mar 1900, p. 9. This coincided with the more stringent enforcement of laws due to the unfolding mad-dog scare.

[24] Evening Star, 18 May 1912, p. 6.

[25] This policy seems to have changed by 1909, when runs began in mid-July (Wash. Post, 9 July 1909, p. 16).

[26] Reminding us that in their very early days the Corporations of both Washington and Georgetown conducted similar house-to-house efforts; Evening Star, 10 July 1910, pt. 2 p. 6.

[27] In the early 1880s the District paid $100-200/year to purchase tags, and $225-375/year in the 1910s (Supt of Property Ann Rpt). Herman Baumgarter won the contract in 1892 – the first year recorded – for $14.50/thousand and supplied the tags (at a diminishing cost) until Lamb & Tilden took it in 1903 ($9.95/thousand, delivered to the Collector of Taxes); Baumgarten won it back the following year (Comm Minutes/Orders, 3 June 1892 and subsequent years; 29 Apr 1903; 23 Sept 1904). The Comm Minutes/Orders for 1941, index, tells us that they were then made at the Tag Shop of the D.C. Penal Institute for $10/thousand. They were called "tags" as early as the 1870s.

[28] (Tag numbers) Nat. Republican, 26 May 1879, p. 4; Evening Star, 9 Oct 1893, p. 8; (other details) Wash. Post, 9 May 1897, p. 21; (number, mailed) Evening Star, 15 Aug 1936, p. 7; (replacements) Evening Star, 9 Oct 1893, p. 8.

Replacement must have been common – a review of letters received by the Commissioners during 1878-1881 (when replacements were requested in this way; after that date such letters probably went to the Tax Office) show literally hundreds of such missives. This might be an indication of wide-spread theft.

The 1903 contract for dead-animal removal required the company to hold dog tags recovered on carcasses for one year and inform the Commissioners of all particulars – the same procedure applied to "articles of special value, as silverware" found in garbage. After a year, the contractor could keep the tags (for whatever use it could find for them).[29]

The necessity of tax-tags led to crimes which would not occur to present-day owners: substitution and theft of tags. When Einstein reported on the 1899 upsurge in captures (and tag sales) he found that "comparing the numbers of the tags worn by said dogs with the register at the tax office it appears that a large number of lost or stolen tags were on dogs that apparently were lawfully licensed [but were not]." Most of these dogs remained unclaimed and so were killed. "The owners of said dogs, Mr. Einstein thinks, probably did not care to risk coming to the pound and explaining how the dog came to be wearing a tag that was purchased for a different kind of a dog than the one impounded." Some folk took their dogs into the suburbs (the working class) or their summer houses on the ocean (the wealthy) during the summer months, when they were most liable to be captured.[30]

Einstein's 1879 testimony about these ruses is amusing: "People borrow licenses from their neighbors when they want to get their dogs out of the pound." Q: "Have you found any dogs wearing spurious tags?" A: "We have had a great many dogs of that kind. One had a trunk check; . . . another was wearing a Centennial badge. We caught one religious dog with a Catholic medal on its collar. Another dog had a beer check."[31]

Owners claiming untagged pets pleaded that the tag had been stolen.[32] "It certainly works a hardship [complained one such] to be afforded no better protection against ill-disposed persons, who are making a business of stealing tags and collars from dogs." The account continued: "Numerous persons residing in the same neighborhood [very near the Capitol, NE] have been puzzled to find the tags missing from their dogs, and believe they have been stolen." Claimed Clark, the license clerk: "Perhaps there are more dog tag thieves in this city than there are thieves of all kinds," and recounted "a prominent army officer" whose dog wore a metal collar with the tag welded to it. As early as 1879 Einstein figured he had taken near 300-400 properly licensed dogs whose tags had been stolen.[33]

And finally, we should note that not all dogs required a tax paid, a fact gleaned mostly from orders of the Commissioners, who decided on the minutest affairs. These free tags included dogs owned by: the Wholesale Market Master (but only "as long as the dog remains with him in his present position,"

---

[29] Street Cleaning Dept Ann Rpt, 1903. Another curiosity: why did the Health Office spend $15 in 1884 for "repairing dog tags" (Supt of Property Ann Rpt, 1884)?

[30] (Switching tags) Evening Star, 15 Mar 1900, p. 9; (suburbs) Wash. Post, 8 July 1901, p. 10. "One of the interesting sidelights of the crusade against the tramp dogs was the great exodus of Washington's fashionable population. To the seashore and country resorts went thousands of prized dogs which in former seasons . . . were left behind in charge of housekeepers and attendants" (Wash. Post, 20 Sept 1908, pt. 4 p. 4). Indignant owners pointed out the loss of tax revenue to the city as they removed their pets ("hundreds of dogs") to safer locales (Wash. Post, 19 June 1908, p. 11).

[31] Nat. Republican, 26 May 1879, p. 4.

[32] "Practically everyone who goes to the pound to [retrieve] their pets insists that their dog's collar and tag were lost or stolen, and in writing to the Commissioners the owners invariably demand the refund of the sum paid. This is likewise invariably refused, upon the recommendation of the Health Officer" (Wash. Post, 8 July 1901, p. 10). See also Einstein's very amusing imitation of such pleaders in Evening Star, 10 July 1910, pt. 2 p. 6. Such petty theft, as well as hustling dogs out of town, continued into the 1930s (Evening Star, 15 Aug 1936, p. 7).

[33] Respectively: Wash, Post, 4 Dec 1900, p. 10; Evening Star, 9 Oct 1893, p. 8; Nat. Republican, 26 May 1879, p. 4.

(Minutes/Orders, 18 Mar 1898), the Fire Department (first noted 17 July 1901, and regularly thereafter),[34] the Naval Battalion National Guards ("Sausage", 16 Sept 1913), the Southeast Street Cleaning Stables ("Mat", 2 Dec 1914 and later years), the Engineers Stables (19 June 1931), the Electrical Department Storehouse ("Blackie", 22 July 1932), the Garbage Transfer Station (a black and white bulldog "Jack Rags", 19 June 1931), the Home for Aged and Infirm ("in connection with rat extermination"; 1941, index) and the pound's own mascot dog (2 May 1916). Kennels were not required to license their dogs; the Board of Health discussed exempting hunting dogs in 1876 but seems not to have acted.[35]

After years of granting tags gratis to foreign legations (e.g., to the Spanish and German embassies in 1915), the Commissioners made this a blanket courtesy in 1921. In 1934 the Corporation Counsel reversed itself and decided that diplomats must pay the tax like everyone else unless the question was specifically addressed in the nation's convention with the U.S., as was the case with Mexico.[36]

And, following some legal jousting, dogs used by visiting theatrical troupes were exempted from the tax inasmuch as they were only in the District temporarily in 1904. (The Health Officer had given allowance for dogs travelling with their owners to remain tagless in 1901.)[37] On the other hand, in 1904 the Assistant Corporation Counsel ruled that even puppies required tags, the 1878 act not specifying otherwise.[38]

The issues of **muzzles and rabies** were closely intertwined. It will be recalled that both Corporations had regularly issued rabies emergencies into the 1860s. How often these reflected true outbreaks of the disease we have no way to know.[39] Muzzling of dogs off of private property[40] was from the beginning viewed as a measure related to rabies rather than simply vicious animals. ("Hydrophobia" was the usual term into the early twentieth century, although I have encountered "rabies" at least from the 1860s; "dog-madness" appeared at least once.)

The District began to experience a sustained fear of rabies in the mid-1850s, when the number of press articles describing tragic deaths from the disease, and police (or public) shooting of apparently

---

[34] Students of Fire Department history should note that these orders generally list the station and describe and name the animal: Tom, Jack, Babbles, Bruiser, Billicken, etc. Fairly extensive lists will be found in orders of 16 May and 10 July 1912, and 27 July 1915.

[35] Evening Star, 15 Aug 1936, p. 7. According to the index of letters received by the Commissioners, Freedman's Hospital requested a complimentary tag in the early 1880s but we don't know the reply. See Comm Minutes/Orders, 22 June 1910 for a discussion of taxing kennels, and Bd of Health minutes, 17 May 1876 for hunting dogs.

[36] Comm Minutes/Orders, 8 July 1921; 27 July 1934. Such requests began in 1880, according to the records of the Commissions letters. A particular friend of diplomats' dogs was Countess Cassini, daughter of the Russian ambassador, who regularly visited Einstein's little kingdom (Wash. Times, 7 Aug 1904, p. 4; Evening Star, 16 July 1905, pt. 4 p. 1).

[37] Comm Minutes/Orders, 23 Sept 1904. "Many acrobats, billed at the local variety houses, where they were assisted . . . by diminutive dogs, have been forced to visit the pound and sadly put up the required 'two' for the release of their theatrical partners" (Wash. Post, 5 Feb 1901, p. 12); (travelers): Wash. Post, 23 Apr 1901, p. 12.

[38] Counsel Opinions 2 Jan 1904 (Vol. 14, p. 189). On the other hand, they could not be impounded: "This is due solely to the fact that, 'at the earliest moment of life,' puppies are physically incapable of doing that which is a sina qua non of lawful seizure and impoundage, to wit, 'running at large without the tax-tag." Such is the close reasoning of the legal mind!

[39] A cursory review of 500 District newspaper items between 1800-1850 that include the word "hydrophobia" show only a very small number actually reporting cases in this city – the majority relate to deaths in other places or to purported cures.

[40] Muzzling acts frequently omit this distinction but it was always assumed in execution. This was not the case with unlicensed (untagged) dogs, which were seized anywhere.

diseased dogs began to steadily increase.[41] This might have been a nationwide phenomenon – the same local newspapers reported similar news from many other places.

Understandably, the public became nervous and demanded government action: "Much alarm has been produced in this city by those aristocratic, or privileged classes, the dogs . . . Is it not time that something was done to guard the inhabitants of Washington from the dog nuisances, and possibly hydrophobia?"; "I take the liberty of calling your attention to the alarming increase of hydrophobia, and the apparent indifference of our authorities in providing against this evil" (from "A Citizen of Washington"); "A few days ago the Star reported two cases of persons bitten by rabid dogs within the city . . . If there were no dogs, would there be hydrophobia among us?" (from "Anti-Dogs"); "Washington . . . has more dread probably from hydrophobia than from cholera."[42]

Under the Corporations, citizens raised a constant cry over the non-enforcement of dog muzzling laws.[43] The public, justifiably or not, had come to think of summer as the season of hydrophobia. "Hydrophobia is coming into fashion again [May]. The curs should be killed."[44] Clearly the expectations or demands – on the new poundmaster were high.

A Board of Health ordinance of 1871 required muzzling from 15 June to 15 September and the execution of all mad dogs at any time. In its 1874 annual report the Board endorsed summer muzzling of dogs, and issued an ordinance in the same year requiring muzzling in 15 June-15 October on a regular basis (i.e., not as a temporary measure), and extended it to 15 May the following year.[45]

Protests arrived from "the Boards of Health in several of the northern cities" that the plan was both ineffective and inhumane. The boards stated vaguely that closer owner supervision, encouraged by licensing and public education, would work better.[46] Muzzling as a protection against dog bites, whether diseased or simply painful, had been controversial since first proposed, though more so with owners than the victim-public. The District Board itself debated the matter at its September 1874 meeting.[47]

The 1878 Congressional act establishing the dog tax also empowered the Commissioners to enforce temporary muzzling during declared hydrophobia emergencies, as had been done by the Corporations. The old Board's summer muzzling edict was restated by Congress in 1880, but, as the Corporation

---

[41] Typical examples: (deaths) Daily Nat. Intelligencer, 29 Dec 1855, p. 3; (a particularly touching account of the death of Richard Staples, perhaps because of its detail) Evening Star, 29 March 1873, p. 1; (shooting) Evening Star, 1 May 1854, p. 3; 20 Mar 1860, p. 2.

[42] Respectively: Daily Union, 21 July 1857, p. 3; Evening Star, 30 June 1854, p. 3; 26 Sept 1868, p. 4; 5 June 1873, p. 2.

[43] "Since the publication of the Mayor's [muzzling] proclamation I have seen . . . hundreds of dogs, and not one with a muzzle or collar" (Daily Nat. Intelligencer, 8 Aug 1861, p. 1); "Will you please explain . . . the use of having laws if they are not enforced?" (Evening Star, 12 Aug 1862, p. 3). One letter-writer explained that the Aldermen had not voted funds for enforcement ("They should at least pay for the powder and ball to kill them"; Evening Star, 30 June 1854, p. 3).

[44] Critic-Record, 11 May 1871, p. 4. Daily Nat. Intelligencer, 2 May 1856, p. 3 gives another example.

[45] The full text of the May-October ordinance of 1875 is included in Counsel Opinions 14 June 1899 (Vol. 9, p. 643). The periods were: 1871 – 15 June-15 Sep; 1874 – 15 June-15 Oct; 1875 – 15 May-1 Oct. This summary comes from Nat. Republican, 18 June 1874, p. 4. Sometime in 1875, "upon my [Einstein's] recommendation," the period was extended to 15 May-15 October (Evening Star, 30 Dec 1885, p. 5; Wash. Times, 7 Aug 1904, p. 4; the first May run was reported 1875, but the ordinance is dated to November, possibly picking up an earlier regulation). See also Evening Star, 1 Apr 1874, p. 4, for a useful discussion of this situation (the proposed ordinance failed; 8 Apr 1874, p. 2). It is a bit tricky to work out these details, but this is my best conclusion.

[46] Nat. Republican, 18 June 1874, p. 4, which gives considerable contemporary scientific observations on the disease.

[47] Evening Star, 23 Sept 1874, p. 4. The Board reiterated the importance of the muzzling ordinance at its 29 June 1877 meeting (Bd of Health minutes).

Counsel noted, "judging from the almost universal failure to observe it, this important ordinance cannot be generally known by the public." And so, with no effective standing muzzling provision the law loosed citizens from that requirement unless an emergency was declared.[48] And indeed, Washington's dogs remained muzzleless from then until the Commissioners ordered their temporary measure of 1899, at the beginning of a second protracted rabies scare.

Dogs taken on the street and showing signs of rabies could, if necessary, be immediately shot (in which case the head was kept for examination) or were taken to the pound for ten-days' observation.[49] Once at the pound suspected dogs were separated from the others as could best be done.[50] Examination of diseased animals was handled by the District's Health Officer until 1887. In that year the Commissioners designated the Chief of the Department of Agriculture's Bureau of Animal Industry (later Animal Husbandry) to serve as veterinarian for the District, giving official opinions regarding the presence of "dangerous communicable diseases."[51] Animals found to be healthy could be returned to their owners; diseased dogs were destroyed.[52]

The Evening Star elaborated in 1910: "Oftentimes the family of the person bitten, usually a child, had a warrant made out for the owner for allowing a vicious dog to run at large. The case would then be tried in a court and if . . . the dog [was] of a vicious nature an order was issued for his death, following which his body would be examined."[53]

Although Einstein spoke of rabid dogs held in the pound, in fact as time went by he became increasingly confident that the disease hardly existed. One source of his skepticism was observation of his own men, who were frequently bitten but never caught the illness. "I have had employed since [1873] 20 or 25 different men as laborers. Every one of them, without exception, has been bitten by dogs, not once but several times . . . Several of the men . . . employed at the pound are dead, but all have died from

---

[48] Counsel Opinions 14 June 1899 (Vol. 9, p. 643). This is helpfully explained in the (otherwise carelessly written) article of Wash. Post, 18 Dec 1899, p. 12, and confirmed by Einstein's comments at the time (Q: "Will dogs have to wear muzzles this summer"; A: "Not unless the . . . Commissioners issue a proclamation to that effect"; Nat. Republican, 26 May 1879, p. 4).

[49] (Heads) Evening Star, 28 June 1910, p. 15. I have found no reports of other animals impounded with the disease, although the later Health Officer rabies reports give statistics for cats, horses and cows examined. We don't know if they were immediately shot or held somewhere. A police officer accompanied the wagon after its earliest years; perhaps he did the shooting. Einstein ceased to carry a pistol on runs early on (after the Lincoln Park riot; Evening Star, 10 July 1910, pt. 2 p. 6), and his men never had them.

[50] "Care is taken to keep the vicious separated from the amiable dogs, and a watchman is in constant attendance to prevent the dogs from fighting" (Wash. Post, 27 May 1908, p. 12). Dedicated quarantine pens were not constructed until 1908. (Wash. Post, 18 June 1908, p. 16).

[51] Comm Minutes/Orders, 18 July 1887. Wash. Times (7 Aug 1904, p. 4) gives a rather gruesome account of the testing method, conducted on guinea pigs. Rabies patients were treated at the Marine Hospital, atop the hill adjacent to the pound, and the Pasteur Institute in Baltimore.

[52] Evening Star, 10 July 1910, pt. 2 p. 6. Whenever a reclaimed dog had bitten a poundman, Einstein reported this to the owner with a warning. "The owner generally seems glad of it, and sometimes says he is glad" (Evening Star, 30 Dec 1885, p. 5).

[53] Evening Star, 10 July 1910, pt. 2 p. 6. The cases were tried in police court and the fine was $2/day "for every day the brute was allowed to live" (Evening Star, 3 June 1872, p. 2).

We might note here that then, as now, certain species of dogs were generally considered especially prone to attack. In an earlier time spitz dogs were universally considered prone to rabies, and a proposed Congressional bill of 1878 would have banned them completely from the District. Later it was bulldogs ("bullies"), and the Commissioners considered special restrictions on them in 1904 (Counsel Opinions 22 Sept 1904, Vol. 15, p. 63; Evening Star, 7 Oct 1904, p. 2), although eventually taking no action.

natural [other] causes."⁵⁴ He also kept abreast of current studies in his field.⁵⁵ And, of course, he was a keen and perceptive observer of dogs, both in the pound and on the street.

When Einstein stated that "I never knew of a case of hydrophobia here," and "I never saw but one mad dog in my life"⁵⁶ he was exaggerating, perhaps for effect, but his analysis of the origin of many reports of rabid dogs on the street is touchingly sympathetic: "I think dogs without a home and kicked about the streets and always scared and sick are more likely to have hydrophobia than licensed dogs that are well cared for." And again: "Once a mad-dog scare is started, every dog that is suffering from the heat or other ailment is looked upon as mad and is killed."⁵⁷ The distinguished Henry Bergh, of New York, agreed with him.⁵⁸

Did the public sometimes see ill-cared-for dogs and panic at the possibility of rabies? Here are items taken from the local newspapers (abridged):

- Some little excitement was created in the northeastern part of the city yesterday evening by the cry of "mad dog". The unfortunate specimen of the canine race was speedily chased by a crowd of men and boys, who eventually succeeded in destroying him. *(Evening Union, 9 July 1864, p. 3)*
- In the continuance of my daily walks I have observed that there are still a great many dogs running at large, a number of which look as though they were in the first stages of hydrophobia. *(Evening Star, 12 Aug 1862, p. 3)*
- Within the past week several dogs have been killed in the eastern part of the city that exhibited some very suspicious symptoms. It was thought that one or two were afflicted with hydrophobia, but it is probable the symptoms were mistaken. *(Evening Star, 17 June 1867, p. 3)*

These excitements probably explain the persistence of citizens shooting dogs themselves (and leaving them on the street "a prize for the big blue flies" for the street-cleaners to pick up – or throwing them into the river.)⁵⁹

From the early 1870s until the mad-dog scare of 1899 the city of Washington seems to have become gradually more relaxed about the danger of hydrophobia. Part of this must be credited to Einstein's pound operations, but other factors contributed also. Pasteur's treatment was much discussed in the Washington press, and commonly with a sense of relief, but also intensifying interest in the disease.⁶⁰ This was accompanied by an increasingly sophisticated understanding not only of rabies and diseases with similar symptoms, but also of canine diseases in general. The press took a more measured view of purported outbreaks, now considering that the complaint might be a misdiagnosis or psychosomatic

---

⁵⁴ Evening Star, 30 Dec 1885, p. 5.

⁵⁵ "On the table in his office are piles of legal documents which he reads to the accompaniment of the strongest potpourri [hubbub] ever arranged for voices" (Wash. Times, 26 July 1903, Magazine p. 5). He regularly spoke in interviews of current theories regarding hydrophobia.

⁵⁶ Evening Star, 30 Dec 1885, p. 5, which goes into length on his theories as to why Washington was safe from the scourge; Nat. Republican, 26 May 1879, p. 4.

⁵⁷ Evening Star, 30 Dec 1885, p. 5; Wash. Post, 27 May 1908, p. 12. The second article continues that of 27 dogs examined for rabies by the Bureau in seven months of 1908 only about half had the disease.

⁵⁸ Critic-Record, 28 Aug 1871, p. 3. A similar protest was raised in 1818 (!) by a Washington letter-writer (City of Washington Gazette, 12 Nov 1818, p. 2) and again in 1861 (Daily Nat. Intelligencer, 31 Aug 1861, p. 3).

⁵⁹ "It is not uncommon to find the body of a dog, attracting a swarm of flies, lying in the gutter or roadway" (Nat. Republican, 25 June 1879, p. 4; also, 19 May 1975, p. 4).

⁶⁰ A "cure" given much ink in the pre-Territorial period was the Mad Stone, an amulet of seemingly magical powers. Its discovery will be found described in Daily Union, 22 Apr 1853, p. 3 and its later career in Evening Star, 28 Jan 1899, p. 14. Government scientist Dr. Melvin felt compelled to discuss (dismiss) the talisman in 1908 and explained what it actually was (Wash. Post, 16 Apr 1908, p. 13).

("spurious hydrophobia") or even the result of mental illness or fraud.[61] Articles about rabies in larger animals almost disappeared in favor of infected cats.[62]

Local newspapers continued to report cases of rabid dogs, but also contrary situations as well: the "worthless cur frothing at the mouth and snapping at pedestrians" which was almost attacked by a crowd until Agent Key of the Humane Society moved the animal to a shady place and poured water over it (the dog was suffering from sunstroke); Mrs. Tyler's pet dog which "snapped and growled every time anyone attempted to pick it up" – again, Key intervened (she had asked the police to shoot it) and found a large bone lodged in the animal's mouth. An article of 1887 felt the need to specify in its headline: "Genuine Hydrophobia". The Evening Star stated the improved mood succinctly in 1887: "As summer heat, dog-days, and hydrophobia are closely connected, though probably without good reason, in the public mind, the magnificent and deserved advertisement of Pasteur . . . comes at a timely season. . . Pasteur will rank among the world's greatest discoverers."[63]

The question of how widespread the incidence of rabies in the 19th century was must be left to medical historians. Certainly there was (and is) a disease of rabies, and very likely its frequency was exaggerated in the public mind, as we see with faddish fears today.

General perception of the danger responded to Einstein's efforts as well as the more moderate attitude toward the disease. In commenting on a verified case of rabies in Georgetown in 1877, the Evening Star observed: "Cases of hydrophobia are so rare in Washington that when one occurs it becomes a matter of public interest. Within the last twenty years this disease has appeared in this city . . . in only six instances. The interval of time between the cases has become less as the population of the city has increased, and as the disease has become more prevalent in all parts of our country, and the average interval at present is about two years." An article of 1885 noted that "no case of hydrophobia has occurred in the city so far this season." An official of the Health Department commented soon afterward: "I do not believe that there has been but one clearly-defined case of hydrophobia in Washington in ten years. . . Since the Pasteur treatment has been receiving so much attention about the country this hydrophobia craze has been given lots of publicity by the press."[64]

---

[61] Evening Star (13 May 1898, p. 16) reprinted an article from the Wilkesbarre Leader: "Frightened to Death" pointing out "the evils resulting from hysterical ideas concerning what is actually a rare disease and yet one that popular imagination has invested with the most horrifying attributes" and much more in that line. Morning Times, 3 July 1896, p. 4: "As a matter of fact, it is pretty certain that what is called hydrophobia is simply an acute nervous malady." In an amusing exchange at the 1909 Senate hearings on the District's budget, Sen. Gallinger asked Commissioner Macfarland: "Did you ever notice in the dictionary the word 'hydrophobophobia'? . . . the fear of hydrophobia. That is what exists. It is not hydrophobia; it is the fear of it" (Hearings . . . 1910 (Senate), 23 Jan 1909, p. 203).

DC's Dr. Greenfell, "considered an authority on such subjects," proposed a counter-hypothesis: "dumb [latent] rabies", which "symptoms . . . are never shown until after some person has been bitten," and which he thought afflicted 4/5 of the city's canines. Dr. D. E. Salmon, of the Bureau of Animal Industry, called this "absurd" (Evening Times, 23 July 1897, p. 3; 25 July 1897, p. 4). See Evening Star, 28 June 1922, p. 6 for more of this.

[62] Occasional reports of hydrophobia in larger animals – usually from other cities – are unconvincing. An early local instance of these will be found in National Messenger (Georgetown), 14 Aug 1818, p. 2.

[63] (Sunstroke) Evening Star, 26 June 1890, p. 2; (bone) 8 Nov 1889, p. 5; ("genuine") 15 Nov 1887, p. 6; (quote) 18 July 1887, p. 2.

[64] Respectively: Evening Star, 24 Dec 1877, p. 2; Critic-Record, 25 Aug 1885, p. 4; 7 Aug 1890, p. 3. Of course, public concern continued. A letter-writer of 1885 opined that "now that hydrophobia is appearing in so many places" the police night-patrols should begin summarily shooting strays – "these creatures are as wild as wolves" (Evening Star, 21 Dec 1885, p. 5). One source mentions "a big mad-dog scare" in 1893 (Wash. Post, 10 Apr 1904, p. B6).

And indeed, the long-serving Health Officer, Dr. William C. Woodward, stated in 1900 that – in spite of regular (if infrequent) press reports of rabid dogs captured and Washingtonians catching or dying from the disease – only seven persons had actually succumbed to hydrophobia between 1874 and that year.[65] The Health Officer's annual reports corroborate this. (See Appendix C6 for statistics.)

The **Mad-Dog Scare of 1899** was preceded by a lesser fright in 1897, fed by the tragic and well-publicized death of 18-year-old Charles Springmann. The man's demise prompted a run of fearful bite-victims on District hospitals. The local Veterinary Association urged the Commissioners to instigate muzzling but city's attorney declared there was no authority for such a measure in spite of the "emergency muzzling" clause of the 1878 act.[66]

In 1899 a much heavier authority weighed in on the question of hydrophobia in the District: the Bureau of Animal Industry. D. E. Salmon, chief of the Bureau, stated in 1897 that "during the past few years [the Bureau had] demonstrated the existence of hydrophobia in about twenty dogs found in the District of Columbia." The Bureau reported in early December 1899 that eleven city dogs had proven to be infected.[67]

The District's Health Officer, William Woodward, initially acknowledged the numbers but persuaded the commissioners to state that they "know of no mad dog being at large [currently], nor have they reason to believe that any animal so afflicted is now at large." In just over a week Woodward issued a second statement explaining that his own figures could be low (due to unreported cases) and giving much higher instances of infection (rising from four in 1896 to ten in the second half of 1899 – this refers to dogs with rabies, not people).[68] Given the steady increase in infected animals and that each was potentially part of a network of spreading infection, Woodward now concurred that "actual cases of rabies exist in this District at the present time, and it is certainly beyond question that there is good reason for believing so." Such authoritative evidence of a hydrophobia epidemic led immediately to a vigorous discussion in the city newspapers about the danger/illusion of the disease and the usefulness/cruelty of muzzling as a preventative.[69]

In the face of official evidence of a rabies outbreak but not wanting to take unwarranted and unpopular actions, the Commissioners on 7 Dec 1899 authorized Poundmaster Einstein to hire extra men (paid from the Emergency Fund), but only to pick up untagged dogs. "This action . . . is not based on the alleged prevalence of hydrophobia . . . but is due to the fact that at the present time there is . . . an unusually large number of dogs running at large without the required tags and collars." District police

---

[65] Evening Star, 28 Apr 1900, p. 15.

[66] (Springmann) Evening Times, 22 July 1897, p. 1; Wash. Post, 22 July 1897, p. 3; (hospitals) Wash. Post, 24 July 1897, p. 2; (muzzling) Counsel Opinions, 14 Aug 1897 (Vol. 8, p. 104). This proposal was opposed by Cecil French of the Washington Canine Infirmary, who will be encountered regularly hereafter. The Counsel concluded that responsibility regarding rabies/muzzling had passed from the Commissioners to the Health Officer and Poundmaster.

[67] Wash. Post, 28 Feb 1897, p. 16; 9 Dec 1899, p. 12. Another report of December 1899 (Wash. Times, 28 Dec 1899, p. 4) said fourteen – either this was an error or the extra three cases represent the nearby suburbs. The Bureau reported 17 cases cumulatively in March 1900 (Wash. Post, 30 Mar 1900, p. 10).

[68] Evening Star, 8 Dec 1899, p. 16; 19 Dec 1899, p. 11. It is not clear if Woodward's statistics were taken from the Bureau or independently developed.

[69] Some examples: (take action) Evening Star, 22 July 1899, p. 8; 12 Aug 1899, p. 12; (there is no problem) Wash. Post, 11 June 1899, p. 6; 8 Dec 1899, p. 6 (which compares the hysteria to fears of yellow fever or smallpox); Wash. Times, 28 Dec 1899, p. 4. The fear was particularly acute at Dupont Circle, where the British ambassador's dog was bitten (Wash. Post, 7 Dec 1899, p. 8).

were ordered to aid this project and the same of the Police Court, which heard such cases.[70] These efforts failed to reassure the hydrophobia-panicked public but did greatly increase the number of (and therefore revenue from) properly licensed dogs, as discussed earlier.

The Bureau of Animal Industry's report of rabid animals in the city and its suburbs declared the region an "infected district" and forbade the transport of unmuzzled dogs in or out of the District – a hardship on Washington's hunters ("local nimrods"), who would then have to hire packs of hunting dogs for their country sports, as one newspaper noted.[71]

The Commissioners wrote Department of Agriculture Secretary James Wilson asking for further information and proclaiming their eagerness to stamp out an epidemic that they had very recently said did not exist. Upon receipt of the Secretary's reply, the Commissioners, Deputy Health Officer and city attorney huddled to decide on a course of action. Attorney Duvall gave his opinion that the 1878 act empowered the Commissioners to declare a rabies emergency and order temporary muzzling.[72]

And so, on 19 December 1899 the Commissioners announced the first hydrophobia emergency in over twenty years, and with it required all dogs not confined on private property to be muzzled. The order was made "with a full appreciation of the unfortunate conditions attaching to the muzzling of dogs, but realizing the responsibility of protecting not only dogs but children and persons from the possibility of being bitten by mad dogs." The muzzling period lasted six months.[73] In fact, enforcement of this provision was delayed to 26 December due to an unlooked-for problem: a near absence of muzzles in local stores. Almost immediately advertisements for the articles proliferated.[74]

In the midst of this legal activity Poundmaster Einstein and his men had been busy. "A few days ago [7 December, Thursday] the District Commissioners summoned Mr. Samuel Einstein . . . to the municipal building. They told him that it was their intent to authorize the procuring of three additional wagons for the work and additional men. He was asked how long it would take to complete the necessary arrangements. Mr. Einstein said one week would be the shortest time possible. The Commissioners declared that the work must be ready to start on the following Monday morning. By working night and day for 72 hours the wagons were procured and rebuilt so as to accommodate the canine prisoners. The

---

[70] (Quote) Evening Star, 8 Dec 1899, p. 16; (police) 12 Dec 1899, p. 8; Wash. Post, 9 Dec 1899, p. 12. "Health officials in the past have been rather indignant because of the tendency of the Police Court judges to dismiss cases of persons . . . charged with keeping unlicensed dogs by advising them to go across the street . . . and procure the required license" (Wash. Post, 9 Dec 1899, p. 12). A Commissioners order of 1911 assigned cases involving unlicensed dogs to the same Police Court; perhaps the responsibility had been shifted elsewhere for a while.

[71] Wash. Post, 18 Dec 1899, p. 12. One man inquired if his dogs would have to stay muzzled during the hunt (Wash. Post, 23 Dec 1899, p. 12).

[72] Wash. Post, 16 Dec 1899, p. 12. They also wrote American embassies asking about muzzling regulations overseas; some replies are summarized in Evening Star, 19 June 1900, p. 3. And see Evening Star, 11 Nov 1893, p. 20 for a lengthy description of the Paris pound.

[73] Evening Star, 19 Dec 1899, p. 11; Wash. Post, 20 Dec 1899, p. 12. A good official account of this process was given by Commissioner Ross (Wash. Post, 27 Dec 1899, p. 10).

[74] Evening Star, 15 Mar 1900, p. 9. "So the muzzle order was drawn up and promulgated, and the hardware dealers, who had been especially disturbed by the fear that a great army of biting, snapping canines might unexpectedly invade their emporiums, breathed a concerted sigh of relief and immediately proceeded to celebrate by ordering signs bearing the device 'Muzzles for sale'" (Wash. Times, 28 Dec 1899, p. 4; see also Wash. Post, 22 Dec 1899, p. 12). One enterprising shopkeeper left a stack of advertising cards at the Tax Assessor's office for the benefit of owners wondering where to find the devices; the practice was soon stopped (Wash. Post, 23 Dec 1899, p. 12).

extra men were engaged and nine extra nets were woven. Last Monday morning, bright and early, the war against unlicensed dogs . . . was begun in earnest."[75]

Health Officer Woodward issued a lengthy and detailed statement describing the types and symptoms of rabies ("hydrophobia . . . is another name for it"). Einstein reported that from 11 December (when his enlarged crew hit the streets – recall that they only took unlicensed dogs until the muzzling order took effect on 26 December) to early March of 1900 he had impounded 2,171 dogs, of which 1,933 were destroyed. "Since the issuance of the Commissioners proclamation . . . the officers have been on the alert for dogs that appear to be affected [with] said disease . . . They discovered several [such] dogs . . ., killed them at once and sent the bodies to the Agriculture Department, the reports . . . proving [that] the dogs were suffering from paralytic rabies."[76]

The Commissioners' muzzling order drew forth a vigorous and informed opposition. Unlike the blue-collar sheep and goat owners of twenty years earlier, who defended their animals with bricks and fists, however, the city's dog owners organized and wrote-wrote-wrote – to the newspapers, to the Commissioners, to Congress. The Washington Times and Washington Post were the great champions of this cause, editorializing early against the alleged seriousness of the rabies threat.[77] Running through these discussions is the assumption that "well-cared for dogs" of the middle- and upper-classes were less likely to contract rabies than "yaller dawgs" and "tramp dogs." ("He [an irate speaker] thought the muzzle cruel and unnecessary for high-class dogs, which are well cared for by their owners.")[78] Health officials admitted that this might be true but they and Einstein aggressively reminded the public that all dogs of any social status would be taken, and then followed up on that threat.[79]

The muzzling order raised a number of interesting legal questions, some related to muzzles themselves: was a dog "with the muzzle attached . . . but not in the proper position" legally muzzled? what about the man who could not find a muzzle that would stay on his flat-faced pug? A visitor from Idaho encountered a miserable dog whose mouth had frozen over because of the muzzle, which he removed: "I suppose I ought to have . . . given myself up to the police as a muzzle thief and a law-breaker."[80]

---

[75] Wash. Post, 18 Dec 1899, p. 12. "The work of the pound was increased very much during the year by the presence of rabies and by the resulting . . . proclamation requiring all dogs to be muzzled and the corresponding necessity for impounding unmuzzled dogs" (Health Officer Ann Rpt ,1900, p. 28).

[76] (Woodward) Evening Star, 28 Dec 1899, p. 5; (Einstein) 15 Mar 1900, p. 9.

[77] Wash. Times, 31 Dec 1899, p. 4; Wash. Post, 22 Mar 1900, p. 6. The arguments, although not new, are well-presented; e.g., "There are some people who can hypnotize themselves into thinking that they have any disease on earth" (Times). And, indeed, the contemporary press reported cases of persons literally dying of fright at the possibility that they had contracted hydrophobia. Both publications later changed their opinions.

[78] Wash. Post, 18 July 1908, p. 2.

[79] Among the prominent citizens to deal with Einstein were Admiral George Dewey, whose dog Prince developed rabies and led the poundmaster a lengthy chase (Wash. Post, 8 Nov 1902, p. 2, and an admiring editorial in the next day's edition), and Sen. Henry Cabot Lodge, whose two untagged Scotch terriers he impounded over the Senator's strong protests (Wash. Times, 24 Mar 1895, p. 12). A letter – presumably from Lodge – regarding this matter appears in the index of in-coming correspondence to the Commissioners (Commissioners letter #209799, n.d.; National Archives, RG 351, Entry 17 "Register of Letters Received").

[80] (Position) Evening Star, 21 Mar 1900, p. 7; (pug) Wash. Post, 13 June 1900, p.10; (frozen) Wash. Post, 4 Feb 1900, p. 6.

Two other legal complications deserve mention. In 1899 Attorney for the District Andrew B. Duvall opined "that policemen are not only justified in using their revolvers to kill dogs displaying evidence of hydrophobia, but it is their duty to destroy the animal."[81]

And secondly, there was the very local issue of diplomatic dogs. It will be recalled that the city furnished tags free to pets of embassy personnel. The 1899 muzzling order, transmitted to diplomatic representatives through the Department of State, asked them "to co-operate in its observance." The British ambassador immediately muzzled all his dogs – he had been a vocal complainer about roving canines – but some others apparently demurred. To round out this matter, Einstein refused to give immunity to such animals, and caused a minor international row trying (unsuccessfully) to capture Klaxin, the Turkish ambassador's pet.[82]

However, written opinions of the Corporation Counsel excused the Argentine legation from the policy (over the protest of an injured neighbor) on the grounds of extraterritoriality, and forced the return of the Belgian minister's unmuzzled pet without payment, using the convoluted reasoning that the normal pound fee was a form of tax (rather than penalty for breaking the law), from which a foreign government was exempt. A 1905 article states: "When a dog belonging to a foreign legation is captured the canine is always returned to its owner free of charge."[83]

At a public meeting on 20 January, citizens organized the **Dog-Owners' Association of the District of Columbia**, the chief opponent of muzzling.[84] Accounts of the meeting summarize their arguments against the practice, some of which echo those of Henry Bergh so many years earlier: muzzling was cruel and even dangerous to the dog; owners had already paid a dog tax and muzzling constituted an infringement of their property rights; rabies ("as it is . . . correctly called") in fact rarely occurred; if the city properly curtailed the population of "tramp dogs" then muzzling would not be necessary; the Commissioners order was not legally supportable.[85] A later (20 March) and more heated meeting added less reasoned complaints: the "youthful" and unqualified Health Officer was "no friend of dogs"; the poundmaster was "an inhuman creature devoid of any feeling"; one Commissioner "despised the sight of a dog"; the British ambassador had instigated the order; a "young scientist" at the Bureau of Animal Industry "was seeking fame," and so forth. The following day the Post begged for calm and defended Einstein as a "mere instrument of the District government" who should not be shot (as one speaker threatened to do).[86]

---

[81] Counsel Opinions 14 June 1899 (Vol. 9, p. 643); Evening Star, 14 June 1899, p. 2. A recent ruling against an officer in such a case (he had, however, used a baton to kill the animal) had had a depressing effect on police actions of this sort.

[82] "I shall take every unmuzzled dog, . . . whether . . . it hails from the Court of St. James or . . . the Crown Prince of Backarawitz – royal blood must produce a muzzle or down to the pound the mutt will go" (Evening Star, 15 Aug 1910, p. 13); see also Evening Star, 19 Dec 1899, p. 11; Wash. Post, 8 Jan 1900, p. 6; 15 Aug 1910, p. 1.

[83] Respectively, Counsel Opinions 25 June 1900 (Vol. 10, p. 688); 4 Aug 1908 (Vol. 19, p. 47); Evening Star, 16 July 1905, pt. 4 p. 1.

[84] The name is variously given Dogowners', Dog Owners', and the form I use here.

[85] For the organization of the Association and extracts of its charter, see: Wash. Times, 21 Jan 1900, p. 5; Wash. Post, 21 Jan 1900, p. 10; the arguments given here are taken from: Wash. Times, 21 Jan 1900, p. 5; 4 Apr 1900, p. 8. Some of them are very similar to ones used in the current gun-control debate.

[86] Wash. Post, 21 Mar 1900, p. 2; 22 Mar 1900, p. 6; 13 May 1900, p. 13. Sen. Gallinger, always skeptical of the scare, agreed about the Bureau's scientists: "We have too many scientists in the Department of Agriculture. If we could get rid of some of them, we would not have this trouble about hydrophobia. They have to have something to do. They . . . examine the brains of dogs or they would be out of work" (Hearings . . . 1910 (Senate), 23 Jan 1909, pp. 203-204).

The guiding force in the Association was **George W. Evans**, a local civic figure and the Association chairman, who in his intensity and single-mindedness seems a rougher version of SPCA's Theodore Gatchel.[87] "The dog question is on again at the District Building, and Mr. George W. Evans . . . has forged to the front with colors snapping from the forepeak. A few days ago Health Officer Woodward, in a report on one of Mr. Evans' frequent communications, states . . ." ran a typical account of his approach.[88]

In February 1900, **T. Edward Clark**,[89] chief organizer of the Association, brought a test case against the order, arguing that it was illegal; the court ruled against him the following month.[90]

After the failure of Clark's challenge, the Association made both a frontal assault on the Commissioners and a flanking attack through Congress. A mass meeting (75 attendees plus several pet fidos) was held and regulations passed and petitions signed (with 2,400 signatures!). One of these resolutions supported an attempt by the Washington Humane Society to assume management of the pound, an issue that will be dealt with later in this study.[91] Letters of complaint, argument and suggestion poured upon the city offices: "The daily communications relative to the dog-muzzling order turn up at the District Building with never-failing regularity."[92] The District Medical Society weighed in on the side of muzzling.[93]

In the U.S. Senate, muzzling's great foe, Jacob Gallinger of New Hampshire, presented the Association's petition and declared that, speaking as a licensed physician, he had "never seen one case of hydrophobia," that it was of "rare occurrence," and that "the community is being constantly fooled by imaginary reports of it."[94] Nothing came of the petition.

If the issuance of the muzzling order in December 1899 aroused the better class of dog owners, its possible renewal in six months drove them to frenzy. During this period, in fact, only one instance of popular fear of hydrophobia appeared in the press: the widely supported campaign of Associated Charities to fund treatment of a little girl from Tenleytown bitten by a mad dog.[95]

---

[87] He was described as prominent, and so was possibly the same Evans who served so outstandingly in the financial office of the Department of Interior from 1864 (at age 16) to his retirement in 1923 (Wash. Post, 1 July 1923, p. 6). He was active in other civic activities and organizations (he later made something of a pain of himself to the city government as President of the West End Citizens' Association), and was regularly asked to recount the assassination of President Lincoln, which he himself witnessed (Wash. Post, 14 May 1905, p. E12; 1 July 1923, p. 6). Evans was also active in local business pursuits, assuming that I am not confusing two men of the same name.

[88] Wash. Post, 13 May 1900, p. 13.

[89] A local businessman (construction/lumber), member of the Board of Education and generally active in civic affairs (Evening Star, 30 Mar 1917, p. 2). He and Evans were both members of the Association of Oldest Inhabitants. He became unbalanced in his last years, and compulsively kept his setter Rhino beside him (Evening Star, 16 Oct 1911, p. 20). The AOI archives contain a very good photo of him (Container 8A/folder 259).

[90] Wash. Post, 24 Feb 1900, p. 5; 13 Mar 1900, p. 12, which quotes all the substance of the ruling.

[91] In regard to muzzling, WHS made an "inquiry" by letter to the Commissioners but took no stand (WHS Ann Rpt, 1899).

[92] Evening Times, 28 Mar 1900, p. 2; Wash. Times, 4 Apr 1900, p. 8; Wash. Post, 31 Mar 1900, p. 8; (quote) 15 June 1900, p. 10.

[93] Wash. Times, 19 June 1900, p. 8.

[94] Evening Times, 28 Mar 1900, p. 2; 9 Apr 1900, p. 1. The complete discussion, including the petition and Gallinger's spirited views on the exaggeration of the rabies threat, will be found in the Congressional Digest, 56th Cong/1st Sess, Senate, 9 Apr 1900. The Washington Humane Society recorded its condolences on Gallinger's 1918 death (WHS Ann Rpt, 1918); the District's municipal hospital was named Gallinger in his honor.

[95] Evening Star, 3 May 1900, p. 16 and several later articles. City officials noted that the disease appeared more in suburban areas than in-town, probably because of "the greater liberty permitted dogs" there. The quarantine areas of 1902 were Brookland, Mt. Pleasant and Congress Heights (Health Officer Ann Rpt, 1902).

And then, on Tuesday, 19 June 1900, the muzzling order expired. No doubt the continuous protests of a distinctly influential interest group were a large factor in this non-action, but two other players had roles also: Dr. Salmon, of the Bureau of Animal Industry, declared that the epidemic had been controlled at least to the extent that it showed no increase, and that "the Department [of Agriculture] is leaving the work of stamping out rabies . . . to the Commissioners";[96] and new Commissioner Henry B. F. Macfarland joined the District's ruling triumvirate. Macfarland, a newspaperman,[97] largely agreed with the "Friends and Owners of the Dog", who submitted the April petition – the fear of rabies was exaggerated, muzzles were harmful to dogs, and problems came largely from tramp dogs. He felt that the scare was fanned by "institutions established ostensibly for the cure of hydrophobia in the name of humanity, but which will not treat a case unless a payment of from $100 to $150 at least is forthcoming." The Friends and Owners' petition was denied but Macfarland prevented the extension of the order two weeks later.[98]

And what of the triumphant Dog-Owners' Association? "The Dog-Owners' Association can now take plenty of time to lay plans for a defensive campaign next season [hydrophobia season]." And George Evans, the victorious general? He quit abruptly, most likely for some internal political/personal imbroglio – such intense and egotistical persons often dramatically jump ship. "I am entirely out of the affair and am no longer connected with the Dog-Owners' Association," he told a reporter. "While my views on the subject have not changed and I have no apologies to make for my past efforts in the matter, I do not care to discuss it further."[99]

With the end of the rabies emergency and discontinuance of muzzling, public concern about both issues waned. The local newspapers saw a distinct drop-off of articles about the disease after mid-1901. Dr. Woodward, the Health Officer, returned to his earlier stance of downplaying the danger.[100] Of the items that made print, some expressed alarm and others skepticism.[101] During these years the District concentrated on elimination of "tramp dogs," as Commissioner Macfarland advised.

Muzzling became quasi-permanent with a series of Commissioners orders beginning **in 1908**. In mid-January, new director of the Bureau of Animal Industry, Dr. Alonzo D. Melvin, reported an alarming increase in confirmed cases of rabies – 86 animals since 1 January – and urged muzzling, something he consistently advocated. Agriculture Secretary Wilson informed President Roosevelt, who wanted to know the Commissioners' planned response. Macfarland vigorously defended his tramp-dog eradication approach. Accounts of attacks by mad dogs proliferated.[102]

The mad-dog scare of 1908 followed the model of its 1899 predecessor with the addition of a presidential directive. The chief of the Bureau's Division of Pathology, Dr. John Mohler, proved the strongest and most persistent advocate of muzzling; support came from the Veterinary Association of D.C., the Marine Hospital Service, and the local Humane Society. Most importantly, on 16 June President Theodore Roosevelt wrote the Commissioners that, based on information from Secretary

---

[96] Evening Star, 19 June 1900, p. 3, with much interesting public reaction.
[97] An active member, with his wife, of the Washington Humane Society.
[98] Comm Minutes/Orders, 3 Apr 1900 and 2 June 1900; Wash. Times, 3 June 1900, p. 4 (with a full account of the three Commissioners' views).
[99] (Association) Evening Star, 6 Oct 1900, p. 6; (Evans) 19 June 1900, p. 3.
[100] Wash. Post, 3 July 1901, p. 6.
[101] E.g., (alarm) Suburban Citizen, 30 Aug 1902, p. 2; Evening Star, 14 Dec 1903, p. 10; (skepticism) Evening Times, 23 July 1902, p. 4; Wash. Herald, 2 Aug 1908, p. 10, in which the case is made humorously as a conversation between several dogs, including a French poodle with a cheesy accent.
[102] Wash. Times, 15 Jan 1908, p. 1; Wash. Post, 16 Jan 1908, p. 9.

Wilson, he strongly urged passage of a six-month muzzling order. "Will you let me know if the Commission intends to pass such a resolution, and if . . . not, what are the reasons? Action in my judgment should be taken without a day's delay." In spite of its earlier resistance, the Commissioners passed such an order that same day, to take effect immediately.[103]

Two days later the Commissioners approved construction of extra pens at the pound, and funds for another wagon and more men. In the next week they for some reason felt the need to formally re-state their muzzling order, and the following month a new police regulation established a fine of $5-20 for owners of unlicensed dogs.[104]

Dog-owners reacted predictably. "Once a dog-muzzling law is passed dog-owners are up in arms, using their time, influence and money to secure its repeal or prevent is enforcement." correctly observed Dr. Melvin.[105] Indignant citizens met in July and formed the Licensed Dog Owners' Association, which heard speeches and formed committees. The moribund Dog-Owners' Association, under its president T. Edward Clark, met a week later, merged with the new group, heard more speeches, formed new committees and planned further meetings. A week later the Dog-Owners' Association morphed into the Citizens' Protective League, dedicated to protection of "the much-abused dog" but which would also "branch out into other matters of interest to citizens of Washington." Clark continued as president.[106]

The new organization was disinclined to a(nother) legal challenge, but veterinarian **Cecil French**[107] refused to muzzle his Great Dane, Capitalus, and forced the issue. He lost his case and suffered the new
$5 fine.[108] No Washingtonians followed the example of the "society women . . . prominent in the fashionable set" of Baltimore's Dog Lovers' Association, who at a hearing on a similar measure in that city "hissed the [city] councilmen, denounced Mayor Mahool, and raised such a rumpus [attacking the legislators with hatpins] that the chairman . . . adjourned the meeting."[109]

During the six-month period of the order Einstein's men busily collected unmuzzled curs of all classes. "The pound capacity has been doubled. Ten men are specifically employed to scour the city day

---

[103] (Mohler) Wash. Post, 17 June 1908, p. 1, among others; (Veterinary) 29 May 1908, p. 3; (Marine) Wash. Times, 18 June 1908, p. 14; Evening Star, 2 July 1908, p. 19, which describes in detail the treatment used at the hospital; (Humane; President) Wash. Times, 17 June 1908, p. 3.

[104] (Pens) Comm Minutes/Orders, 18 June 1908; (wagon) Wash. Herald, 18 June 1908, p. 12; (reinstatement) Comm Minutes/Orders, 25 June 1908; (fine) see text in Health Officer Ann Rpt, 1908, and also in 1909; Wash. Post, 4 July 1908, p. 10, says $5-10. The District's veterinarian visited the pound 81 times in 1909 and 150 the next year (HO Ann Rpt, 1909 and 1910).

[105] Wash. Post, 16 Apr 1908, p. 13.

[106] The Lic. D-O Assn was a southeast DC group, while the D-O Assn was a northwest group; they agreed to hold future meetings in a central location (Wash. Times, 12 July 1908, p. 4; Evening Star, 12 July 1908, p. 22, "Dog Owners on Warpath"; Wash. Post, 18 July 1908, p. 2,` "then came the speechmaking, and there was much of it"; Wash. Herald, 18 July 1908, p. 2). For the Cit. Prot. Lg: Evening Star, 24 July 1908, p. 18; Wash. Post, 25 July 1908, p. 3; Wash. Herald, 25 July 1908, p. 1. The Washington Post thought the broadening of goals ("Now . . . it is the citizen and not the dog who is to be protected") a "terrible mistake" (26 July 1908, p. E4, "Gone to the Bow Wows"); the writing is full of wince-inducing but irresistible puns: "It is barking up the wrong tree"; "dog owners have a real bone of contention," and so forth. Clark apparently thought the new name would have wider appeal.

[107] Prominent local veterinarian, zoologist and environmentalist, at various times active in the Kennel Club, Washington Humane Society, Washington Cat Club, and Fish and Game Protective Association. He once proposed a "National Dog Kennel" at the National Zoo, to hold every species of canine (Evening Star, 2 June 1896, p. 13). As did so many well-to-do men of the time, he dabbled in real estate. He was a Canadian and served overseas in World War I. A photo of French will be found in Evening Star, 7 Aug 1908, p. 11.

[108] Wash. Post, 1 Aug, 1908, p. 5; 8 Aug. 1908, p. 2; Wash. Times, 5 Aug 1908, p. 4; Evening Star, 7 Aug 1908, p. 11.

[109] Wash. Post, 2 June 1908, p. 1.

and night . . . and three wagons are constantly in service." The District government estimated that 12,000 muzzles were purchased in the weeks following the order. "The city is practically rid of unmuzzled dogs," Einstein reported. "'All dogs in the District will be either dead or muzzled a week from now,' remarked one of the dog-catchers." Citizens flooded the tax office to procure tags. "A half-score of clerks, some of them high officials, are forced to suspend their usual duties and hand out dog licenses."[110]

Reported rabies cases declined and medical specialists declared the muzzling edict effective. The President ordered similar action in the Panama Canal Zone. In December the muzzling period quietly expired.[111]

The following year (1909) instances of rabies in Washington almost disappeared. The Marine Hospital's laboratory, adjacent to the miserable pound and where rabies patients received treatment, moved that year into its new building – "of brown vitrified brick and . . . finished throughout with a view to absolute modern sanitation" – but "the rabies section is, temporarily at least, out of a job. There is not a single case on hand." Nonetheless the city continued to produce both dogs testing positive for the disease and humans requiring observation, though mercifully the numbers dropped from the previous year. Three of Einstein's wagons were taken for other use. And yet when Woodward made his report the following year the Health Officer showed a steady annual increase in cases and he declared the six-month decree a failure.[112]

We might say a word here about **muzzles of the period**. This second muzzling order again created a sudden demand for the largely disliked restraint. "The market is being exhausted of its supply of muzzles," reported the Washington Post only one week after the order became effective.[113]

Muzzles came in two types: wire and leather. Authorities trusted only the wire kind but owners (and dogs) favored the leather ones.[114] The chief health concern voiced about muzzling was that it impeded perspiration (panting) and drinking. "Use only large [sufficiently loose] muzzles on our dogs," advised the Washington Humane Society. Health Officer Woodward reminded the public that muzzles must prevent biting and snapping, but should otherwise "interfere to a minimum degree with the dog's freedom." It should be properly fitted, preferably by the dealer, "with . . . as much care as . . . in fitting a pair of shoes on a human being." He added: "A dog can be trained to a muzzle just as a horse becomes accustomed to harness. Its education should begin when it is a puppy." He also advised dealers "against fake muzzles and . . . owners . . . against buying such muzzles."[115] After 1910 only wire muzzles were allowed.[116]

---

[110] (Pound) Wash. Post, 11 July 1908, p.16; (tax office) 23 June 1908, p. 14.

[111] Wash. Times, 20 Sept 1908, p. 11; Wash. Post, 16 Dec 1908, p. 15.

[112] (Decline) Evening Star, 25 Mar 1909, p. 2; 22 Aug 1909, p. 12; (Woodward) Wash. Times, 2 Aug 1910, p. 1. The figures reported here are rather confusing because it is often not clear whether they represent dogs <u>suspected</u> of being rabid or proven so. Likewise were these people entering hospital those merely suspected of having rabies, those actually receiving treatment, or those who died from the disease? Of 32 patients treated at the Marine Hospital in early 1910 none developed rabies or showed any symptoms afterward. Were they cured or never infected? (Wash. Post, 9 Aug 1910, p. 14).

[113] Op. cit., 23 June 1908, p. 14.

[114] "Strap or leather muzzles such as are frequently used are useless"; Dr. N. G. Keirle, Baltimore Pasteur Institute (Wash. Times, 17 June 1908, p. 4). He said that they must be fitted too tight to allow the dog to adequately open its mouth, that they break easily, and can be gradually expanded so as to be ineffective. There was also a "hybrid muzzle, half leather and half wire" that was somewhat effective (Wash. Times, 3 Aug 1910, p. 5).

[115] Wash. Times, 23 June 1908, p. 8; 3 Aug 1910, p. 5; (fakes) 2 Aug 1910, p. 1.

[116] Wash. Post, 5 Aug 1910, p. 2, which gives an amusing if rather uninformative picture of the wealthy looking for stylish gear while the poor improvise from old birdcages, and also the hazard of sales clerks being bitten by unhappy animal-customers.

Certain legal niceties needed clarification. The 1887 Police regulations required that any dog "of a quarrelsome or dangerous disposition . . . be secured by a chain or cord held in the hand of some person accompanying him" when on the street but otherwise dogs were specifically allowed **"at large"** by the 1878 law. This was reiterated in a 1906 Commissioners order.[117]

The Counsel had defined "running at large" in 1901 as "when [a dog] is at liberty to come and go as he pleases upon the public streets," and two years later clarified that dogs on private premises were not "at large".[118] The District government raised the question of whether private property need be fenced in a 1900 legal case; Judge Samuel Church said Yes but this apparently set no legal precedent.[119] When the Commissioners hastily approved the muzzling order in June 1908 they made an inquiry to Corporation Counsel E. H. Thomas regarding the exact parameters of "going at large". "They want to be advised whether having a dog in the arms or in leash while on the streets means 'going at large'." Thomas replied the following day that a **leashed dog** was not "going at large."[120]

Commissioner Macfarland had advocated exactly this approach during the 1908 debates. And in fact, the government in 1899 advised a citizen that his dog could be led through city streets unmuzzled if its owner kept control of it.[121] The new reading opened the way for an alternative to muzzling and in fact to the accepted practice of our own day: either keeping pets confined and on one's own property, or leashed when among the public.

In 1906 the Commissioners tightened the noose on dogs in a new way – the prohibition of dogs "which shall, by barking, howling, or in any other manner whatsoever disturb the comfort or quiet of any neighborhood."[122] Congress had clamped down on females in heat running loose in 1902, following up on a Corporation Counsel suggestion of several years earlier.[123]

The Commissioners **muzzling order of 1910** almost brings us to the end of this long saga. The storyline is by now familiar – rising numbers of people (often children) bitten though by no means all

---

[117] The 1906 decision grew out of a citizen's complaint against bulldogs in general ("unreliable and treacherous") and his suggestion that they be always leashed on the street. Corporation Counsel Duvall opined that this would be within the bounds of legality, citing the authority of the 1887 Congressional act giving responsibility for police regulations to the Commissioners. The bulldog part was dropped (Evening Star, 19 Aug 1904, p. 16; 23 Sept 1904, p. 2).

The question of vicious animals is discussed at some length in the 1907 MPDC Ann Rpt and (for the legalities) in the D.C. Supreme Court decision in Murphy v. Preston of 1887 (Mackey, pp. 514-521).

[118] Counsel Opinions, 7 June 1901 (Vol. 11, p. 549); 8 July 1903 (cited in Counsel Opinions, 16 June 1908; Vol. 18, p. 317). In 1916 the Corporation Counsel opined that dogs running free on private land "undergoing training" were not at-large (Comm Minutes/Orders, 13 Oct 1916, Vol. 27, p. 62), but reversed itself in 1936, then requiring all dogs hunting in the District during the muzzling period to wear the restraint (16 Aug 1936; Vol. 43, p. 30).

[119] Burrows v. District of Columbia (National Archives, RG 21, Entry 60 "Law Case Files, 1863-1938", #43608); but see Counsel Opinions, 16 June 1908 (Vol. 18, p. 317). A jury nonetheless found the District culpable in taking Mr. Burrows' dog, resulting in a series of appeals.

[120] Counsel Opinions, 16 June 1908 (Vol. 18, p. 317); 22 June 1908 (Vol. 18, p. 358); Wash. Post, 18 June 1908, p. 16; Wash. Herald, 18 June 1908, p. 12. The earlier opinion gives much useful background and also leaves open the possibility of legal restraint by "training, habits and instincts." It also ruled that the parking spaces before all District buildings (the seeming front yards, but which are in fact publically-owned land), whether fenced or not, were not permissible areas for unmuzzled dogs.

[121] (Macfarland) Wash. Herald, 16 June 1908, p. 12; (earlier opinion) Wash. Post, 22 Dec 1899, p. 12.

[122] As for noisy animals, "the police can only use moral suasion in such cases" and the complainant had to bring a civil suit (MPDC Ann Rpt, 1907). The Commissioners received regular complaints about this, judging from an index of in-coming correspondence: barking disturbed the meeting of the local Medical Society and the patients at Garfield Hospital in the 1890s. Loud or vicious dogs comprised the most common topic of animal-related letters in this period, followed by reports of dead ones. (One letter is concisely summarized: "Dead dogs and bad boys".)

[123] Counsel Opinions, 2 Apr 1897 (Vol. 7, p. 481).

developing rabies, warnings from the District Health Officer and the federal Bureau of Animal Industry about the advancing threat and pleas for muzzling, and the Commissioners then issuing the order which, on Health Officer Woodward's recommendation, was effective for a full year. Last-minute lobbying added a clause allowing leashing as a substitute, a clause not repeated for several years. (Macfarland was no longer on the Board to object.) Owners were given a week to procure muzzles. On this occasion both Woodward and Einstein – traditionally rabies-skeptics – strongly favored the order.[124]

Public reaction was predictable but feeble – perhaps beaten down by consistent defeats. The newly-formed **Washington Kennel Club** threatened to protest, possibly to President Taft (the Club president was Cecil French, who had brought the test suit against the 1908 order), and several local clergymen spoke out; the earlier, more strident organizations had disappeared. Organized opposition, such as it was, was genteel and entirely upper-class; signatories of the Kennel Club letter included "more than 100 owners of valuable dogs."[125] One cause of this was perhaps the fact that a much higher percent of captured dogs were pedigreed and licensed pets, as the number of street mutts continued to decline.

As usual, the market for muzzles boomed. A panel was appointed (including Einstein and a representative of the cooperative Humane Society) to designate approved muzzles. "Samples of muzzles will be received at the Health Office and turned over to the commission." They approved only wire devices.[126] By that fall Einstein reported that "the dog-catchers simply cannot find any dogs in the streets." The valuable dogs were kept legal by their owners and "stray mongrels are being delivered by residents themselves to the dog pound" as well as the poorer classes continuing to turn in pets they could no longer afford under the new regime.[127] This should not been seen entirely in economic terms: as the city became increasingly both densely populated and sophisticated, the more countrified habit of allowing dogs – as farm animals earlier – to roam free brought disapproval rather than solidarity.

These indicators of civility did not mean that the general public had lost its fear of mad dogs or willingness to lynch them from time to time. The Evening Star that same year carried a touching story of a "little dog . . . playing about on Capitol Hill [which] became frightened for some reason and ran rapidly through the streets. Someone cried 'Mad dog!' . . . and for several hours this unfortunate little animal was bombarded by a mob after it had taken refuge under a box." The poundmen, arriving to take the waif, found it dead from fright and with no trace of rabies.[128]

The year-long muzzling order of 1910 set the later pattern of dog-control in Washington, but we will have to pick up the story in the third section of this report and now turn to the broader sweep of Poundmaster Einstein's efforts to **bring the canine population of Washington to heel**. Einstein's continuing frustration with the District's canine population was reflected in his periodic remarks in the annual reports – pithy and witty – which deserve to be collected here (abridged):

---

[124] Evening Star, 28 June 1910, p. 15; 4 Aug 1910, p. 1; Wash. Times, 2 Aug 1910, p. 1; Wash. Post, 8 Aug 1910, p. 2; Wash. Herald, 8 Aug 1910, p. 7. The fine for keeping an unlicensed dog had risen to $5-20 in 1902. There was at first some confusion as to whether leashed dogs were exempt from muzzling (Wash. Post, 6 Aug 1910, p. 2) but ultimately they were (Wash. Herald, 8 Aug 1910, p. 7).
[125] Wash. Post, 6 Aug 1910, p. 2; 8 Aug 1910, p. 2; 9 Aug 1910, p. 14; Wash. Herald, 8 Aug 1910, p. 7.
Wealthy owners of that time were quite as vulnerable to ridiculous ideas as those of today: see the detailed account of a new establishment offering "Turkish Baths for Dogs" ("[not] a fad"; Evening Star, 8 Apr 1903, p. 20); not only was it scientifically proven healthful for fidos but also helped their masters retain servants, who frequently left over the duty of the weekly dog-bath.
[126] Wash. Post, 5 Aug 1910, p. 2; 6 Aug 1910, p. 2; Wash. Herald, 8 Aug 1910, p. 7, which discusses this quite thoroughly.
[127] Wash. Post, 6 Sept 1910, p. 16.
[128] Op. cit., 13 Aug 1910, p. 4.

- (PM Ann Rpt 1876) The army of miserable curs will be recruited to such formidable strength [by the coming summer] as to demand the marshaling of a sufficient force for their extermination during the next warm season.
- (1878) The question of whence comes the large army of dogs which infest our two cities is still a conundrum. It would seem that the killing of these animals by thousands every year would at least decimate the worthless class; but who among us can say that the 12,474 killed during the past six years are missed? Indeed, it would seem to me, like the adage in regard to gray hairs, two have appeared for every one removed.
- (1879) From whence come the reinforcements to their constantly-thinned ranks is a conundrum which as yet remains unanswered.
- (1887) Washington seems to have some unfailing source of dog supply.
- (1888) Notwithstanding the fact that the canines slaughtered numbered thousands year after year, the supply seems inexhaustible, and its source remains a mystery.
- (1889) There is no dearth of supply as regards the canines.
- (1890) Echo still continues to answer the question as to from whence come the canines.

Appendix B gives the annual figures for dogs captured, destroyed, etc. and can be summarized thus: Generally the number of dogs impounded rose gradually from about 1,000 annually (1873) to 3,000 (1878) before leaping to near 5,000 in 1879, the first full year of licensing, and then ranged one side or the other of 3,000 until hitting over 6,000 in 1900 and again about 4,500 in the 1909-1911 period. After the terrific takes of these early muzzling periods, the numbers declined in the late 1910s back to the 2,500-3,000 level and stayed there to the end of our study period (1940). Not until the 1911 report do the statistics break down dogs captured and those turned in by owners; in that year it was 2:1 ratio captured:surrendered, which was the average for the remainder of our period.

How many dogs – legal or not – resided in the District? Over the period 1873-1908 published estimates generally ranged somewhere between 15,000 and 20,000 (and Einstein's highest figure – 30,000 – in 1893). An 1885 article guessed 12,000-15,000 within the old city limits and 3,000-5,000 in the county. Dr. Melvin of the Bureau in 1908 claimed that 8% of Washington households kept dogs. Einstein, at an earlier time (1879) and more harried by canines, said: "There is hardly a house but has its dog. Some dog fanciers have as many as fifteen." The Post thought the total in 1908 to approximate 20,000, of which 11,000 were licensed. Add to these figures "the visitors from Maryland and Virginia."[129]

Race and class ran parallel in the dog-hunting business: "Large numbers of dogs were kept in those parts of the city inhabited by colored persons." Einstein testified: "I think I may safely say that nine-tenths of the dogs that have met death at our hands had previously found shelter . . . with the negroes who inhabit our alleys and back streets." Especially good dog-hunting was to be had in Uniontown, Hillsdale and Howardtown. Perhaps half the published reports of people bitten or catching rabies referred to

---

[129] Some of the many estimates: Evening Star, 5 June 1873, p. 2; 30 Dec 1885, p. 5; 9 Oct 1893, p. 8; 15 Mar 1900, p. 9; Wash. Post, 23 June 1908, p. 14. (Melvin) Wash. Post, 16 Apr 1908, p. 13; (Einstein) Nat. Republican, 26 May 1879, p. 4; (visitors) Evening Star, 15 Mar 1900, p. 9.

Perhaps there was something to the claim of immigrant dogs. The Evening Star reported in 1893 that in Alexandria "the raids of the dog wagon have . . . rid the city of worthless curs, and a general exodus of untaxed dogs across the river to Maryland . . . has been made, so that . . . homeless dogs are met in all parts of that section" (Evening Star, 19 June 1893, p. 3; Alexandria had 675 legal dogs). How did they cross the river?

African-Americans. More good catches could also be had at the edges of the city: "Dogs are looked upon as an absolute necessity in the county."[130]

In spite of his struggle against the incoming tide of worthless curs, Einstein periodically felt optimism, usually in the flush of one of the larger campaigns resulting from a new licensing or muzzling law. "Last July we used to get 35 or 40 a day . . . Now if we get twelve a day we consider it a good haul. If it keeps up like [this] all the common dogs will be killed" (this in 1879, just at the time of his pitiful complaints quoted above); "It has taken me 29 years to bring about this state of perfection but I can say truthfully that the city today [1902] is as free from stray animals as is possible for any large city to be"; "The idea that it is only the stray dogs that have rabies in entirely wrong. The pet dogs have it now in larger numbers than the homeless ones, for the reason that there are very few stray dogs. We have collected about all the stray and untagged dogs in the city" (1910).[131]

Einstein's perseverance and success catching dogs worked against him in some ways. Street dogs learned to hide from the red pound wagon (and to be alert to the cries of their permanent allies, the local boys). Some came to recognize the poundmen: (Einstein) "'The trouble is, we have been chasing . . . stray dogs so long that they recognize the dog-catchers . . . That black-and-tan that just got away . . . knows John Wells so intimately that every time [he] sees him he will run [away] . . . I guess I'll have to whitewash John,' added the 'General' . . . after a thoughtful pause" (Wells was black). One dog was reported to run to his master for his muzzle whenever he heard the pound wagon approach.[132]

A Washington policeman concurred (1904): "It has been but a few years since it was almost impossible for pedestrians to pass through some of the parks . . . after dark without having to struggle with a dog or two, but now it is different, and very few dogs have been seen hanging . . . about the public spaces." During hearings on the 1914 District appropriation Rep. Albert Burleson challenged Dr. Woodward: "Some people believe that you are catching too many dogs now." "We are unwilling to admit guilt," reposted the Health Officer.[133]

Before leaving the canine question, we should note that citizens occasionally took **private legal actions** against the pests. Most famously, Congressman/ambassador/Attorney General Caleb Cushing brought a civil action against his neighbor, Mr. Kelly, whose "yellow dog . . . was a howling nuisance to his neighborhood" in 1873; the animal moved to a new home as a result. B. H. Collins wrote the Commissioners fourteen years later to complain of <u>his</u> neighbor who kept three (unlicensed) dogs, two cats "now with kittens," and dozens of chickens; "the stench therefrom and the noise at nearly all hours . . . is enough to drive a quiet person crazy." We do not know the outcome of this. And finally, in 1873 Judge Dawson of the Police Court ruled that citizens could legally defend themselves by gun or stone from vicious dogs, restated by the District Supreme Court in a case of 1887. "This decision [1873] will be generally commended by all except the owners of the dogs."[134]

---

[130] (Colored) Evening Star, 30 Aug 1890, p. 12; Poundmaster Ann Rpt, 1878; Evening Critic, 21 Oct 1884, p. 1; (county) Evening Star, 15 Feb 1908, p. 8.

[131] Nat. Republican, 26 May 1879, p. 4; Wash. Times, 13 Apr 1902, Ed/Drama p. 17; Evening Star, 2 Aug 1910, p. 1. He estimated in the second article that 90% of city dogs were tagged, and in the third that nine out of ten dogs examined for rabies had been tagged animals.

[132] (Wells) Wash. Times, 13 Apr 1902, Ed/Drama p. 17; (muzzle) Wash. Post, 19 July 1908, p. A4.

[133] Evening Star, 21 July 1904, p. 6; <u>Hearings . . . 1914 (House)</u>, 3 Jan 1913, pp. 190-194.

[134] (Cushing) Daily Critic, 19 July 1873, p. 1; Daily Nat. Republic, 18 Aug 1874, p. 4; (Collins) Evening Star, 1 June 1887, p. 1; (defend) 3 Sept 1873, p. 2; Murphy v. Preston (Mackey, pp. 514-521). A police order of 1910 cited a recent "[court] opinion relative to a person who maliciously poisons a dog or any other person" but we have no more information (MPDC Ann Rpt, 1910).

Speaking of civil suits, we cannot let pass a curious case from Memphis, 1869: A man's dog bit a passerby on the foot and when the victim kicked his foot loose two of the dog's teeth were embedded in his heel. The victim sued the owner for allowing a vicious dog to run loose; the owner sued the victim for "having a heel tough enough to drag a dog's tooth out" (widely reported, e.g. Charleston, SC, Courier, 21 Oct 1869, p. 4).

CHAPTER TWELVE

Cats

When our doors and gates are shut, neither hog or dog can enter; but to what plan shall we resort to keep cats out of our houses? . . . They steal and devour our chickens, and keep us in perpetual fear lest our Canary birds should meet a similar fate. Not content with this feline felony, they render the night hideous with their unwelcome serenades. A heavy tax should be imposed on these disturbers of our repose; [otherwise] we have been hesitating whether to use buckshot or strychnine. (Daily Union, 28 July 1858, p. 3)

My neighborhood was so overrun with them, and my sleep so disturbed . . . , that in self-defense I provided myself with a parlor rifle, and I have just a dozen notches on the stock to show the number of the enemy slain. And I am keeping up the good work. (Evening Star, 11 June 1896, p. 10)

Pet cats are the craze here just now. They are as numerous as pugs were some few years ago. (Wash Times, 13 Apr 1902, Magazine p. 8)

Corporation-period mentions of cats as street-nuisances in Washington newspapers are either rare or difficult to find. They picked up in the early 1870s: "Since the weather has grown more genial the raving of cats . . . at night is absolutely intolerable. The public call indignantly for a cat pound; and yet that call is hardly judicious, as it might be responded to with a pound of sausages instead of a pound of cure." Apparently there were more such articles, since John Marbury, of the city's Board of Health, commented the following year that "some of the newspapers advocate a war on cats." He did not agree with this, however: "Cats do not bark and bite nor produce hydrophobia." (This statement came the same year that the District Board of Health endorsed a finding that cats carry the disease.)[1]

The coming debate about cats held parallels to those regarding chickens and dogs: cats, like fowl, a rather minor but common animal generally accepted as a useful if sometimes annoying aspect of city life when cows and hogs roamed the streets, became less tolerable once these larger animals disappeared and as the population became more urbane and less rural in experience. And as with dogs, except for some humane individuals or organizations, the general populace felt no sympathy for feral cats but rather the opposite. Even the boys did not protect them. Concern for cats centered on treasured pet felines, and became – at least as far as organized efforts went – largely a cause of the middle- and upper-classes. Ironically a large number of feral cats had been pets whose owners simply turned them out of the house when they went on summer vacation, a common practice at the time.

Cat complaints were (as far as I can find) absent from the Washington newspapers from the mid-1870s to the late 1890s. There were rumblings, however. A short notice of 1893 reported an upsurge in the number of alley cats killed by the populace, not (as was the case with dogs) from fear of rabies but to stop their

---

[1] (Cats) Critic-Record, 6 Sept 1870, p. 2; 22 Mar 1873, p. 4; 24 July 1873, p. 1; (Marbury) Evening Star, 1 Apr 1874, p. 4; (Board) Nat. Republican, 18 June 1874, p. 4.

nighttime noise and "to get rid of fleas"; also "small boys with . . . parlor rifles and air guns are responsible." More sadly, "a large gang of boys" gathered near the LeDroit Park neighborhood in 1882 to hunt cats with trained dogs. "Almost nightly these parties pursue their depredations, and, having tracked a cat to its retreat in some quiet alley, start the chase and often set three or four dogs on a single cat."[2]

The Washington Humane Society complained of feral cats and dogs to the Commissioners in 1896. Health Officer Woodward replied that the pound was doing its best – and successfully – with dogs, but as for cats: "He [cannot] suggest a remedy for the evil . . . Cats which prowl around back lots and over fences and sheds are, undoubtedly, frequent sources of annoyance. And when, in what era of the world, were they not?"[3]

"Judge Uruquhart of Georgetown" the following year vented his astringent opinion of cats to the Evening Star: "Cats should be licensed the same as dogs. They are much more of a nuisance in every way . . ., are kept in larger numbers and much more revenue could be secured than . . . from the dog license tax. There might be some reasons for keeping dogs . . . but there are no reasons whatever for keeping cats. A dog barks now and then [but] cats . . . make ten times the racket . . . As far as hydrophobia is concerned, cats cause it as frequently as do dogs, for, after all, it is a rare, though terrible thing."[4] The judge gives all the arguments against a promiscuous feline population in a nutshell: noise and nuisance; hydrophobia; and the possibility of tax income.

Heading off such aggressions, cat lovers incorporated the **Washington Cat Club** in 1902, headed by the redoubtable Cecil French, who would later try to overturn the dog muzzling order. (Interest in fancy-breed felines had recently travelled to the U.S. from Britain.) The club was only interested in house cats – it planned the first Washington cat show for that December. As for others, "the organization plans to do away with tramp cats," picking them up (somehow) "whenever complaint is made of them" and taking them to one of its planned cat pounds "and destroy them" – "in the most humane manner." "This means the inauguration of a new and peaceful era in the history of the District, the promoters of the new club affirm."[5]

At this time the District had no provision for a cat tax/tag nor, in fact, any other legal restrictions. (Cats have not been restricted in the District to this day.)[6] The first salvo in the campaign to control the cat population came from the Northeast Citizens' Association which, in 1904, sent the Commissioners a resolution deploring "the large number of homeless or back-yard cats," which they saw as a health hazard, and urging the city to institute licensing and otherwise to "provide for their extermination, as is the case with dogs." Dr. Starr Parson, sponsor of the resolution, cited the tragedy of two children recently killed

---

[2] (Killed) Evening Star, 1 Aug 1893, p. 6; 27 were picked up by the dead-animal crew in one day; (hunt) Daily Critic, 20 Sept 1882, p. 4.

[3] Evening Times, 9 Oct 1896, p. 5.

[4] Evening Star, 14 Aug 1897, p. 14. "They break down my flowers, upset my garbage bucket every night, scattering the refuse over the yard, kill spring chickens if not nailed up, fight and squall all night," complained I. N. Hammer, who wrote the humorous poem in Appendix D8 (Evening Star, 9 Aug 1897, p. 9). The proposal to tax cats was, of course, ridiculous since the noisome alley toms were ownerless.

[5] There was also planned a cat hospital. (Evening Star, 1 Oct 1902, p. 10; Wash. Post, 1 Oct 1902, p. 11). The tenor of the club was well expressed by the Post's subhead: "Respectable Felines Will Be Cared for and the Vagrants Dispatched".

[6] Evening Star, 15 Aug 1936, p. 7. Einstein suggested a cat tax in his 1904 annual report.

by the bite of "a germ-carrying cat." Commissioner Macfarland, the friend of dogs, approved heartily; the Health Officer also agreed.[7]

In the same year the District began to **impound cats** – not directly from the street, which would have required legal authorization and was certainly beyond its means – but from owners who no longer wanted them and from those who had caught alley cats themselves. Previous to this unwanted kittens were drowned or simply released in city parks.[8] Citizens now arranged pick-up service merely by writing or calling the pound. The animal needed to be "securely fastened in a box or basket." There was no charge. In 1909 the poundmen discontinued their pick-up service and residents had to deliver unwanted felines to the pound themselves.[9] (The Washington Humane Society also euthanized unwanted pet cats on request at its shelter; "people object very much to have it done in their own home." Such calls reached 70 in one month.)[10]

Impounded cats were killed that day, as the pound had no procedures for redemption or purchase nor separate pens to hold them. Einstein explained this necessity: "Cats, when terrified and caged, seem to revert to their wild state, and if a dozen strange cats were confined in one of the wire netting inclosures . . . pending their possible redemption there would be a dozen balls of fur and blood in the morning."[11]

He also discussed why his men could not chase cats down alleys, going beyond the usual "I don't have enough men" explanation, and demonstrating once again his practical and insightful grasp of his work: "If any citizen . . . advocates the catching of cats in a net by hand . . . I beg him to try it just once. Stray cats are usually bagged with a shotgun, a method impracticable in cities, or put out . . . by poisoned meat, also a method not approved of . . . A man will face and catch a savage dog . . . but it takes the bravest to . . . capture a cornered cat . . . A cat can spring into a man's face and chew and claw it beyond recognition . . . and tear the man's hands and fingers into ribbons at the same time, and then get away. You can't hold a cat as you can a dog."[12]

By July the crew was bringing "a dozen or more" every day. "In some neighborhoods . . . so many cats have been taken away that residents . . . no longer [throw] missiles from their windows at night . . . to secure quiet and be able to sleep." The take of cats grew from 547 in 1904 to 1,005 the following year and 4,038 in 1908, and Einstein requested extra men to keep up with the work. "All day long the pound

---

[7] (Association) Wash. Times, 10 May 1904, p. 4; (Health Officer) Wash. Post, 3 Sept 1904, p. 10. "Pussy Cat, Pussy Cat, Where Have You Been? 'Escaping Macfarland's New Tag of Tin'," headlined the Wash. Times article of 10 May.

[8] "Given to men and boys to drop around vacant lots," as the WHS Ann Rpt of 1898 puts it.

[9] The first mention of this procedure I find is Evening Star, 8 June 1904, p. 16. The pound had long collected unwanted dogs in this way. The other information here comes from Evening Star, 21 July 1904, p. 6 (which mentions only the practicalities as the reason for not taking cats from the street); 4 Aug 1905, p. 5; 23 Apr 1909, p. 24; (delivery) 31 Oct 1909, p. 32. The Street Cleaning Dept's Annual Report, 1909, reports that its crew had begun "collection of live cats and dogs, done without expense to the government" that year, something mentioned in no other source.

[10] WHS Ann Rpt, 1897.

[11] Evening Star, 5 Nov 1905, p. 10; 10 July 1910, pt. 2 p. 6. "At almost every hour . . . people can be seen carrying bundles to the pound, many times . . . small and ragged colored boys. 'What is it?' asks Mr. Einstein. 'Cat.' 'Take it out to one of the men then.' . . . The boy trudges away, sometimes to appear later with another burden of the same character."

[12] Evening Star, 5 Nov 1905, p. 10. John Heap of WHS completely agreed with Einstein: "You know it is not like catching a dog . . . taking into custody a member of the feline family" (Wash. Post, 23 Nov 1905, p. 12). The difficulty of capturing felines was borne out by a description of the New York Humane Society's Night Rider crew of cat-catchers: "Two active young men, much scarred in the face, hands and arms from tussles with East Side cats [form] the regular meow department" (Wash. Post, 28 Aug 1911, p. 8). This very detailed account is highly entertaining. Also described in Evening Star, 11 June 1896, p. 10.

telephone is kept busy, messages being received about . . . stray cats picked up and detained by residents."[13]

Needless to say, this vigorous cat-control did not please everyone. As usual, the local newspapers could not resist mixing some fun in their protest: "After acknowledging that he has murdered 3,788 cats . . ., Samuel Einstein, . . . with shameless effrontery . . . declares that the request 'for removal' of cats by those not in sympathy with their nocturnal concerts are daily becoming more numerous. Instead of endeavoring to instill in the breast of these musical critics a sense of tenderness . . . for the felines who are doing the best they can, he heartlessly [requests] additional means for their destruction."[14]

One article pointed out accurately that cats – now under accusation of spreading disease – are "the most fastidious animals in matters of toilet," while "the dog is as dirty as a boy." A second reminded readers that stray cats catch rodents, while "the pet cat ["fluffy-ruffles in fur" it called them elsewhere] is the symbol of practical uselessness." And a third made the pertinent legal point that cats were not legally defined as property, as dogs had been since 1872 – "most cats are valuable only in affection, and not in coin."[15]

After several years of intermittent discussion,[16] Health Officer Woodward and Commissioner Macfarland in 1908 proposed a revision of District tax on dogs (to $5 for each male dog over one month old, $10 for each female) and the same for cats. Macfarland said that the number of unwanted animals was increasing, that more revenue was needed to deal with them, and that he was moved by "the great suffering among dogs and cats, especially the latter, because so many . . . are allowed to . . . die from exposure and starvation." Better, he thought, that they "be put painlessly to death."[17]

Tellingly, the local community of cat-lovers embraced the proposal. "It was expected that there would be strong opposition to the bill but, strange to say, the communications received yesterday all favored the proposed tax." Nonetheless, the law did not pass, perhaps from practical considerations of how to enforce it, perhaps because of opposition from dog owners.[18] Soon after, three-year-old Mildred Downey was bitten by a supposedly rabid cat. Members of the Public Education Association sent "fuzzy, bright-eyed, playful and cute" be-ribboned and -flowered kittens to three members of Congress to persuade them to include cats in planned legislation calling for "extermination of homeless, sick and injured dogs in Washington." Shelters for homeless cats were proposed and even established. Congress considered adding a cat annex to the pound.[19] The controversy continued . . .

---

[13] Evening Star, 21 July 1904, p. 6; 23 Apr 1909, p. 24; Wash. Herald, 12 Oct 1907, p. 9. Some speculated that people sent cats to the pound for execution from fear of incurring seven years' bad luck themselves.

In regard to superstitions regarding cats, we might mention here that WARL workers of 1934 reported visitors less hesitant than earlier to adopt black cats (Wash. Post, 14 Aug 1934, p. 13).

[14] Wash. Herald, 12 Oct 1907, p. 9.

[15] Respectively: Wash. Post, 12 May 1904, p. 6; Evening Star, 19 Feb 1908, p. 6; Wash. Post, 23 Aug 1908, p. E4.

[16] Wash. Post, 12 May 1904, p. 6 mentions divided opinion among the Commissioners on the subject. Einstein had suggested taxing bitches at $4 in his 1904 annual report, and WARL's Executive Committee discussed the same at its meeting of 29 Nov 1939.

[17] Evening Star, 12 Feb 1908, p. 8; Wash. Post, 12 Feb 1908, p. 14. Discussions of alley cats always specified that the pound euthanized animals painlessly, which was not the case with similar discussions of dogs. This is probably another indication that the cats had no defenders and proponents wanted to head off criticism of control measures on this point.

[18] "A resolution . . . that the [East End Citizens'] Association indorse the plan . . . to increase the tax on dogs . . . met with a storm of opposition and was voted down: Dogs are looked upon as an absolute necessity in the county." (Evening Star, 15 Feb 1908, p. 8).

[19] (Support) Evening Star, 13 Feb 1908, p. 4; Wash. Post, 13 Feb 1908, p. 14; (failure) Evening Star, 19 Feb 1908, p. 6; (Downey) Wash. Times, 4 July 1908, p. 12; (kittens) Wash. Post, 24 July 1909, p. 1; Wash. Herald, 24 July 1909,

In 1911 little William Core was bitten by a rabid cat and Woodward ordered removal of all stray toms. He immediately received strong support from the Washington Cat Club (its president now **Mrs. Henry L. West**[20]), representing "many . . . owners of high-class cats." The Club requested all members of the public to lure strays into their homes for removal by the poundmen, or to take them directly to the pound or Mrs. Beckley's private shelter in southwest, where they would be put down. "I think the owner of every respectable animal . . . will be willing to aid in the extermination . . . All cats found wandering at large should be killed" (West). Both Einstein and his successor, Emil Kuhn, expressed alarm at the possibility of an order to begin clearing out alley toms with their limited crews.[21]

In June 1912 the Commissioners ordered the poundmaster to **seize all stray cats** and destroy them. The order made no provision for redemption, and specified that animals still could be delivered to the pound. The impetus for this move was, again, fear of rabies. Woodward's successor as Health Officer, Harry C. McLean, reported that since the previous summer nine rabid cats had bitten eleven persons. "During the many years the pound has been under his [McLean's] direct supervision [for the Health Department] there has been no year in which cats have developed rabies . . . to the extent they have during the current fiscal year." He also recommended a licensing procedure and gave the interesting information that, after extensive correspondence with other large cities' governments, he could report that of 50 U.S. and 19 foreign cities only New York impounded cats.[22]

This decree did not please the Washington Cat Club, which stated its objections clearly: "We members of the Cat Club are in favor of doing away with cats that are pests, [but] the Commissioners . . . make no allowance for the valuable cats owned by women of Washington."[23] The ladies testified at the Commissioners' 3 July hearing but to no avail. Said Commissioner John A. Johnson: "The demand is very insistent from the people of the District to be relieved of these nuisances," referring to their nighttime noise.[24]

More protests by the Club and other cat-fanciers rained upon the District government, but what saved the city's felines – both prize and common – was a more mundane factor: the pound had no capacity to take or hold them. Men, cages and wagon all would require upgrading. "Poundmaster Kuhn is firmly of the opinion that to order a cat caught is one thing, but to catch it is another." For the time being the city compromised by reinstating its pick-up service. Even this measure brought an unprecedented decrease in

---

p. 2; (shelters) Evening Star, 22 Feb 1908, p. 18; Wash. Post, 18 Oct 1908, p. SM3 (describing the efforts of Sarah Beckley, "the head of the cat propaganda in Washington"); (annex) Evening Star, 19 July 1909, p. 2.

The "kitten" publicity stunt was so saccharine that one feels light-headed reading about it. "The kittens and baskets to match were decorated by an F Street florist after several hours of deliberation and consultation." Each animal came with a little poem attached: "I hope you'll then take care of me when I am old and sick./I only crave death merciful, painless, and quick./We're not just useless froggies/We watch the mouse and rat;/'The pound' takes care of homeless doggies,/Why not the pussy cat?" (Of course, the pound took care of doggies by killing them.) And the Association claimed it only wanted "to prevent children . . . from becoming hard-hearted as a result of witnessing the continued ill-treatment of felines."

[20] Nee Mary Hope White, member of the Board of Trustees of the public schools and a prominent socialite. She served as a Director of WARL in the 1930s. Mr. West was an important and well-connected newspaperman and District Commissioner.

[21] Wash. Post, 19 Aug 1911, p. 2; Evening Star, 27 Aug 1911, pt. 4 p. 3.

[22] Evening Star, 13 June 1912, p. 2. The official notice was published on p. 18 of the same publication. The order, by the way, was an amendment to the Police regulations.

[23] The club was dominated by society ladies. Mrs. W. H. Bixby stated that she had recently paid $500 for her Persian, which she "would not have killed for the world" (Wash. Post, 14 June 1912, p. 14).

[24] See Comm Minutes/Orders, for that date.

the city cat population – almost 3,000 killed in July-October 1912, "practically all . . . of the worthless variety." At the end of 1913 the pound ordered traps to capture alley cats.[25]

---

[25] (Club, pound) Wash. Post, 16 June 1912, p. 17; 18 June 1912, p. 16; 19 June 1912, p. 16; 5 July 1912, p. 6; Evening Star, 21 Oct 1912, p. 9; (traps) Evening Star, 3 Dec 1913, p. 13. In its desperation, the Cat Club embraced plebian tabbies, repeating the argument that they help control mice and rats, and denying that they carry diseases. Said Mrs. West: "The poor, howling tom does more good than harm." The Club now only approved the extermination of "sick and useless cats."

CHAPTER THIRTEEN

Pound Operations and Miscellany

This section details various aspects of pound operations and also some interesting sidelights of that institution.

The Poundmaster

The duties of the poundmaster were listed in the 1872 act that created his position:

> There shall be appointed . . . a poundmaster, whose duty it shall be to take up and impound all domestic animals found running at large . . ., to keep safely and carefully all property pertaining to said pound, and all animals impounded therein; and to report from time to time, through the health officer, . . . the condition of said pound, and what repairs, if any, are needed; and the number and description of the animals therein impounded, and what disposition has been made of the same; and to report all moneys received by him under the provisions of this ordinance. And it shall be the further duty of said poundmaster to pay over, daily, all moneys received as aforesaid to the health officer, taking receipt therefor, and said poundmaster shall give good and sufficient bonds for the proper discharge of his several duties as herein provided.
>
> That the poundmaster . . . shall keep a register of all animals taken up by him, with an accurate description of the same; which shall at all times be open to the inspection of the public; and the said poundmaster is hereby forbidden to deliver any animal taken up and impounded to any person applying for the same, unless such person shall present good and sufficient evidence of his ownership or right to the possession of said animal.[1]

Einstein's salary rose from $1,000/year in 1873 to $1,200 in 1880, and then $1,500 in 1902. It had risen to $2,000 by 1921, when the Health Officer proposed a further addition of $280.[2]

The Pound Staff

We have to suffer much abuse at times for performing our duty, but consciousness of right enables us to bear it calmly. The better class of citizens, I think, appreciate our work, and this is encouragement enough. (Poundmaster Report, 1879)

---

[1] The only other official description of Einstein's assignment, from the Health Officer Ann Rpt, 1904 (p. 44, which describes the work of all Health Department employees), is notable for its unhelpful brevity: "The duties of this officer are those usually incident to the office of poundmaster."

[2] Daily Nat. Republican, 9 May 1873, p. 4; Hearings . . . 1913 (Senate), 16 Feb 1912, pp. 81-82. Hearings . . . 1917 (House), 5 Jan 1916, p. 391, says $1,400 "because of his long experience and in recognition of his very faithful service," – a misprint; Evening Star, 5 Dec 1921, p. 19.

The dog-catcher's job is about the most thankless one on earth. He is looked down upon because he holds a job that compels him to prey on the little cur that frisks at the curb. But let some citizen's youngster get bitten and then the uproar begins. (Wash. Times, 29 Oct 1922, p. 7)

During most of the period under discussion the staff of the pound consisted of exactly five men: Poundmaster Einstein and four poundmen[3] – laborers hired by the Health Officer and then assigned to pound service. In times of unusual activity, such as the extensive sweeps of 1900 and 1908, extra men were taken on and then let go afterward.[4] The Metropolitan Police sent an officer to assist the poundmaster (principally riding on dog runs) beginning in 1878.

In the wild and wooly days of Hoover's contractor pound the poundmen were universally described as ruffians who stole animals from people's yards as often as they legally took them from the street; after all, they were paid by the head. Einstein's men, subject to physical resistance during their duties and legal harassment afterward, were never described so. They were salaried employees of the city, and Einstein's disciplined management of his crew and firm but tactful handling of the public protected them. They also seem to have been sincerely dedicated to their work. Certainly Einstein – punctilious in applying the law to beasts and owners – was not a man to suffer slack employees. But those who stayed with him (and they stayed for very long spells) held a commitment to their work and felt part of a team both with their boss and each other.[5]

All the poundmen were black. "Mr. Einstein says that white men do not make good dog-catchers but that negroes have a natural knack for it." When not on pound duties they could be called away for other Health Department work, such as disinfection of contaminated sites during epidemics (Einstein also participated). "It [should be] remembered that the men engaged in the pound service are . . . appropriated for as laborers in the health department, without particular reference to the pound service," he reminded the Commissioners in his 1898 report.[6]

For his earliest sweeps Einstein was given (temporarily) fifteen men, far more than he ever saw again. A report of 1873 lists six (by name), each receiving $2/day for his work but this sank to four men later that year. He only had more than four in later years when, as in 1893, the District was making a big public push to allay the dog problem.[7]

Poundmen received pay of $30/month for the earlier part of this period. The Commissioners fixed their pay at $1/day in 1888, increased it to $40/month six years later, and $50/month in 1911.[8] The Health Officer requested a further increase from $600/year to $700 in 1918 testifying that "new men are inclined to leave on the slightest provocation . . . We must have larger compensation to hold our men."

---

[3] They were colloquially "hog-catchers" until hogs disappeared from the streets, and then became "dog-catchers".
[4] At $1.50/day in 1899 (Comm Minutes/Orders, 9 Dec 1899).
[5] In 1900 the Commissioners noted that in 21 years of operation only one prosecution had been brought against a pound employee and it ended in acquittal (Evening Times, 28 Apr 1900, p. 8).
[6] (Negroes) Wash. Post, 18 Dec 1899, p. 12; a photo of poundmen from the 1930s includes a white worker but perhaps this was a Depression-era gesture – Ingrid Newkirk, the last poundmaster, found the staff entirely black when she came in. The lower-level staff stayed all black and all male until the Humane Society took over the facility; (disinfecting) Poundmaster Ann Rpt, 1895; Evening Star, 8 Dec 1899, p. 16; Health Officer Ann Rpt, 1904, p. 45. This disinfection project was cited as one cause of the growth in street dog population (it cut into pound runs); see also the 1898 annual report quoted, which elaborates on this task.
[7] Daily Nat. Republican, 9 May 1873, p. 4; 30 Aug 1890, p. 12; Critic-Record, 24 July 1873, p. 1; Poundmaster Ann Rpt, 1877.
[8] Poundmaster Ann Rpt, 1888; Comm Minutes/Orders, 27 Feb 1895; Congressional act of 2 Mar 1911 approving the new pound; Hearings . . . 1919 (Senate), 6 May 1918, p. 77.

Einstein, of course, regularly complained that he did not have enough men ("Nothing has been done to increase the pound service in all these years"), beginning with his annual report of 1876, and repeating it whenever a change of law extended his territory, season or legal definition of animals to be taken – unmuzzled dogs, for example, or cats.[9]

The poundmaster was acutely conscious of his men's worth and the difficulties of their labors. "I am sorry to say, many people look with distrust, even hostility [on the poundmen], while they accept and enjoy the fruits of the faithful performance of the duty . . . It is difficult . . . to select men for . . . the seizure of animals, often in the face of armed aggression, of the requisite activity and strength, who . . . may not sometimes become the aggressor." "The service they perform, while that of a laborer, are to a certain extent expert, the majority of them having been long in the service, and it requires tact and experience to handle the net in the capture of small animals," he stated in requesting a pay raise for his men. "They are on duty often from twelve to fifteen hours a day."[10]

The men who stayed with Einstein (and there must have been those who did not meet his standards and were bounced out)[11] enjoyed his complete loyalty. He supported them in court actions, and fought to get them medical treatment when needed. Discussing his crew with a reporter in 1885, he could name virtually every one of the 20-25 men who had worked for him and the injuries they each had received individually over the years. His many published comments on his men were always underlain with a tone of respect and even affection.[12]

The poundmen seem to have taken to this secure if somewhat limited situation. "On a seat by the large double gates," wrote a visitor of 1875, "you notice as you pass out three or four colored men who recall with manifest enjoyment the adventures of the morning, and who will tell you many a funny tale of dog life." Newspaper accounts of their banter while on dog runs have an earnest but also good-natured tone.[13] They were noted for their frequent singing on the job.[14] Said Joe Burrell in 1921, after his retirement: "Yes sir, it's right smart fun chasing dawgs . . . I've read about rich men that goes over into Africa . . . hunting what they call big game; but give me a dog chase all the time."[15] The regular regimen of dog bites did not bother them.[16]

After discoursing so frequently on the estimable poundmaster, it would be ungrateful not to delineate at least briefly the chief of the poundmen. It is a pleasant surprise to find that the names of all the Health Office laborers can easily be retrieved from the biannual/annual Official Register of the United States, the

---

[9] E.g., Wash. Critic, 27 Aug 1888, p. 1; Evening Star, 8 Dec 1899, p. 16; 29 May 1913, p. 5. His successor faced a cut of funds – and personnel – in his first year (Wash. Post, 23 June 1912, p. 9).

[10] Health Officer Report, 1874, quoted in Nat. Republican, 15 June 1874, p. 4; Poundmaster Ann Rpts, 1888, 1904.

[11] "The poundmaster said he could tell when he got a new man, after very few trials, whether the man would ever distinguish himself as a dog-catcher" (Evening Star, 19 Sept 1885, p. 2).

[12] (Court) Evening Critic, 16 Oct 1882, p. 2; 16 June 1883, p. 1, among others; (medical) Wash. Post, 20 May 1907, p. 4; (injuries) Evening Star, 30 Dec 1885, p. 5. "He is fond and justly proud of his men" (Wash. Times, 13 Apr 1902, Ed/Drama p. 17); "Samuel Einstein . . . takes great pains in pointing out his men and declaiming on their qualities" (Evening Star, 29 June 1901, p. 28).

[13] See Appendix D3 for some samples. "I don't know anything about the men of the pound, but I do not believe they have lost their 'sensitiveness' and grown brutal. They impressed me as straight, clean, manly fellows" (Wash. Post, 29 June 1908, p. 12).

[14] Wash. Post, 30 Aug 1891, p. 9; Evening Star, 27 Aug 1911, pt. 4 p. 3. Both articles indicate the songs sung.

[15] (At the pound) Nat. Republican, 19 May 1875, p. 4; (runs) Wash. Times, 13 Apr 1902, Ed/Drama p. 17; Evening Star, 19 Sept 1885, p. 2; Nat. Republican, 25 June 1877, p. 4; (Burrell) Wash. Post, 25 Sept 1921, p. 10.

[16] "All of the new men have been more or less severely bitten by dogs since they took up the work. These wounds do not seem to worry the men, however. They always have them cauterized" (Wash. Post, 18 Dec 1899, p. 12), and many other testimonials.

detailed list of pound expenditures in the 1880-82 annual reports, and the list of Health Department employees fronting the annual reports from 1903 onward.[17]

- **John Wells**, "The King of the Dog-Catchers", worked for the pound longer than any other, coming on in 1876. Einstein held Wells in esteem and affection: "'John,' enthusiastically declares Mr. Einstein, 'in his best days could take one of the heavy nets . . . and throw it across the street and get his dog every time. I believe he has caught more dogs than anybody else in the business' . . . Mr. Einstein [says] that he is the best in the country." Wells was famously oft-bitten and scoffed at the inconvenience, although he did occasionally take "the Pasteur treatment".[18] He was "as black as the ace of spades."

    When Wells died, still on the job, in 1913 the long-serving District Health Officer, William Woodward, his assistant, Harry McLean, "and other District officers" expressed their condolences, and the Evening Star gave him a brief obituary, something not common for one of his station then or today. "At his special request, Wells turned over the first shovelful of earth in the excavations for the new . . . pound building."

- **Joe Burrell**, "Lynx-Eyed Burrell", came to the pound in 1886. His idyll on the dog-catcher's life, delivered in 1921, has been quoted above. When he "retired" from street work (being injured in the same accident that killed Poundmaster Rae in 1920) he took over day-to-day management as "Keeper of the Pound".

- **Cornelius "Buck" Parker** joined the crew in 1886 also. "Big, broad of shoulder, muscled like a fighting man, and so quick of hand that even the quickest-moving, snappiest of dogs never has a chance to set its teeth in his flesh." He was transferred to the smallpox service in 1894.

- **Shirley Williams** was called the pound's "Dog Jailer and Executioner" from his usual duties.

- **Albert Fortune** and **Joshua Murphy** belonged to the early years of Einstein's tenure.

- **Walter Matthews** and **William Steward** became the chief dog-catchers when Joe Burrell laid aside his net.

Descriptions of pound operations in Einstein's later years mention some other helpers but they were not really dedicated pound employees. Since they are not specified as "colored" we should assume that they were white. E. N. Burgess, described as "his assistant" in 1904, was actually detailed from MPDC; "several inspectors" were mentioned in a 1908 article but this seems to be just another name for his

---

[17] Wells, Burrell and Parker were "the three most famous negro dog-catchers in the United States." These descriptions taken mostly from: Evening Star, 29 June 1901, p. 28; 10 July 1910, pt. 2 p. 6; 27 Aug 1911, p. 48; Wash. Times, 13 Apr 1902, Ed/Drama p. 17; (Wells obituary) Evening Star, 8 Feb 1913, p. 2; (Parker smallpox) Evening Star, 6 Nov 1894, p. 7; 21 Nov 1894, p. 3. Is it possible that he personally captured "50,000 luckless canines," as claimed? For Burrell, Matthews and Williams, see Wash. Post, 25 Sept 1921, p. 10. This article is a sort of paean to Burrell. One wonders if the "very black colored man" described so extensively in Wash. Post, 9 May 1897, p. 21, was Wells.

Good drawings of all these poundmen will be found in Evening Star, 29 June 1901, p. 28; photos – but unidentified – in: Wash. Times, 13 Apr 1902, Ed/Drama p. 17; 7 Aug 1904, p. 4; 29 Oct 1922, p. 7; Evening Star, 20 Sept 1908, pt. 4 p. 4; 27 Aug 1911, p. 48.

[18] In spite of his fortitude, Wells did once claim compensation for injuries from a dog bite (Counsel Opinions, 23 May 1907; Vol, 17, p. 357).

skilled men; and his "clerk" Harry McLean was chief clerk of the Health Office and in fact the pound's direct supervisor.[19]

In 1905 Einstein proposed hiring an assistant poundmaster and a night watchman. (The pound was unstaffed at night, though to that time there had never been a break-in. During runs one laborer always stayed at the facility.) He explained that the only worker who could deputize for him in his absence was the assigned police officer, who was in fact often out on runs with him. Unfortunately, the Corporation Counsel had declared in 1898 that the acts did not provide for a deputy. Nonetheless, the police assistant regularly served as acting poundmaster when the regular master was gone. Einstein's successor repeated this request in his 1914 report and the two new employees joined the pound in 1916.[20]

Pound Equipment/Uniforms

Pound equipment began with the pound wagon – the Brig Catch-'Em-All, as one newspaper wag dubbed it. Here is a description from 1877: "The wagon is a common covered wagon like those used by grocers in delivering goods. There is a grating in front and a grated gate behind like a butcher's cart." In his 1878 annual report Einstein made a plea for a new one: "The purchase of a new wagon . . . cannot be much longer delayed. The one used at present . . . has been in constant service for seven years, and is worn out and well-nigh worthless. A wagon designed expressly for this work should be built at once."[21]

Einstein presumably got a new wagon by 1891, when the cart was described thus: "The dog wagon . . . is not an unsightly vehicle, but is in the shape of a large carry-all, with small iron bars formed into a cage. It is painted in the regulation colors [red], and on the inside of the body in large gilt letters are the words 'Health Department'." Other accounts call it "a cage on wheels, resembling a small circus wagon"; and "closed in the front and rear with iron netting, making a secure cage of the vehicle." Two poundmen rode in the front and a third on a small seat at the rear. In a futile effort to gain surprise on dogs and owners, the wagon was not marked on the outside and the men wore their badges under their coat lapels.[22] For most of this period the pound held one wagon and a buggy, in which the poundmaster accompanied the runs. This number was increased in time of special activity and then dropped back again in periods of tight budgets.

---

[19] (Burgess) Wash. Times, 7 Aug 1904, p. 4; Evening Star, 16 July 1905, pt. 4 p. 1; (inspectors) 20 Sept 1908, pt. 4 p. 4; (clerk) 10 July 1910, pt. 2 p. 6.
[20] (Counsel) Counsel Opinions 17 Aug 1898 (Vol. 9, p. 81); (police) <u>Testimony . . . 1907 (House)</u>, 7 Mar 1906, p. 734-737, giving some detail; (employees) Health Department report, 1916, p. 31. Officer Farquhar served as acting master in 1882 (Evening Star, 13 Nov 1882, p. 4), and Officer Ferrar in 1898 (Counsel Opinions, 17 Aug 1898; Vol. 9, p. 81).
[21] (Brig) Evening Star, 15 Aug 1910, p. 13; (description) Nat. Republican, 25 June 1877, p. 4. Board minutes (6 Apr 1877) list $20 for wagon repair, and (11 Dec) $16 for repair and painting of the buggy.
[22] Respectively: Wash. Post, 30 Aug 1891, p. 9, which includes a drawing of it; Morning Times, 19 Oct 1895, pt. 2 p. 10; Evening Star, 30 Aug 1890, p. 12; (seats) 19 Sept 1885, p. 2; (markings, badge) 27 Aug 1911, p. 48. Good photographs are in: Wash. Times, 13 Apr 1902, Ed/Drama p. 17; Evening Star, 20 Sept 1908, pt. 4 p. 4.

The pound had two wagons and a buggy by 1916.[23] Three of the Health Office's six horses were assigned to (and housed at) the pound.[24]

Equipment used to catch dogs (and perhaps other small animals such as goats) consisted of nets (loose and on eight-foot-long poles) and leashes. The pole nets were stored under the wagon. Only an exceptionally strong and skilled dog-catcher, such as Wells, could fully utilize the loose nets; more commonly one man cajoled or frightened the animal into the open and his partner took it with the pole net. If this was not successful, a foot-chase ensued. Two articles refer to earlier use of a lasso-type restraint.[25]

We are fortunate to have a complete inventory of the pound's equipage, given in a Commissioners order of 1904 that the poundmaster register all such items with the (Health Office's?) Property Clerk.[26] I copy this unique list here:

1 horse collar	6 halters, some straps
4 fly nets	3 saddle pads
5 brushes	2 horse blankets
3 curry combs	1 pair iron hames
2 stoves	2 pieces rubber hose
5 dog nets	2 net rims, with handles
2 shovels	1 pitchfork
1 coal hod	222 unclaimed dog collars 1 carboy

Aside from the badge mentioned occasionally (something useful when one recalls the number of animal thieves posing as poundmen in earlier times) the service's crew had no distinctive uniform until 1945, although published photographs of the 1920s and '30s show the poundmen in identical work clothes. They were described in 1969 as wearing black caps and jackets.[27]

---

[23] "A half dozen wagons are going the rounds both morning and night" – undoubtedly most of them rented or requisitioned from other bureaus (Evening Star, 20 Sept 1908, pt. 4 p. 4; see also Wash. Post, 18 Dec 1899, p. 12); (rental wagon) Comm Minutes/Orders, 30 Apr 1900; Hearings . . . 1913 (House), 11 Dec 1911, pp. 163-164. The pound had only one wagon during the rabies scare of 1913 (Evening Star, 29 May 1913, p. 5); (1916) Hearings . . . 1917 (Senate), 31 May 1916, pp. 118-119.

[24] The other three lived in rented stable space at 224 4 ½ St NW at a cost of $180/year, according to Einstein's 1895 annual report (he was making another plea for a new facility, to include a stable). The pound still used three horses in 1917 (Hearings . . . 1917 (Senate), 31 May 1916, pp. 118-119).

[25] Critic-Record, 24 July 1873, p. 1; Nat. Republican, 25 June 1877, p. 4. The nets were woven by Einstein and his men from heavy cotton rope (Wash. Post, 18 Dec 1899, p. 12). They can be seen in Evening Star, 20 Sept 1908, pt. 4, p. 4; 27 Aug 1911, p. 48; see Wash. Post, 30 Aug 1891, p. 9 for a more humorous depiction.

[26] Comm Minutes/Orders, 14 Oct 1904.

[27] The photos are in Wash. Times, 29 Oct 1922, p. 7 and Evening Star, 2 July 1933, p. 12; 2 Aug 1937, p. 2. Poundmaster Smith, pictured in Evening Star, 15 Apr 1923, p. 59, seems to have no distinctive dress. Gray uniforms were authorized in 1945 (Evening Star, 9 Jan 1945, p. 11), perhaps those seen in a Star photo of 1952 (10 Jan 1952, p. 21). During the MPDC period of the 1950s poundmen wore used police uniforms (memo, 27 Oct 1966, National Archives, RG 351, Entry 21 "District General Files", folder 1-105 "DC Dog Pound"). Their later uniforms were instituted and carefully described in an addition of 29 Nov 1966 to the earlier Commissioners Order 58-1926 of 30 Oct 1958 instituting uniforms for various District government services (National Archives, RG 351, Entry 21 "District General Files", folder 1-105 "DC Dog Pound"); Evening Star, 16 Nov 1969, Sunday Magazine p. 22.

Facilities

The pound is situated on the back of the old Naval Observatory, at the foot of 23rd Street. A little whitewashed hut stands in one corner of a high board fence inclosure, from which a chorus of big and little yelps fall on the ear of a visitor even before he catches sight of the unpretentious institution. (Morning Times, 19 Oct 1895, pt. 2 p. 10)

We have seen that Washington's **first municipal pound**[28] (built and owned by the city) was under construction by May 1871 and in use by that October. It was always described as of temporary intent. The original pound had capacity for 150 dogs, plus "stable for cows and horses, and also accommodations for goats, sheep, geese, etc. Every arrangement has been made to provide captives with food and water." It was "a kolsomined [calcimined/whitewashed] structure of pine boards, like a stockade or a big stable."[29]

The city expanded and improved the largely-outdoor structure over the years: in 1879 (the "rickety old shed" replaced with new pens, creation of an office, a new water supply, all "suitably arranged for the comfort of the unfortunate animals . . . impounded there"; designed by Building Inspector Entwisle) and 1885 (replacing the "yellow pine palings" with iron ones, and a concrete floor laid). The pens were expanded in the early 1890s through a private donation.[30] The pound was sited directly over the intersection of 23rd and C Streets, and New York Avenue NW (where the Institute of Peace is now) "as it is remote from business places or dwelling houses."[31]

A reporter of the Washington Times described visiting the place in 1903: "It stands – or perhaps it is better to say it leans – up against one of the murkiest hills in Foggy Bottom. It is only after a tour of houses full of holes, dogs, cats and oleaginous babies, and through a waste of dog fennel, wild strawberries. . . and pokeberries that you arrive at the most melancholy morgue. . . It is an enclosed structure of pine boards, like a stockade or stable." "To the casual visitor the pound presents the appearance of having stood there for years, with little or no change, and this is the case, with the exception of a few repairs."[32]

The need for new facilities made a regular appearance in the Poundmaster annual reports. The earliest report to complain about the pound buildings was that of 1878, and it also gives the best summary of Einstein's thoughts:

The pound as at present situated is totally unsuited for the purposes required. It is remote from any leading thoroughfare, beyond reach of water-supply or means of proper drainage, and by no way easy to access to the many persons who are compelled to call daily for animals impounded. It should be placed at the most central

---

[28] It was always officially The Pound, but became popularly known as the Dog Pound in the late 19th century, when it came to mostly hold those animals. The term even made its way into official documents in the 1930s.

[29] Respectively: Nat. Republican, 18 June 1874, p. 4; Wash. Times, 11 Aug 1897, p. 8.

[30] Evening Star, 23 Sept 1879, p. 4; 21 Nov 1879, p. 4 (a very detailed description); 29 Jan 1885, p. 5, and Auditor Ann Rpt, 1886, showing the cost as $193; (pens) WHS Ann Rpt, 1897. It also got some improvement with the issuance of the 1874 muzzling ordinance (Nat. Republican, 18 June 1874, p. 4). Repairs and minor additions appear in the Commissioners orders of the early 1900s.

[31] Evening Star, 21 Nov 1879, p. 4. Adolph Sachse's lovely watercolor 1884 map of Washington shows the pound but it was definitely built <u>over</u> 23rd Street and his buildings are not.

[32] Wash. Times, 26 July 1903, p. 5; 7 Aug 1904, p. 4. This "melancholy" theme brought out the inventiveness of newspaper writers, as will be seen later.

Illustrations of the old pound will be found in: Wash. Times, 13 Apr 1902, Ed/Drama p. 17; 26 July 1903, Magazine p. 5; 7 Aug 1904, p. 4; Evening Star, 30 Aug 1890, p. 12; 16 July 1905, p. 45; 27 Aug 1911, p. 48.

point possible where it can be kept free from offense, and where the advantages of water-supply and sewerage may be obtained. The present inclosure is about 40 by 40 feet, and has always been too small. At least one-half as much additional space is required. The yard should be properly paved with stone or concrete, and one entire side covered into a shed for the protection of animals, wagons, etc. during bad weather. A good, substantial stable for the accommodation of two or more horses, and an inclosure for storage of food for same [is also needed]. Two pens for confining the dogs impounded daily, to be supplied with water, and an office-room for use of poundmaster [whitewashed inside] and watchman.[33] If a location could be decided upon where it would be free from complaint and become permanent, I would advise the construction of a good substantial brick building and inclosure. A pound will always be one of the necessities of the District, and as a permanent fixture it should be made substantial and not call for constant repair, as does the present tumble-down institution which bears that name.

He "respectfully renewed" the question of his building again almost every year thereafter. His 1895 report pointed out that the newly-proposed Memorial Bridge would take out his location. In 1908 he wrote: "The pound is becoming more dilapidated each year, or at least would be so were not considerable sums of money spent . . . to prevent that result. The work done by the pound service during the many years that it has occupied its present wretched quarters certainly entitles it . . . to a better home."

The 1910 report reminded authorities of his "previous recommendations for a new pound and for construction therewith of a stable for the accommodation of all horses and vehicles in the service of the health department." The next year he reiterated the need: "It will be a relief to all concerned to have substantial quarters for the pound in place of the frame structure erected as a temporary pound 40 years ago, and now in a state of decay, and the operation of the pound and stable as a single establishment will make for efficiency and economy." The report pointed out that the city owned suitable land "adjacent to the James Creek Canal."

The city government presented a budget request to Congress for a new building in virtually every annual report from 1895 to 1912.[34] The 1903 testimony noted that the streets adjoining the pound had been regraded upward leaving the facility below grade. The only source of water, "a well situated in soil," was constantly fouled by animal excretia and blood; drainage was poor. Continual barking of the dogs kept staff and patients in the newly-built adjacent Naval Medical School Hospital from sleeping.[35] Also the proposed new structure would accommodate the Health Department's horses, which were then housed in rented quarters or livery stables.

Congress included $10,000 for a new pound, sited on any appropriate city-owned property, in the 1912 budget.[36] U. S. Reservation 290 – the South Capitol Street site – was transferred from federal to municipal ownership by the same bill for payment of $4,100 (half the assessed value).[37] As Commissioner Judson

---

[33] If he had a regular watchman at that time he certainly lost the man soon after.

[34] "Revised Estimates for the Support of the Government of the District of Columbia . . . FY 1903" (7 Jan 1902, printed with the DC Appropriations Bill, 1903), p. 58, note 123; Hearings . . . 1907 (House), 7 Mar 1906, pp. 734-739; Hearings . . . 1910 (House), 23 Jan 1909, p. 203; Hearings . . . 1912 (Senate), 3 Feb 1911, pp. 81-82.

[35] Poundmaster Ann Rpt, 1890; Evening Star, 7 Sept 1910, p. 18.

[36] Hearings . . . 1912 (Senate), 3 Feb 1911, p. 82; the act was passed on 2 Mar 1911.

[37] Hearings . . . 1914 (House), 3 Jan 1913, pp. 190-192. The District disputed the charge, saying it had earlier received use of the land. The question almost derailed dedication of the building (Wash. Post, 22 Oct 1912, p. 14), and eventually the city had to pay (Evening Star, 14 Feb 1913, p. 5). These actions were confirmed with the District's 1914 budget, passed on 4 Mar 1913. The rest of this paragraph and the testimony come from the 1914 hearing.

noted: "If you could see the location you would see that it is entirely suitable for a pound and not fit for any other purpose."[38]

Rep. Albert Burleson had qualms about the expense of the proposed building, which he took to the city's Health Officer, Dr. Woodward:

Burleson: That is quite an elaborate pound, is it not, Doctor – $10,000 ought to provide quite an elaborate one.
Woodward: I should not regard it as at all elaborate. It is plain.
B: You think it is very plain. Do you know of any other city that has a $10,000 pound?
W: I think I would have no trouble in locating cities that have pounds and stables that cost a good deal more than $10,000.

The property had been created in the early years of the century when James Creek Canal was filled in. At a later date the site was combined into neighboring Square 644 (previously only the small triangular portion of the square west of the old canal bed – which itself was designated U.S. Reservation 6-L – and adjoining Canal Street) but unnumbered. (In 1912 Square 644 had seen only a few small houses constructed on its western edge.) This new portion of Square 644 was shown only as "Square 644/part" in city tax assessments but in fact given the lot number 809. In 1955 lot 809 was broken unto 811 (the old canal bed) and 810 (the triangle between the canal and South Capitol) which includes the pound and stable.[39] It today carries the address of 9 I Street, SW.

It is pleasant to think that, although he did not live to see the new facility, Einstein did know of its coming before he died.

The **new municipal pound** and stable appeared in the 1911 Engineering Department Report as "in planning," awaiting selection of an appropriate site,[40] and the year following the Municipal Architect's office reported that it had completed the drawings and anticipated completion by 10 September 1912, for a total cost of $9,544. The planning went through several drafts, since the Commissioners order (10 May 1912) awarding the building contract required that all modifications in alternate proposals A-F be included.[41] The Architect's Report of 1913 indicated $45 spent for installation of wire windows and door guards, installed in October 1912.[42] A further $1,000 was spent the following year to pave driveways and grounds and add a screen to dependent wooden sheds (shown on the 1913 Baist map), and in 1916 $2,200

---

[38] "The District dog pound is in an out-of-the-way place... The neighborhood there... is not much. There is a great junkyard across the street, and acres and acres of idle land all about – vacant lots with weeds full grown" (Wash. Post, 25 Sept 1921, p. 10). "Because of the distance from the nearest place of abode, it is stated, no complaints are made of barking or howling dogs at night" (Evening Star, 29 Mar 1920, p. 2).

[39] I wish to sincerely thank Mr. Neal Isenstein of the D.C. Office of the Surveyor for this information.

[40] The selection committee was comprised of the Health Officer, Chief Clerk of the Engineering Department, and the Municipal Architect (Comm Minutes/Orders, 28 Apr 1911, revising the order of 24 Mar 1911).

[41] The building was formally accepted by the Commissioners on 2 Oct 1912. Early photos will be found in Evening Star, 15 Sept 1912, p. 11; Wash. Times, 29 Oct 1922, p. 7.

[42] Op. cit., (1911) pp. 16, 199; (1912) pp. 19, 194; (1913) pp. 14, 203. See also Commissioners order, 7 Oct 1912. A telephone was added at the same time (Comm Minutes/Orders, 8 Oct 1912), and Evening Star, 15 Sept 1912, p. 11. The number of the pound was Main 257.

for heating apparatus, a flag pole, awnings and a fire hose.[43] The yard was of blue stone, "as hard as macadam."[44]

Only a few newspaper articles noticed the new building, but they help fill in some useful details: construction commenced on 18 May 1912, the first shovelful of dirt removed by Health Officer William C. Woodward.[45] Poundmaster Emil Kuhn, long-serving pound property clerk Harry McLean, and "King of the Dog-Catchers" John Wells all watched. The plans were in fact made by Municipal Architect Snowden Ashford himself, and the builder was H. J. Montgomery. Equipment from the old facility was moved to South Capitol Street on 21 October and the place commenced use with no ceremony the next day.[46]

The new building was "one of the best equipped institutions of its kind in the country." It held twelve pens for impounded dogs (holding twelve animals each) plus four separate pens for mad dogs, "an up-to-date asphyxiating plant," the Health Department stables (twelve stalls), an office and an interior court, and sheds for ten wagons. The new building also incorporated "an experiment room for the bacteriological branch of the department" – a function that was not otherwise mentioned either in earlier discussions or later accounts.[47]

To take the municipal pound to its completion, we note that the Engineer's Report of 1918 included plans for a "garage for health department pound and stable," being prepared by the Municipal Architect's office at a cost of $2,641, drawing on a Congressional appropriation of 1 Sept 1916.[48] Completion was planned for July 1917. This is the center hyphen joining the two earlier buildings which first appeared in the 1919 Baist map and remains today.

To its last days as pound the place remained much the same: the Commissioners approved $1,835 in 1928 "to cover structural work and painting at the pound," further work by WPA workers in 1937, and other occasional improvements.[49]

Pound Conditions

The District pound was, as far as feasible, a clean and well-ordered place.[50] (Of course, the noise and to some degree the odor could not be controlled.)[51] The pens were carpeted with sawdust impregnated

---

[43] Hearings . . . 1914 (House), 3 Jan 1913, p. 190-194; Hearings . . . 1915 (House), 24 Nov 1913, p. 552; see also Evening Star, 15 Sept 1912, p. 11. The RFP was published in the Wash. Post, 24 Apr 1912, p. 2. (1916 procurement) Comm Minutes/Order of 16 Apr 1915.

[44] Wash. Times, 21 June 1914, p. 8. This article also describes the internal layout of the place. Paving seems to have been a regular desideratum of the poundmaster; when a further such request was included in the 1919 appropriations bill Rep. Brownlow simply commented: "This is an old friend" (Hearings . . . 1919 (House), 14 Dec 1917, pp. 272-273).

[45] Evening Star, 18 May 1912, p. 5, but the same newspaper (8 Feb 1913, p. 2), in an obituary for John Wells, says that he turned the first shovel of dirt "at his special request."

[46] A police order of 27 Jan 1913 advised all officers of the new pound's address (MPDC Ann Rpt, 1913).

[47] Wash. Post, 19 May 1912, p. 8; Evening Star, 18 May 1912, p. 5; 21 Oct 1912, p. 9; Hearings . . . 1915 (House), 24 Nov 1913, p. 552.

[48] Op. cit., pp. 13, 114. The text reads "1918" but that must be a misprint. See also Hearings . . . 1915 (House), 23 Jan 1914, pp. 179-180, in which the proposed garage will hold vehicles for all the Health Department.

[49] Comm Minutes/Orders, 23 Mar 1928; 20 Apr 1937; Evening Star, 21 Sept 1937, p. 8; Wash. Post, 2 May 1960, p. B1.

[50] "It is kept scrupulously neat and clean, there being nothing which would suggest its purpose except the occasional bark or growl of the dogs." (Morning Times, 28 July 1895, pt. 2 p. 9). It was "immaculately whitewashed"

with resin, which Einstein explained discouraged distemper. Cleaning was surely done by the poundmen, given the shovels and pitchforks listed in the equipment inventory above. In 1891 Einstein experimented with a variety of chemical disinfectants to ameliorate the smell, but without success.[52]

Observers regularly remarked on the humane treatment of impounded dogs, and presumably other animals also. "Really, most of the dogs that come here are better off in these cages than they are in the streets and alleys," one truthfully stated. A newspaper report tells us: "The dogs are fed by contract, entirely on meat. A Center Market butcher has the contract, which nets him two or three hundred dollars a year." The meat (mixed with bran) was cooked at the pound and given out three times a day. "They . . . have water as often as they like."[53]

WHS visited the pound regularly: "Your committee . . . found the animals as well housed and the surroundings as clean and comfortable as the space allotted . . . would permit." "I visited the pound today to bail out my own worthless yellow dog," wrote the Rev. John van Schaick in 1908. "He was awaiting me in a clean, airy pen, containing all the water he could drink. I carefully inspected the whole establishment. Not only was there water for every dog, but it was clean water. Not only were the accommodations comfortable, but they were considerably ahead of our District jail."[54]

Newspapermen relished the moral of the indiscriminate mixing of pedigreed and street pups in the holding cage, "where all dogs are placed on the same level." "Every class of canine society is huddled together in the dungeons." Of course, the poundmaster did regularly pull out obviously fine dogs for likely redemption.[55]

Redemption/Sale of Animals

Impounded farm animals were kept two days for **redemption** by verifiable owners, at a charge of: horses and cows -- $2; goats, sheep, hogs -- $1; fowl – 50 cents.[56] If not taken they were advertised and

---

(Evening Star, 27 Aug 1911, pt. 4 p. 3). The Washington Humane Society in 1883, 1897, 1901, 1907 and 1910 reported the conditions "reasonably clean and the animals . . . fairly well cared for"; "everything . . . as good condition as possible with the restricted space," always adding that the facility was inadequate (WHS Ann Rpts for those years).

[51] "The music of this morgue is portable. You take it away with you . . . It is . . . the composite dying groans and howls of the predestined criminal – mastiff, bulldog, sky terrier, setter, beagle and rat catcher" (Wash. Times, 11 Aug 1897, p. 8) and many other such theatrical observations.

[52] (Sawdust) Wash. Post, 10 Apr 1904, p. B6; (disinfectants) Evening Star, 10 Oct 1891, p. 5.

[53] (Quote) 10 Oct 1891, p. 5; (contract) Wash. Post, 9 May 1897, p. 21; (bran) Wash. Times, 13 Apr 1902, Ed/Drama p. 17; (water) Wash. Post, 10 Apr 1904, p. B6. They received one half pound of meat each per day in 1920 "bought fresh and cooked" (Evening Star, 29 Mar 1920, p. 2). Dogs in the private shelter of the Society for Friendless Dogs got the same mix (Wash. Times, 3 August 1902, Magazine p. 4).

[54] (WHS) "Report of the Special Committee Appointed to Visit the City Pound", 6 Dec 1910 (filed with WHS Exec Comm minutes). Einstein took the Society's recommendations seriously. "So well understood is [the value of WHS oversight] by the Poundmaster that he constantly appeals [for us] to extend the same supervision to his quarters. The rain comes in on his desk and upon the bed of the caretaker. We can only reply that our power ends with the prevention of cruelty to animals"; this report gives some specifics on the place. (Van Schaick) Wash. Post, 29 June 1908, p. 12.

[55] Nat. Republican, 25 June 1877, p. 4, with much philosophical observation; Evening Star, 29 June 1901, p. 28; 20 Sept 1908, pt. 4 p. 4; and Wash. Post, 3 June 1906, p. F3, which last indulges in rather maudlin imagined conversations among the mixed lot of condemned dogs.

[56] Evening Star, 30 Aug 1890, p. 12. The 1878 Poundmaster Ann Rpt stated that the redemption fee for goats had just been raised to $2 "and in consequence thereof the number impounded has decreased considerably and a larger

sold at public auction (at the pound) conducted by the poundmaster.[57] Only diseased animals were destroyed.[58] The Poundmaster annual reports indicate the small number of animals (seemingly all dogs) "returned without fees" but we have no other information on these; presumably released on some legal technicality and with no payment or, after about 1900 dogs examined for rabies but found healthy.

The 1871 Board of Health ordinance set the redemption holding-period and charge for dogs at 24 hours and $1, and that was reiterated in the 1875 ordinance. The 1878 act specified 48 hours to reclaim a pet, for a charge of $2.[59] This fee was always required, even for puppies, but the kindly poundmaster was known to give poor persons extra time to get the money together.[60] Einstein was insistent that the wealthy received no favor.[61] The pound often held fancy breeds for a few days longer,[62] but it was regularly noted that there was a higher redemption rate for mutts than the finer animals, a pleasant but probably incorrect story.

Contemporary writers loved to lampoon the society matron rescuing her perfumed poodle: "Not long ago a very fashionable woman came in and recognized her pet. When returned to her, she was ecstatically wrapping the renegade up in her arms and saying: 'Come back to mommer,' to the intense amusement of the gentleman who would have put the dog to death within the next hour. . . And thus it is that a woman's husband can stay out two nights in the week and may come home by himself, but if mommer's baby stays out one night without a tag 'mommer' will go forth . . . to look him up."[63]

But, of course, the majority of reunions were more touching: "In one instance a young man called for his dog, and on receiving him clasped the dog fondly and wept like a child."[64]

---

percentage have been killed" (see also Bd of Health minutes, 22 June 1878: "together with the reasonable expenses of keeping the said animal"). (On the other hand, the Board proposed reducing the charge for geese to 25 cents the same year; 25 Sept.) Perhaps the charge was reduced later, as the number of animals in the city decreased.

[57] For the legalities, see Hearings . . . 1909 (House), 18 Feb 1908, p. 243. As for what the auctions earned: in 1876 a horse sold for $7, a cow for $9, a goat for $1 and geese for 50 cents each; horses brought about the same thirty years later (Poundmaster Ann Rpt, 1876, 1910, 1912). Some sales were larger: John Southey was compensated $30 for his horse "impounded and [improperly] sold" in 1876 (Bd of Health minutes, 26 May 1876); "He has gotten as much as $50 for a stray horse" (Wash. Post, 9 May 1897, p. 21). Note that while farm animals were auctioned for the highest bid, less-sought after dogs were sold for a set charge.

[58] In 1910-12 (the only years for which we have specific information) no larger animals were destroyed. (Diseased) Wash. Post, 3 June 1906, p. F3.

[59] A Commissioners order of 19 Oct 1891 authorized the Collector of Taxes, the Secretary of the Board of Commissioners and the Poundmaster to review pound fees, and perhaps this is the origin of the redemption charges given in Wash. Post, 4 Jan 1914, p. 16: geese – 50 cents; calves, sheep, hogs -- $1; others -- $2. Wash. Post, 25 Sept 1921, p. 10, says $3, but this possibly is a misprint.

[60] We have seen earlier that puppies required tags. Poundmaster Smith sold puppies for $1 in 1933 (Wash. Post, 16 Dec 1933, p. 27). Wash. Post, 9 May 1897, p. 21 touchingly describes "a very ragged little colored girl" who could only say farewell to her pet: "Good-bye, you Nellie; I won't see you no mo'." Only cash was accepted (Wash. Post, 16 May 1905, p. 8). If Einstein was away one of the poundmen made the transaction (Hearings . . . 1909 (House), 18 Feb 1908, p. 242). To be clear, the owner also had to pay $2 at the tax office for a license if there was none on record.

[61] "'Yessir,' said Joe Burrell [one of the laborers], in his inimitable manner, 'we entertain some of the city's greatest down this way – ladies and gentlemen from the finest sections of the city, society leaders, and . . . diplomats from foreign countries. When they've lost their dogs they know where to come, . . . and we charge them the regular rate – two bucks'" (Wash. Post, 25 Sept 1921, p. 10), although diplomats soon would not have to pay.

[62] They were kept in a special pen; the Health Officer contacted the owners of tagged animals (Morning Times, 19 Oct 1895, pt. 2 p. 10; Evening Star, 20 Sept 1908, pt. 4 p. 4).

[63] Einstein added: "They hug them and kiss them and call them baby" (Wash. Times, 26 July 1903, Magazine p. 5).

[64] Nat. Republican, 18 June 1874, p. 4; for other touching stories, but too long to copy here, see: (a comical Dutchman) 24 June 1875, p. 4; (an elderly black man, at the licensing office) Evening Star, 9 Oct 1893, p. 8; (an army dog rescued when his owner brought mackerel to the pound) Wash. Post, 8 Aug 1909, p. 13.

Newspaper accounts put the redemption rate in the 10-25% range; detailed statistics in the Poundmaster annual reports (Appendix C3) show it at the lower range of that estimate. Dogs turned in by their owners were dispatched the same day,[65] and there was, as noted earlier, no redemption procedure for cats.

Unclaimed dogs could be **purchased** by the public for 25 cents, a charge raised to $2 only in 1905.[66] Over time, the pound became a well-known place to buy good dogs. This was a very popular thing to do (Einstein: "Experience has taught me that such dogs [purebreds] are always redeemed, if not by their owners, by someone else who knows a good thing when he sees it."), and the rise in price was said to have been effectuated to finance a new pound, Congress having balked at the appropriation. (Lesser dogs had a chance: "The pound is a never-ending attraction to the small boy who has saved $2 and wants a dog.") Although we have no information for earlier periods, Poundmaster Marks observed in 1944 that 3/5 of dogs purchased from his pound were taken by out-of-towners.[67]

In fact, an interesting business grew up among "the negroes living in that neighborhood," who kept track of the better dogs being held and when informed by "coachmen and other servants of [wealthy] persons who want dogs and what kind of dogs," bought them at the low pound price and sold them for a higher one. "The profit on these sales ranges from $3 to $20. One man, it is said, has made sufficient money in this manner to buy himself a house and lot."[68]

Until the "Burglar Dog" episode of 1914 (below) we find only one reference to doggie escapes from prison: 15 made it out in 1875 – an embarrassment for Einstein, no doubt.[69]

In 1910, at the height of the vivisection controversy, the Commissioners approved sale of pound dogs to several nearby federal medical facilities (to the Bureau of Public Health and the Marine Hospital on 25 June; the Bureau of Animal Industry on 6 July; and the DOA's Bureau of Chemistry for testing of chemicals "but absolutely not to be vivisected" on 18 November). About a dozen animals were so transferred. The Washington Humane Society investigated the practice but found that no vivisection had occurred. Dead animals were transferred to Walter Reed Hospital with no controversy, as long as there was no dissection performed at the pound itself.[70]

After the required holding period unclaimed dogs were destroyed.

---

[65] Wash. Post, 8 July 1901, p. 10.
[66] "Dogs are sold only on the written order of the Commissioner in charge of the Health Department" (Hearings . . . 1909 (House), 18 Feb 1908, p. 243). This must have referred to some standing authorization, since every sale could not have involved such a high personage, and we have no record of it in the Comm Minutes/Orders.
[67] In 1879 the sale charge had been $2 (Nat. Republican, 26 May 1879, p. 4). (Prices) Wash. Post, 16 May 1905, p. 8; (quote) Morning Times, 28 July 1895, pt. 2, p. 9); (boys) Wash. Post, 3 June 1906, p. F3; (out-of-town) Evening Star, 19 Apr 1944, p. 20. "So universal did the custom become of securing pets from the pound that it was truly an unlucky dog that did not find a master"; a girl once wrote from Chicago requesting to hold a dog for her, which she later claimed (Wash. Post, 16 May 1905, p. 8). Hunters still saw the pound as a good source of bird dogs in 1913 (Evening Star, 15 Nov 1913, p. 9).
[68] Wash. Times, 7 Aug 1904, p. 4.
[69] Evening Star, 22 Sept 1875, p. 4.
[70] (Vivisection) WHS Ann Rpt, 1910; see also Wash. Post, 14 Aug 1910, p. 1; 23 Aug 1908, p. A3; Evening Star, 24 July 1910, pt. 1 p. 6; 25 July 1910, p. 10. On 5 July 1925 the Commissioners authorized the Health Officer "in his discretion" to furnish animals "to the several Government laboratories which may make requests therefor." See also the article by Patricia Gossell listed in Appendix D14; (Dead animals) Comm Minutes/Orders (index 1941).

Killing Animals[71]

In earlier times, as today, everyone pretended a horror of destroying homeless animals while privately feeling a keen fascination with the proceedings; hence the regular descriptions (some melodramatic, some lurid) printed in the local press.

Executions took place every work day (Monday-Saturday) except Tuesday. This latter day was quiet because the law required two days' holding of impounded dogs,[72] and Sunday (the pound being closed) didn't count for dogs brought in on Saturday. No shootings took place during the grace month of July, when dog runs were suspended. Executions occurred about noon.[73]

Until 1898 dogs were shot. This was likely true for larger animals also but we have no specific information.[74] In 1895, Einstein recalled that in the early years "the victim was turned loose in a small yard . . . and fired on [with a musket] until dead. Owing to the obstruction of the [pen's] lattice and the constant motion of the animal . . . the plan was often a prolonged operation."[75]

As early as 1877, however, a more efficient and humane method was used, described by Einstein in his annual report of 1878: "The mode of killing unredeemed dogs is by pistol shot . . . The animals are removed from the pen singly, the muzzle of a . . . pistol is placed against the forehead and a bullet sent directly through the brain."

Here is a typical and more immediate account, from the Morning Times of 1895 (abridged):

> When a batch of dogs have stayed out their time limit one of the helpers takes a rope, at one end of which is a noose, and begins executing them. He selects his victim, slips the noose around his neck, and drops him out of the cage and down to the post. The rope is given a couple of turns around the post, Fido's nose is drawn close up against it, the muzzle of a revolver is placed within a few inches of his forehead, and his trials are over. Death is instantaneous, and the men are so used to it that a second shot is very rarely required.[76]

A few details complete the description: a heavy curtain was drawn over the holding cage to mask the procedure from those awaiting execution; the shooting post was at the rear of the pound and so out of sight of the other pens; and the gun used was a 32-caliber Smith & Wesson.[77]

---

[71] "Killing" or, somewhat fancifully, "executing" were the terms used at the pound. "Putting to sleep" was reserved for the shelters. Poundmaster Marks did use this latter euphemism in Congressional testimony of 1941 (Hearings . . . 1942 (House), 22 May 1941, pp. 55-59), reflecting the increasing influence of the shelter movement. See Appendix D4 for more on killing techniques in other pounds.

[72] Incoming dogs were rotated through "first-day" (wire) to "second-day" (wooden) pens and thence to the yard for execution (Nat. Republican, 26 May 1879, p. 4; Evening Star, 20 Sept 1908, pt. 4 p. 4).

[73] Wash. Post, 6 Aug 1879, p. 2; Morning Times, 28 July 1895, pt. 2 p. 9. A later article says executions occurred every other day (Wash. Times, 7 Aug 1904, p. 4). Dogs brought in by their owners were disposed of the same day, but this might have been a later practice, given the date of its earliest reference (Evening Star, 29 Mar 1920, p. 2).

[74] In 1873 goats were executed by knife to the throat; the carcass was returned to the owner (Critic-Record, 24 July 1873, p. 1). It seems unlikely this practice continued long.

[75] Morning Times, 28 July 1895, pt. 2 p. 9.

[76] Op. cit., 19 Oct 1895, pt. 2 p. 10. This account is mild compared to some, for example Nat. Republican, 25 June 1877, p. 4, and Evening Star, 6 Aug 1887, p. 2, which describes a somewhat more elaborate process and with detail of how dogs die that few readers today would want to know.

For those interested in a drawing: Evening Star, 30 Aug 1890, p. 12.

[77] (Curtain) Evening Star, 30 Aug 1890, p. 12; (post) Wash. Post, 9 May 1897, p. 21; the post was a later addition; (gun) Nat. Republican, 25 June 1877, p. 4. The post was repositioned after 1883, as SPCA (Ann Rpt, 1883) found the method of execution satisfactory "if the pistol is in the hands of a person skilled in its use" but complained of its visibility to the animals; see also Evening Star, 6 Aug 1887, p. 2.

Official and private accounts all emphasize that this was the quickest and most humane end available to the victims. "Practice has made the executioner an unerring marksman," said Einstein. "So it is a rare occurrence when the first shot fails to cause instant death."[78]

Nonetheless, the poundmaster had doubts about shooting and considered other methods. He fixed on electrocution as his alternative: "It is the quickest, surest and by long odds the cleanest and easiest way. Nothing would be easier. By this means the noise, the sight of blood and its offensive odors would be obviated, and besides it would be the most humane of all . . . methods."[79] He made another and very perceptive observation – this one relating not to animals but to his men – in his 1897 report, recommending "destruction of animals by modern methods, which, while probably no less painful than that now employed . . . are certainly less repugnant and have less tendency to brutalize those responsible for their operation."

Let us note that Einstein himself never attended these shootings, betraying a tenderness that was easy to overlook: "Poundmaster Einstein . . . has never had the heart to see one of them killed, much less kill one . . . himself. 'More than 60,000 dogs have been killed here since I took office[80] . . . and I am glad to say that the death of not one . . . can be laid directly at my door.'" He added that he usually left the enclosure during the executions. "In view of the fact that poundmasters are ordinarily pictured . . . as . . . ogres . . . there is something instructive and curious in this statement of the District poundmaster."[81]

The pound moved to asphyxiation is September 1898. "This method of killing is the surest and . . . less painful than any other. The heavy fumes . . . settle at once to the bottom of the box and none of the animals can escape . . . The dogs do not seem to apprehend the danger."[82]

Again, the newspapers give a more telling and detailed picture of the proceedings:

The execution of the unfortunate animals is conducted under a low shed, beneath which is a long gray box [lined with galvanized iron or zinc] with [wire-reinforced] windows in the sides. This death chamber is about ten feet in length, half as wide, and five feet in depth. In the top is a trap door which can be closed tightly. A dozen feet away is a little iron stove, the pipe of which leads to the interior of the chamber. The stove is filled with charcoal, and until the smoke of the kindled fire ceases, it is allowed to pass from a regular chimney. Then a damper is closed and a colorless hot gas, carbon monoxide, fills the box.

---

[78] Morning Times, 28 July 1895, pt. 2 p. 9. See also his remarks in his annual report of 1878.
[79] Ibid. Minter Key, agent of SPCA, agreed (SPCA Ann Rpt, 1884). Bergh, of New York, advocated drowning (SPCA Ann Rpt, 1883). It is not clear whether Einstein's proposal, so similar to that eventually used, was his own or based on some existing system; see the discussion in the section on WARL below. Health Officer Fowler requested purchase of such a system to Congress again in 1923: "Electrocution is a much more modern way . . . and the expense is not very great" (Hearings . . . 1924 (Senate), 12 Jan 1923, p. 74). Poisoning and gassing had been discussed as early as 1873 (Critic-Record, 24 July 1873, p. 1).
[80] The execution of 104 dogs in one day of 1897 set a record to that time (Evening Star, 10 Aug 1897, p. 3). Did Einstein state this from memory or was it a product of his meticulous record-keeping?
[81] Wash. Post, 9 May 1897, p. 21. His account (Poundmaster Ann Rpt, 1879) of watching dogs being drowned by the Baltimore pound reveals real anguish. We have no information on whether or not Einstein kept a pet, although if he had it probably would have been noticed in one of his many profiles in the press.
[82] Evening Star, 16 July 1905, pt. 4 p. 1. This article says 1896, but I follow here Wash. Times, 7 Aug 1904, p. 4, from which the Star article seems to have lifted much of its text, perhaps carelessly. The Washington Humane Society had suggested this method in 1891 (see its annual report for that year), which was then in use at the pound in Evansville IN. In preparation for this decision, Einstein visited the Philadelphia pound in 1897 to inspect its operations (WHS Ann Rpt, 1897). The Commissioners inquired of the New York pound about its methods in 1892, and probably other cities too, doubtlessly in response to Humane Society agitation (Commissioners letters #184455, 184608, 27 June and 5 July 1892; National Archives, RG 351, Entry 17 "Register of Letters Received").

Before the damper is turned the glass-sided box is filled with doomed canines, and the trap door in the top closed. The dogs can be seen inside looking from the little windows. Suddenly one after another is seen to fall over. After a few yelps or two, they lie still.[83]

The 1921 Poundmasters Report stated that victims ("these unfortunate animals") were still euthanized by charcoal fumes and included a budget request for "automatic electrically equipped cages." The pound continued use of its small gas chamber until the early 1960s, as will be described below.

All accounts agree that dogs went to their end docilely ("It is only a matter of a few seconds until they are all dead"), but that cats became restless and took longer to die. "Kittens seem . . . harder to kill, and sometimes outlast their elders."[84]

The carcasses were picked up by "the dead-animal man/the dead-animal collector/the garbage collector/the dead-dog wagon/the man who removed dead animals" (i.e., the city contractor) and "taken down the river to the depot of dead animals," "where all parts of their bodies are used in manufacturing different things." This was mostly fertilizer (from the Washington Fertilizer Company, or Mr. Mann's plant "just below Giesboro Point"), soap (from the fat, perhaps "the rendering factory, at Four-Mile Run"), and driving gloves ("a New York glove manufacturer").[85]

Finances

The earlier contractor-operated pounds were envisioned as financially self-sustaining – the District put no funds into them while the contractor/poundmaster built and equipped his facility, hired his men and made his profit from redemption fees and sale of unclaimed animals. This plan led to aggressive capture of animals from private yards that the public viewed as theft. Einstein and his men, on the other hand, were city employees,[86] worked fixed hours and received fixed salaries.

Under the temporary Commissioners (1874-78) pound proceeds supported pound operations; the incoming permanent Commissioners ordered the money instead turned over to the General Fund, leaving pound operations (except the poundmaster's salary) destitute. A stop-gap accommodation was made.[87]

---

[83] Wash. Post, 18 Dec 1899, p. 12 (abridged). Some articles say the box was red. "Mr. Einstein takes much pride in the death chamber." Generally about 15 were gassed at one time, but as many as seventy could be killed together (Wash. Post, 22 July 1906, p. F9). For a thorough description of this process in its last year see: letter, Helen E. Jones to Commissioners, 10 Sept 1958 (National Archives, RG 351, Entry 21 "District General Files", folder 1-105 "D.C. Dog Pound").

Photos of the death chamber are in: Wash. Times, 13 Apr 1902, Ed/Drama p. 17; 26 July 1903, Magazine p. 5; Evening Star, 16 July 1905, pt. 4 p. 1.

[84] Evening Star, 16 July 1905, pt. 4 p. 1; Wash. Times, 7 Aug 1904, p. 4. The latter article wallows in gruesomeness. WHS, in 1901, minuted its preference for shooting or chloroforming cats, the latter being its own method for dispatching them (WHS Ann Rpts, 1897, 1901).

[85] (Fertilizer) Wash. Post, 22 July 1906, p. F9; (soap, contractor) 6 Aug 1879, p. 2; 25 Sept 1921, p. 10; Wash. Times, 4 Sept 1921, p. 10; (gloves) Evening Times, 4 Mar 1896, p. 6. If anyone wonders, cat carcasses were not skinned because it was not cost-effective (Wash. Times, 2 July 1920, p. 13). A brief but useful review of contemporary practices is given in Wash. Times, 15 Aug 1989, p. B8.

[86] Their names appear in the list of District personnel in the Official Register of the United States, for example, while the earlier Simaker was not included in the city government list that accompanied the annual compilation of Acts.

[87] Wash. Post, 30 July 1879, p. 2. Procedures for handling pound fees (by the Board's treasurer) were outlined in Bd of Health minutes, 16 May 1876.

After 1882 pound expenses – salaries, maintenance, supplies – were carried as a line item of the Health Office. Extraordinary outlays, such as a new wagon or building, required a special appropriation approved by the Commissioners and Congress.[88] Sometimes the District's Emergency Fund was used to cover unexpected expenses, such as increased runs during a mad-dog scare.[89]

Government income from animal laws came from two sources: the $2 tax on dogs, paid to the Collector of Taxes, and the redemption ($2 for dogs; 50 cents-$2 for farm animals) or sale of animals from the pound. (Taxes levied on farm animals as property, dairy licensing fees and any other such fees stayed entirely outside this process.)

Receipts from the dog tax were deposited with the U.S. Treasury.[90] There, per a 1901 Congressional mandate, the funds sat ready to cover deficiencies in the Police and Fire Departments' retirement funds, which ate up over 95% of the money annually, the tiny remainder going into the District's General Fund.[91]

Redemption charges ("pound fees" for dogs and other animals) collected at the pound were deposited with the Collector of Taxes daily, who likewise transferred them to the Treasury. This money went into the District's General Fund.[92]

Proceeds from sale of animals were split: an amount equal to the redemption charge was remitted to the Collector of Taxes for each animal, as above; any money above that amount was weighed against the pound's expenditures in feeding and (for farm animals) advertising and that money credited to the regular pound appropriation to cover the outlay:[93] if any money still remained, it was held for one year (in case the actual owner appeared and claimed his money), and then put into the Health Office's Sanitary Fund.[94] This last couldn't have happened often, since "an accumulation of a number of years" had brought the Fund to a fulsome $37.35 in 1908. Previous to 1895 all money from sales above the deducted expenses (and after the one-year holding period) had been treated as pound fees.

Record-Keeping

The business of dog-catching is hedged about with a lot of red tape despite the fact that it seems like an easy task. (Evening Star, 20 Sept 1908, pt. 4 p. 4)

---

[88] This is lucky for us because we (sometimes) get to read the supporting testimony.

[89] Hearings . . . 1910 (Senate), 23 Jan 1909, p. 203.

[90] This following information comes from: Hearings . . . 1909 (House), 18 Feb 1908, pp. 241-243; Poundmaster Ann Rpt, 1897.

[91] The annual District government financial reports (Auditor, Collector of Taxes) show this division beginning with 1902, when $16,110 went to the Police, $110 to the Firemen's funds, and $786 to the General Fund, the only reported year the Firemen got anything. After 1905 the General Fund got less than $100, and after 1909 nothing. Police fines were similarly used to supply the retirement funds' shortfalls.

[92] The District appropriation bill of 18 July 1888 says (Sec. 3) that money received "from sale of animals" will be split between the federal and District governments; this could refer only to sale of unneeded city-owned animals but the legal compilers Abert and Lovejoy place this reference with other material relating to pound operations.

[93] Einstein pointed out that this bit of bookkeeping trivia exaggerated both pound income and expenses. See Index to Counsel Opinions (referring to Vol. 2, p. 258 of Counsel Opinions undated but probably for the 1880s, that volume missing), which states that pound expenses other than the poundmaster's salary can be paid from pound fees.

[94] The Sanitary Fund had been established in the 1871 act but was not activated until the Comptroller of the Treasury authorized it in 1895.

The poundmaster's meticulous record-keeping was mandated by the Board of Health in 1877: "That the Poundmaster perform such clerical labor as may be necessary for the proper conduct of the Pound Service",[95] and allowed him to furnish on demand figures for: (1A) total number of dogs taken on the street (or, if untagged, also from private property), (1B) those turned in voluntarily by residents; (2A) dogs impounded but properly licensed, (2B) those unlicensed; (3A) dogs redeemed by their owners, (3B) those sold to the public, (3C) those destroyed; (4A) dogs held for observation of rabies, (4B) of those, the numbers found free of or having the disease, (4C) those shot on the street as rabid. The Health Officer and the poundmaster also regularly reported revenue from dog licenses, although this transaction was actually handled by the District's Collector of Taxes;[96] and also income from pound operations. These statistics, in various combinations appropriate to the need and given for the week, the year, or cumulative to date, appeared regularly in his many reports and in the newspapers (and in the Appendixes of this study).

During one period of particularly heavy dog-catching (and therefore particularly frequent complaints) the Health Office clarified its procedures:

> In order to straighten out several rumors that have caused the poundmaster no end of trouble, the following statement as to just what is done to dogs, and how it is done, was issued at the Health Office today:
>
> Daily record is kept of all animals impounded. Kind and number, description, from what part of the District taken, name of owner, the hour said animal entered the pound, number of dogs in pound, how disposed of – whether sold, redeemed or destroyed – and amount derived from said sales, are entered on the record. No dog is sold by the poundmaster without first obtaining authority from the Commissioners.[97] Other animals (horses, cows, mules, etc.) are sold at public auction by the poundmaster, after being duly advertised in the public press, as the law requires. All moneys received from fees and sales are daily deposited with the collector of taxes, and receipt taken therefor. Dogs unredeemed after forty-eight hours are asphyxiated and the carcasses turned over to the dead animal collector, receipt being taken for every dead animal thus disposed of. The record books kept by the poundmaster are always open to inspection. He submits daily, weekly and monthly reports to the Health Officer, covering fully all transactions.[98]

To truly understand the burden this work imposed on Einstein we must turn to the 1905 Poundmaster report:

> The clerical work of the pound service consists of keeping a record of animals impounded; making daily, weekly, monthly, quarterly, and annual reports; keeping a record of requests for the removal of animals from different parts of the District of Columbia; keeping a record of meat furnished daily as food for dogs; giving a receipt to each person for the amount paid as pound fees; and the indorsement of each communication pertaining to the pound service, all of which is performed by myself in addition to my other duties. The result is that I have worked long hours each day and have been unable to take any leave during the summer months.

And one further extract, taken from the Health Officer's "Memorandum Relative to Receipts from Licenses to Keep Dogs, Pound Fees, and Sales of Impounded Animals" of 1908:

---

[95] Bd of Health minutes, 12 May 1877.
[96] Several Commissioners orders of the 1930s permitted the Tax Office to destroy its accumulated records relating to dogs.
[97] Discussed in the section above: Redeeming/Selling Animals.
[98] Evening Star, 15 Aug 1910, p. 13.

All pound fees are paid to the poundmaster, [who] submits each morning to the chief clerk a report of the preceding day's operations, and with it he submits the collector's receipt. At the end of each month the poundmaster submits a sworn statement of the amount collected during the preceding month.[99]

One easily understands his fondness for fishing!

Jurisdiction

In the section on Legalities of the Pound we saw that the purview of pound operations was expanded from only the two Corporations (Washington, Georgetown) to include adjoining suburbs in 1879, expanded again in 1891, and then throughout the District in 1893. But the District of Columbia is a patchwork of local and federal jurisdictions and several of these made their own arrangements regarding unwanted animals.

The best reported of these was the Capitol itself, where the Capitol Police were "kept busy capturing stray dogs and cats." The officers had "a sort of lasso . . . to capture the cats and dogs wild-west fashion." In official records this device was listed: "one dog collar and lead" and, the police, having no nets as the poundmen used, had "to use gum shoe methods" in their work. Occasionally they called in the pound crew for assistance. Untagged animals went to the pound and tagged dogs held for retrieval by their owners. In 1910 the force took 31 dogs, of which 29 were untagged. Six years before they found a stray horse, something which must have been more common in an earlier period. The rule prohibiting unleashed animals on Capitol grounds was "iron-clad" and aimed to protect the "squirrels and song-birds" there.[100]

As far as federal parks are concerned, animal control in these areas seems to have been left to the District government, at least during Einstein's tenure. Einstein requested permission in 1907 of the Commissioners to shoot "tramp dogs" on the Washington Monument grounds, "concerning which there has been much complaint." And in 1907 the Commission forbade the running of unleashed dogs in all public parks in the District, only to rescind the order a few months later in the face of public outcry. They did outlaw dogs from running in Rock Creek Park four years later. In the city's federal parks, where "considerable damage has been done . . . by both dogs and fowls," Park Police held animals for the poundmen.[101]

The poundmen also took dogs from the Washington Market after 1883, when the Superintendent, P. S. Smith, complained of "the habit many persons have of bringing dogs to market, many of them filthy in

---

[99] Hearings . . . 1909 (House), 18 Feb 1908, pp. 242-243. For a very detailed description of the seventeen record files kept by the poundmaster in 1954, see: Memo from Dept. of General Administration, "Records Procedure" (8 Aug 1955) at the National Archives (RG 351, Entry 21 "District General Files", folder 1-105 "D.C. Dog Pound").

[100] Evening Star, 13 July 1904, p. 16; 24 July 1905, p. 3; 1 July 1910, p. 10. These articles indicate that the annual reports of the Capitol Police give statistics and other information on these operations but I have been unable to locate these reports. See Appendix D12 for some examples of their work.

It would be too bad to lose a report of 1974 that the Capitol grounds crew buried a dog killed by a car "under the magnolia tree at the corner of the House Cannon Office Building" near where the animal had expired (Roll Call, 14 Apr 1974, p. 4).

[101] (Monument) Wash. Herald, 16 Feb 1907, p. 12; (Rock Creek) Comm Minutes/Orders, 27 June 1912; Evening Star, 23 Apr 1909, p. 24. Counsel Opinions, 14 Jan 1908 (Vol. 18, p. 246) implies that park regulations prohibited dogs. Police regulations of 1910 forbade unleashed dogs in Rock Creek south of Military Road, and of 1921 anywhere in the park. Congress had given supervision of Rock Creek to the Commissioners.

their habits and a source of terror to ladies and children."[102] The staff of St. Elizabeths Hospital received permission to shoot stray dogs on their grounds in 1918, and the Humane Society noted that dogs found at the Soldiers' Home, Walter Reed Hospital, the Zoo and "other Government reservations" could be similarly killed, not stating by whom, but most likely their own staffs.[103]

Relationship with MPDC

Congress's granting the Commissioners authority over the pound in the 1879 act and over Police regulations in 1887 clarified control vis a vis MPDC.[104]

The Metropolitan Police aided the poundmen from almost the beginning. (The 1871 law creating the pound said nothing about police assistance.) An officer routinely accompanied Einstein on his rounds, as reported in the 1878 Poundmaster report: "The moral effect of having a . . . police officer accompany the poundmaster has been great. Disturbances of the peace have been prevented, the annoyance of boys following the wagon and alarming animals stopped, interferences of all kinds avoided, the general working of the service much advanced, and the number of captures increased." He repeated this observation in 1900 ("materially aided by police officers detailed for that purpose"). When the poundmaster was absent the same officer deputized for him at the pound, leading us to think that his assignment there was full-time. Such officers were those deemed unfit for regular duty.

MPDC discontinued this service in 1906, to Einstein's extreme regret. "The assistance rendered . . . through such details never completely answered the needs of the [pound] service, . . . but it enabled the poundmaster better to supervise the work of his men, and . . . tended to prevent unlawful interference . . . by bystanders." At this time the Police Department was eliminating a number of such special details apparently for budgetary reasons.[105]

There is no evidence of tension or overlap between the two services, MPDC not being anxious to undertake the poundmen's duties. When complaints about nighttime animal noise flooded the department in 1907, officers referred callers to the pound. "People . . . fail to appreciate that fact that a barking dog or crowing rooster cannot disturb the man who is doing his duty on the streets during the late hours of the night."[106]

From time to time – 1893 and 1899, for example – MPDC officers canvassed all households on their beat to remind citizens of the dog tax law; this invariably led to a spike in tax received (which went to the Police retirement fund) and in fines collected.[107]

---

[102] The index of letters received in the 1881-1885 period includes a notice of the appointment of a man to catch dogs at Center Market but the original letters are lost.

[103] (Market) Evening Critic, 20 Apr 1883, p. 3 – they had long been banned, of course; (St. E) Counsel Opinions, 23 July 1918 (Vol. 29, p. 5); Comm Minutes/Orders, 26 July 1918; (other institutions) WHS Ann Rpt, 1924. See Wash. Post, 4 May 1934, p. 8, in which a dog loose on the grounds of the Soldiers' Home was shot. On the other hand, the DC library system, which had previously not allowed dogs in its buildings (Library Ann Rpt, 1906), was given permission in 1940 to allow them in as it saw fit (Comm Minutes/Orders, 9 Feb 1940).

[104] The 1887 act specifically gave the Commissioners authority over Police regulations relating to the driving of animals through city streets and over stray dogs.

[105] Poundmaster Ann Rpt, 1906.

[106] Evening Star, 3 Nov 1907, p. 13. Appendix D5 gives some examples of the public's interaction with MPDC regarding animals.

[107] Evening Star, 9 Oct 1893, p. 8; 8 Dec 1899, p. 16. The earlier instance was described as the first "systematic effort . . . to compel the owners of dogs to take out a license." Einstein had proposed such a project in 1878.

There was one minor point of contention: to quote from the Poundmaster report of 1878: "I would call your attention in regard to the animals taken up estray by Metropolitan police officers. It would seem perfectly natural that all animals taken up by them should be turned over to the poundmaster, but as a rule with them when a horse is found astray considered to be worth $40 or upward it is turned over to the property clerk . . . to await the appearance of the owner, who must pay charges. . . All should, I think, be turned over to the poundmaster, as the pound is the proper place for animals . . . regardless of value."

Whether the poundmaster saw this practice as a money-grab by the Police Department or simply a defective procedure, the MPDC annual report of 1897 indicates that it viewed the arrangement as more of a pain than a privilege: "During the year many animals [are] picked up estray . . . and their disposition has long been a matter of contention. The establishment of a District pound . . . clearly confirms the . . . manner for receiving and disposing of such property, and that the police . . . can only render assistance to the pound service." The MPDC Superintendent noted that then-current regulations (which I could not find) required animals (and all confiscated property?) worth over $40 be kept and disposed by the Property Clerk; he proposed sending all strays to the pound. "This suggested by reason of the frequent embarrassments occasioned the clerk . . . in the disposition of animals taken up by the police."

MPDC statistics (Appendix C3 and C4) show a gradual but steady shift in handling of animals taken by the police – whereas until the mid-1890s the Property Clerk kept as many or more than were sent to the pound, by the 1910s the Clerk had very few, and much larger numbers went to the Foggy Bottom establishment. Whether this reflects a change in the types of animals taken (from more valuable farm animals to dogs) or that the Superintendent got his wish that only animals known to have been stolen would remain in MPDC custody I cannot say.[108]

Legal Challenges

The city endured regular legal threats, mostly from irate animal owners reporting complaints against the pound staff for purported disrespectful treatment or demanding exemption from the dog tax, and of course challenges to muzzling and other regulations, all described above. The only direct legal attack on the 1878 licensing act itself was made by "owners of dogs under the leadership of O. B. Lester" in 1911, who argued that street-capture of dogs as a question of tax delinquency was inappropriate and unconstitutional. He wanted the office of poundmaster abolished; the Commissioners disagreed.[109]

Four tangential legal imbroglios might be noted also:[110]

- The claim by Mr. F. J. Nee in 1900 that a poundman broke his bicycle trying to net a dog (he lost);
- The considerable (and successful) efforts of Dr. James Morgan Barber three years later to save his fox terrier Yankee from execution ("the subject of writs, attachments, appeals, replevins, and other legal formalities"), the dog having reportedly bitten a man and Barber refusing to turn him over;

---

[108] Possibly the former: as late as 1913 the MPDC Property Clerk was recorded as selling an abandoned mule (Commissioners orders, 9 Dec 1913).
[109] Wash. Post, 30 Oct 1911, p. 9.
[110] (Bicycle) Wash. Post, 15 Mar 1900, p. 12; (Yankee) 25 Jan 1903, p. 9. "Yankee enjoys the distinction of being the only dog in the history of the pound . . . wrested from the executioner by legal means," and retired to a farm in Loudoun County; (rabbit dog) Evening Star, 10 July 1910, pt. 2 p. 6; (compensation) Wash. Herald, 15 Apr 1911, p. 2. The latter two are most amusingly written ("It was discovered that Teddy had taken things into his own paws").

- The owner of a rabbit dog ("not particularly valuable," according to Einstein) who refused to pay the pound fee and then sued for several hundred dollars compensation after the animal had been destroyed (he lost, and also lost two appeals);
- And a three-party hearing (District, first and second owners) regarding an unclaimed dog sold at the pound, and which then escaped from the new owner, the original owner then demanding compensation.

Pound Mascots and Escapees

Not all animals reaching the pound left it either alive (to a new home) or dead. A fortunate few, by fluke or pluck, endeared themselves to the poundmaster and his men to become pound mascots. Here are some mentioned in the various newspaper accounts (abridged):

- (1874) [The pound kept] one little rat terrier [which] early developed his ruling passion by seizing a rat and made short work of him. The poundmaster said that dog is worth his keeping. He has already killed fifteen rats at the pound, and is looking around for more. (Nat. Republican, 18 June 1874, p. 4)
- (1901) The bull terrier "Ring" [is] the watch dog of the pound. Ring's heart is as hard as his looks. He is the autocrat of the dogs – the only one that can defy the law with impunity; the only one that can go abroad day or night; the only one the dog-catchers know with respect. (Evening Star, 29 June 1901, p. 28; a picture of Ring is included.)
- (1905) [Einstein:] There is one cat in Washington that will not come within the provisions of an ordinance, and that is the boss of the pound lying over there sunning himself. Jim is a remarkable cat. He wandered into our inclosure when no bigger than a ball of fur. He can whip any dog twice his weight. [Jim killed snakes – moccasins – around the fairly rural old facility.] (Evening Star, 5 Nov 1905, p. 10)
- (1910) A small boy appeared with a chicken under his arm: "It's sick and a lady done ask me to bring it to you." He has become the mascot of the establishment. His chief claim to fame is his willingness to fight upon the slightest provocation, and this he is kept doing at all times. [Einstein declared it would never voluntarily leave its new home.] (Evening Star, 10 July 1910, pt. 2 p. 2)
- (1913) A little dog, unlicensed, had been taken to the pound. He was an affectionate animal; they called him Chum. [He was scheduled to follow his fellows to the smoke chamber but] the attendant looked up and saw the superintendent [Kuhn] standing there. There were tears in the eyes of each. Chum is still living, but instead of being nobody's dog he now is everybody's. (Evening Star, 9 Nov 1913, p. 46)
- (1916) [The Commissioners ordered a free tag for a rat terrier kept at the pound,] said dog being needed to prevent continuance of injury by rats in public property. (Commissioners Minutes/Orders, 2 May 1916)
- (1939) Wimpy, neurotic Toy Spitz, pride of the Pound and pooch with a purpose was put through his paces yesterday [doing clever tricks] in advance of "National Be Kind to Animals Week". The poundmaster [Marks] thought the performance extraordinary and marvels whenever Wimpy, the pound officeboy, so performs. (Wash. Post, 12 Apr 1939, p. 15, with a picture)
- (And to show that the tradition continued: 1958) [Retiring Poundmaster Marks'] most touching good-bye was reserved for Topper, a pointer who has served him as watch-dog at the pound for the past five years. Marks says he has made express provisions for a continuance of Topper's favored treatment under his successor. (Wash. Post, 27 June 1958, p. A3)

And we cannot overlook a white bulldog dubbed "The Burglar Dog" by the Washington Times, which actually escaped the pound in 1914, if not the only instance of such a feat at least the only recorded one. "'I take my hat off to him,' said [Poundmaster] Rae. 'He is a wonder. He deserves to be free.'"[111]

---

[111] Wash. Times, 21 June 1914, p. 8, which recounts the animal's truly ingenious exploit in detail and with gusto.

CHAPTER FOURTEEN

Einstein's Last Years: The Pound as an Institution

The daily experience of the dog-catchers presents a long record of adventures, insults and fights with humanity, to say nothing of bites from the beasts. Not one man of corps but carries scars, but Mr. Einstein says the public is getting educated to the pound. (Evening Star, 29 June 1901, p. 28)

The dogs in the pound barked a merry welcome to this day of days, and the homeless cats mewed pleasantly, for 37 years ago today Samuel Einstein was made poundmaster. (Evening Star, 23 Mar 1910, p. 9)

Samuel Einstein would surely never have admitted that his work was easing up (and the statistics of animals impounded – with the same number of men he had 30 years before – show only an increase), but in fact as the new century approached, the pound and its place in the District community was entirely different than in the poundmaster's earliest years: **the District pound** and its goal of a city largely free of unrestrained animals **had become generally accepted** (even if the specific methods were still in debate).

This laudable development rested to a high degree on the shoulders of the worthy poundmaster, but other players contributed vitally: his fine crew of workers were – unlike their predecessors – honest and hard-working; city officials – Health Officers Townshend and Woodward, Commissioner Macfarland, Police Superintendent Sylvester, even in his own way Theodore Gatchel of SPCA – all promoted the effort. But the chief actor that made Einstein's labor successful was the populace of Washington itself, gradually moving from a semi-rural life turning out their horses to graze in city parks to a fully urbanized class not tolerant of even stray chickens or cats.

Einstein enjoyed the full support and protection of the District government throughout his career. The Board of Health's annual report for 1873 (his first year) stated: "The service has been well performed. The Board in their selection of poundmaster have been particularly fortunate. Being a thankless office, and its incumbent subject to constant hindrance and misrepresentation, it is difficult to find a man . . . combining sound judgment with the necessary energy and courage, [and] men for the actual labor of seizure . . . of requisite activity and strength who, in the resistance to such opposition, may not sometimes become the aggressors. The comparative freedom of the two cities from animals running at large marks how well the work is done." Added the National Republican: "Probably very few of our citizens know of the . . . existence here of perhaps one of the most perfect pound services in the country."[1] In spite of his frustrations, Einstein himself spoke with confidence of the pound's work and its gradual but spreading influence: (Poundmaster Report, 1878) "For the small force employed, I am convinced that our pound system is the most effective of any in this country, certainly far superior to that of any of the large

---

[1] Op. cit, 15 June 1874, p. 4. In his 1878 annual report, Einstein made this comparison covering 2½ months of that year: Washington DC's pound service: 4 men/over 2,000 dogs captured/expenses of $575; Brooklyn NY: 10 men/1,200 dogs/$2,300.

Eastern cities with which I have become acquainted. We are constantly on the alert, working night and day, and few animals running at large . . . escape us. Owners are becoming more and more careful and instances of damage to public and private property less frequent." His report the following year repeated this assessment, claiming the District's operation was "fully equal to, if not superior to, those of many cities where the force employed and expenditures made are more than double ours."

By the end of the century the work of the pound had become an accepted and appreciated part of Washington's life, and **the poundmaster** had become something of **a personal institution**. The first notice of the anniversary of his appointment appeared in 1908 – beginning his 35th year: "Congratulations were showered on him when he made his regular rounds of the Health Office yesterday." This anniversary was celebrated (there is no better word) every year thereafter until the newspapers had to report his death.[2]

A telling indication of the growing status of the pound is the increasing frequency of profiles appearing in the local papers, listed in Appendix D2. After its earliest years the pound was only mentioned in passing by the press until the 1890s. In later times, however, a visit to the place and a long chat with the poundmaster or one of the poundmen[3] became standard for Sunday supplements, sometimes with long portions of text copied from earlier profiles. Oddly, such articles almost entirely disappeared after Einstein's death.

In these articles, the poundmaster enjoyed bragging about his men (individually), discoursing on the canine population of Washington and its origins, explaining his theories of hydrophobia, and recounting glorious battles of times now safely past. His favorite stories were the famous Battle of Lincoln Park, the owners who shot him and his men,[4] and taking President Grant's cows. Sometimes he embroidered these tales, or confused them with others, but that was a privilege he had earned.

Indeed, "General" Einstein (as he was commonly called, replacing the earlier "Professor" or "Colonel") gained a minor celebrity status that would take him onto late-night talk shows today. Complaining of an increasing difficulty catching dogs he opined that the curs had come to identify him and his wagon. "He proceeded to buy a set of fake whiskers. To his dismay, the dogs were not deceived, and as a further resort he had his wagon repainted." We must imagine him smiling as he announced his imaginary plan to a Post reporter – he would buy an airplane! "I shall get into my aeroplace in the morning, take my lunch and a large net, and proceed to business. . . When I see four or five stray dogs I will throw [out] a piece of meat . . . and when the dogs are grouped around it I shall drop the large net over them . . . and dump them into a large box under the seat. Then when my lunch hour comes I can take a short run down Chesapeake Bay" (to fish?).[5]

Once, when he and his wife did get away (and during the mad-dog scare of 1908) – to a resort in "the extreme fastness of Virginia" – local pranksters filled his hotel room with dogs ("on the bed and under the bed, tied to the chairs, washstand and bureau"). Einstein was initially upset but later, upon departing,

---

[2] Wash. Post, 24 Mar 1908, p. 16; "When he called at the Health Office this morning he was presented with a handsome bouquet of flowers [from the Health Officer], and during the day was the recipient of congratulations by telephone, letter and personally" (Evening Star, 23 Mar 1909, p. 19), among others.
[3] Supplemented by a grisly description of the killing chamber, melancholy musings on the fate of unwanted dogs, or humorous sketches of desperate owners.
[4] The poundman refused to release a horse to Mr. Lynch, "who later served time in the penitentiary" (Wash. Times, 7 Aug 1904, p. 4).
[5] Wash. Post, 7 May 1911, p. 14.

good-humoredly satisfied himself by promising "no mercy" if those animals ever came into his DC jurisdiction.[6]

The daily work aside, there were a few bumps in the poundmaster's later period. In 1891 "at least one dozen men" applied for his job "although there is as yet no vacancy and the incumbent has not been asked to resign" – a curious incident. The following year Congressional budget-cutters threatened to reduce his salary to $800 (unsuccessfully). And the Washington Humane Society made an abortive effort to take over pound operations in 1900, vaguely claiming that they could do a better job but actually wanting a profitable contract.[7]

More commonly Einstein of these last years enjoyed the affection of his official and extended community. Caught up in the firestorm resulting from the muzzling order of 1908, a local minister defended him in the press: "In this case [the criticism] is a peculiar exhibition of unreason, for Samuel Einstein . . . is an unusually courteous, kindly man, as well as an efficient official." "He is regarded as one of the most faithful employees of the District," stated the Post the following year. In Congressional testimony of 1906, Rep. Frederick Gillett questioned the proposed raise of Einstein's salary to $1,500/year: "What kind of a man receives this $1,500?" Replied Commissioner Macfarland: "He is a man who has been there for years, a very faithful and efficient officer who has carried on this service . . . to the general satisfaction of all." "We have never had a complaint against him," testified Commissioner Cuno Rudolph two years later.[8]

His unexpected death in 1911 stunned the local government. "He was 25 years of age when he was selected . . . to organize the District pound service," wrote the Evening Star in its lengthy obituary, "a service that was extremely unpopular many years ago and one which today does not tend to increase the popularity of those engaged in it."[9] The 1912 Health Officer Report noted: "Samuel Einstein, who had served as poundmaster since March 23, 1873, died on July 9, 1911 . . . Mr. Einstein's intelligent, tactful and energetic administration of the duties of his office during the 38 years of his service is a matter worthy of record here for the influence it may have on those who come after him."

---

[6] Wash. Times, 13 Sept 1908, Society p. 6.
[7] (Applications) Evening Star, 17 Sept 1891, p. 8; (salary) Wash. Post, 10 Mar 1892, p. 4; (WHS) see below.
[8] (Defense) Wash. Post, 29 June 1908, p. 12; (faithful) 24 Mar 1909, p. 14; (testimony) Hearings . . . 1907 (House), 7 Mar 1906, p. 735, and Hearings . . . 1912 (Senate), 3 Feb 1911, pp. 81-82.
[9] Evening Star, 10 July 1911, p. 3.

CHAPTER FIFTEEN

Amazing Adventures of the District Poundmen

Containing tales of bravery, ingenuity and occasional foolishness on the part of our brave boys of the District Pound, as taken (and sometimes abridged) from the local news outlets and designed to induce both admiration and amusement in our readers:

- **An Unhappy Dog-Owner** Eliza Jenkins charged John Wells and two other colored men employed by Poundmaster Einstein as dog-catchers with using profane language toward her. The men pursued dogs in the Division and she had come to the window and told them to let the dogs alone, when they began to curse her. The men were returning to the wagon when the complaining witness [Jenkins] began to curse them and throw missiles at them until they were required to beat a hasty retreat. Judge Snell dismissed the case. *(Evening Critic, 31 Mar 1882, p. 4)*
- **A Crazy Mule** In his report of the work done last week, Poundmaster Einstein says that 152 dogs, 2 horses, 2 steers and 1 mule were captured. The mule appears to have made a record as a kicker and gave more trouble than all the other animals. This particular animal, says the poundmaster, was crazy. "He actually tried to climb a telegraph pole," the chief dog-catcher said to a Star Reporter. "The animal broke away from the bazaar [horse market] and had to be killed." *(Evening Star, 21 Aug 1893, p. 8)*
- **An Embarrassing Mistake** Yesterday evening, while out on their usual tour of capture, one of the poundmen espied a little way off a fine-looking canine asleep on a porch [on F Street SW]. Preparing his net, he started for the animal, thinking of an easy capture. He drew nearer to the noble-looking fellow but the dog did not even so much as raise his head. Thinking him sleeping the dog-catcher approached nearer, but still no movement of the animal was perceptible. Making one more step forward and preparing to cast his net, he took a final look and to his disgust found that he was attempting to capture a bronze dog. Some of the neighbors roared with laughter, and the canine capturer departed quickly out of sight. *(Nat. Republican, 28 July 1874, p. 4)*[1]
- **The President's Cow** Mr. Einstein recalled an exciting incident shortly after his appointment. A complaint was made that cows were running at large over the stony, ungraded lot now known as the White House ellipse, in 1873. When he gathered the herd, he discovered that he had impounded a cow belonging to Col. Babcock, then Superintendent of Public Buildings, and another belonging to President Grant. He wanted to collect $2 for each cow before releasing the animals. The Superintendent

---

[1] Some readers might recall the mock advice given by "veterinarian" James Thurber (reprinted in <u>The Thurber Carnival</u>) to a couple complaining that their dog neither eats nor exercises; "Doctor Thurber" concluded from the accompanying drawing that they had been caring for a brass statue.

protested, but when he called on President Grant to collect, the chief executive praised him for discharging his duty. *(Evening Star, 23 March 1909, p. 19)*[2]

- **An Evil Woman** Some days ago Johanna Quill had a warrant sworn out for Mary Walker, one of her neighbors, for keeping a barking dog, though, as it afterward proved, not only the bark but the dog was in the plural. Mary heard of the warrant and "vamoosed the ranch" till she could see about getting bonds or bail. While she was absent Johanna [broke] into the Walker house, set all the furniture on the street and sent for the pound master, and, beguiling Mr. Einstein, induced him to kill all of Mrs. Walker's dogs. When Mrs. Walker returned she found a woeful vacuity of dogs and had Mrs. Quill arrested on charge of destroying private property. *(Wash. Post, 29 July 1894, p. 8)*

- **Another Embarrassing Mistake** One of [the poundmen] saw a dog in the gutter on a South Washington street last week. He sneaked slowly and stealthily along with the net, and finally got near enough to throw it over the animal. "Come along!" he yelled, "I've got him." The driver came and when the two attempted to lift the pup, they discovered they had captured a dead dog. *(Wash. Post, 18 Dec 1899, p. 12)*[3]

- **Wise Dr. Fowler** Health Officer William Fowler was unexpectedly called upon today to enact [the] role that made King Solomon famous in determining the master of a fine German police dog. The dog was brought to Dr. Fowler's office and the claimants notified to be present – a young colored boy, Whitfield Cobb, and an unidentified white woman. The dog was placed in the bacteriological laboratory and the door closed. The boy on the outside puckered up his lips and whistled several shrill notes. The dog barked vociferously and licked him affectionately. The woman was put to a similar test but the dog showed little affection for her. Dr. Fowler turned the animal over to the boy [and] said he is confident he made the correct decision. *(Evening Star, 31 Dec 1925, p. 6)*[4]

- **A Clever Ruse** A well-known Washingtonian has a pet bulldog, and both have congenial prejudices against muzzles. In this dilemma, the owner used paint and brush to good effect, and gave doggie an imitation muzzle that looked like the real thing and fooled everybody. The scheme worked brilliantly until a day or two ago. Then the bulldog forgot himself, playfully strolled up to a hobbie skirt and gave a cute little tug with his teeth. The result was complete wailing and gnashing of teeth at the home of the canine. The poundmaster does not know whether he ought to prosecute or have a laugh on himself. *(Wash. Herald, 15 July 1911, p. 7)*

- **A Reporter Takes the Fall** Many years ago a young and guileless newspaper man got in a buggy with the poundmaster and proceeded into the county to a neighborhood [where] stray cattle had been frequent. After some trouble the offending cows were found and started toward the city. Anticipating trouble, Mr. Einstein got out of the buggy to help the men, leaving the reporter to come along behind. Suddenly they heard angry cries and beheld two or three irate women owners bearing down upon them. The poundmaster hurried the cattle along and yelled to the women: "I've got nothing to do with it. You'll find the poundmaster in the buggy. Go and see him!" Back down the road they sallied with renewed imprecations to the unfortunate journalist, his protestations of innocence in vain. The

---

[2] See also Wash. Times, 7 Aug 1904, p. 4 for a fuller account. By the way, President Taft also owned a (milch) cow, Pauline, which can be seen in Wash. Post, 29 May 1910, p. E1.

[3] To show that these things are not confined to the Old Days: "The Washington Humane Society received a call about a dog that appeared to be frozen and dead in the yard of a residence [on Ft. Davis St SE]. [An] officer found, instead, an alert pet with access to shelter. It was determined that the dog probably had been sleeping" (Wash. Post, 7 Dec 2014, p. C4); "Responding to a call about an injured owl on the side of the road [in Arlington County], an officer found a large mushroom" (Wash. Post, 27 Nov 2016, p. C3).

[4] The same test memorably staged in the 1937 Cary Grant-Irene Dunne comedy The Awful Truth.

Amazons set upon him tooth and nail and had not the poundmaster deserted the cows and interfered, the young man's career would have been abruptly terminated. *(Morning Times, 19 Oct 1895, pt. 2 p. 10)*[5]

☐ **A Third Embarrassing Mistake** Walter R. Smith, poundmaster, was riding on the pound wagon yesterday when he and his trusty men spied a dog without the muzzle required by law. The chaser quickly reached the dog and slapped the net on the animal. Then Mr. Smith discovered his own dog had fallen into the hands of the law. The dog was taken to the pound where Mr. Smith deposited the $2 required for the dog's release. *(Evening Star, 19 May 1921, p. 1)*[6]

---

[5] See also Wash Times, 7 Aug 1904, p. 4.
[6] In 1937 the pound crew by chance picked up Poundmaster Marks' own dog, Foxie, which had wandered from home several days earlier. "If a poundmaster's dog isn't safe from the dog-catchers, whose dog is?" (Evening Star, 2 Aug 1937, p. 2).

CHAPTER SIXTEEN

Theodore Gatchel and the Establishment of the Society for the Prevention of Cruelty to Animals

By the 1860s concern for animal welfare had grown throughout the U.S. to the point that citizens of New York City, under the energetic leadership of Henry Bergh, in 1866 formed an effective SPCA organization, clearly modeled after Britain's of 1824.[1] Philadelphia, Boston and Montreal soon followed New York's example.

Press articles and official MPDC statistics from the mid-1860s indicate that police regularly prosecuted cases of cruelty to animals. Nonetheless, a growing chorus of opprobrium over the public mistreatment of horses assumed the eventual establishment of a local effort similar to that of New York, which was widely reported in Washington newspapers.[2] In April 1870 public-spirited citizens met at City Hall to organize such a society.[3] Congress approved the charter for "an Association for the Prevention of Cruelty to Animals in the District of Columbia" the following June.[4] This act not only set the organizational structure of the group but mandated that the Metropolitan Police would "arrest offending parties without a warrant" in any part of the District upon information from any member of the association, who could establish their bona fides by "the exhibition of a badge or certificate of membership." Any fines collected through the intervention of the Society were split between the organization and the public schools. This financial arrangement will require attention in the later history of SPCA. An order of the police superintendent of September ordered officers to assist Society members "without waiting for a warrant from a magistrate."

In its first session (August 1871) the Territorial Legislative Assembly passed "An Act for the More Effectual Prevention of Cruelty to Animals". This law attacked animal abuse directly out of the gate: "Whoever overdrives, overloads, drives when overloaded, overworks, tortures, torments, deprives of necessary sustenance, cruelly beats, mutilates, or cruelly kills, or causes or procures to be so overdriven . . ." It covered lack of care whether during service or enclosed, the confining of animals in transit through the District, animal fighting, and abandonment of sick or aged animals. Both the perpetrator and owner or supervisor were liable to one year's imprisonment and a fine up to $250. As in its chartering act, the local

---

[1] Most of the local groups changed their name to some form of "Humane Society" in later years; perhaps, like Washington's organization, they added concern for children to their purview.

[2] See, for example: Nat. Republican, 6 Sept 1867, p. 2; 20 Aug 1869, p. 4; 12 Oct 1869, p. 4.

[3] Daily Nat. Republican, 9 Apr 1870, p. 4. The original by-laws and later amendments can be found in the office of the Washington Humane Society and a copy deposited with these papers in the Washingtoniana Division. I thank Ms. Alexandra Feldt of WHS for helping me find the Society's materials. Washington's was the twelfth such organization in the U.S. (WHS Ann Rpt, 1898).

[4] 21 June 1870. The acts specifies the name as "Association for . . ", and this form appears also in the 1885 law changing the name to "Humane Society" and in the by-laws of 1870. Nonetheless, the organization's annual reports all used "Society for . . ." as invariably did contemporary newspaper reports, and here I bow to common usage in this question.

SPCA was designated the agent of enforcement and the city police as their helpmates. The Society was required to attempt to locate owners for redemption. The act specifically excluded scientific experimentation from its strictures. This law became the touchstone of later city anti-cruelty laws.[5]

Public expectation seems to have been high: the Critic-Record complained in August that "we have not seen any steps to put such a society in actual operation" in spite of "a pressing and immediate necessity for such an organization." It is somewhat disappointing that the first reported meeting of the new organization (November 1870) discussed only diseased beef.[6]

The Congressional charter act listed over 60 men as charter members, including Mayor Matthew Emery, black civic leader John F. Cook and future Governor Alexander Shepherd. (Ladies entered as members the following year.)[7] The last member on this list, Theodore Gatchel, a real estate and insurance agent, served as president of the Society at its November 1870 meeting and dominated the organization through its first iteration to 1879.

Theodore F. Gatchel (1844?-1901),[8] originally of Maryland, was a clerk in the District's Second Auditor's Office in 1869, and promoted to Sanitary Inspector General two years later.[9] He was an active member of Wesley Chapel and participated in various worthy civic and business groups – religious education, an organization "for the suppression of vice [gambling]," another proposing establishment of an exchange in the capital.[10] Notices of his real estate activities peppered city newspapers in the 1870s. He was "an intimate friend of [Ulysses] Grant . . . and managed many of Grant's business affairs."[11] It is noticeable that reports of SPCA actions, including direct intervention in abuse instances on city streets, invariably describe Gatchel as the agent. It is easy to see him as a dedicated and sacrificing citizen, but the intensity of his many causes and his near-death grip on a slowly diminishing organization brings to mind the self-righteous and egocentric self-appointed community leaders so often met today.

Gatchel served as sanitary inspector for the Board of Health in 1871-74,[12] attracting the expected criticism from cattlemen. In 1877, already a private in the Metropolitan Police as president of SPCA,[13] he was appointed president of the Board of Police Commissioners as part of a reform faction. Within eight

---

[5] This act was tangentially cited in an important civil rights decision of the Municipal Court of Appeals in 1951 (John Kelly in Wash. Post, 15 Feb 2018, p. B3, taken from Wash. Post, 25 May 1951, p. 1). Critic-Record, 25 Mar 1876, p. 4, briefly reported a proposed Senate act (Mr. Conkling) regarding cruelty to animals that seems very similar to this one but with lower fines.

[6] (Expectation) op. cit., 9 Aug 1870, p. 2; (meeting) Evening Star, 2 Nov 1870, p. 4. Mr. Bernard Unti tells me that unhealthy meat was a much-discussed issue of the period.

[7] Evening Star, 18 Jan 1871, p. 4. A later source says that the Society was "organized in 1870 by about ten men" (Washington Times, 4 May 1902, p. 7), possibly a more realistic figure than 60. Shepherd sat on the Executive Committee. "William R. Woodward" was also a founding member – was he the later District Health Officer?

[8] Frequently misspelled Gatchell in the newspapers and even in later WHS Reports; this is the spelling used in his numerous realty ads. Several other Gatchels appear in these materials, including another SPCA charter member. At his death he was 57 years old.

[9] Heap, "History"; Nat. Republican, 14 Aug 1869, p. 1; Evening Star, 7 Sept 1871, p. 1. "He was a man of powerful build, being some six feet, four inches in height, and of splendid proportions" (Heap).

[10] (Wesley) Daily Nat. Republican, 13 Feb 1872, p. 4; (education) Daily Nat. Republican, 20 Nov1969, p. 1 ("Mr. Gatchel is a zealous worker, and has done much to advance the cause of Christ"); (vice) Nat. Republican, 1 Jan 1874, p. 1; (exchange) Nat. Republican, 27 Oct 1876, p. 4. "Theodore G. Gatchel" belonged to the Morton Cadets, a quasi-military fraternity, in 1896 (Evening Star, 23 Nov 1896, p. 1).

[11] Minneapolis (MN) Journal, 8 Nov 1901, p. 17. We must remember that Grant died almost bankrupt.

[12] Evening Star, 6 Sept 1871, p. 1. His reports to the Board appeared in the press through 1873.

[13] (Complaint) Evening Star, 4 Jan 1873, p. 8 ("M. Gatchel is Verey good in Catching bayd boys in beating Horses or Cows; but nose nothing about diseace in Animals which the publick eats" – evidently a German writer); (police) Nat. Republican, 25 Sept 1874, p. 4.

months he was forced to step down as president and in the following spring (March 1878) a number of members threatened to resign if he stayed on the Board at all, complaining of "his insincerity, his want of discretion, his fondness for such execution of the law as will invite publicity." That same month he had ordered a botched police raid on two gambling houses that resulted in lawsuits against the city; there were also charges of corruption against him. Under intense pressure he resigned, claiming innocence in all matters.[14] When he personally intervened in the alleged abuse of boy acrobat Zanlo Poole, demanding custody of the child himself, the Evening Star noted: "The general opinion is that Mr. Gatchel is in the wrong in his proceeding."[15]

Gatchel left the moribund SPCA in 1879[16] and moved to Des Moines, Iowa, sometime after 1881. There he continued his civic works: "Comrade Gatchell [sic] was the founder of the splendid Methodist Hospital . . ., which owes its inception and organization to his persistent efforts and self-sacrifice."[17] At his death the Washington Humane Society memorialized: "Unaffected by . . . discouraging conditions, Theodore F. Gatchel prosecuted the work with remarkable zeal and vigor . . . . The Society desires to record . . . its lasting debt of gratitude to [him] and to recognize and extol the moral and physical courage exhibited by him in the prosecution . . . of the pioneer labors in behalf of the humane treatment of God's dumb animals."[18]

The **early history of the Society** was neatly summarized in its 1881 annual report: "Mr. Gatchell's [sic] zeal and activity was great . . . but there was no general interest in the work . . . When Mr. Gatchell left the city in 1878 [sic], his successors . . . found the Society without public support or private encouragement, and not withstanding repeated efforts made by these gentlemen and others, its active operations ceased for nearly three years."

These earliest years of Washington's SPCA show considerable activity but of a rather unfocussed sort and mostly – especially after the first two or so years – performed by President Gatchel.[19] Topics discussed (and occasionally acted upon) included: drinking fountains for animals; humane transport of cattle in railroad cars; a devilish device called a "bit bur" fastened to horses "to make [them] appear frisky and rear up" (by pressing nails into the animal's mouth); the close shaving of horses' coats ("getting to be very fashionable"); horses abandoned because of age or illness; "bagging" of cows (preventing elimination of milk to make them attractive to buyers); pigeon-shooting; dog and cock fighting; stoning birds; an essay project; and improved veterinary training.[20] At the 1876 annual meeting little Zanlo Poole was introduced to great applause, an event which indicates that (considering that child abuse was not a charge of SPCA) Gatchel could not distinguish his personal causes from those of the organization.[21]

The Society claimed credit for 556 arrests between 1871 and 1876. In one month (July 1873) Gatchel "turned twenty-three horses out of harness"; he caused eleven arrests and destruction of unsalvageable

---

[14] Evening Star, 16 Jan 1877, p. 4; 29 Jan 1877, p. 4; 1 Aug 1877, p. 4; 4 Mar 1878, p. 4; 21 Mar 1878, p. 1.
[15] Op. cit., 13 Nov 1875, p. 4; 15 Nov 1875, p. 4. See also 30 Nov 1875, p. 4, in which he filed for control of two abused children.
[16] Evening Star, 22 Sept 1879, p. 4; WHS Ann Rpt, 1901. Newspaper articles place him in Washington for a few years.
[17] Nat. Tribune, 10 Apr 1902, p. 5. "Comrade" refers to his membership in the Grand Army of the Republic.
[18] WHS Ann Rpt, 1901.
[19] "The conclusion of the report [the 1876 annual report] makes most complimentary mention of the president, Mr. Gatchell [sic], through whose energy most of the cases have been prosecuted" (Nat. Republican, 1 Feb 1876, p. 4).
[20] Accounts of the Society's annual meetings, from which this information is taken, will be found in: Evening Star, 18 Jan 1871, p. 4; Nat. Republican, 28 Jan 1875, p. 4; 1 Feb 1876, p. 4; 1 Mar 1879, p. 4.
[21] Bergh, in New York, had similar concerns, and founded a Society for the Protection of Children there.

horses in the last two months of the same year, and 33 prosecutions in July-October 1875.[22] In 1875 Gatchel arrested a man for setting a rat on fire, and single-handedly stopped a pigeon shoot the following year.[23] Retentive readers will recall that he served for a short time as "Superintendent of Pounds" for the Board of Health.

At the Society's 1875 annual meeting, Gatchel enthused "that public sentiment had grown strong in the society's favor" – the decreasing number of arrests indicated an increasing awareness of the cause. He anticipated that Congress soon would enact a cruelty-to-children bill, one of his intense concerns.[24] In 1876 Sen. Roscoe Conkling of New York introduced – unsuccessfully – a bill that would have greatly strengthened the Society's powers, allowing members to <u>without a warrant</u> seize, hold and sell abused animals along the same lines as the pound. The Board of Health, presented with complaints about brutality to cattle held overlong at the city market, referred the question to SPCA.[25] But in fact the Society was running out of steam.

Part of the problem stemmed from its financial arrangements with the city. A writer of 1875 began his public letter by wondering "if there is a society for the prevention of cruelty to animals in this city, and if that society has a president." He proceeded to the crux of his concern: "Much is said . . . of the work done by the . . . society, but careful examination is hardly able to distinguish any acts of disinterested kindness as simple philanthropy. Arrests . . . are most commonly made in cases where fines can be . . . collected, and not simply to save helpless animals from acts of needless severity. When more acts of pure kind-heartedness and less of gain are discovered, the community will have more confidence in the professions of the actors."[26] The Society reported disputes with the city over claimed payments, and in turn the Society was investigated by the city for not turning over half the collected fines to the school system.[27] In 1880 the District government (somewhat illogically) decided that in the future all fines would be paid directly to the Society rather than through the District treasurer.[28]

The 1879 meeting which accepted Gatchel's resignation called for the Society's complete reorganization. "The Society is badly in need of funds." Referring to the noted head of the New York organization, the Washington Post in 1880 titled a letter regarding poor enforcement of anti-cruelty laws: "A Washington Bergh Wanted", and in 1881 the new secretary of SPCA admitted that the local group had become "almost powerless for lack of support."[29] Noted a later member (John Heap, op. cit.): "It was without means to pay rent for offices or employ agents, and what little was done . . . was made possible by a few members, who had the courage of their convictions."

---

[22] Nat. Republican, 2 Aug 1873, p. 4; 2 Jan 1874, p. 4; Evening Star, 23 Oct 1875, p. 4.
[23] Evening Star, 23 Oct 1875, p. 4; 10 June 1876, p. 4.
[24] Nat. Republican, 23 Mar 1876, p. 4.
[25] Bd of Health minutes, 7 July 1876.
[26] Nat. Republican, 14 Jan 1875, p.4.
[27] See the 1876 and 1879 annual meetings; Evening Star, 21 Dec 1875, p. 1; 2 Feb 1876, p. 2.
[28] Nat. Republican, 28 Oct 1880, p. 4.
[29] Evening Star, 22 Sept 1879, p. 4; Wash. Post, 22 Sept 1879, p. 1; 26 Dec 1880; Nat. Republican, 4 June 1881, p. 2.

CHAPTER SEVENTEEN

SPCA and WHS

Whether the number of dollars collected [from fines] or the number of cases investigated . . . is greater or less some years compared to others, we . . . can see the gradual growth of the humane sentiment in this city . . . and believe that societies to prevent cruelty to animals in common with other benevolent orders of which this nineteenth century is so fruitful are influential factors in our advancing civilization. (WHS Annual Report, 1886)

"In January 1881 Mr. [George T.] Angell, President of the Massachusetts SPCA, second only to Mr. Bergh himself, was in Washington, and after some inquiry found the remnants of this Society, then numbering 20 persons, and immediately engaged in restoring it to activity. An informal meeting was held at his house, January 25, General Graham, president, in the chair, 43 persons were elected members, and the annual meeting of the Society appointed for January 29."[1]

The Society accordingly met at the office of Fitch, Fox & Brown (presumably the same R. C. Fox who followed Gatchel as president) and Gen. L. P. Graham resigned as president in favor of the Hon. Arthur McArthur, a justice of the District's Supreme Court.[2] Angell oversaw the proceedings. Fifty people attended this meeting, and 200 a special meeting the following month. In spite of shaky finances, the local SPCA was re-launched.[3]

Two initiatives of 1881 distinguished the revived SPCA from that of President Gatchel:

- The Society **hired two agents**, Robert Ball and Maj. John H. King, who had assigned territories and warned or caused to be arrested offenders. The twin effects of this move were: to immensely broaden and professionalize SPCA's efforts (as opposed to the volunteer and largely individualized work under Gatchel); and to create a need for constant funding, which only grew as the desire for more agents grew;[4]
- A general plan developed to move the Society into the **protection of children**. This same discussion proposed the new name of "Humane Society".[5] Proponents pointed out that there was then no District law specifically protecting minors (a proposed act had failed in Congress only the year

---

[1] SPCA Ann Rpt, 1881.
[2] Now U.S. District Court for DC.
[3] Evening Star, 4 Jan 1881, p. 4; 8 Feb 1881, p. 4; SPCA Ann Rpt, 1881. Henry Bergh and George Angell were made honorary members in 1883 (Evening Star, 22 Jan 1883, p. 4).
[4] "The Humane Society, on account of the larger number of agents employed and increased expenses, is in need of additional funds and appeals to the members and friends of the Society for financial assistance" (Wash. Times, 9 Mar 1904, p. 5).
[5] "Uniting with an inchoate society [i.e., unincorporated; the Society for the Protection of Children] for the protection of children started two years ago." The 1881 annual report cites precedents in Chicago, Cleveland, Cincinnati and other cities. In other places, such as New York, "the two institutions [SPCA and SPC] stand only a few feet apart" (ibid.). See also WHS Ann Rpt, 1883.

before) and that existing institutions – various church-sponsored asylums, houses, hospitals and "Sunday schools" (?) – were all passive in nature, waiting for abused victims to come to them, while the new Society would actively seek out offenders.

In 1885 Congress passed "An Act for the Protection of Children . . . and for Other Purposes" relating to the District. This act generally paralleled the existing cruelty to animals law inasmuch as it laid out rather general prohibitions against abuse (as well as a lot of specific ones – children working as gymnasts in circuses, prostitutes, beggars, street singers, scavengers, etc.) and established enforcement, prosecution and appeal procedures, and penalties. It changed the name of SPCA to the **Washington Humane Society**,[6] empowered its "proper officers or agents" to bring complaints to local courts, and required MPDC to aid the Society's agents. The act says nothing about the disposition of resultant fines but in fact the Society took nothing from child-related fines; fines from animal-related cases went to WHS, as before to SPCA.[7]

The general history of SPCA/WHS lies beyond the scope of this study but can be easily followed through its annual reports fleshed out by newspaper articles. Before describing its "street" operations protecting animals, however, let us at least sketch out the **Society's organization and operations** during this period, taken from WHS annual reports.[8] (Since these reports are so extensively used in this section, material taken from them will be sourced in-text by year, as: ". . . (1903).")[9]

- **Presidents:** 1870-79 – Theodore F. Gatchel;[10] 1879-80 – R. C. Fox and Gen. L. P. Graham; 1881-87 – Arthur MacArthur; 1888 – Thomas Riggs; 1889-1900 – Adam S. Pratt;[11] 1900-1909 – Chester A. Snow;[12] 1910-18 – Walter Stilson Hutchins;[13] 1919 – Thomas Featherstonhaugh and James P. Briggs;[14] 1920-28[15] – Rev. C. Ernest Smith (1927 – Mrs. Truman B. Palmer[16]); 1928-29 – Maj. Gen. George Barnett; 1929-32 – Mrs. Herbert W. (Victorine B.) Elmore; 1932-33 – Col. Laurence Halstead;[17] 1933-43 – Mrs. Herbert W. Elmore.

---

[6] The Society's announcement/appeal in its new incarnation was printed in Critic-Record, 26 Feb 1885, p. 2. The incorrect name "Humane Society of Washington" is frequently encountered.

[7] Evening Star, 17 Nov 1907, p. 5, lists thirteen other cities in which these fines were assigned to the local Humane Society and four also making direct government subsidies to them.

[8] See Appendix D2 for a list of good newspaper overviews. Evening Star, 24 Mar 1912, p. 26, by the way, tells us that SPCA records before 1881 were lost in a fire, thus our reliance on newspaper accounts for those early years.

[9] The reports are dated to the year covered; they were issued very early the following year, after the January annual meeting.

[10] Many sources give Gatchel's resignation (and move) as 1878; this chronology is based on contemporary SPCA documents, however.

[11] He died in mid-1900. The WHS Ann Rpt, 1899 has a good photo of Pratt, and that of 1900 a memorial.

[12] See Wash. Times, 1 Nov 1903, Magazine p. 2 for a photo of Snow, and Evening Star, 30 July 1913, p. 8, and Wash. Post, 31 Mar 1937, p. 11 for bios.

[13] Not to be confused with his father, Stilson Hutchins, founder of the Washington Post.

[14] Featherstonhaugh moved from Washington, replaced ad interim by Vice-President Briggs and in December by Smith (Evening Star, 23 Nov 1919, p. 5; 3 Dec 1919, p. 25). Briggs is described at length in relation to the Humane Education Society later in this study.

[15] Prior to this SPCA/WHS annual meetings were held in mid-January, at which time new terms of office commenced. Sometime in Smith's presidency the meetings were moved to April, leading to a repeat of the year in this list.

[16] Contested and removed after legal action.

[17] Encountered once as Holstead, but this apparently an error.

- **Membership:** For most of this period the membership was about 300. Members paid $1/year before 1884 and $2/year (children 50 cents)[18] thereafter. The annual reports regularly complain about the difficulty of collecting dues. In 1901 a couple took a membership for their dog.

  Finances: The Society's funds came largely from membership fees, donations and fines from animal-cruelty prosecutions.[19] In 1892 (to take a typical year) these three sources were: $560/$170/$628 respectively, of total receipts of $1,970. Expenditures mostly went to pay agents and office rent – in the same year $$1,292/$300 of total $2,159. Donations (including memorials) and bequests noticeably rose in value over the years. The 1911 report noted sourly that other large cities allocated income from their dog tax to the local Humane Society, unlike Washington.

- **Agents:**[20] SPCA employed no agents until 1881, when two were taken on, reduced two years later to one. In 1885 an agent came on to handle only cases involving children, and from then on WHS had one agent for children of a total of 2 in 1887, rising to 6 in 1905 and 10 in 1908, then dropping steadily back to 2 in 1919. Agents carried badges and after 1899 wore uniforms. Animal agents had territories to work ("divisions") which by 1906 numbered eight – the same as MPDC. Before that year each stayed in one division but thereafter rotated every month so that each would have a similar workload over the year. They did not work on Sunday, and both patrolled their districts and responded to complaints called into the WHS office. Key's salary was $25/month his first year, raised to $830/year until 1887, when it was increased to $1,000/year. In the earliest years King received a percentage (20% in 1881, 5% in 1886) of the "fines, fees and contributions" he caused (plus expenses), but this was discontinued.[21]

- **Equipment/Facilities/Staff:** Equipment in 1887 consisted of one bicycle (later a covered carriage), and in 1898 a derrick (to lift incapacitated horses)[22] and a camera. In 1889 the Society obtained use of a wagon ("ambulance") which it had to periodically repair or replace. This vehicle was housed and operated by the Knox Express Company as a service to WHS, and charged $5 per run: $2 for the Society and $3 for the company, although very poor people did not pay.[23] WHS constantly sought better office space. It established its first full-time office in 1884 (with a telephone; the office was shared with the Newsboys' and Children's Aid Society),[24] and in 1895 established a building fund to buy or build its own place, but was still pleading unsuccessfully for support in 1900. Besides the agents, the Society employed an office secretary (Mrs. Kate Barlow at $10/month in 1887) and a School Visitor (Helen Armour). All other workers were volunteers, including the two veterinary surgeons who offered aid on the street and testimony in court.

---

[18] In 1907 the two sons of the Turkish Minister joined the Children's Branch.

[19] The standard fine for the first offense was $5. "The judge is often lenient to poor offenders and releases them on personal bonds. Persons arrested deposit collateral for appearance at court and frequently forfeit the collateral rather than appear" (1886).

For an interesting comparison of WHS's expenditures with those of the New York organization, see Wash. Post,
1 May 1908, p. 9.

[20] They were called "police agents" in later years. For photos of the agents at work, including one identified as Agent Rabbitt, see Wash. Times, 30 July 1905, Magazine p. 6

[21] WHS Ann Rpts, 1881, 1886, 1906, 1907; "Mr. King . . . stated that he is paid $25 per month . . . and one-fourth of the fines" (Evening Star, 19 Aug 1881, p. 4); Wash. Times, 30 July 1905, Magazine p. 6, give other specifics of their procedures.

[22] Used, for example, to rescue a horse from the river (Wash. Times, 4 Dec 1920, p. 8).

[23] Good photos of the ambulance appear in WHS Ann Rpt, 1895; and Wash. Times, 30 July 1905, Magazine p. 6. It was also used for dead animal removal, and provided a minor source of income for the Society.

[24] A list of the office furnishings ("two window shades," etc.) was given in the 1884 report.

- **Structure:** The organization consisted of a president, several vice-presidents, treasurer and secretary, an Executive Committee, and standing committees. These latter, naturally, changed over the years but generally included: Fountains; Legal Proceedings and Legislation (chaired at one point by future Commissioner Henry H. B. Macfarland); Humane Education (Prof. Edward M. Gallaudet was a member); Finance and Membership; Agents/Rooms/Meetings; and (for a while) Vivisection. The revised WHS by-laws were printed in the 1887 annual report, and all annual reports after 1910.
- **Cruelty to Children:** WHS's long-standing agents for children's welfare (Charles W. O'Neill, served 1885-90; Samuel B. Wilson, 1890-98; George T. McGlue, 1901-05)[25] handled cases of children abandoned, neglected, abused or inappropriately worked. A far smaller proportion of prosecutions resulted than from the animal agents' work, the large number being "amicably adjusted" (in 1895, for example, of 337 cases investigated: 327 adjusted and 10 prosecuted). A large number of children clients ended up in institutions (153 in the same year). Congress created a Board of Children's Guardians in 1892 (26 July) which had legal protection over all such minors and authority to commit them to orphanages, adoptions or apprenticeships.[26]

    The number of juvenile cases investigated by the Society fell from over 300 in the early 1890s to 81 in 1898. Wilson – a member of the police force assigned to WHS – was recalled for other work in 1898.[27] That same year President Pratt admitted: "It seems to me the work of our Society for children is drawing to a close." In 1906, President Snow reported: "We have not in the last year given much attention to the prevention of cruelty to children. In attempting to take care of children . . . we frequently find ourselves overlapping the work of many excellent charitable institutions and mixing problems. In defense of animals, we have a clear field and can work without arousing the jealousy and hostility of church or State or Boards of Children's Guardians or Asylums or parents." The last annual report to include statistics on work for children was that of 1906.[28]

    The Society occasionally took stands on such issues as underage drinking (in which it worked with the Women's Christian Temperance Union) and spanking in schools.[29]
- **Special Projects:** Long-standing efforts of the Society included: provision of **drinking fountains** for horses[30] (there was a standing committee concerned with this which received designated donations every year, although the Society kept hoping fruitlessly that the city would take over their provision);

---

[25] They were regular officers of MPDC detailed to the Society and remained on the District payroll. They contributed regularly to the MPDC Ann Rpts in the Commissioners Reports, beginning in 1888. This detail was discontinued in 1906, the same year many other such special assignments (including that to the pound) were ended by MPDC. The Society toyed with the idea of hiring its own men in 1907 but had in fact begun simply referring reported cases of abuse to the Board of Children's Guardians or MPDC.

[26] For a useful description of the new Board see Evening Star, 22 May 1893, p. 10.

[27] "A recent investigation . . . raised a question as to the legality of the acts of such a [MPDC] representative, and it was deemed expedient to withdraw the officer thus detailed" (MPDC Ann Rpt, 1898).

[28] The Society wanly mentioned 15 cases the following year. For some capsule descriptions of cases involving children, similar to those for animals given below, see WHS Ann Rpts, 1887-91, 1897, 1902.

[29] (Drinking) Wash. Post, 12 Sept 1910, p. 2; (spanking) 29 Nov 1910, p. 9.

[30] The fountain was designed by Agent Key and cost $22. By 1923 the Society had installed 160 at a total cost of $4,450, of which 145 were still functioning (Heap, "History"). Washington Post founder and ardent WHS supporter Stilson Hutchins erected his own horse/human fountain outside the paper's headquarters in 1885; for a history and photo see the website GreaterGreaterWashington: https://ggwash.org/view/71685/fascinating-story-of-washignton-dc-benjamin-franklin-statue-old-post-office.

education in public schools (which largely disappeared from the annual reports after 1913), including an annual essay contest; and a junior branch, the **"Bands of Mercy"**, (established in New York by Angell in 1882 and coming to Washington in 1884, booted out of the public schools in 1900, revived in the schools in 1910) in many public schools and expanded to Boy Scout troops in 1913.[31] WHS also held occasional public lectures, handed out awards to worthy citizens and companies, published articles (the Washington Times was its favorite venue) and brochures, distributed useful books to various public venues (in 1900 it sent a copy of Black Beauty to every city fire station), and encouraged ministers to give sermons on humane treatment of animals.

The Society regularly interacted with sister branches throughout the country and internationally, and sent representatives to the annual meetings of the American Humane Society.[32]

- The **Barber Refuge for Animals:** The Barber Refuge will be discussed in the next chronological section, under "The Early Shelter Movement".
- **Cruelty to Animals Issues:** Our interest here centers on WHS's efforts to aid animals in public places, but many, many other concerns occupied its thoughts for long or short periods. Here is a sample: fox hunting;[33] pigeon shooting; care at the Zoo (including close confinement of eagles and of Dunk the elephant); the Horse Bazaar;[34] treatment of animals in rail transit through the city (which resulted in several federal restrictions);[35] winter horse racing at Ivy City ("jeopardizing at this time of year . . . the most noble of the animal creatures"); dropping animals and young girls (!) from low-flying balloons at circuses; "a passing taste for horse flesh"; skinning live fish at the wharf market;[36] crowding horses on ships bound for South Africa; inhumane treatment of crabs at the Atlantic City docks; "cruel bits" used in the 1901 inaugural parade; crowding of fowls in market cages; docking (cutting short) horses' tails and coats (including at the White House stable);[37] blinders and checkreins on horses; loss of wild birds (working in cooperation with the newly-established Audubon Society); feeding meat to dogs and cats, which the Society considered "repugnant, immoral and abhorrent"; improper shoeing of horses; slippery streets in winter on which pack horses could not get footing; injurious horse whips ("a long heavy and tortuous knout"); protection from rain for cab horses at Union Station; installation of squirrel houses in public parks; fireproofing stables; installation of brakes on wagons; screening of a film on bullfighting in Congress Heights; export of horses to Europe during the Great War; and provision of hats for horses.[38]

Standard filler material used in later annual reports included exhortations to take proper care of pet dogs and to provide for cats when on vacation. The Society supported Prohibition, hoping that it would mean fewer drunk drivers crashing into horses, and naturally opposed vivisection. This last

---

[31] For a good account, see Evening Star, 8 Jan 1911, p. 52.
[32] For a most useful list of U.S. and foreign sister societies see WHS Ann Rpt, 1899.
[33] For an essay on fox hunting in the District and environs see Wash. Post, 11 Aug 1929, p. SM9.
[34] These were privately-operated markets; the largest was in the 900 block of Louisiana Ave, NW (when that street ran past the old Center Market). For a good, detailed profile see Evening Star, 17 Jan 1891, p. 12.
[35] E.g., 29 June 1906.
[36] The MPDC Ann Rpt of 1910 shows four cases of cruelty to animals reported to police by the District's Harbor Master, but they are undefined.
[37] Evening Star, 22 Nov 1894, p. 1.
[38] For a harrowing description of treatment of animals in Center Market in 1922, see that of the humane movement's dedicated advocate Virginia W. Sargent (Wash. Herald, 18 Jan 1922, p. 6).

issue – particularly intense from about 1895 to 1910 – demanded much of the organization's energy (including scrutiny of the pound's sale of animals to government laboratories) and required a dedicated committee, which made unsuccessful attempts to secure Congressional legislation controlling experimental use of animals in the District of Columbia.[39]

For its early period SPCA/WHS operated under the 1870 charter granting its members and designated agents the power to cause the arrest (by its own agents or police officers) of violators as defined by separate legislation. After an unsuccessful attempt in 1888, Congress clarified and amplified this procedure in an **act of 1892**, which became the instrument of the Society's subsequent dealings. This law specified procedures at police court, the detailing of assisting officers, defined some words (for legal purposes), outlawed docking of horses and animal fights, and allowed agents to take charge of or to put down abused animals if they deemed that necessary.

Once WHS hired its first paid agent **operations "on the street"** predictably gravitated entirely to professional staff. Any member could in theory cause an arrest but such actions, rare in the days of Gatchel (except by Gatchel himself), entirely ceased as volunteer workers turned to the more genteel work of fund-raising, community education and lobbying.[40]

Reports of these agents in the annual reports were consistently favorable: "[The Society's] special agents . . . have rendered valuable assistance by their energy and skill in the prosecution of their work";[41] "I take great pleasure in commending these Agents for very faithful service, and . . . I . . . bear testimony to their patience and forbearance under provocation, often most trying.[42] Day and night these men are ready to respond to any call of duty, and frequently one or another of them is on watch into the small hours of the morning" (1898). Of particular note were agents: John H. King (served 1881-83), Minter P. Key ("a faithful and efficient officer," 1883-92),[43] Cpt. John Paine (1891-93), Joseph R. Rabbitt (1891-1906),[44] William R. Haynes (1898-1923), and James E. Thomas (1907-1928).

WHS agents had varied and taxing assignments. "It is the practice of each agent to thoroughly investigate every case of cruelty reported to him, formally or informally, or that comes under his own observation. [Their duties] have involved going long distances, making frequent visits to witnesses or to the alleged offender, and working early and late" (1881); "In his work the Agent [Key, whose report this is] has travelled over 8,000 miles since March 1 and wishes to make his humble acknowledgements to the tricycle which has carried him at such a rate as often to outrun horses, and to enable him to arrest the driver" (1884). Key estimated that he spent "nearly 200 half-days" at Police Court in 1884. As with the poundmaster, WHS agents held special unpaid commissions from MPDC and could make arrests on their own authority.[45]

---

[39] The proposed bill was reprinted in WHS Ann Rpt, 1895 and several years thereafter.

[40] We do read of William Pallas, a "volunteer agent," who had to stand down in 1903 due to his pending move (WHS Ann Rpt, 1903).

[41] From a report of a meeting of the Executive Committee (Nat. Republican, 12 May 1881, p. 4). "It is but just to say that the agents, although inadequately paid, have performed every duty readily and promptly, and chiefly by their zeal and efficiency the Society has been able to accomplish the good it has done" (WHS Ann Rpt, 1881).

[42] The same quality also ascribed to the poundmen.

[43] In 1888 Mr. J. R. McLean donated $25 "in recognition of the bravery of Agent Key, whom he had seen fight his way through strong opposition to the rescue of a suffering horse" (WHS Ann Rpt, 1888). An interview with this worthy man was published in Wash. Critic, 16 Dec 1886, p. 3.

[44] For his obituary see Wash. Post, 4 June 1906, p. 2. A "well-known society woman" once gave him a horse "for rescuing a tortured horse from a driver." He had been a liveryman and had some veterinary skills.

[45] WHS Ann Rpt, 1888; Evening Times, 13 June 1902, p. 8.

The annual reports consistently show about 200 or more prosecutions brought by each agent[46] but do not indicate their many special investigations (observing horses working the canal, for example), reports and suggestions (proper shoeing of horses) beyond specific cases. It is disappointing to find the Society in 1899 publically advertising for the public to "report any dereliction of duty or incivility on the part of its agents."[47] Perhaps the large number of new hires brought in less-motivated men, since the 1904 report admitted: "Our fine agents are perhaps not as active as they should be"; and the question was again addressed in 1907.[48]

WHS prided itself that most cases were resolved short of prosecution. "Prosecutions . . . are only a part of the work which the Society is doing. . . A warning is often deemed sufficient in cases where the abuse arises from ignorance or thoughtlessness" (1883). An instance from the 1894 annual report (abridged) gives a particularly nice example of this approach:

> Last October Mr. Rabbitt found that the loads hauled up the 14th and 7th Street hills were too heavy for the animals used, and he insisted upon the teams doubling up. The Washington Brick Co. manager, Mr. Holbrook, was sent for and came, accompanied by our Secretary. He informed us that such overloading was entirely against the company's orders, and at once had extra horses put on. When he saw how vigorously we were prosecuting this branch of our work he subscribed $10 monthly and stated that if our agents or members of the society saw any of his drivers whipping or driving their teams faster than a walk and . . . inform him he would discharge the man at once.
>
> This is only one instance in which the persistency of our agents in the performance of their duty has done good service both to the Society which they represent and also to the owners of horses.

Court-ordered fines, as reported in the 1881 report, generally ranged from $1 to $10.

Three annual compilations of agents' case work are given in Appendix D9 to illustrate the range of complaints they met. The 1881 list is the only one to specify every one individually (and the only one short enough to allow that); subsequent reports are more statistical in nature and always include a standard menu of horse-related abuses plus a few eccentric cases that happened to occur in that year. Some of these less-frequently encountered abuses, gleaned from a review of the annual reports, are:

> Stocking (tying) cow udders; breaking horse's/dog's head with a stone; cats/dogs/rabbits/opossums humanely put to death; calls made but unable to catch animals; home found for cats/dogs; failing to blanket horse in winter; cruelly shooting cat; breaking dog's hip with bottle; cutting mule with knife; throwing lye in cat's eyes; killing squirrel with whip; dragging horse with chain attached to jaw; shipping chickens with legs tied/with heads down; inciting cats/dogs to fight; overcrowding chickens/calves/sheep in pen; neglecting sick horse; killing pigeon with crowbar; tying horse's tail to post; beating pet bear with gun stock; killing snakes by biting off head (in circus); locking cat in house two weeks without food; working horses with Cuban itch; chaining dog in yard; chaining bear with ring in nose; cruelty to performing pig (in circus); scalding dog; tying live duck on ice; kicking cat; breaking cow's horn with brick; killing horses for insurance.

---

[46] The earliest statistics do not include instances resolved by a simple warning, which were much more numerous than prosecutions. For example, of 28,778 animals examined in 1906, only 1,977 cases went to court. See Appendix C7. Agents made daily and monthly statistical and textual reports.

[47] Evening Star, 5 July 1899, p. 3.

[48] The comments on agents and their work in the 1906 report give some idea of the problems.

And to give a more immediate feel for the agents' work, here are a few accounts of specific cases selected almost at random from the annual reports (abridged, as always):

- A man was found driving a horse which had a sore seven inches in diameter upon his back. Upon this the man had sprinkled a handful of salt. The harness rested directly upon the raw place, rubbing in the salt with every movement, rendering the poor creature stupid with pain. The judge fined the man $10. *(WHS Ann Rpt 1895)*
- Henry Wayne, for failing to provide his horse with proper shelter, allowing it to lie out on a vacant lot all night without food or protection from the weather, was arrested and forfeited $10 instead of standing trial. *(1914)*
- A young man hired a team of horses and drove them so fast and so long a distance that one of them fell dead in the street. The man was arrested and fined $50. *(1893)*
- Daniel Pinkney, driver for the Washington Brick Co., was arrested for most cruelly beating a team of mules he was driving because the animals were unable to pull a load of brick too heavy for them. They had been hauling heavy loads all day and were nearly exhausted when discovered by the Society's agent. Pinkney was tried and fined $10. *(1911)*
- A cow belonging to a dairyman escaped and was wandering in the open fields when a neighbor caught her, tied her to some bushes and went to notify the owner. While he was gone a brute in human form came along and thought to have some sport by throwing bricks at her, breaking off one of the cow's horns, which was hanging down the side of her head and the wound bleeding profusely when agent Thomas arrested the culprit, who forfeited $10 rather than risk a trip to the workhouse. *(1924)*
- Robert Hayes, a fancier, brought chickens to market in a bag and when found by Officer Finn some of the chickens were dead of suffocation and the others nearly so. Hayes was allowed to deposit $6 security to insure his appearance for trial. *(1910)*

Agents were also authorized to humanely put down badly injured animals on the street.[49]

As in the earlier period when Theodore Gatchel arrested a driver of Poundmaster Wheelock for overdriving his horse, so later agents prosecuted employees of the city's dead-animal contractors Felix Draney and Patrick Mann (discussed below.) The only record of WHS actions against Einstein's poundmen come from 1883: two instances of unnecessary roughness in capturing dogs.[50]

One victory for modern society attributable at least partly to WHS agents was the extinction of (public) animal fights. "They have driven cock and dog fighting out of the District" (1881). "In condemning this practice [pigeon shoots] the Society is quite well aware that they are interfering with the amusements of men who are not otherwise cruel but who . . . indulge in a sport which inflicts unnecessary cruelty upon an innocent animal. Of cock fighting, the law is so stringent and the sense of community so generally opposed to its practice that [it has] been driven into cellars or lofts, admission to which is gained only by passwords furnished to a few of the lowest sporting fraternity."[51]

And one last service of the agents: "Our agents are always willing to give advice in regard to the care of animals, thus aiding people who are too poor to consult a veterinarian" (1894).

---

[49] 1912 saw the first instance of a judgment against WHS for such an action (Wash. Herald, 5 Apr 1912, p. 2).

[50] (Draney) Evening Star, 21 June 1881, p. 4; (Mann) 10 Sept 1901, p. 3, and regularly thereafter; (poundmen) WHS Ann Rpt, 1883. The Society registered similar concerns regarding dog-capture to the Commissioners in 1896, to no effect (Evening Times, 9 Oct 1896, p. 5).

[51] Nat. Republican, 12 May 1881, p. 4; "Chicken fights are uncommon today in the District. Whenever chicken fanciers arrange a fight they make plans to go into Maryland" (Wash. Times, 30 July 1905, Magazine p. 6). For a typical account of a dog fight, see Daily Nat. Republican, 15 Apr 1874, p. 4. The annual reports of the District's Attorney for the period show about two prosecutions per year for dog fighting – far fewer than "bathing in river" or "profanity". See the Congressional anti-cruelty law of 25 June 1892.

Not all cases of cruelty were brought to Police Court by the Society – any citizen witnessing such acts could call in the police and some officers apparently had an eye open for abuse. The annual reports on 1884 and '91 actually list officers sympathetic to this work.[52] However, "the number of such cases is not great, complaints generally being referred to the Society" (1886) – only 32 in 1883 (1883). Key, in his report of 1884, found 66 cases brought outside of SPCA and noted that these "yielded to the District $545 in fines." Since money paid as a result of citizen-police action (rather than the Society) went only to the District coffers, one can understand the tone of territoriality running through SPCA/WHS pronouncements on this matter.[53]

WHS several times published "How to Proceed in Cases of Cruelty" in its annual reports[54] (and most likely as a separate pamphlet also), giving fairly detailed guidance to Society members (members only – "show . . . your card of membership") on steps of action ranging from "a word of caution and reproof" for the "thoughtless" abuser to the exact method to bring about and facilitate prosecution "if the abuse is willful or malicious." These instructions emphasize that the complaining member would not be inconvenienced by this civic act in a resulting trial.

Here is a shorter version, from the 1918 annual report (abridged):

> Be on the lookout for cases of cruelty in the streets. Take quick action *yourself* and bring every offence to the immediate attention of a policeman. If no policeman be handy keep the offender in sight until you find one. Then insist upon an arrest. Pay particular attention to cases of overloading and to carts drawn by decrepit horses unfit to work. Policemen are required to take notice of all acts of cruelty witnessed by them whether the immediate complainant is a member of the Humane Society or not.

The 1870, 1885 and 1892 acts authorized the Commissioners "in their discretion to detail from time to time one or more members of the **metropolitan police force** to aid [WHS] in the enforcement of laws relating to cruelty to animals as well as children" (1892). MPDC did regularly assign an officer to act as the agent for children's cases (and paid him also). The Police Department never detailed officers to corresponding duties on animal abuse, as was done for the pound. A policeman arresting an animal abuser, whether on the complaint of a Society agent or not, was simply arresting a criminal.[55] In 1902, perhaps arising from disputes we no longer know, the City Solicitor clarified that MPDC officers made animal-abuse arrests as police officers and not as WHS agents. The children's agent, Officer Wilson, on the other hand, after 1898 took abused children into custody on the authority of WHS, not MPDC.[56]

---

[52] 1884: Bailey, Breen, Kirby, Mills, Rhodes, Shank, Slack; 1891: Moore.

[53] Wash. Post, 2 Feb 1902, p. 10. The police achieved a good rate of success with their cases. Key (1884) said that of the 66 cases brought by the police, 50 resulted in convictions. Of the 263 cases prosecuted by SPCA that year, 238 ended in some kind of fine or punishment. The 1911, 1913-16 reports give comparable statistics for police-instigated arrests with similar ratios of conviction.

[54] E.g., 1895.

[55] Animals impounded by WHS agents while their owners were booked, etc., were kept at the local police station rather than the pound (Wash. Post, 16 Nov 1902, p. 12). Proceeds from animals then sold by MPDC went wholly to the District treasury. MPDC's Hack Inspector made at least one cruelty arrest (MPDC Ann Rpt, 1905).

[56] (Animals) Wash. Post, 2 Feb 1902, p. 10; (children) 29 Sept 1898, p. 10. Procedural brouhahas were inevitable – when a runaway horse fatally impaled itself near Farragut Square, should the reporting police officer shoot the writhing animal on the spot or wait for the WHS agent? (Wash. Post, 20 May 1904, p. 6; 24 May 1904, p. 6). "Invariably when there is a horse to kill the police call upon the [WHS agent] to do it" (Wash. Times, 30 July 1905, Magazine p. 6, which also describes the technique of shooting). "The relation between the Humane Society and the police department is a little puzzling to a layman trying to obtain speedy succor for a disabled, suffering animal" (Sarah Porter letter, Wash. Post, 22 Apr 1908, p. 12).

The relationship of the Society with the Police shows a love-hate quality frequently seen in volunteer organizations toward entities that they need for success but which they can blame in defeat. Early reports included commendations to the police and courts for their eager support: "It is gratifying to note that citizens and members of the police force are co-operating with the Society in a greater degree than heretofore" (1886); "We have the confidence and support of the Commissioners, . . . of the Chief of Police and his officers, . . . [and of] the judges of the Police Court, prompt and fearless in meting out justice to the guilty" (1892). MPDC returned the compliment: it was "to the credit of the [police] force and the agent of the Humane Society" that cruelty arrests were up, its 1892 annual report noted.

From the late 1890s onward the tone became more uneven, sometimes stating "our great indebtedness" to the District government (1903),[57] but increasingly chiding the police for not putting their hearts and backs into the work: "The Humane Society has seven agents. The city police force numbers about six hundreds" (1909); "The attention [that MPDC] pays to offenses against animals is notoriously slight" (1913).[58] During the 1905-14 period the Chief of Police regularly issued orders for his men to be more respondent to abuse cases.[59] His successor received thanks for increased support in the President's Address of the January 1916 general meeting (1915), but President Hutchins returned to bitter complaints the following year. Grumbling spread in 1912 to the uncooperative Police Courts, with their "political hack" judges and venal court officers; the Society appointed a special committee to investigate the situation. The issue resurfaced spasmodically into the 1930s.[60]

This same darkening tone pervaded WHS reports' **view of the city's population**. Here we must be careful not to confuse the personal attitude of an individual – even one as well-informed as the President of the Humane Society – with the actual situation. In spite of increasingly shrill cries of public abandonment from Presidents Snow and Hutchins, statistics of cases proportionate to the number of agents remained steady over this period. The "Nobody-Loves-Me" theme of these speeches probably reflects the frustrations of truly dedicated men that fundraising and membership, through relatively constant, never met their personal goals, and that large numbers of the citizenry – and especially those of their own class and background – had not followed them in adopting animal rights as their principal cause.

Annual keynote speeches must, by common tradition, initially sound a hopeful note so as to not discourage their audience who will only later be warned of present and coming problems. Even Gatchel,

---

"Tying of horses to trees" was also a punishable offense, but probably as a traffic-control rather than humane issue (MPDC Ann Rpts, various years, including 1906, which gives the relevant regulation).

[57] This to Chief of Police Sylvester, who was also a great support for Poundmaster Einstein.

[58] It is not impossible that the President's criticism of the police in 1909 was connected with the active proposal to turn all cruelty enforcement (and resulting fines) over to MPDC and away from WHS; see Wash. Times, 21 Feb 1910, p. 1; 3 Feb 1912, p. 5. The Congress agreed: "It is a notorious that such arrests [for cruelty] are rarely if ever made," concluded the Senate Committee on the District in rejecting the same proposal (Senate Comm on DC, "Prevention").

[59] Other related police orders from these years – the only period when new regulations (= laws) and orders (= internal announcements and instructions) were given in MPDC annual reports – relate to overloading of wagons (1909); prevention of dogs "from destroying birds and squirrels in parks and reservations," protection of birds and small game from being shot, and poisoning of dogs and other animals (all 1910).

I cannot resist observing how interesting it would be to have the background on these varied orders – what was the origin of the order regarding "seduction by a teacher" (1911), or prohibiting the use of "skipmobiles" by boys (1914)?

[60] WHS Ann Rpt, 1912; Evening Star, 3 Feb 1912, p. 4 (Hutchins' letter to MPDC); Wash. Times, 25 Mar 1913, p. 12 (in which we learn that the Society's allegations "fell flat" upon investigation); Evening Star, 27 Dec 1921, p. 4; 13 Mar 1930, p. 30.

as SPCA was dwindling to nothingness, regularly proclaimed growing public enthusiasm. The revived Society inevitably heard of the spreading awareness of its work and its worth.[61] And as we have seen throughout this study – in the public repudiation of animal fighting, for example – this was true, and SPCA/WHS properly claimed a strong role in this development.

When President Pratt stated in 1891: "We need more members who will take an active interest, and more money . . . to employ agents [and] to educate our people," he was reporting a universal truth of voluntary organizations. President Snow, in 1909, saw a much gloomier situation:

> When I became President ten years ago, I thought I had a great opportunity to do something for the much wronged and oppressed work animal. . . But I little knew then the prejudices, powers and interests that stood between us and justice to these animals. I then knew nothing of the attitude of obstinacy and indifference of some upon whom we rely for the enforcement of humane laws. I did not then know that the sentiment of altruism . . . could be a subject for indifference and even for derision.

WHS members who called complaints of cruelty to the office but then refused to testify in court ("they do not want to be . . . 'mixed up in it'") he castigated as "boudoir or sanctum humanitarians."[62]

President Hutchins (1910) spread his complaints to the entire city population: "The trouble is that Washington takes the Humane Society for granted and gives itself no further concern about it." In 1913 he pointed out that the Society numbered 300 of 300,000 inhabitants. "In no other large city . . . is the work horse worse treated than in the national capital. This disgraceful fact is a source of wonder to visitors, Americans and foreigners, but it concerns the local citizens very little." He repeated these feelings in 1916.

One factor that hindered the popularity of WHS was a perception – probably justified – that it was **an organization of wealthy do-gooders**. In 1881 President MacArthur had to deny that the humane movement was animated by "the sentimental impulses of a few tender-hearted enthusiasts." Hutchins demonstrated his class bias in appealing specifically to "kindly people of the better sort" for their participation (1916). "I wish that more society girls would take up this crusade," declared Snow. Complaining about the organization's ineffectiveness, a letter-writer of 1908 to the Post opined: "To many . . . the Humane Society . . . is but a name for a small group of more or less meddlesome rich persons."[63] Certainly the individual members identified by profession all seem well-placed, and the generous donations and bequests received point in the same direction.

Adding to the impression of an elite organization was **the class of most targets** of the Society's actions: the working poor. Of course, large construction/hauling/supply/transportation operations felt the

---

[61] "The work of the year would seem to indicate increased sympathy with our cause and a growing purpose to aid its advancement" (1884); "The interest in our work is growing every year, and we are greatly encouraged by the help given us" (1894). In 1921 President Smith ironically claimed that dwindling interest demonstrated the triumph of the cause.

[62] Even the 1881 annual report complained of this.

[63] (Snow) Wash. Times, 13 Feb 1909, p. 1; (complaint) Wash. Post, 22 Apr 1908, p. 12. The latter writer, Sarah Porter, describes the Society as a basically closed organization, citing its near total absence of outreach to the larger community ("The Society never brings itself before the public . . . by means of fairs, parades, prizes, lectures, house-to-house canvasses . . . or similar advertising devises . . . Such means may be undignified – even occasionally in bad taste, but . . ."). In old age Mrs. Henry Moses, a founding member of WARL, recalled: "At first everybody made fun of us. They just thought we were a lot of hysterical women" (Evening Star, 26 Apr 1962, p. 23).

sting of WHS prosecutions but they could easier pay the fine and continue business.[64] And many of the activities the Society deplored – sports hunting, inhumane treatment of race horses, pigeon shoots, fashionable docking and shearing of horses – were those of the upper classes; but the Society largely focused its street work on draft horses, and that meant lower-class private wagon operators and bottom-level employees of large companies.[65]

In its earliest reports SPCA/WHS carefully stated that it pursued abusers of horses "white and colored" and the 1886 report referred only to "the poorer classes of our population," but as time went by criticism was increasingly directed at the city's African-American population. "Peculiar conditions exist here. The colored people flock into the city . . . seeking easier employment than tilling the soil, and as horses can be bought for one dollar up, the ash [removal] business proves very attractive. To supply this demand, car-loads of worn-out horses are shipped here from Maryland and Virginia" (1899). These carts – used to transport ash or any other material for individuals or companies – were most commonly operated by poor blacks ("expressmen") trying to eke out a living,[66] and they often ran afoul of Society agents. "They [the horses] are driven by colored men almost as forlorn as themselves" (1896). "His lawyer pleads that the horse is his only means of support, that he is not able to buy a better horse or to give this one more or better food and care, and that our solicitude for the horse results in cruelty to the owner. Thus it becomes a serious question whether a wretchedly poor man has a right to make a horse joint partner in his misery" (1903).

Later statements by Society officials were less understanding: "I have found that the best and most lasting lesson for the negro who delights to whip, lash, kick and otherwise torture and torment his horse is to be fined" (Agent Paine, 1892); blacks are "idle, shiftless and intemperate . . . unfit for steady work or . . . to secure remunerative employment" (Snow, 1908); "The colored people here are poor, unthrifty, and, as a rule, ignorant. They do not know how to take care of themselves. It is to them that the care of approximately twelve thousand horses in [DC] is relegated" (Snow, 1909).[67] When Anna Thomas, a prominent member who did step forward to testify at a cruelty trial (in 1906), was questioned by the black defendant's black lawyer she refused to answer him, not caring to acknowledge the prerogatives of a man of color. (She was fined $10 and the Society stated that she testified as a private citizen rather than as its representative.)[68]

---

[64] "Of the large contractors and . . . horse owners of Washington, not one would know his horses if he should meet them on the street; not one in ten would know the drivers of his horses" (1909); "Many times [the] poor are warned and let off . . . or their cases are dismissed by our agents. On the other hand, corporations and those able to pay receive attention when they violate the law; and our records will show numerous cases against street-car companies, express companies, coal dealers, sand dealers, contractors, etc." (1894).

[65] The organization was cognizant of this feeling: "Many persons . . . think we do nothing but prosecute poor people, but could they see our records they would change their opinion" (1894); "Right here it should be said that wealthy people who clip the coats of their handsome horses . . . during the winter months, and those who still drive docked horses . . . are quite as deserving of condemnation and punishment as heartless horse owners who maltreat their animals in the streets" (1913).

[66] This is not an anecdotal surmise but attested fact: see Evening Star, 28 Jan 1899, p. 20 for a very good overview of the trade. Einstein noted of stray horses taken: "The animals [belong] to the poorer classes . . ., and [are] used during the day in carts and other vehicles" (Poundmaster Ann Rpt, 1878).

[67] "The work of the Society is difficult because there are so many poor, ignorant colored people in Washington" (Evening Star, 24 June 1911, p. 6).

[68] Wash. Times, 29 Sept 1906, p. 9. The case was dismissed on technical grounds.

It is difficult to think that WHS had any African-American members,[69] although the by-laws say nothing about that and the organization's school outreach entered both the white and colored divisions of the system, as did its humane work with abused children. And we should note the testimony of the city's black Evangelical Ministers Alliance when voting to support the Society in its 1910 struggle with establishment horse-owners: "While the Washington Humane Society causes many arrests . . ., except in rare instances [it] does not prosecute for the first offence but seeks by counsel . . . and by warning to turn the offender from the error of his way . . . and make arrests unnecessary."[70]

In spite of these personal prejudices[71] (surely typical for that time), there can be little doubt that the city's black population did account for a disproportionate number of animal-cruelty cases, mostly because of the work they did. Police statistics from the first decade of the century show a ratio of arrests for cruelty to animals of about 2:1 white:colored when the city's population was closer to 2.5:1; by 1914 the arrest rate for blacks had passed that of whites.[72] Of the individual cases handled by WHS in 1912 and 1915 (two years for which we know the race of offenders), well over half involved African-Americans. We also have the testimony of Einstein and of the Washington Fertilizer Company official (below) that much of their work came from the Negro parts of town.

During this period the Society came under pressure to address the basic nature of its efforts: was it concerned chiefly with its traditional cause, the betterment of **street horses** and other working animals, or should it take its activities more aggressively to the cause of smaller, pet animals – **dogs and cats**? With the city increasingly middle-class and the troublesome population of farm animals rapidly disappearing (even stray dogs coming under control, due to the good work of the pound), societies for pet-owners formed around issues such as muzzling requirements, and they turned to WHS for support.

Britain's RSPCA was founded in 1824 particularly to combat abuse to draft horses, and similar concerns animated Henry Bergh of New York in 1866. The Washington organization continued this focus while deploring – and working against – abuse of any species. The President's address of the January 1884 annual meeting called out inhumane treatment of horses, but also mistreatment of dogs ("fighting, baiting, hunting, . . . starved and frozen"), any animals improperly transported, and "the nobler animals of the forest" (including birds) killed in hunts; plucking of live fowls; muzzling calves; vivisection; and inhumane slaughtering methods.

Nonetheless, annual statistics of prosecutions for this period show that at least 95% of such actions involved abuse of horses and mules, estimated to number about 11,000 in 1900. For this focus, WHS began to feel heat from a growing chorus of citizens wanting to protect their pet dogs and cats while ridding neighborhoods of mutts and toms. In answer to one such complaint Snow challenged the writer to find "a person guilty of overloading, overdriving or beating a cat, working it when lame or tying it in a stall without food or bedding."[73]

---

[69] WHS Ann Rpt, 1888, made the only reference to a neighborhood branch (in Anacostia) but the three sponsoring churches were all white congregations. At the 1904 annual meeting the Society considered a proposal to establish a "colored branch" (1903) but nothing was reported thereafter about this. An article of 1911 – mostly WHS propaganda – simply assumed that only whites would be members ("Out of 200,000 white persons in Washington . . . there are only 235 . . . members"; Evening Star, 24 June 1911, p. 6).

[70] Wash. Bee, 12 Mar 1910, p. 1.

[71] Although complaints about careless or heartless horse-owners remained constant, the racial animus of Snow's years disappeared entirely under succeeding President Hutchins.

[72] The numbers of total such arrests are given in Appendix C7; see MPDC Ann Rpts. From the same tables we find that arrests for ignoring the dog licensing requirement changed from 1:2 to 1:1 white:colored, while for "keeping a dangerous dog" (a very small number) was always much higher for whites than blacks.

[73] (Number of horses) 1901 Street Cleaning Dept Ann Rpt; Wash. Post, 1 May 1908, p. 9.

This issue absorbed the Society, or at least its president, in the first decade of the new century and led the ever-quotable Snow into some of his most trenchant observations. His arguments were that:

- Abuse of horses, mules and to a lesser extent cows ("useful animals") remained rampant and easily observable in the District: "When I think how dependent are the wageless workers whom we represent, how painful, helpless, and pathetic their sufferings, how heavy their burdens, how endless their task, all human suffering . . . grows smaller in comparison. Beggars can ask for food . . . ; the human laborer is thought worthy of his hire . . . Those whom we represent . . . have no wages or limitations of hours. Their insufficient bed and board are never of their own choosing. Their fortitude and their unresentful patience are an example and a reproach to us" (1905); "It has been the aim of the . . . Society to prevent cruelty to all animals. But our time, energy and money have been *mainly* directed to the . . . suffering of *useful* animals – . . . work animals and animals used for food. Because man's need of these animals is most urgent, the result has been . . . that they are most abused.[74] Our work has been and must be mainly in the alleviation of the lot of these animals" 1906);
- Cruelty to dogs, cats and other house-bound pets ("animaux-de-luxe"), while deplorable, was of less concern and less consequence: "Dogs and cats require our attention only incidentally . . . These animals are not useful. They are pets or animals of luxury. They appear to have little place in the economy of urban life. Let loose in the city they are a menace and a nuisance, while to confine them in the house or the back yard is cruel" (1906); "I have little patience with alleged humanitarians who would have us turn aside from this Calvary and crucifixion [of horses] . . . to the imagined wrongs of dogs and cats, pets . . . that do nothing and suffer nothing" (1907);
- Abuse of horses, etc., in the street was amenable to action (including prosecution) while that of pets was almost impossible to ferret out and deal with: "Dogs are of little or no use to the city, and ninety per cent of them would be better out of the way. In my opinion, the Humane Society should continue to prosecute those guilty of cruelty to dogs and cats, just as it has . . . to rats, monkeys, fowl and fish; but I think it has too much serious and real work to do to spend time and money in coddling and fondling dogs and cats" (1905);
- The universally acknowledged problem of feral dogs and cats was not a matter of abuse but of nuisance – rounding them up and eliminating them, which the city was already doing: "In my opinion the city pound is the proper place for unclaimed dogs and cats, and at least nine-tenths of them are unnecessary" (1905);
- As a subhead to this, he strongly disapproved of the movement to establish "homes" or "hospitals" for such strays, which will be discussed later in connection with WARL.

Although he never directly said this, and several times directly stated otherwise, Snow simply felt that horses and larger animals were of a higher order than smaller pets. In his continual reiteration of these points, and the reversal of the Society's views later (at least on the matter of cruelty to pets and of the value of shelters) we see also the influence of one strong and well-placed individual can exercise over an organization, as so frequently occurs in such situations.[75]

---

[74] In his reply to Miss Porter (ibid.), who took umbrage at the distinction between "useful" and "useless" animals, Snow elaborated this point: that he was not making a value judgment (which he clearly was) but that animals <u>used</u> in work were more liable to ill-treatment.

[75] He was also a consistent and important contributor.

As WHS maintained its concentration on the condition of draft animals, a new player – **motorized vehicles** – threatened the central pillar of the Society's raison d'etre, and with the Society's enthusiastic welcome.[76]

The first mention of mechanized transport came in the 1898 annual report, referring to trolleys: "In common with a large number of our citizens, I fully believed that the change of motor power from the horse to the electric system on our principal street railways would materially lessen the work of our agents, but . . . our hope has not been realized."

The appearance of motorized trucks received a hopeful announcement in 1909, and again in 1915: "There is no more encouraging sign of the times than the steady growth in the number of motor vehicles in commercial use in Washington . . . The rapid increase . . . of motor-drawn coal wagons, express, baggage and delivery carts and trucks used in heavy hauling, entitles us to . . . look hopefully to the day when work horses will vanish from city thoroughfares altogether."[77] President Hutchins went on to urge members to only patronize merchants who used such vehicles, and suggested that if the District's animals could do so they would erect "a tribute to gasoline" in some city park. The following year he wittily and tellingly compared horses to automobiles:

> Motor cars cost money and a frozen engine will not work. But a freezing horse is a different matter. He will work after a fashion until he drops dead and his comfort meanwhile is a secondary thing. The automobile on the contrary has well-defined rights and does not respond to blows; hence its owner coddles and protects it.[78] Happy the day when the work horse can say as much. Happier still the day when he disappears from the streets of every city in the world. Modern man is not to be trusted with flesh and blood; his helpers need to be made of steel.

Two further events must be recounted to draw a full picture of WHS's work during this period:

In early 1900 WHS offered the Commissioners to **take over operation of the District pound**. This move seems to have come virtually out of the blue – the Society had always had a cordial relationship with Einstein's pound. The 1898 annual report noted that at an Executive Committee meeting of that year "Mr. [Wallace W.] Hite asked that some measures be taken to secure the dog license [revenues] for our Society." A newspaper account of the annual meeting of January 1899 reported that "it was the consensus of opinion that [the pound] should be under the management and supervision of the Society."[79] And the 1900 report briefly mentioned a Committee on the Pound which had met with Sen. Gallinger and sent inquiries to other large cities to inquire how they operated their pounds.

No further word of this idea appeared in WHS or news publications until the organization actually presented its proposal to the Commissioners in March of the following year. "The Society . . . has been induced to make such an offer because . . . representations have been made to it . . . in regard to cruelty and unnecessary suffering attendant upon the seizure of . . . dogs, and their detention and destruction at the pound." President Pratt pointed to the still-large number of unlicensed dogs at large, the result of

---

[76] I will not document here the self-evident rise of the automobile and truck occurring in Washington in the first two decades of the twentieth century. The number of licensed automobiles in the city can be tracked from the annual reports of the Automobile Board in the Commissioners Reports. See also Matthew B. Gilmore's two fine articles "Washington Welcomes the Automobile" in the May and July 2019 issues of the local journal The InTowner.
[77] In 1909 the Society wrote the Commissioners urging adoption of motorized fire engines (1909).
[78] He probably paid more for it also.
[79] Wash. Times, 11 Jan 1899, p. 5.

"previous neglect."[80] He promised "unremittent watchfulness" by WHS agents to eliminate this population, and also better treatment and more humane execution of impounded dogs. New York, Philadelphia and Baltimore had turned their operations over to their Humane Societies.[81]

The Society's proposal seems a solution to a non-existent problem. Neither WHS nor newspaper records reported such complaints about the pound but rather the opposite. And, as we have seen, the Society had little interest or experience in the question of dogs. An observer must speculate that WHS was really interested in the fee it would receive for this work: it proposed using half the dog-tax revenue, or about $8,000 for that year. The Commissioners were unimpressed ("Mr. Einstein has . . . performed his work . . . to the entire satisfaction of the Commissioners"), even when the Society dropped its asking price to $5,000. Ultimately the District managed to kill a Senate bill[82] favoring WHS and also put in their usual request for funds for a new pound.[83] And with that this curious episode ended.

Several years later WHS itself came under attack itself from its natural enemy, the **Horse Owners' Mutual Protective Association**.[84] Throughout its existence the Society constantly lobbied Congress for strengthened humane laws of various sorts – an expected position. Its efforts in 1890 to see enlarged powers and subsidies came to nothing. By 1894 the organization began to experience push-back – "about a score of coal merchants, brick manufacturers and others . . . visited the office of the Humane Society . . . yesterday morning and protested loudly, unanimously and contemporaneously against . . . the interference of the Society in their business." Reminded of existing laws they backed down and agreed to "an amicable agreement" regarding both treatment of draft animals and procedures for enforcement.[85]

Charles E. Myers, "a local expressman and drayman," in 1902 made a legal challenge to: WHS's privilege of seizure of purportedly abused animals and of bringing actions against owners;[86] unconstitutionally interfering with private property rights; and harassing his business specifically.[87] He added ironically that in some instances his animals, impounded at police stations,[88] were left all day on the street without food, and pointed out that WHS agents had a pecuniary interest in bringing prosecutions. The Post's account of this suit said it was the first to directly challenge the Society's prerogatives, and

---

[80] Einstein and his men had been pulled from pound work to help disinfect contaminated residences during an outbreak of smallpox (Evening Star, 8 Dec 1899, p. 16).

[81] Evening Star, 24 Mar 1900, p. 2; Wash. Times, 25 Mar 1900, p. 4; 30 Apr 1900, p. 4. A longer list will be found in WHS Ann Rpt, 1907, which also includes the very limp reasoning of WHS member Mary Howe Totten justifying the plan. It is noticeable that Washington's organization always followed the lead of New York's.

[82] S 4232, introduced by Sen. Lodge; it will be remembered that the Senator had been highly upset when his pet dogs were seized five years earlier. This bill had dropped the proposed remuneration to $4,500.

[83] (Commissioners) Evening Star, 26 Mar 1900, p. 8; ($5,000) Wash. Times, 27 Mar 1900, p. 8; (Senate bill) Evening Times, 28 Apr 1900, p. 8.

[84] "So vigorous and unrelenting were the activities of the Society that it became a terror to evil-doers and an association was formed . . . calling itself the 'Horse Owners' Mutual Protective Association'" (Heap, "History"). In the many news notices of the Association not one mentions any activity beyond its battle with WHS.

[85] WHS Ann Rpt, 1891; Wash. Post, 14 Feb 1890, p. 4; Wash. Times, 24 Oct 1894, p. 1.

[86] "There has never been any valid law . . . in the District of Columbia which created, defined, prohibited or punished . . . the offense of cruelty to animals."

[87] This part of the complaint covers six legal pages and indicates his frustration: "The defendants, and especially the defendant agents [Rabbit, Haynes], have often threatened . . . to cause your complainant all the expense and trouble they can, and to do all they can to injure him in his reputation, property and business, and have most arbitrarily, tyrannically, oppressively and insolently, and with the greatest persistence and frequency, and without any authority or warrant of law whatever, persecuted, harassed and annoyed him by forcibly stopping, seizing and detaining his vehicles . . . [etc.]"

[88] At the recommendation of the MPDC Property Clerk, housing of such strays was centralized in one Department stable in 1887, saving $46 the first year (MPDC Ann Rpt, 1887).

that the Congressional act giving such authority to the group had been modeled on acts of New York and Maryland. Myers received an injunction from further Society actions while the two sides carried the case up the chain of courts, which process was still underway in 1907.[89]

The Society was certainly cognizant of the "private property" concern. To quote from President Hutchins' address to the 1917 annual meeting: "Gently nurtured and kindly-hearted men and women seem . . . consumed . . . that cruelty to helpless beings, while regrettable, is not lightly to be interfered with by the private citizen. Shall not a man do as he wills with his own, and if he own a horse or a mule shall he not beat it when he chooses? Who are these sentimentalists and what right have they to thrust themselves between an owner and his live stock?" (1916).[90]

The storm broke in March 1907, when 200 horse owners held an "indignation meeting" to organize against alleged persecution by WHS. They organized the Horse Owners' Mutual Protective Association,[91] with Charles Myers as president. WHS's strong-willed president Chester Snow attended, regularly interrupting the proceedings only to be consistently shouted down ("Put him out!" "Shut up!" "You are not in this!"). Another surprising attendee was George W. Knox, presumably the son of that G. W. Knox (then deceased) whose company had cooperated with the Society for years in the operation of its ambulance, but who now spoke against it. Several District officials sat as spectators.[92]

Two observations help set this new organizations in perspective: (1) it was not, as WHS claimed after its later victory, "a few horse owners" (1909),[93] but a collection of important companies anxious to protect their interests; and (2) like WHS itself, it was a group of only prominent businessmen – if many horse-owners were not represented it was because they were small independents at the bottom of the professional scale.

As is typical of mass meetings held in the heat of passion the cascading complaints about the Humane Society took on a life of their own. It was true, as stated, that WHS largely lived off revenue from court fines, and possibly true that agents were evaluated at least in part on "cases" – warnings and prosecutions – reported,[94] but demonstrably incorrect that agents' pay was tied to the fines they produced, although this last was repeated regularly ("Perhaps they have families to support"). Other charges thrown out were: that agents were unqualified to judge horses; that the Society pressured them to bring prosecutions for the income (a complaint made rightly or wrongly against the old SPCA); that "mental weaklings" were called as witnesses; that the courts habitually favored the prosecution; and that the District's Corporation Counsel who handled these cases was a paid WHS legal adviser. Snow challenged the horsemen to pay $2 and

---

[89] And dismissed the following year (Wash. Post, 15 Feb 2018, p. B3). WHS Ann Rpt, 1902; Wash. Post, 16 Nov 1902, p. 12; Wash. Times, 22 Mar 1907, p. 10. Myers' legal complaint will be found at the National Archives (RG 21, Entry 69 "Equity Case Files, 1863-1938", #23616); my sincere thanks to Mr. Robert Ellis, one of many wonderfully helpful staffers at NARA, who found this for me. (Mr. Ellis told me that the annual indexes to these files indicate many other cases involving WHS.)

[90] See also WHS Ann Rpt, 1912.

[91] Often seen without the "Mutual".

[92] Wash. Times, 22 Mar 1907, p. 10. The announcement of the meeting is in 19 Mar 1907, p. 13.

[93] Snow claimed after the initial meeting that the men present represented only 1,800 out of 12,000 horses in the city: "The horse owners . . . last night were by no means a representative body" (Wash. Times, 22 Mar 1907, p. 10). The Association claimed 300 members representing 3,500 horses (Wash. Times, 1 Nov 1907, p. 10).

[94] Remember that after 1906 agents rotated territories so that they all worked the lightest and heaviest loads, "thus giving each one equal chance, and avoiding the old complaint that some . . . had better territory than others, and were enabled to make a better record" (1906).

join the Society; the horsemen bandied the idea of doing exactly that en masse and then "elect the right kind of officers on election day."[95]

After such huffing and puffing the new Association devised a more subtle attack on WHS — through its pocketbook. In the fall of 1907 it proposed to the Commissioners that the 1885 WHS Charter law be amended to strip the Society of money from court fines and direct the funds instead to the District treasury. "The Society is developing into a money-making institution, and . . . its agents make . . . arrests for trivial causes for the purpose of adding to its revenues." Enforcement would be given entirely to MPDC, a demonstrably dubious proposal.[96]

This approach went nowhere with the Commissioners, who were not anxious to see MPDC saddled with work then being done by WHS agents.[97] The Society rejoiced: "Two or three years ago a few horse owners who . . . had been arrested . . . for cruelty to horses . . . formed an organization to oppose the Humane Society . . . They argued that the horse's best protection is the self-interest of the owner. This is fallacious, for the interest of the owner is not in the horse, but in the profit they can get from the labor of the horse" (1909).

Undaunted, the Association took their bill to Congress in 1909, with the support of the Chamber of Commerce and (this time) the Commissioners.[98] In reply, the Society testified, rallied and collected endorsements: from the (African-American) Evangelical Ministers Alliance, a plethora of prominent local worthies, and sister societies from around the country. (Washington hosted the national convention that year.) The bill died in committee.[99]

After these titanic struggles, the Humane Society faced only slight legal provocation. Commissioner John A. Johnson proposed reducing the maximum penalty for cruelty infractions to $40 in 1912; such a low amount would put cases below the monetary level triggering a jury trial and require only a simple verdict by the Police Court judge. This appealed to the District government because jury trials were expensive but made a problem for the horsemen, who got more favorable results from juries than judges. The Horse Owners' Association wanted to keep jury trials (naturally) but in a poke at WHS suggested taking away the organization's revenue from fines and giving it instead to the Police and Firemen's Pension Fund (also the recipient of fines resulting from breaking dog licensing and muzzling laws).[100]

A second professional association, the **District Team Owners' Association**, agreed, deploring the proposed loss of jury trials. (The Team Owners', organized in 1907, possibly represented small owners: it regularly advertised available jobs, and when it demanded a raise in rates in 1910 – due, it claimed, to

---

[95] Wash. Times, 22 Mar 1907, p. 10; 1 Nov 1907, p. 10.

[96] WHS Ann Rpt, 1907; Wash. Times, 1 Nov 1907, p. 10; Wash. Post, 2 Nov 1907, p. 16. Further accusations of a technical nature were piled on a few days later (Wash. Post, 7 Nov 1907, p. 16).

[97] Evening Star, 17 Nov 1907, p. 5. The Association's vigorous testimony before the Commissioners (1 Nov 1907) will be found in Comm Minutes/Orders, Vol. 28 p. 848a.

[98] Senate Comm on DC, "Prevention"; Wash. Post, 21 Feb 1909, p., 12; WHS Ann Rpt, 1909 gives the Commissioners report.

[99] (Evangelical) Wash. Bee, 12 Mar 1910, p. 1; (worthies) Evening Star, 15 Mar 1910, p. 16; (other societies) Wash. Post, 12 Mar 1910, p. 2, which includes interesting comparative statistics on the finances of each city's organization. These are only a few of the many newspaper articles from that time describing this event. See WHS Ann Rpt, 1910 for a concise report of the bill's demise after an unfavorable committee report. There was a less-publicized attempt to strip the Society of such funding the following year, but outmaneuvered in Congress (1911).

[100] Wash. Herald, 20 Mar 1912, p. 12; Wash. Times, 29 Nov 1912, p. 3. In April-August 1910 of sixteen jury cases involving cruelty to animals only two brought in verdicts of guilty; the average fine was $10 (Evening Star, 14 Mar 1912, p. 15). A court official estimated the Society won only 10% of its jury cases (Wash. Times, 17 July 1912, p. 3, which gives one attorney's closing statement).

the expensive demands of WHS – it was able to take 725 teams on strike!).[101] Nothing came of this last legal fling from the two organizations, which were quickly heading toward extinction anyway.[102]

During this same period WHS also withstood attacks from the Retail Grocers' Protective Association and the Milk Dealers' Association, both complaining about "unwarranted arrests," "persecution" and so forth, to no effect.[103]

---

[101] Evening Star, 10 Oct 1909, p. 2; Wash. Post, 2 Apr 1910, p. 5; Wash. Times, 22 Feb 1911, p. 4.
[102] Wash. Herald, 20 Mar 1912, p. 12; 4 Apr 1912, p. 2. "This was a death blow to the Horse Owners' Association and further opposition on its part waned" (Heap, "History"). The Horse Owners' Protective Association did not appear in the newspapers again. The Team Owners' Association was last mentioned in 1917, when it claimed to represent 500 teams (Wash. Post, 30 Jan 1917, p. 9). Another group, the DC Liverymen's Association, did not enter the fray.
[103] (Grocers) Evening Star, 27 Sept 1912, p. 3; (Milk) 9 July 1913, p. 2.

CHAPTER EIGHTEEN

Summary

During the Territorial and early Commissioners periods the cities of Washington and Georgetown and a good deal of Washington County moved from their rural adolescence to urban maturity. Development of an effective mechanism of animal control – established by the government and accepted by the citizens – was one aspect of this change.

Chief among the factors driving this development (as this paper has regularly emphasized) was the steady shift in the city's economic and social make-up:

- Land used for farming within the District's bounds decreased from 11,600 acres in 1870 to 6,100 in 1910. Farms, and then individually-owned farm animals were gradually squeezed out of the two Corporations and more and more toward the edges of the county;[1]

- The District's increasing middle- and upper-class had little use for animals kept for work/food purposes or as casual (untended) pets, but focused only on their own cared-for dogs and cats. Work animals became the province of the lower classes, while all the animal-centered organizations discussed here (except for the contractors' associations) represented well-off pet-owners, bringing a class aspect to the issue.

The establishment by the Territorial Government of a centralized, government-operated pound (in place of ineffective MPDC tasking) signaled the city's determination to actually tackle a problem that was increasingly felt to be intolerable. After misfires both in the arrangements of a contractor-pound and in selection of contractors, the appointment of Samuel Einstein proved fortuitous and perspicacious, as was his selection of his poundmen. The continuous support given by the police, Health Officer and Commissioners ensured the success of his efforts. This success both bred and benefitted from the increasing support of the city's populace. (These factors are specified in the chapter Coralling the Population of Farm Animals.)

Some specific developments in animal control in the District during this period should be pointed out:

- Loose or untended animals kept for husbandry purposes by local families virtually disappeared during these years as this activity was pushed out of the populated areas by legal and social forces;

---

[1] I will not belabor the steady and inevitable decline of farming in the District, but refer the reader to Appendix C1, which documents this fact with the usual anomalies found in such statistics. I thank Ms. Michele Casto, of the Washingtoniana Division of the ML King Library, for bringing these Census reports to my attention.

- The appearance of these larger animals used directly for work (draft horses and mules, for example) or in transit (taken from railroad yards to abattoirs) also disappeared due to economic and technological (i.e., mechanization) developments;

- The District's efficient pound operation plus increasing public disapproval began to bring actual diminution of its problem of stray dogs and cats, so that by 1912 the population of street dogs had largely been tamed;

- As the city's middle classes came to distinguish a culture of pet animals (which they approved of) separate from unwanted strays (which they didn't) an accepted code of pet control developed:

    - *Licensing*: conceived in the early days of the District as a means of control of the dog population and a source of revenue (and certainly not, even in 1912, as a guarantee of good care of the animal – there were no requirements for shots to get a license, for example) became standard for most animal-owners;
    - *Muzzling*: although later abandoned by the city, was imposed in the face of a real threat of rabies, and further accustomed owners to control of pet dogs;
    - *Leashing*: the increasing popular and legal acceptance of leashing led to our present understanding of proper pet etiquette: animals confined to their owner's property or leashed when off of it (as a substitute for muzzling);

- In spite of the regular hand-wringing of WHS, the city's population did in fact express an increasing abhorrence of public cruelty to animals. Even in the Territorial period patently inhumane treatment of animals in city markets and animal fights had begun to disappear. Urbanization brought citizens into closer contact with the remaining work animals while it pushed the businesses that were most likely to abuse them (slaughtering, for example) out of the District. Mechanization of transport and other processes ended most sources of obvious abuse by 1912.

By the end of this period the role of animals in the District's life more resembled that of our own time than that of 1871 – all the important trends that we take for granted today had firmly taken hold. In the next period it is not the animals but the governmental and private organizations that will show greatest change, as they respond to the new situation.

CHAPTER NINETEEN

Dead Animals

I [wish to note] the innumerable number of carcases [sic] of dead rats, cats and dogs, which have all Summer been tossed into our alleys, . . . emitting odors more disgusting and unhealthy than all the garbage which collects . . . Let each person or family . . . bury them at least a foot deep at the roots of their grape vines or trees, where they will cease to . . . make sick any one, and will prove an excellent fertilizer. I charge nothing for this advice. Truly yours, Richard Roe. (Daily Critic, 30 Aug 1878, p. 4)

[Patrick Mann defending his rendering plant:] He denied that the perfume arising from the works [where carcasses were boiled down] was injurious to health or that it contained poisonous gases. He pointed out . . . a corps of herculean examples of stalwart manhood, and added that they had been employed at the factory for twelve years, that they had never even had the toothache, never contracted any doctor's bills, utterly refused to die and continued to grow fat. (Evening Star, 12 Aug 1893, p. 16)

Collection of dead animals from streets of the growing and increasingly dense metropolis during the Territorial and Commissioners periods was closely intertwined with collection of garbage. The 1871 act creating the Territorial Government returned this responsibility to the re-constituted Board of Health. The Board restated its authority over nuisances at this time (including dead animals) and laid out procedures for reporting, removing and penalizing them: if the perpetrator did not remove them himself within 24 hours the city would do so and charge him the expense.[1] A news report of that year mentions that Police Superintendent Richards pledged the force's cooperation with the Board, and suggested that the contractor ("the party") which had previously collected carcasses for the Corporation be contracted to resume this work. The Board adopted this plan: we find William Wolf listed as "Remover of Dead Animals" in 1872 with an annual salary of $600.[2] No matter which District agency managed the operations, and whether a public or contractor force performed it, the District police played a tangential but regular role also.

---

[1] The Board's Nuisance ordinance of May 1871 and later additions invoked fines for allowing carcasses or "animal . . . substances in a state of decay" to remain exposed for 24 hours, and required the Health Officer to remove the same as a last resort. The consolidated 1875 ordinance (incorporating earlier regulations) is a useful compendium of procedures and penalties then in force.

Unlike the Board's reluctance to take on pound operations (cited above), trash and animal removal proved a natural for the organization: "The work of the Board of Health has met with such success as to exceed the most sanguine hopes of its friends. It has proven that sanitary measures could not be effected by a little squad of ten policemen [the Sanitary Company], headed by a lieutenant devoid of any knowledge or cause of disease" (Daily Nat. Republican, 23 Nov 1872, p. 4).

[2] (Richards) Evening Star, 5 July 1871, p. 1; (Wolf) Anonymous, "Affairs . . .", p. 184. The increased expense of this arrangement caused some controversy (Daily Nat. Republican, 23 Nov 1872, p. 4).

Garbage collection, including that of dead animals, was described in detail by the Evening Star in 1873.[3] Some was burned and some carried to Broad Creek as landfill. The bodies were taken to the rendering plant at Four Mile Run. "It may be, however, that the small carcasses of . . . dogs, goats, etc. are thrown overboard downstream to save trouble and that they float ashore, creating nuisances."[4]

Complaints about the service led the Board of Health to investigate and recommend reform. "The Board . . . determined that the best riddance of it [garbage] was to give it to Mr. [F.] Sawyer, to be conveyed away with the animals and excretia."[5] The Board also considered the advisability of an ordinance requiring reporting of "any undressed dead animal" within twelve hours. Member Dr. Bliss "explained that many persons who owned such animals failed to report them promptly."[6]

And in September 1873 the Board did indeed issue such an ordinance: that carcasses within the two cities "or in the immediate suburbs" constituted "nuisances injurious to health." Anyone owning "or having charge or knowledge of" such dead animals were required to inform the Board within eight hours under pain of a $5-10 fine. District policy, reflected in the periodic compilations of police regulations, made it illegal to deposit dead animals (along with other types of refuse) in any public land (1887), on any private "vacant lot or open space" (1902), or in the Potomac or other waterways (1921).[7] The Commissioners required transport in a closed wagon by an order of 1893.

Responsibility for collection of garbage officially passed from the City's garbage-master to the Board by a Commissioners order of 1874; the Board immediately contracted the work out. The task shifted from the Health Officer to the Street Cleaning Department in 1900. Both offices continued using private firms for this work, as with other public cleaning, but the news article announcing this change also mentions another player: "the contractor who is said to derive a profit by converting [animals'] bodies into certain materials. But it is understood that his business is concerned almost entirely with animals of the horse kind."[8] (We will hear much more of him shortly.)

Most references tie removal of dead animals to garbage collection rather than street cleaning. A full profile of the city's sanitary operations lies beyond the scope of the present paper, and we will skirt the larger picture to focus only on the removal of carcasses.

The Board's first contractor, Henry and William Turner, proved unsatisfactory,[9] and in 1877 **Felix M. ("F. M.") Draney**[10] received the Board's contract to collect and transport garbage, including dead

---

[3] Op. cit., 14 Apr 1873, p. 4. Researchers of the history of refuse hauling in Washington will want to read this article, and also: the Commissioners order of 1 Dec 1891 specifying the equipage and supplies ordered for the Health Officer's trash crew and other interesting details; the minutes of 18 June 1902 summarized later in this section; and Evening Star, 19 Aug 1891, p. 10. Before 1881 "Washington possessed a 'horse heaven' [burial ground] located on the outskirts of the town" (Wash. Post, 14 Aug 1893, p. 8).

[4] William Wolf, the contractor in 1872, declared that he engaged only in "boiling the carcasses . . . for fertilizer and saving the oil for other purposes," rather than feeding them to his own hogs as alleged (Evening Star, 2 Mar 1872, p. 4). Another irritant: "the fact that the collector of dead animals is in the habit of carrying the carcasses of putrefied horses at a snail's pace along Pennsylvania Avenue . . . and that the stench . . . is too horrible for description" (Evening Star, 19 Sept 1873, p. 4).

[5] He apparently had a general contract for garbage collection (Evening Star, 23 July 1873, p. 4).

[6] Evening Star, 21 May 1873, p. 4; 20 Aug 1873, p. 4. Sawyer imprudently accepted a $1 tip for removing a carcass from a site "which necessitated the remover to be placed at extra trouble"; the citizen then complained to the Board about his own unsolicited offer! (Daily Nat. Republican, 3 Dec 1873, p. 4).

[7] An opinion of the Corporation Counsel (1893) supported the Commissioners' proposed police regulations "concerning the transportation, deposit and disposition of dead animals" but we have no further information on this.

[8] Comm Ann Report, 1875, pp. 20, 456; Evening Star, 20 July 1900, p. 3.

[9] The Turners' contact is included in the Board of Health Ann Rpt for 1875; complaints spangle the Board's minutes of 1876.

animals. John McCauley underbid Draney in 1878 but "set to work making a most signal failure of it" and the Board gave the work to another contractor (H. Clay Jones), who was not much better.[11]

After two underfunded and unprepared contractors (McCauley had to lease equipment from Draney), the city returned to Draney, whose earlier work (at $17,500/year, though now for $15,000/year) "had been very satisfactorily executed." Draney kept this appointment to 1891, when, having just been granted a new five-year contract, he had a payment dispute with the government and withdrew.[12]

From this point on the responsibility for taking up dead animals (and other refuse) became diffuse. A newspaper article of 1891 states that the Health Officer "assumed the business of collecting garbage" that September and was disputing the charges of its new contractor Benjamin W. Clark. A listing of his vouchers showed at least three subcontractors at work collecting garbage and one – "Mr. Mann" – dead animals. Clark also did spot work: the Commissioners approved hiring Clark to remove dead animals and garbage from wharves in December 1891 for $12.50/day, taking the material beyond the District boundary.[13]

Clark sub-contracted collection of dead animals to **Patrick "Patsy" Mann**,[14] who owned a "guano [fertilizer] factory", and had a definite use for animal bodies, particularly horses. Clark charged the city $8/day for animal removal and paid Mann $6/day (including Sundays) for services of one wagon and crew.[15]

By 1893 the subcontract for dead animal removal had passed to Mann's rival, the National Sanitary Company. Mann, however, continued his carcass-collection privately. "It is well known that Mr. P. Mann has been hunting for dead animals for years . . . [for] his bone-boiling establishment down the river." National Sanitary complained, without result.[16]

---

[10] Draney had been a Weigher of Hay, Straw and Fodder in 1873 (Critic-Record, 26 Nov 1873, p. 1) and later worked in the Board of Health itself (Evening Star, 4 June 1892, p. 15). He also received contracts to remove night soil, sprinkle and sweep streets, and livery District government horses. He was active in the local horse-racing scene, being president of the Jockey Club (Wash. Post, 1 May 1881, p. 1; 1 Apr 1890, p. 5; among many) and died in 1892. He was first approved by the Board at its 9 March 1877 meeting; see also Wash. Post, 14 Aug 1878, p. 4, which lists rival bidders for the extension, including Wm. Wolf & Co.

[11] Evening Star, 2 Sept 1879, p. 4; "Mr. McCauley's contract goes into effect today, and up to 12 o'clock he had not reported for duty, and complaints thick and fast were coming in for the delay in removing dead animals" (Evening Star, 2 Sept 1878, p. 1). He had worked for "the Commissary department" (Evening Star, 23 Aug 1878, p. 4). See also Wash. Post, 3 Sept 1878, p. 1 (his men and Draney's struggle over use of the storage dump); 8 Mar 1879, p. 1; and Health Officer Ann Rpt, 1879, p. 129. For Jones, see Wash. Post, 4 June 1880, p. 4. He took garbage and carcasses to a storehouse at 1st and N Streets SW, along the James Creek ("the place designated by the Health Officer" for Draney's use; see Bd of Health minutes, 23 Mar 1877), for shipment downstream. Before 1877 it had been loaded straight onto boats rather than collected on shore.

[12] Evening Star, 2 Sept 1878, p. 1; 7 Sept 1891, p. 2 (the best discussion); 2 Feb 1892, p. 6; Wash. Post 3 Sept 1891, p. 2.

[13] (Vouchers) Evening Star, 24 Oct 1891, p. 6. He worked also at the Department of War, and was an officer of the Washington Fertilizer Company, described below (Evening Star, 6 Jan 1892, p. 3). The wharf-contract was approved by the Commissioners on 1 Dec 1891. Note that several of these contractors had federal or District government jobs.

[14] Born in Baltimore, 1838; died in Washington, 1905. He had a farm implement store on 7th Street NW, and patented an animal trap and harness improvement (Wash. Post, 1 May 1879, p. 4). See his obituary, Evening Star, 19 June 1905, p. 16.

[15] Evening Star, 24 Oct 1891, p. 6; 5 Nov 1891, p. 7. "Every year from 1,800 to 2,000 horses die in the District" (Wash. Post, 14 Aug 1893, p. 8).

[16] (Quote) Evening Star, 5 Nov 1891, p. 7; (legal complaints) 5 Aug 1893, p. 4; 30 July 1895, p. 2. The Health Officer proposed making garbage, offal and dead animal collection monopoly concessions but apparently the Corporation Counsel did not support him (Evening Star, 6 Jan 1892, p. 3). For an interesting account of the

When Washington Fertilizer Company won the contract to remove garbage and carcasses in 1900, the Commissioners minutes noted that several contractors were then splitting this work.[17] It was in 1905 that the District's contract for removal of dead animals was separated from that for other types of rubbish.[18] Patrick and Robert E. Mann won back the contract to collect dead animals (five years at $2,360/year) in 1905, renewed (Robert only) for a similar period and a slightly higher rate in 1910.[19] By 1905 Mann had moved his plant to Four Mile Run, Virginia. The Street Cleaning report for that year tells us that he used one-horse vehicles to collect small animals and two-horse wagons for larger ones.

Citizens took complaints of carcasses to the Health Office before 1900 and after that to the Street Cleaning Department. Beat cops reported dead animals to the MPDC Telegraphic Office rather than directly to the Health Officer; an order of June 1893 that they contact the Health Officer was rescinded three days later, inasmuch as the Superintendent of Police felt "that the present system is more serviceable and expedient." Only in 1910 did the Commissioners require the police to notify the Street Cleaning Department or the contractor of such nuisances.[20]

Carcasses were transported to various companies for use in manufacturing: "We will probably take them to some factory" stated M. H. Chamberlain to the Commissioners when bidding for the contract in 1900.[21] Patsy Mann's plant was well documented because complaints from his (surely very few) neighbors brought on an inspection in 1893. Carcasses were transported to a wharf "at the foot of South Capitol Street" (Buzzard Point) by wagons (not properly air-tight) and taken by scow ("exposed . . . for hours to open air and heat and giving off an intolerable stench") to the plant "about four miles . . . below Giesboro" – "a dilapidated, partially-brick and frame structure." There the bodies were skinned and cut up "in a rough shed on the wharf" and the meat and offal boiled in two iron vats – "turned [into] bone dust, glue and other such useful but not particularly attractive commodities." Mann cleared about $8 on each carcass.[22]

---

unlooked-for complications found in this work see the Harbor Master's Annual Report, 1895, in which he describes his heroic efforts to break up ice on the river "in order to remove the great number of dead horses and other dead animals that had accumulated during the hard freeze."

Joshua N. Warfield, of Cumberland, Maryland, is listed in the 1895 Engineers Ann Rpt as having a five-year contract to collect and cremate garbage and dead animals.

[17] These contractors took different types of material: night soil was generally discussed as a separate task from other refuse, and the Washington Fertilizer testimony discusses the annoyance of finding broken pottery in their "garbage," which should only contain organic matter.

The ambulance of the Washington Humane Society also picked up large dead animals on request and presumably for its usual $5 charge, but we don't know what they did with the remains or why anyone would use this relatively expensive service (WHS Ann Rpt, 1893).

[18] Osborn, "Disposal of Garbage", p. 15, and the Street Cleaning Div's annual reports for this period.

[19] Commissioners Orders/Minutes, 1 Dec 1891; 4 June 1900; 18 June 1902; 6 June 1905; 1 Apr 1910. This is the last such contract mentioned in the minutes but the story can be followed through the annual reports of the Street Cleaning/City Refuse Divisions. An analysis of the cost of this service and an evaluation of Mann's work will be found in the 1909 Street Cleaning Dept Ann Rpt.

[20] Comm Minutes/Orders, 27 June 1893; 19 Nov 1910. A police order of 1909 reminded officers that the work had passed from the Health Department to Street Cleaning.

[21] Per city policy; carcasses not removed within a stated time were taken by the contractor and burned (Evening Star, 30 July 1895, p. 2). This article cites the Commissioners' recent revision of garbage-related regulations (Comm Minutes/Orders, 1 Apr 1895), which in fact says nothing specific about dead animals. "The soap factory" got dead horses.

[22] (Report) Evening Star, 5 Aug 1893, p. 4, with much gruesome detail; the article only mentions horses and cows, but Osborn "Disposal of Garbage", p. 15, says small animals were also "reduced"; Wash. Post, 14 Aug 1893, p. 8, providing more details for both the companies' operations and its use of the carcasses; (response) 12 Aug 1893, p. 16. See also Evening Star, 18 Oct 1893, p. 10; 27 Oct 1893, p. 3; and 30 July 1895, p. 2, in which a rival company

The District moved to incineration of all garbage in 1895 (before that it had been hauled out of town) and ordered construction of two plants, one at long-suffering Buzzard Point in southwest Washington and another where 23rd Street NW met the river (just south of the pound). The former, a "Brown furnace" (the type of system) located "at the site of the old reduction plant at the foot of South Capitol Street [and T]," came onto operation in March 1895. The other, and smaller, facility opened few years later. The South Capitol plant disposed of both garbage and dead animals, probably the smaller ones since the contractor continued to deliver horses to rendering plants.[23]

"City Refuse Regulations" printed in the 1895 Health Officer and the 1903 and 1912 Street Cleaning Department annual reports, along with the work specifications for prospective bidders in the latter two documents and an actual contract in the 1896 report give a good outline of the **legalities** of these procedures. Of course, the details changed over the years:

- Dead animals were collected from 6 AM to 9 PM daily (including Sundays) and at other times if required by circumstances and approved by the city. Failure to do so resulted in a fine. (By 1903 large animals were collected individually upon notification.) The carcasses were required to be "within the digesting tubs" by 6 o'clock the following morning and "completely disposed of" within 24 hours. The contractor should have two vehicles available for collection: "covered wagons . . . as nearly air-tight as possible;"
- The regulations allowed only the city contractor to take carcasses from public spaces but permitted other companies to take them from private property if they used approved vehicles. In acknowledgement to the continuing and successful competition offered by unofficial haulers, the 1912 contract specified that the District government, informing the contractor of a reported dead animal, could not be held liable if the company wagon made the run only to find its prize taken by someone else;
- It is probable the official contractor also made regular collections (on the same contract) from some approved places including the pound and the District's own animal hospital, and (perhaps a separate contract) WHS's Barber Refuge. A proposal of 1892 would have allowed residents to leave bodies of small animals with their trash for collection by the garbagemen, but I have seen no evidence that this was adopted.[24]

Congressional appropriations for the District from 1895 onward authorized five-year contracts specifically for this work until it was taken over by the city in 1923.

We are fortunate to have very detailed testimony on this specialized business from officials of the **Washington Fertilizer Company**, defending the company's performance before the Commissioners

---

(the National Sanitary Company, founded by a former Chief Clerk of the Health Office) located its plant next to Mann's and then lodged vigorous complaints against his facility. Its facility had been at Buzzard Point until it burned. (That earlier factory, by the way, was a lesser creation of Paul Pelz, who had just designed the majestic Library of Congress building; Wash. Post, 23 Oct 1892, p. 10.)

[23] Commissioners Ann Rpt, 1895, p. 14; Health Officer Ann Rpt, 1896, which includes a good photo of the plant and a sectional drawing.

[24] (Pound) see Appendix C9, in which pound-provided carcasses were included in the official count of 1915; (Hospital) Wash. Times, 15 Aug 1897, pt. 2 p. 18; (Barber) WHS Ann Rpt, 1898; (garbage) Evening Star, 6 June 1892, p. 3. For a personal but broader overview of the business see Norton, "A History of Four Generations", written long after these times and from memory by a rendering plant owner, a unique source but not entirely reliable in its details. I have followed the contemporary record here.

in 1902 and illustrating the timeless government-/private-provider argument perfectly. Any serious student of dead-animal-removal-ology will want to review the full text,[25] but here are the chief points:

- Washington Fertilizer's five-year contract (1900-05) required it to collect "all dead animals" throughout the District seven days a week and remove them to a place "within convenient hauling distance" approved by the government. It removed the hides for an unspecified use,[26] and "then there is fat." If the company removed all dead horses in the city (and the testimony says nothing about other animals at all) they would turn a profit. The problem (and their complaint) was that private hauler Patrick Mann was getting their horses first: the company estimated "he gets on the average three or four to my two or three" and at times an even higher ratio. The company figured it had lost 90 horses per month in this way;
- How did this happen? First of all, Mann paid people $1 for each horse while Washington Fertilizer simply picked up the carcass; and second, the company was contractually obligated to take reported bodies from anywhere in the District while Mann just skimmed the more productive areas, mostly the old city. "I had to ride five miles over here just this side of the District line, once on the Bennings [sic] Road, near the Soldiers Home, and out to Tenleytown, and then down pretty near the Mann factory;"
- The company had equipped two cars ("built on sanitary lines") to pick up the carcasses and each run (the "freight") cost it $7, which was not profitable for just one horse. "Q: How many cases do you find where a horse dies and the owner refuses to give him up? A: About two-thirds of the cases. They have found out that they can get a dollar and they refuse to give the horse up. Sometimes the horse is shot in the streets and taken over onto a vacant lot, and unless it is on government ground I just can't get them. We find that Mr. Mann has been notified before we have been notified." The company official admitted that Mann's service was every bit as efficient as his.[27] While sympathetic, the Commissioners had no legal help to offer (exactly as in 1893) – an animal body was in fact private property and the owner could dispose of it in any way he wanted, as long as he did dispose of it.

Washington Fertilizer did get all dead District-owned horses, held by the District veterinarian. As for the ones the company picked up from the street: "These were all an inferior class of horses – colored people worked them to death."

Before leaving this arcane but oddly interesting topic, let us add some **miscellaneous notes**, all gleaned from orders of the Commissioners:

- Transport of dead animals "or any part of any of the aforesaid dead animals" through the District had to be done in an approved sealed container, which could not be left in a public road (16 Aug 1893; for earlier discussion see Daily Nat. Republican, 7 May 1873, p. 4);
- No dead animals "not intended to be used for food" were allowed to be transported in the District without a permit (4 June 1901).

---

[25] Comm Minutes/Orders, 18 June 1902. It must be read from the original volume in the National Archives, but I have left a copy in the Washingtoniana Division.
[26] Ladies shoes, according to Wash. Post, 14 Aug 1893, p. 8.
[27] "Mr. Mann can be reached by telephone whenever his wagon is wanted for the removal of a dead animal" (Evening Star, 5 Nov 1891, p. 7).

Some unlooked-for situations required special arrangements to take up animal bodies:

- In 1894 the Commissioners authorized the Chief Engineer of the Fire Department to hire men on the spot to remove bodies of "persons or animals . . . buried in the remains of large fires," specifying a salary of $1/day for laborers and $3/day for the ad hoc foreman (26 Sept 1894). Previously such removal – of the animal corpses, that is – had been given to the District's garbage contractor (Evening Star, 17 June 1885, p. 5; 25 July 1894, p. 2).
- The Harbor Master two years later was granted funds to hire men to take up dead fish floating at the wharves "for removal by the garbage contractor" (23 Apr 1896). According to the 1902 Washington Fertilizer testimony, that firm had committed to collect "fish offal" from the harbor wharf at no expense to the city. "It was a favor to us" said Commissioner John Ross, but this was unfortunate because the fish mixed with other garbage and so prevented the company from making profitable use of the material: "It prevents us from getting oil out of the other matter that goes in."

The Poundmasters

Samuel Einstein in his prime . . .
Evening Star, 30 August 1890, p. 12

. . . and in his last years
Drawing by Laura Friend Smythe;
Evening Star, 21 March 1909, pt. 7, p. 6

Emil Kuhn
Wash. Times, 14 July 1911, p. 18

George W. Rae
Wash. Times, 21 June 1917, p. 8

The Poundmasters (2)

Walter R. Smith
Evening Star, 16 May 1936

Frank Marks
Evening Star, 15 June 1958, p 17

John R. King, Jr.
Evening Star, 16 November 1969, Magazine, p. 22

Ingrid Newkirk
Evening Star, 8 Sept 1978, p. D2 (Evening Star Collection, Washingtoniana Div)

The Poundmen

Mastiff and John Wells, Best Dog Catcher.

Evening Star, 29 June 1901, p. 28

KING OF DOG CATCHERS DEAD.

John Wells, for 30 Years Employed at District Pound, Succumbs.

John Wells, "king of dog catchers," is dead. For thirty-seven years he was employed on the pound force of the District of Columbia government, where he earned the reputation of being one of the most expert dog catchers that ever engaged in that work in Washington, or any other city. It is estimated that approximately 70,000 luckless canines were captured by him and consigned to the pound during that time.

Regret for his death, which occurred Thursday at his home, 431 20th street, was expressed today by Dr. William C. Woodward, health officer; Harry C. McLean, chief clerk of the health department of the District, and other District officials. At his special request, Wells turned over the first shovelfull of earth in the excavations for the new ten-thousand-dollar pound building, which recently was completed. Funeral services will be held at his residence tomorrow.

Evening Star, 8 February 1913, p. 2

Fox Terrier and Cornelius Parker, Dog Catcher.

Bull Dog Who Has Been in Trouble and Joe Burrell, Dog Catcher.

"Ring," Pound Watch Dog, and Shirley Williams, Dog Jailer and Executioner.

Evening Star, 29 June 1901, p. 28

Scenes from the Dog War

THE BOYS ARE HERE

Evening Star, 30 August 1890, p. 12

A lady saves her dog
Wash. Post, 11 March 1900, p. 22

> RAID ON THE POUND MEN.—On Saturday evening, Poundmaster Einstine and his forces, while raiding on dogs in Swampoodle were set up on by over a hundred residents in that neighborhood, male and female, and for a time the paving stones flew lively. The wagon used in carrying captured animals was completely riddled, and the horses and driver injured. Einstine finally had to call upon Lieut. Kelly for protection and aid, which resulted in the arrest of two of the assaulting party and one pound man.

Evening Star, 10 August 1874, p. 4

Episodes of the Hunt
Wash. Post, 30 August 1891, p. 9

HIS LAST CHANCE

YOU DARE TOUCH THIS DOG

Boys vs. Dog Catchers

Evening Star, 27 Apr 1890, p. 12 (courtesy of Washingtoniana Div, ML King Library, Mansfield Collection; thanks to Ms. Sandy Schmidt for finding this gem.)

Pet Paraphernalia

DOG MUZZLES.

A LARGE ASSORTMENT
OF
DOG MUZZLES,
All sizes, very cheap, at
E. G. WHEELER'S,
Seventh and B streets,
Je12-F,M,W6t   Opposite Centre Market.

Daily National Republican, 12 June 1874, p. 2

FOR SALE—SINGING BIRDS, BIRD FOOD AND Cages, Gold Fish, Aquariums and Fish Food. Largest assortment in the city, at SCHMID'S Bird store, 12th st., two doors south Pa. ave.   n27-1m*

Evening Star, 30 November 1886, p. 2

Buy Your Xmas Present At
C. Schneider's Sons
1207 F Street

Toy Dogs	50c
Dog Sweaters	$1.50 up
All sizes.	
Dog Blankets	$1.50 up
Dog Harness	$1.00 up
Dog Collars	15c up
Dog Leashes	25c up
Dog Whips	25c up

Combs, Brushes, Bells,
Locks and Whistles.

Wash. Times, 9 December 1914, p. 3

Drawing by Laura Friend Smythe;
Wash. Post, 15 April 1900, p. 26

BARBER & ROSS

DOG MUZZLES

The Kind the Authorities Approve

All dogs must be muzzled at once—that's the decree of the Commissioners. And the muzzles must be the right kind. We anticipated this decree and ordered an immense stock of muzzles. They are the kind the authorities approve. They are now on sale. Muzzles for all kinds of dogs at low prices.

BARBER & ROSS
11th and G Streets

Wash. Times, 3 August 1910, p. 3

The Old Pound

Evening Star, 30 August 1890, p. 12

"the present tumble-down institution"
Wash. Times, 26 July 1903, Magazine, p. 6

Evening Star, 26 July 1903, Magazine, p. 6

Einstein and the Pound Wagon
Evening Star, 20 September 1908, pt. 4, p. 4

Evening Star, 30 August 1890, p. 12

The Gas Chamber
Drawing by Laura Friend Smythe;
Evening Star, 26 July 1903, Magazine, p. 6

The New Pound

Evening Star, 15 September 1912, p. 11

Kids look at dogs and dogs look at kids
Drawing by Laura Friend Smythe;
Evening Star, 5 November 1951, p. 21

The Pound's annual Christmas Feast for dogs
Evening Star, 24 December 1930, p. 3

DOG OWNERS' ATTENTION—A meeting of the Dog Owners' Association will be held on Friday, July 24, at 8 p. m., in the parlors of the Chamber of Commerce, Brentano building, 12th & F sts. nw., by courtesy of the Washington Chamber of Commerce. Every member, those who wish to become members, and every friend of the much abused dog, ladies and gentlemen, are cordially invited to meet with us, to take such action as may be deemed best for the preservation of our rights and for the defense of our property in dogs. Be sure to bring with you the blood and spirit of 1776. T. EDWARD CLARK, President.   jy21-4t

The antagonist –
Dog Owners' Assn
Wash. Times, 21 July 1908, p. 2

Dog Catchers
Drawing by Laura Friend Smythe
Evening Star, 2 August 1937, p. 2

Einstein at Rest

Photo by author

WHS Notices

☞ **OFFICE OF THE WASHINGTON SOCIETY FOR THE PREVENTION OF CRUELTY TO ANIMALS,**
CORNER OF ELEVENTH AND F STREETS,
WASHINGTON, D. C., Dec. 22, 1876.
All members and friends of the society are requested to report, by post or otherwise, any cases of cruelties coming under their observation, particularly where animals are confined in obscure places without proper food or shelter, to
THEO. F. GATCHEL,
de22-1w   [Star&Critic1t.]   Pres. S. P. C. A.

Daily National Republican, 30 Dec 1876, p. 4

☞ **THE ANNUAL MEETING OF THE** Washington Humane Society will be held TUESDAY EVENING, the 10th INSTANT, at the rooms of A. S. Pratt & Sons, Sun Building, 1315 F street, at 7:30 o'clock.
ARTHUR MacARTHUR, Prest.
J. B. T. TUPPER, Cor. Sec.

Wash. Critic, 10 Jan 1888. p. 2

THE WASHINGTON HUMANE SOCIETY, rooms 10 and 12 Corcoran Building, 1430 F Street northwest, will thank citizens who will report any dereliction of duty or incivility on the part of its agents.
jy4tf   A. S. PRATT, President.

Evening Times, 6 July 1899, p. 3

THE EXECUTIVE COMMITTEE OF the Washington Humane Society offers a reward of $100 to the person who will furnish the evidence leading to the apprehension and conviction of any one who has hitherto docked a horse in the District of Columbia by cutting the solid part of the tail. AMELIA S. STOWELL, Secretary.

Wash. Post, 13 Feb 1900. p. 2

NOTICE

Please Blanket Your Horses

To leave them standing without shelter or covering is a violation of the law and will be prosecuted as such.

HUMANE SOCIETY.

Wash. Times, 10 Jan 1912. p. 12

Washington Humane Society

1231 New York Avenue N.W.
Tel. National 2846

Organized 1870 under special Act of Congress. Only organization in District of Columbia authorized by law to initiate prosecutions for cruelty.

The Society invites and carefully investigates, through its agents, complaints of cruelty to children or animals.

It is dependent upon dues of members and gifts to carry on its work.

Membership Invited.

Evening Star, 20 Jun 1937, p. 13

NOTICE TO DOG OWNERS
The dog muzzling law is now in force and all dogs when on the street or in other public places must wear a muzzle, unless on leash accompanied by some one. The Humane Society regards this as a cruel and unnecessary law, but it should be obeyed until October 1 next. Therefore the society earnestly advises all owners, when taking their dogs out, to leave off the muzzle but have the animal on a leash and under full control.
WASHINGTON HUMANE SOCIETY.

Evening Star, 6 June 1930, p. 3

TEAMS FOR HIRE.
TEAMS SUPPLIED FOR ALL PURPOSES AT short notice.
TEAM OWNERS' ASSOCIATION.
1047 Jefferson st. n.w.; phone W. 44X.
ja3-tf,4

The antagonist
Evening Star, 8 Jan 1910, p. 15

WHS Graphics and Shelter

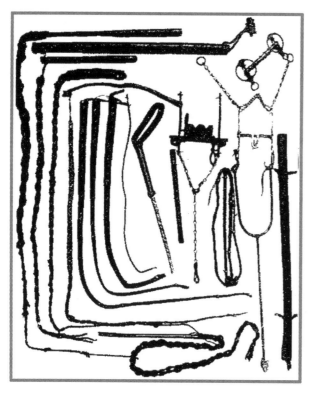

Horse-control implements
WHS Ann Rpt, 1900

WHS Ann Rpt, 1891

WHS Annl Rpt, 1901

WHS Annl Rpt, 1906

WHS Graphics and Shelter (2)

WHS Ann Rpt, 1892

WHS Archives

The Barber Shelter
Drawing by Laura Friend Smythe;
Wash. Times Magazine, 13 April 1902, p. 8

1895 Municipal Trash Incinerator

Health Officer Ann Rpt,, 1896

PART THREE

The Later Commissioner Period
(1913-40)

Folks have dogs but don't buy tags. A crowd collects to watch the chase. A little colored fellow runs up to the house. "They're after yo' dawg, Mis' Caroline," he yells. (Evening Star, 3 Aug 1924, p. 11)

The first half of the twentieth century saw two important developments in the District's (and probably nation's) animal-control situation (wandering farm animals having already largely disappeared):

- The regular threat, or at least fear, of rabies outbreaks largely disappeared, converting homeless dogs from dangers to pitiable waifs in need of help;

- Citizen-organized shelters, oriented more to the welfare than control of strays, bred and flourished. These shelters cared for cats as well as dogs.

These trends grew in urbanized Washington until they overwhelmed the traditional pound operations and ultimately subsumed them. Important official studies and new laws and regulations of the late 1930s and early '40s cemented these changes.

Sources: For this period our sources remain the same as the previous one but generally become scantier. Commissioners Annual Reports shrank back to one volume by the early 1920s and WHS annual reports have been lost. Many local newspapers are not available on-line (and therefore searchable) because of copyright restrictions.

CHAPTER TWENTY

The Pound Under Later Poundmasters

Samuel Einstein died on 9 July 1911, succeeded as poundmaster by **Emil Kuhn** on 13 July.[1] His appointment seems to have been a patronage effort; Kuhn was an active Republican, earlier employed by the Pittsburg "department of charities" (sic), but for the previous three years an elevator operator in the House of Representatives office building until a change of administration there. His acknowledged inexperience with the work and ignorance of such issues as rabies and muzzling ("He said he never had paid much attention to the question") led to skepticism of his abilities. In spite of this unportentous start, press references picture pound operations continuing smoothly and we have no reason to think that Kuhn performed unsatisfactorily. In 1914 Kuhn resigned and moved to New York.[2]

Kuhn's successor, **George W. Rae**,[3] had worked as a Health Department inspector since 1896 and had just been appointed master carpenter at the Capitol when he was recommended for the position by Health Officer Woodward, the Postmaster General and a number of Congressional and business heavyweights. He was an active Democrat and belonged to the Shrine and Knights Templar. Rae was "the kindliest of persons, who will put down a little gray kitten that has clamored upon his shoulder and . . . tell you about the pound."[4]

Rae died on 16 February 1920 when the pound truck was broadsided near Dupont Circle by a speeding Army truck. (Several poundmen were injured in this accident; Joe Burrell, the longest-serving man at the pound, could not return to street duty and was made on-site manager of the facility.) Rae, both professionally and socially popular, was much mourned. The city provided a pension for his widow, for he had died on duty. In all his years of public service he had taken only one day of annual leave. "Mr. Rae's death came as a shock to employees and officials at the health department, who had been laughing and joking with him . . . only an hour before the accident."[5]

Upon Rae's tragic death the Health Department assigned an inspector (Walter Smith, below) to oversee pound operations before appointing local veterinarian **Edgar R. Sando** (often "Dr. Sando", noted as the first licensed veterinarian to hold the post) poundmaster on 1 March 1920. "A strong advocate of

---

[1] Kuhn's picture will be found in Wash. Times, 14 July 1911, p. 18; Evening Star, 27 Aug 1911, pt. 4 p. 3. Inspector C. H. Welsh, of the Health Department, filled in as poundmaster in the intervening week; his photo appeared in Wash. Times, 29 Oct 1922, p. 7. There were twelve applicants for the vacancy.

[2] Evening Star, 13 July 1911, p. 5; Wash. Times, 14 July 1911, p. 8; Wash. Post, 15 July 1911, p. 14; 4 Jan 1914, p. 16. Testimony relating to the District's 1913 budget capsulized Kuhn's situation: "There was not any man in the pound service who was competent to succeed the late very capable poundmaster. The present poundmaster has proved to be a very efficient man" (Hearings . . . 1913 (House), 11 Dec 1911, pp. 163-164).

[3] Sometimes misspelled Ray. The courtly Rae's image is in Wash. Times, 21 June 1914, p. 8; Evening Star, 16 Feb 1920, p. 2.

[4] Wash. Post, 4 Jan 1914, p. 16; Wash. Times, 21 June 1914, p. 8. His appointment began on 3 January 1914 (Comm Minutes/Orders, 3 Jan 1914) and he was reported as "doing good work" at Congressional budget hearings in 1916 (Hearings . . . 1917 (House), 5 Jan 1916, p. 391).

[5] Wash. Herald, 17 Feb 1920, p. 2; Evening Star, 16 Feb 1920, p. 2; 17 Feb 1920, p. 2; 18 Feb 1920, p. 7.

handling impounded animals in the most humane manner," Sando stayed on the job only two months, resigning on 4 May for reasons not now known.[6]

Sando was succeeded immediately upon his resignation (perhaps because the Health Department knew the vacancy was coming) by **Walter R. Smith**,[7] an inspector in the Department since 1905.[8] A farm boy from Virginia "raised with dogs and horses," he combined a sincere love of his animal wards (as he viewed them) with a strict enforcement of the law reminiscent of his predecessor Einstein.[9] His tenure seems to have been a successful, well-managed period publicized mostly when he gave dogs to children and civic groups at Christmas or advised citizens on good pet care.

Smith was "a civilized human being," a "friend of dogs," "a genial man [who] gives both the dog and owner the benefit of the doubt when any one accuses him of unrightfully holding a dog."[10] His salary was raised in 1930 "in recognition of his knowledge and interest in dog lore." Smith died after several months of failing health in 1936. "A kindly faced, elderly man, with graying hair and twinkling eyes died here yesterday and all the dogs whose ribs are spare, whose eyes are stark with hunger, lost the best friend they'll ever know."[11]

The vacancy drew 21 applicants "and each has a series of endorsements," probably because of the now-generous salary. The Commissioners vowed that political support would not sway their decision – that they were looking for a cynophilist (dog-lover), preferably one already within the District government – and in July chose **Frank B. Marks**, a native Baltimorean who had most recently served as Chief of Watchmen at the District Building.[12]

In Marks the city found the ultimate dog-lover: "My chief aim in life is to help dogs," he declared; "the District's most militant dog lover," as the Evening Star called him. He is the only poundmaster on record disparaging his predecessor: "When I took over the pound . . . it was the dirtiest, filthiest mess I ever saw . . . I rebuilt [it] and made it so the dogs had a little comfort." Whatever the pound's condition in 1936, a visitor in 1953 reported the place "clean and orderly . . . and Mr. Frank Marks . . . politeness itself."[13]

In fact, over the years Poundmaster Marks became the darling of local animal-lovers and an annoyance to his District employer. He publicly complained about supervision of the pound by MPDC,

---

[6] Wash. Herald, 17 Feb 1920, p. 2; Evening Star, 29 Mar 1920, p. 2; 4 May 1920, p. 1. A "Dr. Edgar R. Sando, District dairy farm inspector" died in 1933 at age 35. It is possible that at age 22 this was the same man in 1920 (Wash. Post, 21 Apr 1933, p. 3).

[7] Photos in Evening Star, 24 Dec 1930, p. 3; 23 Dec 1933, p. 10; Wash. Post, 16 May 1936, p. 26.

[8] Evening Star, 16 May 1905, p. 16. Articles reporting his death say 1907 but this earlier notice seems decisive.

[9] (Kindness) Evening Star, 2 July 1933, p. 17; (enforcement) Evening Star, 6 May 1921, p. 1; 27 June 1928, p. 39; 30 July 1931, p. 10. Smith had his adventures: he was once "arrested in line of duty" as an apparent dog thief (Wash. Times, 6 May 1921, p. 1).

[10] "The late W. R. Smith . . . brought a tiny, new puppy to [his friend C. M.] Towers in the palm of his hand one day. The terrier had been born at the pound without part of a leg. 'I can't put this puppy in the gas chamber,' Smith said." Towers adopted it (Evening Star, 15 Aug 1936, p. 7).

[11] (Quotes, respectively) Evening Star, 2 July 1933, p. 17; Wash. Post, 16 May 1936, p. 26; 16 Dec 1933, p. 27; Evening Star, 15 May 1936, p. 14; for an earlier paean, see Evening Star, 20 Mar 1922, p. 2. The 1930 Congressional act raising the poundmaster's salary also reinstated his status as an MPDC special officer.

[12] Joseph I. La Salle acted as poundmaster in the interim. Wash. Post, 5 July 1936, p. M1; Evening Star, 5 July 1936, p. 13; 5 Aug 1936, file clipping Wash. Div; 15 Aug 1936, p. 7; 15 June 1958, p. 17; Comm Minutes/Orders, 4 Aug 1936 (his appointment; the job just about doubled his salary). Good photos of Marks are in Wash. Post, 19 Dec 1949, p. B1; Evening Star, 9 May 1957, p. 68; 15 June 1958, p. 17. His assistant, Clyde Underwood, can be seen in Evening Star, 14 Oct 1936, p. 25, recounting his contretemps with a dog-loving messenger boy.

[13] Evening Star, 9 May 1957, p. 68; 15 June 1958, p. 17; (letter) Wash. Post, 13 Feb 1953, p. 22.

gummed up the works of the Animal Allocation Board (of which he was a member; both these developments are discussed briefly in the Afterword), quarreled with the principal of neighboring Randall Junior High School, and vociferously allied himself with all anti-vivisectionists. His mandated retirement in 1953 (because of age) was withheld for four successive years due to enthusiastic support from the public. On 30 June 1958 Marks retired, leaving behind daily stress from his 22 years work and the recent requirement that some of his cherished dog friends be turned over to medical laboratories ("It has been an emotional strain to face daily this difficult situation"), succeeded by his assistant, John R. King.[14]

The poundmasters of this later period all, as far as we can tell today, handled their responsibilities competently and with sensitivity. Compare this record to the collection of thieves and non-entities appointed by the Corporations and Territorial Government to operate the contractor pounds. A striking point of each, beginning with Rae, was his well-publicized love of dogs. It is hard to think that earlier Health Officers specified "dog-lover" as a job requisite, as was done in 1936 – "dog-hunter" was then the more desired qualification.[15]

The larger shifts in Washington society that enabled this new posture have been already indicated and will be summarized again, but in speaking specifically of these 20th-century poundmasters we must acknowledge their enormous debt to their progenitor, Einstein. The worthy Einstein likewise appreciated animals, but he also knew his duty to the human population of the District. His successors worked upon a structure that he had built patiently and carefully over 39 years, and they inherited established procedures and standards to guide them, a luxury Einstein had not enjoyed. It was his stern enforcement of District laws over many years and the inevitable urbanization of Washington that permitted the softer, more loveable personas of Rae, Smith and Marks.

Before investigating the pound and its activities in this later period it would be good to review the key legal document relating to animal control in the District after the turn of the century, a **special committee report from 1939**.[16] In October 1938 the Commissioners, responding to continued citizens' complaints of "barking dogs, cackling chickens, etc." (as one letter-writer put it), appointed a select committee to review police regulations regarding "so-called nuisance conditions arising from keeping of dogs, fowls and pigeons in the District," composed of an Assistant Corporation Counsel, the Director of the Bureau of Sanitary Inspection, and the Assistant Superintendent of Police. This blue-ribbon group studied the legalities of District policy and received public opinion in a series of hearings, issuing its report on 23 January 1939. The report made comprehensive and very specific recommendations regarding dogs, fowl, pigeons, wild animals and bees, all of which were enacted on 24 February and will be described below.

The particular interest of the committee's work regarding the city's ordinances up to its own time is its close legal analysis of their foundation and authority, which helps explain a certain persistent looseness

---

[14] Above references, and ("emotional strain") letter, Commissioners to Rep. George Andrews, 16 Apr 1958 (National Archives, RG 351, Entry 21 "District General Files", folder 1-105 "D.C. Pound Master"), which continues: "This [record] is unprecedented in the history of the District . . . Government and is a tribute to the high regard in which Mr. Marks is held." This file contains many letters testifying to the admiration and support of local animal-support organizations ("I believe that Mr. Marks has made one of the finest and most unanimously-liked pound masters in the United States"; letter, John L. McMillan to Commissioners, 28 Mar 1956). He was "the embodiment of Commissioner Hazen's ideal of a dogcatcher" (Wash. Post, 16 Oct 1936, p. X19).

[15] In further contrast to Hoover et al., the Health Officer specified in 1912 that the new poundmaster must be "a man of industry, intelligence, and courtesy in dealing with the public" and have some knowledge of dog breeding (Hearings . . . 1913 (Senate), 16 Feb 1912, pp. 81-82).

[16] National Archives (RG 351, Entry 21 "District General Files", folder 1-100 "Animals, Fowl & Wildlife"). A copy has been deposited with the Washingtoniana Division. The Commissioners appointed the committee on 22 July 1938 and approved its recommendations on 24 Feb 1939.

that runs through the successive regulations. "The difficulty encountered by the committee on this question [control of dogs] arose from the fact that Congress itself has withdrawn from the Commissioners all but a general power to carry into effect the former's own specific enactments on this subject." That is, the Commissioners could not initiate regulations of broader import than those already approved by Congress, a handicap doubtless felt throughout District governance.[17] Nonetheless, the committee in its recommendation on leashing took city regulations into new territory, as shall be seen.

Pound work after about 1900 centered largely on pets, **farm animals** having largely disappeared from the District. Capture of these animals fell steadily from 105 in 1896 to 17 in 1905 and stayed at about that number into1940 (Appendix C3). Such events became a matter of curiosity rather than routine, meriting occasional brief filler articles in the local papers.[18] This condition was reflected in District regulations also; a review of Commissioners orders and police regulations after the 1890s shows no new rules regarding larger animals, and the important 1939 District-government review of animal laws did not mention them.[19]

The only new regulations issued related to smaller animals, specifically the continuing issue of **chickens**. (Note the increasing number of registered "chicken houses" recorded in Appendix C1 – from 1,232 in 1915 to 2.424 in 1923, not a development expected by modern readers.)[20] These rules saw seven revisions in 1939-40 and others into the 1950s, always further restricting their latitude, but in 1939 dropping restrictions for **homing pigeons**.[21] The pigeon question carried unique considerations. As early as 1896 the Police Court (which seems to have regularly issued eccentric rulings) declared that the "fowl" of standing restrictions "means the common domestic chicken or hen, and does not apply to pigeons,"[22] although in fact the birds remained under the regulations. Furthermore, these birds had a small but intense circle of owner-supporters,[23] and the military trained them in its Washington facilities for its own

---

[17] For an illuminating analysis of the tangled results caused by conflicting authorities as they applied to dog-related regulations, see Evening Star, 31 Oct 1943, p. 42.

[18] We must record that the pound took a coyote in 1916 (Poundmaster Ann Rpt, 1916), and in 1937 a monkey and an alligator (Hearings . . . 1938 (Senate), 18 May 1937, pp. 4-5). The bag for 1945 consisted of three rabbits, two goats and four pigs (Evening Star, 23 Dec 1945, p. 8).

[19] Quite unexpectedly, the Corporation Counsel was asked in 1944 whether the pound could charge a fee for redeemed "stray horses and other animals." What prompted this query – from the poundmaster himself – we do not know; perhaps a few horses still pulled milk carts through the city. The Counsel responded that this long-practiced fee was not justified by local law and that such charges were only legal if levied by MPDC for its holding of the animal. Surely the question was moot by this time, and the practice itself seems to have gone out of memory (Counsel Opinions 17 Mar 1944; Vol. 54, p. 762).

[20] At least one cote – used for breeding squabs – still stands in the District, at the Tudor Place mansion in Georgetown.

[21] Much interesting background material on the chicken question will be found in the National Archives (RG 351, Entry 21 "District General Files", folder 1-113 "Fowls"), including a summary of the legal questions involved, citizen input pro and con on proposed restrictions in 1926, and a full set of papers relating to the case of a resident keeping fowls at his residence in the 3700 block of Northampton Street NW covering 1931-38. There is also record of a 1955 discussion on the conditions of chicks kept in pet stores.

[22] Cited in Counsel Opinions, 3 Oct 1896 (Vol. 7, p. 137). This curious document equivocates on the question under review – whether the neighbor of a pigeon-owner was culpable for putting out poison on his own property to permanently quiet the birds' annoying cooing. The Counsel had declared in favor of another neighbor-poisoner in a similar contretemps involving murdered chickens in 1897 (Counsel Opinions, 16 Nov 1897; Vol. 8, p. 222).

[23] In 1926: Washington Racing Pigeon Club – 24 members, D.C. Racing Pigeon Club – 22, Aero Racing Pigeon Club – 32 (National Archives, RG 351, Entry 21 "District General Files", folder 1-113 "Fowls"). And I must record this curious factoid, that in 2016 the state of Maryland hosted 109 licensed falconers (Wash. Times, 28 Dec 2016, p. A12.).

use ("The 25-foot [proposed restriction] might have [a] disastrous effect upon the flying of pigeons belonging to the U.S. Army").[24]

In 1939 the Commissioners issued an order prohibiting the keeping of "**captured wild animal[s]**" as pets without a permit.[25] Raising **bees** came under restriction in the same year.[26]

The tale of the city's **dogs** in this later period continued as before but with less passion, the rabies/muzzling/get-your-license/catch-dogs pattern set since 1900 persisting, and would be tedious to recount here year by year. Annually, after new testimony from the Health Officer describing the danger of **rabies** and the number of people bitten, the Commissioners extended their **muzzling** edict – for full years in 1911-20, July-September in the next five years, June-September from 1926 until 1934, and May-September then to 1944.[27]

A scan of typical headlines through the period shows the continuity of the dog question in Washington:

1911: "Muzzle Law Not Well Enforced"; "[Experts] Raises Doubts of Rabies"
1912: "Crusade Upon Dogs"
1913: "Rabies Suspect Cases Are on the Increase"
1914: "Order Muzzling Dogs Is Extended for Year"
1916: "Dog-Bite Epidemic Rouses Authorities to Seek Cure"
1917: "Failure to Muzzle Dogs Means Arrest"
1918: "Police to Enforce D.C. Law Against Unmuzzled Dogs"
1919: "D.C. Dogs Bite 208 Persons in Year"
1921: "Pets Free to Bite for 9 Months"
1924: "Police Kept Busy by Vicious Dogs"
1925: "Dr. Fowler to Urge Muzzling of Dogs"
1926: "Extra Dog-Catcher Force Advocated"
1930: "Muzzling of Dogs Is Opposed by [WHS]"
1931: "Saturday Deadline for Licensing Dogs"
1933: "Dog Owners Warned to Obtain Muzzles"; "'Mad Dog' Cry Seldom Justified, Records Show"

Against the background of this familiar routine, the pound's operations showed some differences from Einstein's time. With the intense pressure to take in illegal canines generated by continuous publicity of bites and rabies but the pound force back down to four men and one wagon,[28] the Health Officer declared that the poundmen could do no better than their best and pleaded for police help. MPDC Superintendent Sylvester ordered his men to arrest owners of unmuzzled mutts in 1912 but they also

---

[24] Ibid. Echoed a representative of the clubs: "Homing and carrier pigeons serve [a] useful purpose. Other pigeons are [a] nuisance" (from the 1926 testimony cited above).
[25] The first victim of this regulation was a legless news vendor, Eddie Bernstein, who lost his attention-grabbing monkey Gypsy (Evening Star, 30 June 1939, p. 20; for a good profile of Bernstein and Gypsy see John Kelly's columns in Wash Post, 18 Aug 2019, p. C3, and 25 Aug, p. C3). The District's General Files (National Archives, RG 351, Entry 21 "District General Files", folder 1-109 "Animals in Public Space") contain a 1958 letter from a downtown resident asking permission to walk his pet ocelot along M Street NW "in the same manner as any dog . . . owner would want to do" – turned down.
[26] National Archives (RG 351, Entry 21 "District General Files", folder 1-118 "Keeping of Bees and Hives").
[27] The shortened period was ordered over objections of Health Officer William C. Fowler. Explained Commissioner Rudolph: "We feel that the poor bow-wows lead a curtailed life for three months and that they should be allowed to run free the other nine months" (Wash. Times, 20 June 1921, p. 9).
[28] Blame for this decrease was always assigned to an indifferent Congress.

faced limits on what could be accomplished. Soon authorities began encouraging private citizens to bring civil suits against owners in cases of attack.[29]

Other proposals floated (without resulting action) included: prohibiting dogs from running at large overnight, as was then common practice;[30] and requiring owners to justify possession of such pets.[31] The Health Officer also took a new tack in fixing blame for these perennial problems on a new culprit: "There are two causes of dog bites – vicious dogs and vicious children." That youngsters regularly teased dogs was shown by the preponderance of injuries among children, he pointed out. "A dog is bound to resent too severe mauling and may bite," agreed MPDC Superintendent Raymond Pullman.[32]

The muzzle problem reappeared in the guise of the "figure-eight muzzle" – "which is merely a strap passing over the nose and under the mouth." "Entirely inadequate," according to authorities.[33] The absence of lobbying on these various issues by citizens' groups, as had earlier happened, is striking.[34]

Leashing remained an uncertain area because, as seen above, the District could not extend regulations beyond that allowed by Congressional fiat, and established laws only required restraint of vicious dogs. The District Corporation Counsel's 1908 declaration that dogs "in leash" were not "at large" and therefore not required to wear muzzles during emergency periods was written into the muzzling orders of 1923 and thereafter.[35] Leashing as a required year-round restraint was finally codified in 1939, at the suggestion of the special committee, but absence of any reference to the practice in the 1878 Congressional law made it ineffective until the 1945 legislation.[36]

During this same period leashing on the street became the norm of respectable society (hunters had long known it). Newspaper articles referring to pedestrians with their leashed pets increasingly appeared, and also complaints of dogs not restrained, beginning about 1910 and seemingly the standard practice after 1920 (although ads for leads never reached the number of muzzle ads).[37]

To take this story of city canines to its end, in 1941 the Commissioners authorized the Health Department to seize any dog suspected of rabies for observation, and two years later leashed dogs were

---

[29] Evening Star, 26 May 1912, p. 5 is the earliest instance of this suggestion that I find. Woodward: "If some of the people bitten by vicious dogs would sue owners . . . it would be a great step in preventing future cases" (Wash. Times, 27 Sept 1916, p. 5).

[30] A "pernicious practice . . . followed to considerable extent in this city" (Woodward; Evening Star, 5 June 1911, p. 1). It was difficult for the poundmen to take them in the dark (Evening Star, 26 May 1912, p. 5).

[31] Was Woodward serious in this, or simply expressing his frustration? He complained furthermore that they ate food fit for humans (Wash. Times, 30 Oct 1917, p. 4).

[32] Wash. Times, 27 Sept 1916, p. 5. John Heap, of WHS, strongly agreed and added a blast at the whole concept of rabies (Evening Star, 11 June 1930, p. 8).

[33] Wash. Post, 31 Oct 1917, p. 4; Evening Star, 24 May 1933, p. 37.

[34] The Safety-First Association supported muzzling in 1917 (Wash. Times, 13 Dec 1917, p. 8).

[35] See Evening Star, 29 Mar 1920, p. 2; Wash. Herald, 10 June 1922, p. 4, et al. for later references to the new practice.

[36] This glitch is explained in Evening Star, 24 Oct 1943, p. 19; and 31 Oct 1943, p. 42. And even after that – see the Afterword, in which Congress again tackled this momentous question in 1961.

[37] On the odd side of leashing: Two fashionable New York ladies were reported in 1907 thus accessorized: "A little gold clamp fastened to the bottom of the skirt at one side is snapped into the rings of the dog collar . . . A good many persons wondered what would happen if two of the skirt-leashed dogs took a notion to mix it up" (Wash. Times, 21 Apr 1907, Woman's Magazine p. 8); 1922 saw a new fashion trend: the "dog-collar belt" or "dog-leash belt", which was quite thin (Evening Star, 12 Apr 1922, p. 30); and for "the latest freak of society," the baby leash, see Wash. Times, 4 Aug 1909, p. 7. (I cannot resist passing on this tidbit: In 1922 Parisian ladies dyed their pets to match their ensembles; Wash. Times, 6 Aug 1922, Magazine p. 5.)

made exempt from the muzzling requirement during the annual rabies emergency.[38] (The 1943-45 period was the last major rabies scare. Inoculation of dogs had become common by then.) At the urging of Health Officer George Ruhland, the Commissioners sent to Congress proposed **amendments** to the 1878 law requiring vaccination for issuance of dog licenses and authorizing leashing in public places. This act passed on 5 July **1945**. Leashing became compulsory on 23 July 1945 and muzzling ended in the District on the same day. Vaccination against rabies entered the city's regimen with the same legislation, bringing dog-control regulations largely to those of today.[39]

Judging from the occasional references to passengers taking their pets on streetcars and trains there was no restriction in this regard. A Corporation Counsel memo of 1944 tells us that the District itself had no regulations on the question at that time but that the Capital Transit Company allowed animals to ride only if restrained (held, leashed, muzzled or in a carrier), to the annoyance of many passengers.[40] The 1939 act banned dogs from private property without the proprietor's permission. And for the inevitable doggie habit of chasing cars, the only notice I find is a 1939 amendment to the District's traffic regulations (suggested by the special committee) exempting drivers from dog-injury claims involving unrestrained pursuers.[41]

We should note that as the urban fabric grew the problem of rabies and dogs became an inter-jurisdictional concern. Alexandria, Arlington and Staunton (in **Virginia**), and Chevy Chase, Takoma Park and Prince George's County (**Maryland**), all reported similar efforts between 1907 and 1926.[42] Statistics from the 1910s show that about half those taking the Pasteur cure at the Marine Hospital lived outside of DC.[43]

Just how many provable cases of rabies occurred remained a matter of debate. Newspapers continued to write of the "rabies season" and the Health Officer and Police Superintendent (strongly supported by Commissioner W. Glynn Gardiner) warned regularly of "the continued presence of rabies in the District." Increasingly, neighboring jurisdictions with looser muzzling laws were blamed for this problem.[44]

The Health Officer's meticulous statistics (Appendix C6) included in the Commissioners annual reports show only a handful of actual deaths from rabies before 1917 and none after then. Of course, Dr. Pasteur's treatment presumably saved many bite victims. The more salient figures are the number of animals and humans found to have actually contracted the disease, a determination made by the Department of Agriculture's Bureau of Animal Industry laboratory (for animals) and the Marine Hospital

---

[38] During an exceptional winter rabies emergency of 1943, dogs were required to wear both muzzles and leashes on the street; those brought into the District without a veterinarian's certificate of health were quarantined; Marks suspended sales at the pound (Evening Star, 24 Oct 1943, p. 19).

[39] Evening Star, 12 Jan 1941, p. 3; 8 Feb 1945, p. 17; 19 Apr 1945, p. 32; 13 July 1945, p. 1; 23 July 1945, p. 16 (for an illustration of the difficulty of implementing new procedures in a town full of lawyers); Wash. Post, 2 Dec 1943, p. B1. Evening Star, 14 July 1945, p. 17 describes the vaccination plans in detail, including the difficulty of obtaining sufficient vaccine. District-sponsored vaccination clinics became common at this time, including at the pound (see, e.g., Wash. Post, 7 July 1948, p. B2).

[40] Counsel Opinions, 29 July 1944 (Vol. 55, p. 65). Seeing-eye dogs were exempted by the company from muzzling.

[41] Comm Minutes/Orders, 24 Feb 1939.

[42] Respectively: Wash. Post, 6 Aug 1907, p. 5; Wash. Times, 3 June 1922, p. 4; Evening Star, 21 Oct 1921, p. 37; Wash. Herald, 17 Dec 1910, p. 16; Evening Star, 30 June 1926, p. 26; Wash. Times, 30 Oct 1917, p. 4.

[43] These are given in Appendix C6. As with all rabies-related statistics, the numbers are confused; for conflicting figures see Wash. Times, 30 Oct 1917, p. 4.

[44] Reminding one of the present debate over illegal guns in the city. The continuing crisis also fueled a constant demand for more money for pound operations. A useful summary of local dog-regulations will be found in Wash. Post, 22 Mar 1972, p. C1.

(for people).[45] Suspicious animals caught on the street were quarantined at the pound under observation by a Health Department veterinarian.[46] If found healthy but tagless they then entered the standard holding-execution process, while those taken directly from owners were returned to their masters.[47]

The Health Officer made painstaking compilations of "suspected rabid", "confirmed rabid", "bitten by suspected rabid", ". . . by confirmed" and so forth under the title "Communicable Diseases Among Animals". Newspapers also often reported such statistics, generally accompanied by accounts of recent attacks. In spite of this documentation it is difficult to get a feel of the rabies situation in Washington for the period with any confidence. This is due to the unpredictable fluctuations in official statistics, compounded by direct contradictions between these figures and those cited (on attribution to the Health Officer) in contemporary newspaper accounts.

Why was the number of patients given the Pasteur treatment nearly twice that of reported bite victims in 1912? Why did Woodward claim two deaths from rabies in 1915 when his own report for that year shows none? Or that in 1914, 67 District residents were treated when the official report showed 16? And many more of the same.[48] Probably the safest thing to say is that a good number of persons – in the several hundreds – were bitten by dogs every year, that a disproportionate share submitted to the painful Pasteur treatment (it was given on any suspicion of rabies),[49] and that fortunately very few actually died. The public and official fear was probably exaggerated but certainly real.[50] "Washington has been virtually free of rabies since 1931," we read from a later article, and the last authenticated case occurred in 1946, although minor, localized scares occurred for years.[51] Only occasional reports of bites by rabid cats appeared.

Licensing procedures, longer established than muzzling, proceeded smoothly in this later period. The Police Court in 1911 unhelpfully ruled that tags need only be worn when off the owner's property, a view challenged by the Corporation Counsel in 1911 and again in 1914.[52] We have no information on how this affected impoundment. Otherwise the licensing process, handled by the Tax Office, continued with no interruption until 1931, when the Auditor (overseeing tax collection) tried to foist the duty onto the District Assessor, unsuccessfully. The ensuing confusion led to a short period of non-issuance due to lack of proper forms.[53] Poor management of the work led to dismissal of several staff in the late 1930s.[54]

---

[45] Some sources say the Hygienic Laboratory, U.S. Public Health Service (Health Officers Ann Rpt, 1912, p. 35; Wash. Times, 30 June 1919, p. 13).

[46] "This service requires the greater part of the time of a veterinarian, who is also detailed to the inspection of dairy farms" (Health Dept Ann Rpt, 1935).

[47] Wash. Times, 30 Oct 1917, p. 4; Evening Star, 28 June 1922, p. 6. Eighteen were returned to their owners in 1913 (Wash. Post, 4 Jan 1914, p. 16); see Appendix C3. There was no charge for properly licensed animals returned.

[48] Official figures from Health Officer Ann Rpt, "Communicable Diseases of Animals"; others: Wash. Post, 4 Aug 1915, p. 12; Wash. Times, 3 Aug 1914, p. 5; 30 Oct 1917, p. 4; 29 Jan 1918, p. 3.

[49] Especially after the Marine Hospital Service began offering it for free in 1909. "Many persons have availed themselves of the opportunity of receiving treatment" (HO Ann Rpt, 1909).

[50] See Wash. Post, 25 Sept 1933, p. 18 for a brief rebuttal of the scare.

[51] Evening Star, 15 Aug 1936, p. 7; 13 Apr 1971, p. 1. "No dogs were found to be suffering from rabies during . . . 1932. Rabies has been steadily declining for several years past and at present seems to have practically disappeared in the District of Columbia" (Health Dept Ann Rpt, 1933). Indeed, after 1938 the Health Officer ceased to report on rabies at all, describing examination of suspect canines under the rubric of "duties of the laboratory staff" rather than investigation of communicable diseases. Rabies after the 1940s were believed carried by foxes and other wild animals rather than dogs (testimony, Paul L. Romig, 8 May 1973;`` National Archives, RG 351, Entry 45 "Hearing Files, 1967-1974", "Dogs, Stray"); this testimony is very interesting – Romig headed Animal Disease Control for the District's Department of Human Resources and gave many useful details.

[52] Counsel Opinions, 25 Sept 1911 (Vol. 22, p. 43); 17 Oct 1914 (Vol. 25, p. 65).

[53] Evening Star, 12 July 1931, p. 1. Evening Star, 15 Aug 1936, p. 7, gives a good picture of the office's procedures.

(An article of 1936 tells us that during the Harding administration the District Collector of Taxes, C. M. Towers, began holding the first 100 licenses for prominent Washingtonians, #1 being gold-dipped and reserved for the president, if he had a dog.)[55]

The only change in licensing procedure during this time is that by 1936 these funds were deposited into the U.S. Treasury.[56] The 1945 law revised the dog tax to $3.

The number of dogs impounded annually by Smith was actually greater than by Einstein – while the latter took curs in the range of 2,500-3,000 (other than the exceptional years of muzzling or licensing campaigns), Smith's haul averaged 4,500-5,500 yearly. About 25% of these were brought in voluntarily by owners.[57] How many dogs did the District hold in these years? The number of licensed dogs in 1921 was 10,947, and in 1931, 19,123; it reportedly doubled in one year (1936) to 25,000, and the 1939 committee report estimated 40,000 total, of which about 10,000 were unlicensed. "This . . . figure is not believed to be an overstatement in view of the present population here of over 600,000." Marks pessimistically estimated 65-70,000 dogs in Washington in 1941, of which only 25,000 had tags.[58]

The matter of **cats** showed very little change after 1913; all cats at the pound had been captured by citizens or delivered directly by their owners. "The District has no authority to capture stray cats, so residents are denied the fun of seeing a perspiring man with a long-handled net scale fences and climb trees after elusive cats."[59] Every cat reaching the pound went into the gas chamber, as before.[60] The total number impounded rose from about 500 in 1904 to over 4,000 in 1915 and then declined steadily to 1,200 by the end of our study period.

One innovation in cat-catching was the introduction of traps, described by the Washington Times in 1914: "An ingenious device called a cat trap has recently made an appearance . . . It is an oblong wooden box fitted with a trap door, and when the inquiring cat enters for a tempting morsel . . . the door is sprung." The pound supplied these devices to homeowners upon request and then picked up the captured tom. 183 cats were taken this way in 1914 and 231 and 204 the following two years.[61]

The 1939 committee found no public interest in instituting cat laws or legal foundation to do so.

Basic **pound operations** continued **after Einstein** much as they had under him; a brief – and rare – description of a pound run from 1937 could have been written in 1900 except that the wagon was

---

[54] Memo, National Archives, RG 351, Entry 21 "District General Files", folder 1-104 "Dog Tags".

[55] Evening Star, 15 Aug 1936, p. 7. We have no information whether the President paid the tax but can guess not.

[56] Ibid.

[57] It is difficult to compare this rate with that of Einstein's time – we only have figures from his last years, but the various written accounts of earlier pound operations seldom speak of voluntary surrender of dogs. Marks gave the same proportion as Smith. He also said the pound held about 50 dogs on the average day (Hearings . . . 1938 (House), 9 Feb 1937, pp. 88-91).

[58] Evening Star, 4 Oct 1921, p. 2; 12 July 1931, p. 1; 15 May 1936, p. 14; Hearings . . . 1942 (House), 22 May 1941, pp. 55-59. "The Nation's Capital, being a spot where the unmarried, childless and itinerant are likely to yearn for a dog about the apartment" (Evening Star, 15 Aug 1936, p. 7). Dr. Milton Bosley, a prominent local veterinarian, estimated there to be 100,000 pet owners throughout the metropolitan area in 1936 (Wash. Times, Jan 1936, date unclear, file clipping Wash. Div).

[59] Wash. Times, 2 July 1920, p. 13, a very wittily-written article ("Cats Lead 'Dog's Life' Here – 30 Tons of 'Em Made into Soap"). In fact the Commissioners order of 1912 required such (amusing) procedures; the writer should have said "has no capacity to capture". Poundmaster Kuhn's take on District cat policy is given in Appendix D8.

[60] Summarized Health Officer Woodward: "We put them in a covered cage, turn on a little poison gas, and it's good-bye cat." In 1917 the DC Congress of Mothers and the District PTA proposed the charming little campaign: "Kill a Cat for Your Country," saying felines gave children mange (Wash. Herald, 24 Apr 1917, p. 5).

[61] Wash. Times, 21 June 1914, p. 8; 27 Sept 1916, p. 5; Wash. Post, 4 Jan 1914, p. 16; Poundmaster Ann Rpt, 1914-16.

motorized and at least one of the poundmen appears to be white.[62] The labor force available remained a persistent question. Although in Einstein's last years his workers had been increased spasmodically as rabies scares/muzzling enforcement ebbed and flowed, his successor Kuhn had dropped back to one wagon (from two)[63] and four – and at times three – poundmen. Health Officers and succeeding poundmasters complained energetically to a stingy Congress, which cut funding for the poundmen from $3,000 to $2,000 in 1912, and in 1937 slashed the poundmaster's salary. "With our present equipment, we can never hope to overtake the work," moaned Woodward. In 1914 the poundmaster operated three wagons, but this surely was temporary, since he had only three men two years later.[64]

Several factors besides the growing number of Washington dogs in the city and repeated muzzling edicts contributed to the distress of Kuhn and Rae. Reported the Washington Post in 1912: "The new pound now being built . . . will require a larger force of men than the old one," without explaining why.[65] A very measurable burden was the obligation to pick up unwanted pets and captured cats from residences. "The removal of animals in this way . . . imposes an enormous amount of labor on the [Health] department, 4,573 visits having been made during the year . . . As the requests that come in during one day are . . . scattered over the entire District . . . and as all require reasonably prompt attention, the time consumed in . . . such visits can readily be conceived."[66]

The Health Officer, in his 1936 annual report, recorded that "inasmuch as the dog pound is not primarily a health service," the Commissioners had removed the service from his jurisdiction and placed it directly under their own supervision. This threw more clerical work on the poundmaster, work which had previously been done by Health Department staff.[67]

Woodward's 1914 annual report made three specific recommendations to improve the pound service: appointment of an assistant poundmaster[68] and night watchman; higher wages for the force; and purchase of "a proper motor vehicle" to replace the horse-drawn wagons. With the increasingly scanty records of this period it is difficult to know what became of the first idea, although we have noted earlier that in 1920 the disabled Joe Burrell was made "Keeper of the Pound", the highest level an African-American achieved at the pound in our study period. By 1926 the pound staff included a chauffeur and watchman (paid

---

[62] Evening Star, 2 Aug 1937, p. 2.

[63] The pound owned two wagons (heavy and light teams), "but we have only horses enough to haul one team at a time." With this restriction the poundmaster sent the heavy team out in the mornings and evenings and the light team in mid-day (Wash. Herald, 26 May 1911, p. 6; Evening Star, 29 May 1913, p. 5). Hearings . . . 1914 (House), 3 Jan 1913, p. 193, has a good description of the street operations: the heavy wagon (worked by a driver and two runners) handled captures from the street; the lighter one (one or two men) made pick-ups from houses.

[64] Wash. Post, 1 Sept 1911, p. 2; 23 June 1912, p. 9; Wash. Herald, 26 May 1911, p. 6; Wash. Times, 21 June 1914, p. 8; 27 Sept 1916, p. 5; Evening Star, 30 Mar 1937, p. 6. Unfortunately the Health Officer and Poundmaster annual reports begin to lose their detail at about this time, so we have to rely more on chance newspaper notices.

[65] Op. cit., 23 June 1912, p. 9. Wash. Times, 27 Sept 1916, p. 5, mentions a stableman, probably attached to the Health Department directly, which kept all its horses there.

[66] Poundmaster Ann Rpts, 1913, 1914. The 4,573 trips of 1914 retrieved 7,042 animals, to give an idea of how tedious these many one-stop runs must have been. They averaged 5,000 in the late 1930s (see Appendix C3). Marks testified in 1941 that about 25 such runs were made daily, covering on average 50 miles (Hearings . . . 1942 (House), 22 May 1941, pp. 55-59). The Animal Rescue league had the same complaint (below).

[67] This was a recommendation of the U.S. Public Health Service. Health Dept Ann Rpt, 1936; Comm Minutes/Orders, 23 June 1936. From this point on the meager Poundmaster Annual Reports appear as independent items at the very end of the Commissioners Annual Reports.

[68] Whose salary was proposed at $720 annually in the 1917 District budget request (Hearings . . . 1917 (Senate), 31 May 1916, pp. 118-119).

$1,020 annually between the two;[69] $1,320 and $1,260 respectively in 1936). A clerk was paid $1,260 in 1936.[70] Health Department financial reports show that salaries for poundmen stayed at $510 yearly to at least 1920, and had risen to about $1,100 by 1936.[71]

The poundmaster's pay rose from $1,500 to $1,680 in 1917, and to $3,080 by act of Congress in 1930 after an extremely flattering report by the Senate Committee on the District (below). However, the 1938 budget dropped his salary by over one-third to $2,000. This drastic decrease originated partly from the separation of the pound and its budget from that of the Health Department; now the pound's expenses came under detailed scrutiny of Congress, and the poundmaster's salary was seen to be near that of even high-ranking MPDC officers. But Marks' rough handling by Rep. Ross Collins in the 1937 hearings is inexplicable:

Collins: What are your qualifications for this job, Mr. Marks?
Marks: I think –
C: We do not want any thinking.
M: I mean I feel the bill –
C: We do not want your opinion of it. We want to know what your qualifications are.[72]

The Commissioners bemoaned this decision every year thereafter[73] and Committee members in 1941 could not explain it (Rep. Young: "I understand his salary for some reason . . . was reduced."). Marks continued his work conscientiously but naturally resented the loss ("He is complaining very much, Senator"). Perhaps his later antagonistic relationship with the District had some roots here. By a sort of financial legerdemain the poundmaster's salary increased a pitiful $200 in 1941.[74]

As for the motorized pound truck ("an old [1914] Cadillac chassis with a body put on it"),[75] it was included in the District's FY1918 appropriations and entered service in the summer of 1917. Alas! No advance comes without its own problems: by the end of that year the pound had expended its gasoline funds and threatened to shut down all runs for want of fuel, something that never occurred with the horses. It also had mechanical trouble: "It breaks down nearly every time it goes out," complained Fowler in Congressional testimony of 1921.[76]

---

[69] The watchman made $600 in 1917, when Health Officer Fowler pleaded with Congress for a raise: "It has been very difficult to keep anybody there at all" (Hearings . . . 1919 (House), 14 Dec 1917, p. 265). The 1910 WHS report on pound conditions referred to a "caretaker" with a bed at the facility ("Report of the Special Committee Appointed to Visit the City Pound", 6 Dec 1910; filed with WHS Exec Comm minutes).

[70] Perhaps this is the "assistant poundmaster" whose position was upgraded by the Commissioners in 1937 (Comm Minutes/Orders, 15 Oct 1937).

[71] (Burrell) Wash. Post, 25 Sept 1921, p. 10; (salaries) Health Dept Ann Rpts, various years; Schmeckebier, The District of Columbia, p. 368; Comm Minutes/Orders, 23 June 1936 (which lists all pound employees and their salaries); Evening Star, 30 Mar 1937, p. 6.

[72] Hearings . . . 1938 (House), 9 Feb 1937, pp. 88-91. Collins was particularly upset that Marks was not a veterinarian, something that had never been required.

[73] Sen. Thomas: "Do you mean you cannot get a dog-catcher for $2,000 a year?" Harry F. Wender (President of the Southwest Citizens' Association): "You can get a man for $1,000 . . . because times are such that you could get a man to work for almost anything, but that man [Marks] is worth $3,080 for the type of work that he does. The efficient work that he performs . . . is worth the additional $1,080" (Hearings . . . 1939 (Senate), 8 Feb 1938, pp. 456-457).

[74] Hearings . . . 1939 (Senate), 8 Feb 1938, pp. 78-82; Hearings . . . 1942 (House), 22 May 1941, pp. 55-59. Both explain how this was accomplished.

[75] The new 1940 truck was a 1½ ton Chevrolet model with a special body (Comm Minutes/Orders, 11 Oct 1940).

[76] Hearings . . . 1923 (House), 12 Dec 1921, p. 474. Hearings . . . 1914 (House), 3 Jan 1913, pp. 193-194 – the earliest incidence of this proposal – gives a detailed discussion, including Woodward's assurance that the new

A few minor changes in procedure might be noted: Food for the pound dogs now came from the National Zoo – "all their bones and scraps," an expense figured at $637 in FY 1940; dogs redeemed or purchased from the pound had to have tags and vaccinations to be taken (per the 1945 act); newspapers advertised pound pooches gratis, as they perhaps did also for shelters; the pound service received a two-way radio in 1944. On the other hand, complaints about too-few men and breaking-down trucks continued as before.[77]

The Senate District Committee's **1930** report on the proposed raise of the poundmaster's salary[78] painted a picture of that gentleman's **duties** that Einstein would have immediately recognized:

"The qualifications for the position are tact, judgment, administrative ability, and knowledge of the diseases of dogs." – "He is frequently called upon to perform dangerous tasks and on numerous occasions has been attacked." – "If several claimants appear for the same animal, the PM must act as judge and jury in ascertaining the true owner." – "The PM has supervision [of] seven employees and the pound comprises a group of buildings covering almost a quarter of a city block. To do his work well [he] must possess administrative ability." – "The PM [has] the duty of enforcing the pound laws. An error of judgment may involve him as well as the District in a court action." – "The PM is practically always on duty. He is subject to calls at all hours, and is practically a 24-hour man. The clerical work must frequently be done at home at nights or on Sundays." – "If no claimant appears the animal is killed or sold. In case of public sale the poundmaster acts as auctioneer – a quite frequent occurrence." – "The field duties of the [PM] are frequently more hazardous than those of the police. [He] is given neither a pistol nor a pension. The present incumbent has on several occasions been assaulted and injured."[79] – "The PM must render daily, weekly, monthly, quarterly and yearly reports. A report of fees collected must be made every day."[80] – "The PM is twice a bonded officer. Yet [he] must pay the premiums for both bonds out of his meager salary."

The report continued that in spite of these onerous tasks Poundmaster Smith had steadily increased the number of animals taken, fees collected and dogs licensed, all this "in large measure, attributable to the activity of the poundmaster . . . and . . . accomplished without additional facilities or cost to the Government and only after a hard fight against stern opposition from the public."

The separation of the District pound service from the Health Department in 1936 led to appearances by Poundmaster Marks at annual Congressional hearings on the proposed DC budget, and this testimony gives us our first direct view of any poundmaster since Einstein wrote his own reports thirty years earlier. In preparation for hearings on the 1942 budget (in May **1941**) Marks prepared a précis of his **duties**, followed by requests (and justifications) for increases in support. As a final nod to one focus of this long research – the District poundmaster – I copy verbatim his very brief and, I think, incomplete job description:[81]

---

vehicle could not be used "for pleasure" by off-duty employees; Hearings . . . 1923 (Senate), 13 Feb 1922, p. 137; Wash. Times, 18 Dec 1917, p. 3 has a good photo. The District bought a replacement in 1928.

[77] (Food) Hearings . . . 1938 (House), 9 Feb 1937, pp. 88-91; (ads) Hearings . . . 1942 (House), 22 May 1941, pp. 55-59; (radio) Hearings . . . 1938 (Senate), 18 May 1937, pp. 78-81; Evening Star, 23 May 1944, p. 6. Irate dog-owners remained a constant, even to the 1970s; see Evening Star, 12 Aug 1977, p. B1.

[78] Senate Comm on DC, "Giving Police Power".

[79] The Commissioners rejected (on legal grounds) Poundmaster Marks' request that his men be given the same police powers that he carried (Comm Minutes/Orders, 30 Mar 1937). The poundmaster's MPDC Commission, suspended at some earlier time, had been re-instated with the 1930 pay raise.

[80] These procedures were revised in 1941. Comm Minutes/Orders, 26 Mar 1941 gives all specifics.

[81] Hearings . . . 1942 (House), 22 May 1941, pp. 55-59. Several of the hearing transcripts cited in this section include Marks' verbal descriptions of his work.

- Enforcement of laws relative to impounding of domestic animals at large in the District of Columbia;
- Supervision and responsibility for administration of work of the pound, maintaining all records, actively directing the operating activities, handling of correspondence, preparation of annual and other reports, budget estimates, etc.;
- Supervises investigations concerning complaints regarding vicious animals and in his discretion directs the impounding of all such animals;
- Collects and captures unlicensed and unlawful stray dogs and impounds for redemption, sale or disposal. All known vicious animals or those suspected of having rabies are held in quarantine in the pound for examination by a District of Columbia veterinarian.

Rep. Karl Stefan kindly added remarks to the poundmaster's testimony that would have much gratified Einstein so many years earlier: "I want to remark here, Mr. Chairman, that . . . an ordinary layman looks at a poundmaster as the old-fashioned dog-catcher. That work has been really raised to a very high level in recent years in that the dog-catcher now has become the boys' friends instead of the boys' enemy. They have got to be highly scientific men today where they really teach the public to be not only kind to animals but make the animals useful to the public. And . . . they can eliminate an epidemic here – look at this man handling 60,000 dogs in this community ten miles square, and innumerable cats and other animals . . . And you know he really becomes a very important man in our community rather than the old-fashioned dog-catcher with the iron hoop that we all used to see."

And so the District pound after Einstein, with some modernizations (new building, motor truck), in its basic procedures (mechanics of runs, method of holding and killing animals, rabies protocols) looked very much like the pound under Einstein, certainly in his last years. But a more **basic transformation was changing the pound** both in its own outlook and its perception by the public: the pound was gradually moving from a stern enforcer of laws and executioner of unwanted animals to a friendly place where happy if unfortunate four-legs and kind-hearted two-legs came together.

We have seen that poundmasters from Rae on were publicized for their warm love of animals. Beginning with the 1920s the pound itself took on this image. What factors brought about this transformation?

- Farm animals had essentially disappeared from the District. Those that remained (it is safe to conjecture) were confined to proper farms, such as the Soldier's Home, and no longer bothered average citizens, certainly not on city streets and their front yards;
- Gradually the reality and perception of rabies subsided, and with it the fear of unfamiliar dogs and cats;
- Public habits changed: the custom of turning dogs outdoors overnight and while on vacations slowly disappeared,[82] and the popular and legal acceptance of leashing on the street allowed people to keep dogs without seeming to threaten others or inadvertently add to the stray population. We can assume also that the increased traffic and density of the city made owners less inclined to allow dogs to run free;
- Most importantly, the number of loose mutts living in alleys and fields had greatly diminished, to the point that most residents probably were unused to seeing the packs of "mangy curs" which their

---

[82] Discussed at more length below in the section on WARL. The 1939 regulations requiring leashing on-street would have made this (in theory) illegal. How would you turn out a dog overnight from a large apartment building?

grandparents had accepted – perhaps resignedly – as normal. Einstein himself had declared that the stray population had been largely brought under control. In 1897 Einstein estimated the ratio of licensed to unlicensed dogs to be 7:6; the 1939 committee estimated it at 3:1.

The broad effect of these developments was that by the 1920s the general populace of the District no longer looked upon animals a source of food or work (farm animals and street horses), or a common nuisance (loose dogs and cats), or dangerous (rabies). Increasingly animals in the city played the role of lovable pets, and as such generally deserving of the public's – and poundmaster's – care rather than control.

Over these years the pound morphed from "the Gehenna of the city's dogs" to a cheery place to buy a pooch, and even an object of charity. In the early 1930s claims appeared in the local press that virtually all pound dogs were adopted. "The public thinks of the establishment as a death house. But . . . it really is a house of life. Only those dogs that are incurably diseased are destroyed. . . For others found to be ill careful nursing and medical treatment are arranged, while dogs in unimpaired health [find] new homes . . . Some are sold and some are practically given away but the great majority are placed . . . Thus the trip to the pound is the beginning of a new lease on life."[83] When dogs remained untaken in late 1933 Smith broadcast an appeal by radio which "about cleaned the pound of stray dogs"; a generous businessman chipped in $20 so that "ten dog-loving children . . . could each get a pet."[84] The pound saw a run of purchases each December for Christmas gifts: "We would like to accumulate as many as possible to meet the Christmas demand," declared Smith in 1933.[85]

The growing demand for pets and the evolving views of successive poundmasters of their responsibilities toward their furry wards brought a change in sales practices that would have astonished Einstein: "Persons purchasing dogs from the poundmaster are required to give satisfactory evidence that the animal will be properly cared for" (1920). Warned Poundmaster Marks in 1948: "Prospective purchasers must pass a rigid inspection . . . We are as careful in putting out our dogs as if they were babies offered for adoption."[86]

By 1930 animal lovers began to donate funds to the pound in touching if rather sentimental ways. In that year "a kindly-disposed woman of Vermont" provided Thanksgiving dinner for the inmates: "a menu fit for a king – of dogs . . . liver, pork and sausage, [and] extra rations of milk" for pups. Smith erected a (donated) Christmas tree at the pound annually, decorated with sausages and cakes for each dog ("provided by a local dog lover"). Local radio station WMAL's Jim McGrath broadcast live from a

---

[83] Evening Star, 2 July 1933, p. 17. The article says that Poundmaster Smith had a waiting list for some breeds and sent dogs as far as to Arizona!

[84] Evening Star, 22 Dec 1933, p. 17. "Good dogs are never destroyed at the pound, purchasers being numerous. In fact charming stray mongrels find homes when the pound exhibits them" (Evening Star, 15 Aug 1936, p. 7). The claim that almost all dogs were placed seems incredible and is not borne out by the annual reports (see Appendix C3); perhaps this applies only to those taken on the street, surrendered animals being destroyed with no waiting period.

[85] Wash. Post, 16 Dec 1933, p. 27. "Poundmaster W. R. Smith said Cabinet officers, senators, socially prominent women and troops of boys and girls are among those demanding dogs for Christmas gifts." Rep. Frank Boykin once purchased 100 pups for his friends in Alabama, where there apparently was a shortage (Evening Star, 15 June 1958, p. 17). See also Evening Star, 22 Dec 1926, p. 3; 14 Oct 1928, p. 3.

[86] Evening Star, 29 Mar 1920, p. 2 (this included proper licensing and a signed statement that the animal would not be used for "scientific or experimental purposes"); Wash. Post, 7 May 1948, p. B2. By the way, the writers of this time had not yet taken on the word "adopt", as is commonly used today; the earliest use of the word I have found is from 1948.

pound run in 1936. When the Post reported on two pound dogs apparently dead from heat the following year an "avalanche of calls and offers of aid" flooded Marks, allowing him to purchase sun-shading awnings.[87]

In intent (and in publicity) the pound was moving toward the Shelter model then coming of age.

---

[87] (Thanksgiving) Evening Star, 27 Nov 1930, p. 17; (Christmas) 24 Dec 1930, p. 3; 23 Dec 1933, p. 10 (both with photos); (radio) Evening Star, 6 Aug 1936, p. 14, Wash. Post, 8 Aug 1936, p. 9; (awnings) Wash. Post, 15 July 1937, p. 4.

CHAPTER TWENTY-ONE

The Washington Humane Society
(Continued)

When we last left the Humane Society (1912) it had beaten off a series of legal and legislative challenges by various enraged animal-owner associations and seemed at the peak of its influence. In fact, the organization was beginning a long period of stagnation.

From the moment that the Society turned over its street work to paid agents (with gratifying results) it tied itself to a relentless fund-raising regimen. Although WHS regularly portrayed itself as dependent solely on donations, court fines from successful prosecutions actually provided a substantial if decreasing part of its income.[1] With the numbers of both horses and its own agents decreasing, this was a dead end, as acknowledged by WHS Secretary, John P. Heap, in 1923: "Owing to the advent of the automobile . . . the work of the Society has been greatly lessened, and its income curtailed to such an extent that it now employs only two agents . . . This is unfortunate, but the Society has no money to spend in advertising either itself or its needs."[2]

In response, several lady members planned to form a "Women's Auxiliary" from among their friends ("some of the best-known social leaders will be on the 'force'") to protect horses on the street. Nothing came of this, but it did produce some amusing caricatures in the local press.[3]

In the late 1910s WHS began greater outreach, mostly to raise **funds** but also to increase **membership**. Its traditional grass-roots projects continued – 1912 saw the effective revitalization of elementary school-based Bands of Mercy, and in 1916 a plan to enroll all local Boy Scouts as junior members.[4] New efforts included a Christmas candy sale (1919); an annual Thanksgiving appeal (from 1919); a "musical fairy play" (beginning 1920, which became for a few years a major society event); and

---

[1] 1901 – $3,064 (= 60% of that year's income); 1911 – $4,114 (48%); 1917 – $2,453 (30%); 1925 – $85 (sic; 3%).

[2] Heap, "History". pp. 64-65. "According to [President James P.] Briggs, the fines have greatly diminished during the last few years as a result of the decline of the horse as a medium of transportation" (Evening Star, 23 Nov 1919, p. 5).

As for the claims of all-voluntary financial support, see for example the statement of President Smith in declaring the annual Thanksgiving appeal in 1923: "the Society, which received support only from public contributions" (Evening Star, 17 Nov 1923, p. 30), although there continued a thin trickle of court fines coming in.

[3] Wash. Times, 12 Mar 1914, p. 3. A faint echo of this plan was a later dust-up between a group of WHS ladies and Poundmaster Smith, who they accused of roughness to dogs ("If you beat them, we'll beat you; if you choke them, you'll get choked"; clipping labelled Wash. Times, 27 June 1922 but apparently mismarked, in a Health Department Scrapbook, D.C. Archives).

[4] (Schools) Evening Star, 6 Jan 1912, p. 18 and many other after that; (Scouts) Wash. Times, 2 Mar 1916, p. 16. Re-establishment of the Bands began in 1910 but the first stable group only formed in 1912 (Evening Star, 24 Mar 1912, p. 26).

a vaudeville show (1922). The Society joined its colleague-organizations in celebrating "Be Kind to Animals" week every April from 1916 on.[5]

Throughout this period membership statistics for WHS remained reasonably stable (285 in 1917, rising to 413 in 1921, and then drifting downward to 356 in 1925, and 285 in 1932).[6] Available funds reported by the Treasurer in the first half of the 1920s also show healthy if varying levels (1919 – $7,347; 1922 – $10,722, to give the parameters). Nonetheless, newspapers of the early 1930s carried pathetic pleas from the Society's members for funds ("As a friend of all animals, . . . I appeal for aid in behalf of the Washington Humane Society in its efforts to secure new members now, acutely feeling the effects of the general business depression in its rapidly decreasing funds"). In 1936 WHS began to place general ads in the papers trolling for members ("The Society invites and carefully investigates . . . complaints of cruelty to children or animals. It is dependent upon dues of members and gifts to carry on its work. Membership Invited").[7]

The number of horses in Washington dropped rapidly in this period. Heap estimated the population at 13,050 in 1911 and 4,350 in 1921. WHS agents killed 315 irredeemable animals in 1911 but only 45 in 1919 and 27 in 1923, almost all horses.[8] The number of stables, liveries and other horse-related business in the District fell from 68 in 1900 to 19 twenty years later; the last commercial stable closed in 1932. Nonetheless, it was only in the early 1930s that dog-work definitely replaced horse-work as the focus of WHS.

An ancillary casualty of the dwindling number of horses was the increasing disuse/misuse of the Society's precious drinking troughs, which dropped from a high of 145 in 1923 to 108 in 1938 – "which the [District's] Water Division feels is 108 too many." Widened streets, new streetcar tracks, careless motorists, neglect and age all took their toll. And, of course, they had fewer equine customers. Press accounts listed other, more contemporary uses of the installations: "Handy footrest . . . supply of water to wash the car . . . ammunition for children's squirt-guns . . . water to fill radiators with" and so forth.[9]

WHS had always pursued **issues** beyond those of draught animals; as the post-World War I period progressed the organization was forced to look to these for a new raison d'etre. The most obvious was the anti-vivisection movement, which commanded much of its efforts in the 1920s, working with the Society for the Humane Regulation of Vivisection. (WHS President Smith was also president of the International Conference for the Investigation of Vivisection.) The Society's great foe in this question was the Friends of Medical Progress.[10]

Sporadic campaigns included: feeding birds and squirrels during winter months; opposition to sale of chicks and baby rabbits at Eastertime; the annual muzzling orders, of which WHS disapproved but

---

[5] (Thanksgiving) Wash. Post, 30 Nov 1919, p. E15, and later years; (candy) Evening Star, 23 Dec 1919, p. 2; (play) 17 Apr 1920, p. 5, and later years; (vaudeville) 6 Nov 1922, p. 3; (Be Kind) 26 Feb 1916, p. 12. Newspaper articles about the organization drop noticeably after 1913.

[6] WHS Ann Rpts, and Evening Star, 12 Jan 1932, p. 8.

[7] Evening Star, 12 Jan 1932, p. 8, et al. For an example of the ad, see Evening Star, 20 June 1937, p. 13. This decline of interest was a nationwide trend even in 1921, according to President Smith (WHS Ann Rpt, 1921).

[8] Extrapolated from Heap, "History"; WHS Ann Rpts. In 1919 all animals so killed were horses (Wash. Times, 22 Mar 1920, p. 9). The WARL Executive Committee stated the obvious at its 31 May 1939 meeting: "There are very few old horses seen on the street at the present time."

[9] Evening Star, 9 May 1929, p. 24; 20 Mar 1935, p. 5; 23 July 1937, p. 17; Wash. Post, 13 Aug 1938, p. 13. "Approximately 25 old horse troughs throughout Washington . . . are maintained – now – for the use of birds" (Evening Star, 5 May 1963, p. 46). One entered the collection of the Smithsonian Institution.

[10] (Intl Conf) Evening Star, 14 Nov 1926, p. 27. See WHS Ann Rpt, 1922 for an excoriating account of the opposing group.

acquiesced to; and a few less sustained interests such as the shooting of dogs by thieves (WHS called for gun control); hit-and-run drivers "who fail to stop after injuring animals";[11] branding of police horses; the condition of bald eagles displayed in institutions such as the National Zoo; cropping dogs' ears; and care for animals stranded by a marooned rodeo. In 1940 the Society offered free identification tags to "all animal owners."[12]

The Society realized its long-held goal of purchasing a motorized ambulance in 1917.[13]

This gradual change of focus led a letter-writer of 1932 to point out that much cruelty to horses continued in the city (citing the Highway Bridge over the Potomac and the Horse Bazaar), concluding: "The activities of the Society seem to be confined to pet cats and dogs. No notice seems to be taken of the faithful and long-suffering horse. Before the Humane Society asks for help let it help the horse."[14]

In 1919 WHS proposed to revive its work with abused children, revisiting its role in that issue discarded several years earlier. The Society did indeed hire a children's agent in 1925 (William J. Moore, of the New York Society, who seems to have acted as a legal counselor rather than a street agent) while noting that virtually all cases of child abuse were handled by the District's Board of Children's Guardians (the same situation that had taken the Society out of the matter earlier). This effort must have been fairly anemic – the lack of later annual reports does not allow us to study statistics but it never made the local papers. WHS still advertised this service in 1936.[15]

As the Humane Society struggled to find its way in the evolving cityscape of motorized Washington, the organization entered a stormy period of unhelpful internal squabbles typical of decaying volunteer groups.

One sign of WHS's basic weakness was its increasing reliance on its paid secretary and (volunteer) treasurer, **John P. Heap**,[16] who served in one or both of these capacities from 1905 to his final illness in 1936. Through his constant writing (he edited the Society's newsletter) and public testimony Heap was the steadying force and public face of WHS through its troubles of the 1927-33 period, and in that way a great benefactor. Nonetheless, when an organization comes to depend for such a long time on the presence (and direction) of one (salaried) individual it indicates a rot in both its ostensible governing body and general membership, whose roles he has come to fill.

In 1927 WHS began a series of internecine battles that left much blood on the floor. I will outline these here without too many specifics, more to illustrate the dynamics of Washington's humane movement at the time than to record the full history of the Humane Society (which is not my purpose anyway). The sister organizations mentioned are described in the next section.

The first great battle in this **Time of Troubles** occurred at WHS annual meeting of 1927, when former president Hutchins, supported by Heap and Mrs. Truman G. Palmer, president of WARL, deposed Smith in a disputed election (Palmer taking his place) and then declared a union of the two organizations,

---

[11] Also a concern of WARL (Evening Star, 26 Aug 1939, p. 9).
[12] (Birds/squirrels) Wash. Times, 16 Jan 1912, p. 3 (MPDC officers were pressed into service); Evening Star, 10 Jan 1930, p. 8; (chicks) 18 Apr 1922, p. 14; 19 Apr 1935, p. 16; (muzzling) 6 June 1930, p. 3 (an annual announcement); 11 June 1930, p. 8; (shooting) 26 Apr 1933, p. 8; (drivers) 16 Feb 1927, p. 3; (branding) Wash. Post, 16 May 1915, p. 12; (eagles) Evening Star, 13 May 1924, p. 4; (ears) 12 July 1925, p. 56; (rodeo) 16 Apr 1931, p. 3 (see also Wash. Post, 27 May 1923, p. 2); (tags) Evening Star, 17 Oct 1940, p. 35.
[13] WHS Ann Rpt, 1917.
[14] Wash. Post, 13 Jan 1932, p. 6.
[15] WHS Ann Rpts, 1921, 1925; Wash. Herald, 23 Oct 1919, p. 3; Evening Star, 11 June 1925, p. 25. Remember that the earlier agent for children had been on the MPDC payroll, while Moore – as long as he remained on staff – further drained the organization's straitened resources.
[16] For his obituary, see Evening Star, 19 July 1936, p. 10.

neither of which was in particularly good shape. "The activities of the Humane Society . . . have been diminishing for several years and there has been inefficient duplication of work [between the two organizations]." Smith objected that a merger put the Society's greater treasury at risk; more importantly, he strongly disapproved of WARL's practice of killing animals it could not place.[17]

It is a pity that we don't have the 1927 annual report, for Smith opened the meeting with a great blast at his opponents. The published exchange between Smith and Hutchins seems amusing to us today but surely saddened those of their time:

Smith: We are going to lose our trust funds.
Hutchins: Kindly put my motion.
S: Kindly stop interrupting.
H: I'm going to keep on interrupting as long as you keep on talking.
S: I'm going to keep on talking as long as I wish.
H: I'm sick of your insinuations.[18]

Smith's friend James P. Briggs, vice president and former acting president of the Society took the new officers to court as illegally elected. After some legal shoving the court apparently agreed with Briggs, since Smith was listed as president in later articles. Incoming President George Barnett proposed a cooperative arrangement with WARL the following year, admitting that the Humane Society "was not justified in asking the public for financial support because 'the results obtained are not equal to the expenses' [Barnett's words]." One year after that, Smith's supporter Briggs was arraigned in Police Court for mistreating dogs in his care.[19]

The next battle occurred solely within WHS, in 1930, when then-President Victorine Elmore accused the same Briggs (a vice-president) and ten members of the Executive Committee (including John Heap) of improperly transferring Society funds to Briggs' other organization, the Humane Education Society, and other similar causes. Needless to say Briggs et al. objected; all were eventually cleared.[20]

Mrs. Elmore continued as president of WHS to 1943 (with one year out). Ernest Smith returned as first vice-president in 1933. No further disturbances were reported, but in a sad last look at WHS the organization's secretary reported to the 1940 annual meeting that fewer complaints of cruelty reached the office "largely [due] to the fact that the Society did not continue to advertise its efforts."[21]

---

[17] But who didn't execute them at this time? The Humane Society itself put down unwanted cats at its earlier Barber Refuge.
[18] Evening Star, 13 Apr 1927, p. 2; 29 June 1927, p. 2; 24 July 1927, p. 41; Wash. Post, 29 June 1927, p. 1; 19 July 1927, p. 18. This affair is well documented in the minutes of the WHS Executive Committee.
[19] (Challenge) Wash. Post, 29 June 1927, p. 1; 19 July 1927, p. 18; 24 July 1927, p. 6; Evening Star, 29 June 1927, p. 2; 24 July 1927, p. 41; 24 Apr 1928, p. 5; (Briggs) Wash. Post, 28 Nov 1929, p. 24.
[20] Evening Star, 14 Nov 1930, p. 3; 22 Nov 1930, p. 4; 20 Feb 1931, p. 17.
[21] Evening Star, 14 Apr 1932, p. 54; 13 Apr 1933, p. 11; Wash. Post, 11 Apr 1940, p. 25.

CHAPTER TWENTY-TWO

The Early Shelter Movement

One of the charities of which the women of wealth in Washington interest themselves is in caring for homeless and friendless cats and dogs. (Nat. Tribune, 19 Mar 1903, p. 7).

Until 1897 the only institution in the District that actually took in homeless or stray animals was the pound, which handled all kinds. Of course, it also disposed of them one way or the other. Beginning in 1897 a variety of kindly organizations and individuals organized private homes for strays with a more animal-oriented approach. These **shelters** (as we shall call them)[1] differed from the pound in that they operated without the city institution's legal underpinning or financial backing and that, except for the WARL animal farm, they concerned themselves solely with dogs and cats. The obvious rationale for this second factor is that the pound had both the mandate and resources to take in farm animals and could almost always place them with their old or new owners; the less obvious cause is that the citified organizers were basically pet-oriented. All of these groups except poor Sarah Beckley reveled in their upper-class make-up.

Before working through a succession of animal shelters it would be good to lay out their virtually non-existent **legal framework**. Until 1908 there were no effective regulations of private (human) hospitals at all.[2] (See the Health Officer annual report of 1907 for a discussion of this.) In that year Congress authorized the District Commissioners to institute a licensing regimen for hospitals and asylums intended for either "human beings or domestic animals." The Commissioners approved such procedures the following year. Regarding animal asylums, this order required the approval of 2/3 of neighbors within 100 feet of the facility and attendance of a licensed veterinarian.

A memo from the Corporation Counsel in 1936[3] discussed "whether an institution for the housing of pet cats and dogs may be established in the residential use district," referring specifically to charitable efforts. The Counsel concluded that as an eleemosynary (charitable) project it could locate as a matter of right, but added that inasmuch as "an institution for the care of animals . . . is likely to become very objectionable in a residential district" the Zoning Commission might consider establishing restrictions.

---

[1] In their earliest years they went under the names of Refuge, Asylum, Station, Home, Farm (if rural) and colloquially Animal Poorhouse. "Animal hospital" frequently appears in records and newspapers (seven in the Health Officer's annual report of 1911) but these were veterinary clinics, which sometimes also boarded pets.

[2] Licensing of veterinarians was established about the same time – the first annual report of the Board of Examiners in Veterinary Medicine is in the 1909 Commissioners annual report. For a very detailed account of the District's chief animal hospital, with much other interesting information, somewhat before this period see Wash. Times, 15 Aug 1897, pt. 2 p. 18.

[3] Counsel Opinions, 31 Dec 1936 (Vol. 47, p. 344). The Commissioners instructed the Zoning Commission to prepare a "suitable amendment to the Zoning Regulations to prevent the establishment of homes of this character [in a residential area] in the future" (Comm Minutes/Orders, 15 Jan 1937).

(Current zoning regulations – effective 13 Mar 2015 – require that shelter buildings be at least 25 feet from any residence, external facilities 200 feet removed, and include provisions for hygienic maintenance.)

Cat Shelters

In 1896 the Washington Humane Society began plans to establish "a home for lost and starving animals"[4] and the following year inaugurated the **Bertha Langdon Barber Refuge for Animals** in refitted property at 19th Street and Columbia Road NW recently willed the Society by Maria S. Stoddard. (Barber was the daughter of a project supporter.)[5] The shelter dealt almost exclusively with cats (19 dogs were received in 1899 compared to 1,791 cats) and, like the pound, put down virtually all of them immediately.[6] ("Many are under the impression that this is a hospital or home for cats. This is not the case.") In 1898 the shelter ceased accepting cats unless "sick or disabled . . . to do justice to the animals at that place." As at the pound, "those of fancy breed are retained with the hope of finding homes or the owner." The shelter also offered a paid boarding service.[7] The boarding and (very infrequent) sale of cats and dogs produced a small income, but in fact it was "totally dependent" on donations from WHS and individuals. The salaried caretakers, **Mr. and Mrs. Frank J. Buckley** ("cat papa and mama") lived at no charge in the old Stoddard house ("a poor one and small").[8]

The Buckleys became a regular component of charitable shelters for the rest of this early period. Frank Buckley, so generously described by that friend of animal causes the Washington Times in 1901, seems a tenderer version of Samuel Einstein: "a small man with rough clothing but a kindly face that is all smiles and a manner that is all softness and gentleness."[9] But when duty demanded the execution of unloved toms Buckley did his work manfully. In the second WHS shelter he also made cat pick-ups from houses, operated a small dispensary, vetted would-be purchasers, and organized the boarding service (perhaps keeping the fees). Judging from his disappearance from the city directory in 1904 he died about that time and, as noted below, his widow assumed his duties.

---

[4] "Similar to those in New York, Philadelphia, Indianapolis, [also Boston] and various cities in Europe" (WHS Ann Rpt, 1897).

[5] This name created an unexpected problem for the institution: when its agent appeared at a house to pick up an unwanted animal the owners, seeing the name of the wealthy Miss Barber, would conclude the shelter was well endowed and refuse to pay the 25-cent charge!

[6] Including all kittens, by chloroform followed by drowning, according to WHS annual reports. The replacement shelter used an asphyxiating chamber similar to the pound's and chloroformed only the kittens (Wash. Times, 7 Apr 1901, pt. 2 p. 17; a fairly gruesome account).

In its earliest days the ladies who organized that effort "were compelled not only to select the victim [for euthanasia] but to personally execute the work of dispatch" until a paid HSW agent took the twice-weekly duty, the Board feeling it was "unfitting and an unnecessary tax upon them." It is difficult to imagine these well-intentioned society ladies stuffing kittens into the gas box. (Wash. Post, 24 July 1898, p. 10).

[7] This was not a new idea: "The summer 'home' for the pet bow-wow and the gentle tabby, where they could be left during vacation time with a feeling of absolute assurance that they would be well cared for, is an institution of long standing" (Evening Star, 8 Apr 1903, p. 20). See also Evening Star, 16 May 1891, p. 7 for many specifics of the business.

[8] WHS Ann Rpts, 1896-99; Wash. Post, 24 July 1898, p. 10; Evening Star, 2 Aug 1898, p. 12. One article calls him T. J. Buckley, a confusion with a local businessman of the time.

[9] Op. cit., 7 Apr 1901, pt. 2 p. 17, from which the rest of this paragraph is taken. Photos of the Buckleys are in Wash. Times, 13 Apr 1902, Magazine p. 8; 3 Aug 1902, Magazine p. 4.

The Society severed its connection with the Barber Refuge in 1899, in view of the imminent widening of 19th Street through the property, but it continued operations into early 1900 "on account of its having become nearly self-supporting," a claim that was not explained. After that, the Society continued to euthanize animals on request until 1905. (There was a 10-cent charge after 1902.)[10]

A **replacement shelter** opened in upper Georgetown (2007 32nd Street NW, also a donated property) by 1901. Operations there proceeded largely as at the Barber Refuge, including the death of most charity inmates. Society boarders (usually during the summer vacation season) had separate quarters and ate very well indeed.[11] Although it was a WHS project the Society's annual reports never mentioned it and perhaps it was some sort of auxiliary or semi-private effort. Buckley, managing the new facility, became a salaried agent of WHS. The shelter closed sometime after 1905 "for want of funds." WHS discussed re-establishing its shelter occasionally in the 1910s but without obvious enthusiasm or means.[12]

As early as 1902 the newly-established Washington Cat Club expressed its interest in taking over the Humane Society's faltering cat shelter. Washington, it claimed, was almost the only large American city without such a place. Socialite Maria Peet had earlier (1898) offered WHS land "a little outside of the city" (the Brookland neighborhood) to transplant the Barber Refuge, and this is probably where the Washington Cat Club began construction of an unrealized facility in 1902. However, in spite of regular talk and sporadic fund-raising nothing came of the project.[13]

The redoubtable Mrs. West could not be happy with this lack and about 1907 she and Mary A. Peet (daughter of Maria) established a private cat shelter in "an old frame structure" at 126 D Street SW. To manage the venture she hired "an old negro aunty" away from the Friends of Homeless Dogs (below), **Sarah L. Beckley**.[14]

Among the society names of the Friends' shelter one notices "Mrs. Sarah Beckley" of 505 Twentieth Street NW, who "will gladly receive any stray dogs for the shelter, or can be communicated with in regard to them." Beckley demands our attention as an interesting outlier in the Washington humane movement of her time – a working-class mulatto accepted by so many fine ladies apparently on the basis of her complete devotion to the cause. The 1905 city directory listed Lewis Beckley (at the 20th Street address) as "laborer". Two years later the couple moved to 126 D Street SW where Lewis was a waiter and Sarah dressmaker.

---

[10] (Closing) WHS Ann Rpt, 1899; Wash. Times, 3 May 1899, p. 8; (euthanasia) Wash. Post, 25 Nov 1905, p. 12 (the Audubon Society considered taking up this task, for the protection of birds). Agents occasionally put down rabbits also (Wash. Times, 1 Nov 1903, Magazine p. 2, which gives useful statistics).
"The Society has a plant on 32nd Street where these animals are killed if . . . it [is] impossible to get homes for them" (Wash. Times, 30 July 1905, Magazine p. 6). Special agent Frank Buckley, Collector of Small Animals, had this assignment. In 1899, 2,128 animals were collected and 2,135 humanely killed [sic]; in 1904, the comparable numbers were 4,866 collected and 3,677 killed. It was noted that after it stopped euthanizing animals itself, WHS failed to publicize that the pound still performed this service (Wash. Post, 22 Apr 1908, p. 12).
[11] Good descriptions, including photos of the house and Buckleys, and an unexpected account of the killing chamber, will be found in Wash. Times, 13 Apr 1902, p. 8; 7 Apr 1901, pt. 2 p. 17; see also Evening Star, 10 Feb 1903, p. 1; 10 Feb 1907, p. 16.
[12] (WHS) Evening Star, 24 Mar 1912, p. 26; WHS Ann Rpts, 1912-15.
[13] (Peet) WHS Ann Rpt, 1898; Peet bequeathed $5,000 to the Society (WHS Ann Rpt, 1911); (shelter) Evening Star, 1 Oct 1902, p. 10; 10 Feb 1907, p. 16; Wash. Times, 13 Apr 1902, Magazine p. 8; 30 July 1905, Magazine p. 6; 20 June 1912, p. 12; Wash. Herald, 12 May 1911, p. 12.
[14] Evening Star, 20 Sept 1908, p. 46, the only account that specifies its origins; Wash. Post, 1 Feb 1912, p. 2. Regularly misspelled Berkley, even in the Bee's tribute. Wash. Post, 18 Oct 1908, p. SM3 has a very appealing picture of her with feline friends.

Although under the initial supervision of West and Peet, Beckley became so identified with the shelter ("This woman has become very much attached to her charges") that it was commonly referred to as **Mrs. Beckley's cat shelter**. The institution opened in 1907, was licensed under the new regulations in 1911 and finally saw its license revoked in 1916.[15] Her shelter was modeled on the earlier cat and dog operations – homeless strays and paid, upper-class boarders with separate quarters and provisions, animals gratis to good homes, and shaky finances. She did put down unwanted pets on request (how difficult this must have been for her!) for "a nominal fee" of 25-50 cents. The home was licensed to accommodate 50 cats and 10 dogs, but the 1908 Post profile reports "well-nigh a hundred cats of all social grades," of which 40 were charity cases.[16]

As had the pound for dogs, Beckley's shelter gained a loyal following of concerned cat-aficionados ("To her place come the cat devotees from all over the city. Some of them . . . ride up in their automobiles [wealthy ones – this was 1908], and in company with Mrs. Beckley, gloat in joy over the multitude of cats"). Beckley was "the head of cat propaganda in Washington." The Washington Cat Club routinely referred inquiries to her, and no printed reference condescended to mention her race.[17]

Although we want to admire Beckley's dedication to animal welfare, it is impossible to overlook its obsessive quality. The Post's description (somewhat snide but no more so than most newspaper articles about animal-related matters) gives the general feel of her operation: "Here is a comfortable inn, wherein cozy beds ensconced in comfortable corners await the weary feline; even the most irritable cat must needs gurgle a purr of utter content when it finds itself housed in these comfortable quarters." When we read that the cats ate better than her waiter-husband one wonders how the couple stayed together. A longer extract of this profile, paired with a somewhat syrupy appreciation of the lady, are given in Appendix D10.

The cat shelter suffered a disastrous fire in 1912, during which Beckley, at considerable risk, rescued all her wards but two fearful dogs. It did not appear in local newspapers after that date. We read that in 1929 Sarah Beckley, "a colored servant" of Mary Peet (who like her mother left much of her estate to humane organizations), inherited $2,000 from her deceased mistress. She was still living in 1935 when she attended a friend's funeral.[18]

(A similar, individual-operated and informal cat shelter was reported by the Evening Times in 1899 at Ellicott City, Maryland, at the country home of an unnamed "kind-hearted women." "Persons who know of her humane treatment of stray cats have for years imposed upon her good nature by dropping their superfluous felines on the public road as they drive past her home until now the lady finds herself sorely taxed to provide for the expatriated animals." She fed them "gallons of milk" through "a feeding trough out in the back yard."[19])

---

[15] Comm Minutes/Orders of 19 Apr 1911 and 19 May 1916 respectively. It was listed in the Health Officer annual reports for 1911-15; no other shelter appeared in these lists.

[16] "The institution is not self-supporting, but many cat lovers voluntarily contribute and these enable Mrs. Beckley to sustain the hobo branch of her hotel" (Wash. Post, 18 Oct 1908, p. SM3, which gives specifics on the place); (fee) Wash. Post, 19 Aug 1911, p. 2. There is no evidence of how involved West and Peet were at this point; they both were forming the new Friendly Hand by 1908 and had perhaps spun off Beckley to operate independently.

[17] I only learned this from the Washington Bee article (a colored newspaper). The 1929 notice of her inheritance – this not in the context of her cat-work – also gives her race, as was customary at the time.

[18] Wash. Post, 1 Feb 1912, p. 2; 14 Mar 1929, p. 22; Evening Star, 14 Apr 1935, p. 9.

[19] Evening Times, 5 July 1899, p. 5. Note also Mr. R. H. Montgomery, a "scenic painter", whose wife left him in 1921 "saying the painter seldom came home at night and tried to turn the house into an animal rescue yard" (Wash. Times, 6 May 1921, p. 5).

Undaunted by the regular demise of earlier cat shelters, the ladies of Washington met once again – in 1908 at the New Willard Hotel – and formed yet another cat-centric organization, **The Friendly Hand Society**, with the stated purpose of establishing a lasting shelter. The Washington Herald made no attempt to disguise its opinion in one of the funniest bits of writing encountered in this research (abridged):

O felines, chant peons of thanksgivings and praise! Lift your melodious chorus to hail your champions!

Assemble, both worthies and hoi-polloi of the cat world. Convene en masse today, aye, every day, and particularly every night, proceed to the peaceful abodes of your defenders and there beneath their windows evidence your appreciation of their devotion to your cause, and serenade them as only cat can.

Retreat never till your song be sung, even though the night air be thick with bootjacks, alarm clocks, hair and tooth brushes, bottles and other missiles, armed by those who love neither your song nor your being.

Thus will you grasp the glad mitt, tendered you by "The Friendly Hand".[20]

West was the president of this organization also, and Peet the treasurer. Locating the proposed shelter was much discussed ("Everyone knows that if any neighborhood hears a cat home is to be established . . . there will be a great hue and cry"). The question hardly mattered – nothing was heard of the society after that. To add insult to injury, Peet, who had started keeping cats (about 40) at her property in Cherrydale, Virginia, was evicted by complaints of her sleepless neighbors ("The loud talking of the cats at unreasonable hours is objectionable, the neighbors declare").[21]

Dog Shelters

When Mr. W. B. Biddle of Cincinnati wrote the Commissioners in 1901 asking how the District dealt with its loose canine population he was informed "that there has never been any provision made in this city for the care of homeless dogs in the manner that he [Biddle] doubtless has in mind – a place of refuge, where they are cared for and kept indefinitely."[22] And this was true – at that time only cats received such attention.

Humane shelters for dogs began in Washington the following year (1902) when a committee of prominent ladies – many of them already familiar to us (Macfarland, Chandler, Cassini) – formed the **Society for Friendless Dogs**.[23] Frank Buckley, WHS agent and manager of the Society's cat shelter, found a property at 2025 32nd Street NW (part of the cat shelter site at 2007).[24] The goal of the Society was to house homeless mutts until they could be placed (free to the original owner or sold "at a minimal sum" to a suitable family, who were carefully screened), but of course "in case of incurable disease or

---

[20] Wash. Herald, 25 Feb 1908, p. 7. Intermixed with the satire is quite a bit of actual information, including the alternate – and often silly – names proposed.

[21] (Friendly) Ibid; Wash. Times, 6 May 1908, p. 7; (Cherrydale) Evening Star, 20 Sept 1908, p. 46, with a description of the country operation.

The Society wrote the Capitol's Superintendent of Ground the same year urging him to put out water for "these dear little creatures" the squirrels in winter (AOC archives, "Animals").

[22] Evening Star, 16 Dec 1901, p. 16.

[23] The name was also given (most likely from careless writing) as The Dog Home Society, and Washington Society for Homeless Dogs.

[24] For photos and a detailed profile, see Wash. Times, 3 Aug 1902, Magazine p. 4. Photos of the cat shelter (Wash. Times, 13 Apr 1902, Magazine p. 8) and this profile seem to show the same building.

injury" the dogs would be "painlessly put to sleep in the gas-box." In fact, this last happened surprisingly few times. "Vivisectionists [are] specially guarded against." The facility also boarded pets for a fee.[25]

Within three months "some crank" nearby filed suit complaining of the noise and Mrs. Macfarland began to desperately look for an alternate location. "No neighborhood has been found that is willing to tolerate a dog chorus." The shelter housed about 30 strays at the time. In October 1902, after three months of "complete paralysis," the fencing and sheds were moved to donated land in the Brookland suburb (another account says Mt. Ranier, Maryland, which is fairly near Brookland).[26]

The Society initiated a series of fund-raising home concerts/dramatic readings (for "a fashionable crowd of women"); Miss Alice Thaw, "the fiancée of Lord Yarmouth," donated $5; owners took out memberships for their pets. For a time "the Society [was] becoming quite a fad . . . The movement has appealed very strongly to the better class of people of the District."[27]

The Society lost its shelter again when the Brookland/Mt. Ranier property was sold, probably in 1904. It had only been "a summer home" there anyway. The Board re-organized, changed its name (confusingly, to us modern readers) to the Animal Rescue League of Washington "in view of the widened scope of the work," and the following year found new property on Tennleytown Road (Wisconsin Avenue) in Bethesda, Maryland. (An earlier plan to move to Hyattsville, Maryland, apparently fell through.)[28]

This final shelter also took in paid boarders, and so had separate kennels and runways,[29] under the care of a live-in manager (who may or may not have been Mrs. Buckley).[30] "Pets for nothing to good homes" – the heading of its classified ads – indicates the shelter's laudable intent. The last public notice of the place appeared in 1907, and it closed in early 1908. "Interest in the enterprise was on the wane, and . . . funds to continue . . . were lacking . . . Twenty-three dogs were in the shelter when the fiat went forth: homes were found for thirteen. Ten just 'skiddoed'." The last press notice of the Society appeared in 1909 referring to its opposition to muzzling two years earlier, when Mrs. Henry L. West served as president.[31]

And with this, the first period of efforts to establish humane shelters for homeless animals in the District of Columbia came to an end.

---

[25] Evening Star, 9 Apr 1902, p. 16 (the first notice); Wash. Post, 29 Apr 1902, p. 12; 2 June 1902, p. 10.

[26] (Complaint/move): Evening Times, 17 July 1902, p. 3; 23 July 1902, p. 8; Wash. Post, 19 July 1902, p. 7; 25 Oct 1902, p. 12; (crank) Nat. Tribune, 19 Mar 1903, p. 7; (Mt. Ranier) Wash. Post, 5 June 1905, p. 9).

[27] Wash. Times, 3 Aug 1902, Magazine p. 4; Evening Star, 10 Mar 1903, p. 6; 17 Mar 1903, p. 12; Nat. Tribune, 19 Mar 1903, p. 7.

[28] Wash. Post, 8 May 1904, p. 12; 5 June 1905, p. 9.

[29] "Made attractive by the trees, shrubs and vines with which they are surrounded"; "pet dogs may here find a pleasant home until sought by their owners."

[30] Evening Star, 25 Apr 1904, p. 9; 25 May 1905, p. 16; 27 May 1905, p. 7; Wash. Post, 25 May 1905, p. 11; 5 June 1905, p. 9. As for Buckley, as of 1903 it was she who provided the required shelter statistics to the Society rather than her husband. Nat. Tribune, 19 Mar 1903, p. 7 specifies an unnamed lady manager – widow of a dog-handler – and tells a silly story.

[31] Wash. Times, 13 Nov 1905, p. 11; Evening Star, 7 July 1907, p. 14, among others; 20 Jan 1908, p. 16; Wash. Post, 21 May 1909, p. 2.

CHAPTER TWENTY-THREE

Washington Animal Rescue League[1]

Don't let little animals suffer when there is a place for them. This [WARL] is not the pound. Women run this place. (Wash. Post, 23 Oct 1916, p. 7)

The Animal Rescue League works with the object of treating the stray animal along humane lines. The District pound believes in protecting the citizen from the dangers that travel along with the homeless, half-starved animal. Both institutions are doing splendid work in the same direction while working in different directions. (Wash. Times, 29 Oct 1922, p. 7)

The shelter movement in Washington lay dormant for a few years after the demise of these early efforts. Here is the **genesis** of its later and more successful stage, taken from an account of June 1914:

> Several months ago two Washington society women, seeing horses mistreated on the streets of the National Capital, had their owners taken into court, where they appeared personally against them. From this action they interested their friends in the misfortunes of cats, dogs and horses in the District.[2]

One of these determined ladies was Mrs. Peter Goelet Gerry,[3] who became the leading force in the renewed effort at its beginning. The group of friends invited Mrs. Huntington (Anna Harris) Smith, founder of Boston's Animal Rescue League and crusader for the movement, to meet them informally and outline the possibilities. Smith served as the keynote speaker at the public organizing meeting of the new Washington Animal Rescue League held at the Woodward & Lothrop Department Store auditorium on 31 March 1914.

If the earlier shelter societies had been high-society clubs the WARL organizing meeting was a veritable Congress of Vienna for the Washington upper-crust. Newspapers gushed their awe: "many of the most prominent society women in Washington"; "100 women and a score of men prominent in Congressional, diplomatic and social circles"; "Washington's most exclusive social set." Smith outlined the goals and activities of the Boston League and challenged Washingtonians to raise $2,000 to establish their own effort. WHS President Hutchins promised his organization's sincere cooperation while explaining why his Society needed help eradicating cruelty to the city's animals (using the usual rather

---

[1] I express my deep appreciation to Ms. Susan Strange, archivist of WARL, for her provision of so much unpublished material used in this section.
[2] Evening Star, 20 June 1914, p. 9.
[3] Sometimes erroneously written Goelet-Gerry. She was a local beauty (Matilde Townsend) married to Rep. Gerry of Rhode Island, and later to diplomat Sumner Welles. See her interesting interview and very attractive photo in Wash. Herald, 9 Apr 1914, p. 2, and another photo in Wash. Times, 31 Mar 1914, p. 1. She was not a League charter member, however.

unsatisfying arguments – lack of public and police cooperation – found in his annual addresses). The meeting adopted resolutions of basic purpose and future actions and appointed an organizing committee.[4]

A second meeting the following month formally enrolled members and elected officers, and the organization adopted by-laws and incorporated in the District of Columbia on 14 April. The goal of the initial resolutions was "that an animal hospital and shelter be established in Washington," which work was vigorously begun, but let us first turn to some underlying fundamentals of the new WARL:

Three assumptions guided WARL at its beginning:

- That the League would be primarily concerned with horses: "My love of all animals has drawn me into this work but particularly my great devotion to horses, and they will be the primary and first care of the League," stated Gerry, a noted horsewoman.[5] The earliest League record gives its purpose as "the proper disposition of decrepit and injured horses and other animals." But in fact this was never the case – dogs and cats provided the bulk of the League's work; horses were already disappearing from Washington streets. This development spared WARL from the dead-end that rendered WHS nearly irrelevant in the same period;
- That the League would be largely an organization of women: The organizers had specified a "mixed board of men and women to assure business-like management," and were "especially anxious to have representative men as vice-presidents . . . to assure standing in the community". Nonetheless, the by-laws always referred to the president as "She". Gerry indicated this truth in the same Herald interview when she expressed her hope that "every woman – and man, too – in Washington . . . should become a member of the League." Although men were generally represented among WARL officers the preponderance was always female, and there were years in which every officer and the entire Board of Directors were women;[6]
- That the League was an effort of the affluent and socially well-connected:[7] This is clear from reading the oft-published lists of event organizers and attenders, of officers and members, of the prestigious venues of meetings and fund-raisers. Nowhere do we read of any approach even to the city's middle-class, not to mention the laboring population.

---

[4] "Scores of members were registered on the spot and cash was freely given . . . Several women were kept busy for an hour after the meeting enrolling members." Evening Star, 1 Apr 1914, p. 10; 20 June 1914, p. 9; Wash. Post, 1 Apr 1914, p. 4; Wash. Herald, 1 Apr 1914, p. 2; Wash. Times, 1 Apr 1914, p. 3; WARL Ann Rpt, 1919. Both speeches and the resolutions will be found in these sources. The first ARL – Boston – had been established in 1899. Smith stated that before that there had been such shelters in Philadelphia and in Brighton, Massachusetts. "Washington is the only large city in which such a society does not exist" (WARL General Meeting minutes, 31 Mar 1914).

Use of the acronym began after our study period (i.e., after 1940) – in its earliest years the organization used the short name "the Rescue" replaced in the 1930s by "the League".

[5] WARL Directors minutes, 28 Mar 1914; Wash. Herald, 9 Apr 1914, p. 2. "Friends of Horse Form Rescue Club" headlined Wash. Times, 31 Mar 1914, p. 1.

[6] Said Hutchins at the March meeting: "The men of Washington . . . could not bring this matter to a successful conclusion. So I put the matter up to the women. This afternoon you see the result" (Wash. Times, 1 Apr 1914, p. 3). There was a special Men's Advisory Committee in 1932, which provided much useful service the ladies could not (WARL Sec Ann Rpt, 1932). (Quote) WARL Directors minutes, 28 Mar 1914.

[7] We seem to be entering a period in which ladies of social standing no longer felt that a public life centered on parties, clothing and home decoration was adequate, and that some beneficial cause needed to be part of the mix, but this is the subject of a different study. Note also the beginning of celebrity endorsements (even more pronounced for the Tail-Waggers' Club, below), heralding the wide-spread practice of today.

We might also say here something about the League's **relationship with** its older sibling, **WHS**. That Society's opinionated president of the 1900s, Chester Snow, had been much opposed to the very idea of humane shelters, at least for dogs and cats (animals he seems to have detested). "We should . . . avoid the mistake of cruel kindness. Those who impound dogs or cats together in so-called homes regardless of the fact that they are not gregarious and where the weaker live in terror . . . have doubtless the best of intentions but . . . the habits and tastes of these animals [make] the homes so-called [a] prison." And again: "It is impossible either economically or humanely to maintain asylums for cats or dogs or even for horses."[8]

A change of leadership brought a change of attitude. Succeeding President Hutchins spoke encouragingly at WARL's organizing meeting and told his own group at its annual meeting of 1915: "It [WARL] should be encouraged in all possible ways and its membership rolls enlarged by the addition of every one . . . whose desire to extirpate cruelty to dumb animals is expressed in something more practical than sighs and groans."[9] Indeed, WHS presidents Snow, Hutchins, Smith all served at some time as officers or benefactors of the League and (at least in its earliest years) often strove to bring WHS issues and attitudes into WARL. The two organizations worked together closely in various publicity/outreach projects (such as Be Kind to Animals Week) and lobbying for humane causes (horse protection, for example). WARL President Palmer re-stated "the friendly relations now existing" between the two groups in 1924's annual meeting.[10] The League's unsuccessful attempt to merge with WHS is discussed in the previous chapter.

The **primary object** of the new League was the rescue of friendless horses, dogs and cats from city streets, or – in the case of horses – from abusive owners, usually by direct purchase. It would see their injuries treated and then return them to their original or new, suitable owners. The organization was clear from the beginning that irredeemable or unwanted wards (generally meaning mongrels) would be humanely put down. "It is our plan, instead of sending the poor dears [that is, dogs] to the pound, to have a humane method by which we will chloroform them," said Gerry.[11]

From its earliest time the WARL shelter also operated a (contractor) medical clinic – initially open one hour every morning and geared toward horses, free for minor services and at "moderate charge . . . for medicines and for surgical operations." A boarding service was also envisioned, as had been done at its predecessors. More ambitious plans considered at the March meeting included purchase of "a horse ambulance and a dog ambulance," an automobile, and "a special bicycle" ("for carrying injured cats") and a rest home "for run-down horses."[12]

It is worth considering just why these well-intentioned people felt the need for a new organization at all – the pound not only humanely disposed of unwanted animals but actively took them off the streets. Anyone wanting a pet could – and often did – travel to South Capitol Street and bought one. It is true that cats could not be adopted from the pound, but WARL organizers were frankly concerned primarily with horses, and consistently treated cats as an afterthought; Gerry admitted in her Herald interview that she had

---

[8] WHS Ann Rpts, 1905, 1906; see also 1907.
[9] WHS Ann Rpt, 1915.
[10] (Horses) Wash. Times, 12 May 1914, p. 4 – there are many other examples; (Palmer) Evening Star, 13 May 1924, p. 4.
[11] Wash. Herald, 9 Apr 1914, p. 2.
[12] Evening Star, 27 May 1914, p. 24; Wash. Times, 1 Apr 1914, p. 3, with quite unflattering caricatures of some founding personalities.

little sympathy for them.¹³ The simple answer is that they had little confidence in the pound without being quite able to articulate why. Organizers promised to hold animals longer than the pound and to advertise orphans, but in fact simply and vaguely assumed that they would handle things in a nicer way. Said Smith in her rousing speech: "[A humane shelter] must be something more than the ordinary ill-conducted dog pound." ¹⁴

The new League made a quick start on its work. A **shelter** opened "in a few rooms [the hay loft] over a stable" at **20 Decatur St., NE** (between N and O) on 10 May with Mary E. Coursey as manager. Coursey, a capable and kind lady, had run the Boston shelter for fifteen years. She was joined by an assistant, Joseph Parker,¹⁵ in June and some time later by another assistant, Mrs. Sacrey. A large box earlier used for grain served as office furnishing. Mrs. Mundrum R. Blumenberg, a WARL vice-president, was an important and constant volunteer. Even in its first full month of operation (June 1914) the shelter took in 19 dogs, 365 cats and two horses. The dogs and cats all met a chloroformed end either at the shelter or on site; the horses were sent to new owners or, if decrepit, disposed of.¹⁶

Clearly many people agreed with WARL founders that their shelter offered some improvement over the District pound. "As soon as the public learned that the station was caring for cats and other animals, notification by telephone poured in [and] Miss Coursey . . . has been a very busy woman collecting the stray cats and kittens." Undoubtedly the prominent names attached to the organization bolstered this confidence: Mrs. Henry L. West of the Washington Cat Club and Mdm. Hussein Bey, wife of the Turkish ambassador, were members. So was Mrs. Woodrow Wilson and her daughter, initiating a line of First Lady supporters. Prominent actor George Arliss championed participation by men but feared (how different from today!) that "people wouldn't listen to an actor off the stage." There was reported to be work in the Takoma suburb "done along this line."¹⁷

With business booming (so to speak) the League needed larger quarters and moved to a rented "small house" (for a rather expensive $25/month) at **1355 Ohio Avenue, NW**, in December 1914. Here operations continued as before but on an increased scale. In the single month of August 1915 the shelter took in 743 dogs and cats. The large number of these continued to be chloroformed but League reports increasingly spoke of animals given to new homes. Unsurprisingly, there was a distinct preference for animals of good

---

¹³ "The object of the organization is to provide painless deaths for stray animals, principally cats" (Evening Star, 6 Aug 1914, p. 15).

¹⁴ "The object of the League is to rescue cats, dogs, etc. from starvation, and to dispose of them instead of having the dog pound outfit do it" (letter, Wash. Times, 10 Mar 1915, p. 8). No one ever explained how being killed at WARL was better than being killed at the pound.

¹⁵ "On meager pay, Miss Coursey plunged into her work. Because of her self-sacrificing devotion, her disregard to her own personal comfort and her straightforward common sense and clear headedness [WARL] today is a monument to the devotion, leadership and vision of its founders" (Evening Star, 25 Oct 1931, p. 14). She returned to Boston in 1920 with a gift of $65 from the grateful League (WARL Directors minutes, 8 May 1920). Coursey's photo is in Evening Star, 20 June 1914, p. 9, and perhaps is the lady in Wash. Post, 30 Mar 1919, p. S13.

Parker was "the faithful colored man . . . to whose devotion and intelligence high credit is due" (Wash. Post, 30 Mar 1919, p. S13). He is probably the man pictured with a dog in the 1919 Annual Report.

¹⁶ Evening Star, 20 June 1914, p. 9; 9 Oct 1921, p. 59; WARL Ann Rpt, 1919; WARL, New shelter dedication brochure.

¹⁷ Evening Star, 20 June 1914, p. 9; 5 Mar 1916, p. 8; Wash. Herald, 2 July 1914, p. 10; Wash. Post, 6 Aug 1914, p. 14; WARL Ann Rpt, 1919. Arliss continued his remarks by suggesting, with disarming innocence, that "some politician be asked to make an appeal for the League [as if the populace held politicians in higher esteem than celebrities] but he was told by some of the women . . . that 'a politician in Washington' was more or less an everyday 'occurrence'". Arliss was an active member for many years and later made an honorary WARL Vice-President (Evening Star, 27 Apr 1933, p. 2). Another celebrity supporter was actress Minnie Maddern Fiske.

breed: "None of the dogs . . . have been at all valuable, and so have been chloroformed at once." Occasionally, as at the pound, a particularly fetching inmate won the matron's heart and stayed on as a mascot – Nellie, a temperamental dog, merited a photo in the 1919 annual report in this way. Another, Mickey, appeared in the 1924 report.[18]

The smallish Ohio Avenue facility housed cats on its second floor and dogs on its first, but the modest number of horses taken in had to be placed at nearby commercial stables. These received medical care and then, ironically, were put down.[19] Purchase of "a small country farm" would have alleviated this situation but was beyond the organization's means. Horses commonly came to the League by purchase, negligent owners offered $1-10 for worn out nags; 69 were bought in 1915. This practice, laudable as it was, opened the possibility of hucksters buying broken-down animals and then taking them to WARL as a sort of hostage, a misuse the group promised "was well provided for; . . . no such deception could be practiced."[20]

Other efforts during this earliest period included the provision of "a kind of carpet slipper" allowing horses to get traction on snow-covered streets,[21] and encouraging MPDC officers to report abused animals to the shelter. In general, operation of the shelter remained the focus of WARL's work.[22]

A visitor of 1915 wrote: "The system is remarkable . . . I was so impressed by the place that I feel every man, woman and child should visit." Nonetheless, a headline of two years later tells the usual story: "Residents of Ohio Avenue Opposed to Rescued Animals in Neighborhood". Among other complaints in the residents' petition to local government was that dead animals were not taken up for days "and that it is impossible to keep out the sickening odors from the homes in the vicinity. The lives and pleasures of human beings should be considered before animals."[23] Both its own growth and neighborhood opposition soon brought about a move to WARL's third shelter.

In July 1917 WARL purchased "a roomy old mansion" at **349 Maryland Avenue, SW**[24] for $14,000, a four-story brick building with a two-story rear extension then serving as a dispensary of the Miner Institute. This substantial expense was generously covered by Chester A. Snow (the former WHS president earlier so opposed to animal shelters) and Miss Martha C. Codman. Codman, "a member of a distinguished old Massachusetts family . . . well known in Washington, New York and Newport society," and at that time only "a winter resident" of Washington, also donated the new heating system ($2,100)

---

[18] (Rent) Evening Star, 25 Oct 1931, p. 14; (statistics/mascots, of which many others are mentioned) Wash. Times, 3 Sept 1915, p. 2; 29 Oct 1922, p. 7; Wash. Post, 30 Mar 1919, p. S13; Evening Star, 9 Oct 1921, p. 59; 24 July 1927, p. 5 (Jerry, a goat); (dogs) Evening Star, 20 June 1914, p. 9.
[19] WARL members in 1916 discussed the desirability of finding a place for this procedure "where a group of small boys will not be able to act as interested spectators" (Evening Star, 13 Dec 1916, p. 17).
[20] (Housing) Evening Star, 6 Apr 1915, p. 5; (farm, purchases) 13 Dec 1916, p. 17; (fraud) 5 Mar 1916, p. 8.
[21] "The ridicule of those who scoffed at this simple idea turned to approval when experience proved its effectiveness" (WARL, New shelter dedication brochure).
[22] (Slippers) Evening Star, 6 Apr 1915, p. 5; (police) Wash. Post, 16 May 1915, p. 12 (officers were given contact cards for ready use). It is noticeable that WHS officials speaking at League meetings were generally critical of the police, while WARL members were much more complimentary.
[23] (Visitor) Wash. Times, 10 Mar 1915, p. 8; (petition) Evening Star, 14 June 1917, p. 17.
[24] At the corner of Maryland and 4½ Street. The house had once been the brothel of the city's leading madam, Mary Hall. Wash. Times, 28 July 1917, p. 4; Wash. Post, 1 July 1917, p. R1; Wash. Herald, 1 Apr 1914, p. 2; WARL Ann Rpts, 1919, 1924. Good photos of the building will be found in the two annual reports, and also in Evening Star, 18 Nov 1917, p. 9; Wash. Post, 30 Mar 1919, p. S13. WARL Ann Rpt, 1924 lists a number of necessary repairs to the facility, coincidently giving a few more details of the place.

and electric killing cages (about $1,000, described later). Codman funded an addition the following year.[25]

As with its earlier move, the new and larger facility allowed the League to amplify its core work: over 6,700 animals passed through its hands in the 1918-19 year (April-March), and 12,200 in 1921-22 (!). The new home had stables for two horses and a run for dogs. More employees were taken on: a bookkeeper and an extra summer agent. Staff generally consisted of a daytime clerk to run the office and answer calls, a live-in matron, and the on-street agent. In 1924 their combined salaries of $2,625 comprised the largest item of WARL's nearly $6,000 annual budget.[26] In 1920 J. Joseph "Billy" Smallwood replaced Parker as agent, making pick-ups.[27]

Along with the numbers of animals processed, so did their range expand, though only of smaller types. We never read of farm animals going there, but reports show minor numbers of squirrels, wild birds, rabbits, monkeys, foxes, turtles, guinea pigs, opossums . . . in 1921 someone dropped off 104 white rats. Almost all of these animals were injured and brought in to be euthanized.[28]

Animal pick-ups (which by 1924 "not only cover the entire city but reach out into the suburbs [the former county]") were made during the day but deliveries accepted at any time. After several years of the League's agent taking cats from houses in a basket by streetcar ("a wonderful performance") WARL acquired an ambulance[29] in the summer of 1918 through the efforts of Walter Stilson Hutchins. Even with this, emergency runs in members' cars or taxis were not uncommon.[30] The ambulance averaged 19 collection runs daily in 1921, and in 1933 travelled 14,665 miles, supplemented by 688 taxi trips.[31] In 1931 the shelter still had only one ambulance and the president wrote annoyedly of citizens who demanded immediate pick-up of animals ("It would seem possible that . . . people . . . would bring in their own dog or cat, thus releasing our one car to the calls of those who have no conveyance"). Persons turning over animals received a receipt and signed a release.[32]

A sample of emergency street runs made by WARL personnel reported in the two annual reports and the press mostly concern cases of retrieving stranded or abandoned animals (cats in trees or sewers, an

---

[25] Wash. Post, 30 Mar 1919, p. S13; Evening Star, 9 Oct 1921, p. 59. Later Mrs. Maxim Karolik. She was also a generous benefactor of the Boston organization.

[26] The salaries in 1914 were: Manager -- $45/month; night watchman -- $40/month; veterinarian -- $30/month (WARL Directors minutes, 14 May 1914).

[27] Wash. Herald, 26 Apr 1919, p. 3; Evening Star, 31 Jan 1918, p. 23; 9 Oct 1921, p. 59; WARL Ann Rpts, 1919, 1924; WARL Directors minutes, 19 Oct 1920. Smallwood's photo is in the 1924 Annual Report with Micky, the mascot.

[28] Evening Star, 28 Apr 1921, p. 10.

[29] A photo of this vehicle is in the 1919 Annual Report, and of later trucks in the 1924 report; Evening Star, 3 Aug 1930, p. 4; Times-Herald, 7 Jan 1941, p. 17. Replacements were purchased in 1920, '24, '33 and '36, and perhaps also years whose minutes are lost. "A new one will be needed every few years" (WARL Exec Comm minutes, 18 May 1933). The 1936 model had a built-in gas chamber (WARL memo, "Outstanding Achievements", 29 Apr 1936). There was a standing Ambulance Fund.

[30] "Before the League had an ambulance . . . it was no uncommon occurrence for a member to leave a dinner table on receiving a telephone call . . . and drive to some remote section of the city to bring in some injured or suffering creature" (Evening Star, 25 Oct 1931, p. 14).

[31] The number of taxi runs actually increased over the years: 1936 – 1,454; 1938 – 2,004 (WARL Sec Ann Rpts, 1936, 1938). The League "has a special cat rescue gadget to fetch Toby out of a tree" (Times-Herald, 27 Apr 1941, p. E2).

[32] Evening Star, 28 Apr 1921, p. 10; 9 Oct 1921, p. 59; Wash. Post, 30 Mar 1919, p. S13; WARL Ann Rpt, 1924; WARL Sec Ann Rpts, 1921, 1933; WARL, "A Few Facts". See also Palmer's extensive complaint about demands for the ambulance "by thoughtless and selfish people" in the 1924 Annual Report, and also in WARL, "A Few Facts".

injured horse beside the road) and not the instances of direct cruelty handled by WHS agents. In fact, WARL reported abuse cases to WHS for action.[33] The 1919 report gives an interesting example of the legal complications this work could entail: a starved horse taken while its (still legal) owner resided in the insane asylum.

Conditions at the shelter were exemplary, by all reports. WARL regularly advertised its approval by the District Health Department. In one of those stories that no writer could invent, two men searching for recruits for their "troupe of trained fleas . . . performing at a carnival at a nearby city" combed dogs for an hour, locating only two insect-performers for their company. "The Animal Rescue League is quite proud of this record" – understandably.[34]

WARL remained frank in its policy of **executing animals** not readily adopted.[35] Virtually all horses met this fate. "The horses are given a few days of comfort in the . . . stable before they are led into the stall . . . called The House of Blessed Release." They were at the shelter because of their decrepit condition, after all. Recall also that, unlike WHS, WARL did not prosecute offenders; it only bought their nags with its Horse-Purchase Fund.[36]

Of dogs and cats, clearly diseased or otherwise undesirable animals were killed on receipt. The large number stayed on for four or five days while the League attempted to locate their owners (both searching Lost and placing Found notices in the local papers)[37] or find new families. "We would like to be able to place more animals in homes . . . but good homes appear difficult to find," explained the League's secretary. Only males were put up for adoption; all unredeemed females (dogs and cats) were put down.[38] There was no fee for the animal and the League bemoaned how few persons made any donation for the service. A charge of $2 for animals eventually was instituted.[39] Potential new owners were screened and signed a contract to care for the pet, obtain a tag (for dogs) and not allow them to be used for experimentation. Animals could be returned and any donation remitted.[40]

The earliest reports mention only chloroform for killing animals, although probably horses were shot; the League spent $50 a month in 1918 for the chemical. The shelter continued to chloroform any animal put down at residences or on the street (for example, seriously injured ones) and, at the shelter (in a "chloroform box"), all animals with injuries and all puppies and kittens.[41]

---

[33] In 1937 WARL asked the Commissioners for police powers for its employees, as WHS and the poundmaster had, but the Corporation Counsel advised that only Congress could grant this (Comm Minutes/Orders, 9 July 1937).

[34] Evening Star, 29 May 1921, p. 6. See also Evening Star, 23 July 1923, p. 6; and Wash. Post, 22 Sept 1940, p. 74, for further details of operations.

[35] WARL Pres. Palmer: "I wish to emphasize that we are neither a hospital nor a boarding house for animals" (WARL Ann Rpt, 1924), and many other such statements.

[36] Evening Star, 9 Oct 1921, p. 59; WARL Ann Rpts, 1919, 1924. These purchases were still advertised in 1936 (Evening Star, 20 Dec 1936, p. 3).

[37] "The League people are experts in detecting a stray from a homeless dog" (Wash. Post, 30 Mar 1919, p. S13). The cost of classified ads (always in the Evening Star and the Post; WARL Directors minutes, 29 Oct 1919) must have been a major expense – they appeared in the press almost daily – unless they were run gratis (see WARL Ann Rpt, 1924's thanks to the press, "which have been most generous in giving us notices"). WARL Exec Comm minutes, 30 Sept 1936 mentions a standing contract with the Washington Herald.

[38] WARL's Executive Committee considered releasing spayed females on 27 June 1934, and 29 Nov 1939.

[39] At least by 1941 (Times-Herald, 27 Apr 1941, p. E2).

[40] Evening Star, 9 Oct 1921, p. 59; Wash. Post, 30 Mar 1919, p. S13 ("Careful investigation of the proposed home is made, and decision always is rendered on whether the dog would like that kind of home, and not whether the applicant would like that kind of dog"); WARL Ann Rpt, 1924; WARL "A Few Facts"; WARL Sec Ann Rpt,1923. They seldom went to homes with small children (Wash. Post, 24 July 1927, p. 5) or apartments without exercise yards (Wash. Post, 22 Sept 1940, p. Amusements p. 12).

[41] Wash. Post, 31 Jan 1918, p. 7; 17 Oct 1920, p. 46; Evening Star, 9 Oct 1921, p. 59.

With its move to Maryland Avenue in 1917 President Codman donated an electrocution system invented the previous year by Mr. Huntington Smith and used in 32 other shelters at the time. There were three sizes of these machines – a stall for horses, a cage for dogs equipped with a specially fitted metal collar, and a small box for cats. "Only a second is required to accomplish the result. The animal does not even close his eyes. His face is as peaceful and happy as before." The agent was the "official executioner," and an electrician checked the mechanism monthly. This system had been "endorsed and recommended by men of the highest standing in humane and scientific standing in the country," and contrasted well with hanging, which was how human prisoners met their end in the District jail at the time.[42]

The 1931 WARL publication "A Few Facts" states that small animals were then chloroformed and larger ones dispatched "in the gas lethal chamber." In fact, the League had discontinued use of its electrocution box in early 1930, the result of regular mechanical problems and doubts about its effectiveness. The Board considered purchase of a newer box in 1932 "similar to the one used in SPCA in New York, but of a smaller size." This led to an unexpected evaluation of the different types of gasses used and their contrasting virtues.[43]

The League's policy of destroying unwanted animals ("at the League headquarters 'putting to sleep' is the accepted description of the process")[44] brought increasing criticism in the 1920s. This practice had both practical and philosophical underpinnings. The practical problem was obvious and the same dilemma that led its predecessor shelters and the pound to regularly destroy animals: space/resources/finances. "Collecting, as we often do, a thousand animals in a month, immense area, buildings, kennels and a great number of attendants would be necessary and the income required . . . would be far more than the public would be willing to provide."[45] Today, when far fewer animals are collected by a much larger number of organizations, the truth of this argument can be easily overlooked.

The philosophic argument was, of course, less clear cut and probably more legitimate on both sides. From its founding the League made clear that a painless death served homeless strays better than a painful life. "The League believes that it is far more humane mercifully to dispose of sick and diseased [and simply unwanted] animals than to keep them alive and prolong their suffering." Indeed, WARL never put any female animals up for adoption, and actively advised cat owners to keep "one or two of the strongest" kittens of their pet's litters and drown the rest. "It takes but a moment." This approach went beyond the limits of practicality and confirmed the organization's stated goal not only of helping distressed animals

---

[42] Poundmaster Einstein had endorsed this method in 1895. Evening Star, 31 Dec 1913, p. 8; 18 Nov 1917, p. 9; 9 Oct 1921, p. 59; Wash. Post, 17 Oct 1920, p. 46; WARL Ann Rpts, 1919, 1924. Most of the newspaper accounts include fairly graphic descriptions of the apparatus and its operation, but none compete with the gruesome details of Wash. Herald, 11 June 1916, p. 22 (regarding Boston's shelter). A good photo is included in the 1919 Annual Report.

[43] Op. cit.; Evening Star, 21 Feb 1930, p. 8; WARL Exec Comm minutes, 23 Apr 1932; 21 July 1932.

Purchase of a "lethal chamber" in 1937 generated considerable, and sometimes surprisingly frank, discussion; e.g., WARL Exec Comm minutes, 13 Oct 1936, again detailing the properties of various gasses and the prohibitive expense of injection and electric cages. From 27 June 1934 minutes we learn that WARL had recently written prison officials in Canon, Colorado, "asking what kind of pills were dropped in the pail of water under his chair when William Cody Kelly was executed in their new gas chamber." There was also a "dead box", described in the minutes of 3 May 1935, which apparently was different from the lethal chamber (for holding carcasses?). "The dead box is worn out and must be replaced" (WARL Exec Comm minutes, 25 July 1934).

[44] Wash. Post, 17 Oct 1920, p. 46. The earliest use of this phrase I found was in 1902 (Wash. Post, 2 June 1902, p. 10), but from the 1920s on it was the standard terminology of humane organizations. "Euthanized" appeared in the 1960s.

[45] WARL Ann Rpt, 1924.

but of ridding the District of strays with their deleterious "effect on sanitation" and potential danger to children.[46]

Needless to say, some opposed the very idea of putting down any creature, as they do today. "Many there are who believe that all humane workers are fanatical sentimentalists," wrote President Palmer. "There are some, but there is a long difference between sentiment and sentimentality We are not in sympathy with those persons, of whom there are still some left, who hold that no animal should be deprived of life." This controversy grew in the 1920s and explains a certain defensiveness in League pronouncements over the period. The Humane Education Society was founded in 1920 explicitly to avoid euthanasia (below). President Smith of WHS, a former League official, opposed the proposed merger with WARL precisely on the grounds that it killed unwanted wards.[47]

Following the League's 1928 execution of the pitiable collie Pal, which the organization made into a poster child for its cause, a flood of critical and often caustic letters poured into the local press. "Why should an organization with the experience of thousands of dogs' executions behind it suddenly become foolishly and tearfully affectionate for just another dog, all in the days' work?" wrote George Page pungently. "Did it not select this occasion . . . for the purpose of self-serving publicity? Does slobbering over a dog and then killing him justify the League's duplication of the poundmaster's work, or make the lot of the unfortunate dog easier?" He concluded by rejoicing that there was "no 'rescue' organization for . . . children." All of this the League bore with equanimity and, ultimately, success.[48]

A factor causing great seasonal strain on the League's resources was the distressing habit of many citizens to simply **turn pets outdoors** when they left **for vacations**, creating an annual summer bump in waif dogs and cats. While the wealthy could take their pets with them or leave them in the care of animal hospitals or servants or private establishments,[49] a large part of the population simply tossed them out, and whether or not expecting to find them again later is unclear. This habit was so common that it was unremarked upon in Washington until 1911.[50] WARL advertised regularly each summer against such thoughtlessness, and reminded the public that they could leave (board) their animals at its shelter. These notices continued through the 1930s, indicating a continuing problem.[51]

Other unhappy sources of discarded pets came from families moving out of town or from houses to apartments; from unwanted litters and pets lost at suburban tourist camps or left at beach resorts; and those whose "usefulness is gone or [are] no longer beautiful or attractive." During World War I League workers searched out pets abandoned by belligerent alien families expelled from the country. "Some of them have gone to new homes . . . to become good naturalized American dogs and cats," while others "have

---

[46] Wash. Post, 12 Aug 1934, p. 7; WARL Ann Rpts, 1919, 1924. The policy on female dogs was adopted in 1932 (WARL Exec Comm minutes, 30 Nov 1932). Much later – 1963 – WARL had changed this policy, but, echoing the District's policy of taxing females more than males to depress their number, the League charged $3 for a male and $10 for a female dog (Evening Star, 5 May 1963, p. 46).

[47] WARL, Ann Rpt, 1924.

[48] (Pal) Evening Star, 15 Aug 1928, p. 2; (criticism) 13 Aug 1928, p. 8 (a short, typical example); 20 Aug 1928, p. 8 (Page's letter).

[49] Classified ads of the late 19th century occasionally listed boarding available at "animal hospitals". A superb description of one such place is in Evening Star, 16 May 1891, p. 7, which took in all kinds of animals including birds, squirrels and goldfish. The article goes into charges, facilities, and its related business: selling and stuffing animals.

[50] By Health Officer Woodward (Evening Star, 5 June 1911, p. 1).

[51] "With the departure of people for the summer vacation and consequent turning of pets adrift, the work of the League will undergo its annual seasonal increase" (WARL Ann Rpt, 1924). Some typical examples: Wash. Times, 11 June 1919, p. 22; Evening Star, 18 July 1927, p. 2; 30 July 1939, p. 52. WHS complained of this practice also (Evening Star, 4 Aug 1921, p. 21).

journeyed to the happy hunting grounds by the happy, painless way." It also publicized reminders of good pet-care, such as the danger of summer heat and the need of canaries for exercise.[52]

Horses and mules received well-publicized if largely symbolic support by WARL's annual **Christmas feast**, modeled on Boston's project and initiated in 1915 by member Mrs. Ira Bennett. Held at various locations over the years but eventually settling at the shelter, horses munched hay and corn before selecting an apple or carrot from a large Christmas tree, all this donated by members and sympathizers. Drivers found coffee and doughnuts, a gesture these hard-working men undoubtedly appreciated.[53] In some years dog biscuits awaited accompanying canines. Take-out was available, and deliveries made by a roaming truck. The League's winter horse-slippers and even leather bridles (to replace painful wire ones) were given out free of charge.[54]

These events fed 102 in their first year and 150 in 1919, but numbers dwindled with the population of potential customers to 30 in 1928 and a disappointing three in 1933, its last year. Besides this lack of obvious need, WARL had opened itself to criticism that it was using money to feed horses "with so many human needs to fill." As an alternative, drivers could pick up grain at the shelter.[55]

In 1927 WARL advertised free summer boarding "to poor, disabled horses and mules" at a farm near Silver Spring, Maryland, but we have no further information on this venture, unfortunately.[56] Perhaps this referred to the Humane Education Society's farm.

Aside from its curious and aborted union with the Humane Society in 1927, WARL worked well with its humane colleagues all of this period. The Boy Scouts, Women's Club, Washington Riding Academy, WHS – all contributed to the effort. The annual "Be Kind to Animals Week", instituted in 1916, presented a good vehicle to publicize its work, and WARL participated in HES's "animal parade" (below).[57] In the late 1920s it joined other organizations on the issues of vivisection and safe horse stalls.

The League made sporadic efforts to educate children on humane practice but not as successfully as WHS. Its most successful juvenile program was made in conjunction with the District playground manager, Susan Root Rhodes, who encouraged the organization of Junior Animal Rescue Leagues in the very early 1920s. Sometimes children formed their own support groups, such as The Happy Four, which raised $35.23 for the League in 1922, and "another club of young girls" called The Animal Friends Society. Apparently this movement withered but was revived briefly in 1934, again under the initiative of the youngsters themselves.[58]

---

[52] ("Usefulness") WARL Ann Rpt, 1924; (Alien dogs) Evening Star, 16 Feb 1918, p. 7; (advice) 1 May 1918, p. 3; 18 Apr 1932, p. 17. A stretch of Ontario Rd NW was a favorite place to toss unwanted cats (Evening Star, 23 July 1923, p. 6).

[53] Needless to say, reporters could not resist the satirical possibilities: "Menu: Oats au naturel; Cornstalk fodder, Illinois style; Apples, carrots; Doughnuts a la life preserver; Coffee au lait" (Evening Star, 26 Dec 1916, p. 2).

[54] Evening Star, 26 Dec 1916, p. 2; 24 Dec 1918, p. 2; 24 Dec 1919, p. 2; 28 Dec 1923, p. 6; but every year earned an account.

[55] Ibid.; Evening Star, 5 Jan 1933, p. 17; 3 Jan 1934, p. 17; unidentified publication, 30 Dec 1928, file Wash. Div. These newspaper figures apply to the morning customers only and those coming to the premises, before the Star's reporters had to write up their articles but are comparable with each other; WARL Sec Ann Rpt, 1933, states that 50 horses benefitted the previous December.

[56] Evening Star, 3 July 1927, p. 3.

[57] (Women's Club) Evening Star, 14 Sept 1924, p. 26. The club offered a delivery service of unwanted pets to the shelter. (Be Kind) Evening Star, 26 Feb 1916, p. 12. The Executive Committee on 8 Mar 1933 did discuss a complaint that WHS was accepting unwanted animals, along with monetary donations, and then leaving the orphans with WARL while pocketing the money.

[58] (Education) Evening Star, 19 June 1920, p. 3; Wash. Herald, 27 Oct 1938, p. 15; (Jr ARLs) Evening Star, 11 Sept 1920, p. 10; 28 Apr 1921, p. 10; Wash. Herald, 18 May 1921, p. 16; WARL Ann Rpt, 1924; (Happy, Friends)

WARL **finances** came largely from members' dues (standard: $1-5, with higher levels to Life: $100, and a 25 cent Junior membership; somewhat revised in 1924), and the League solicited donations in honor of deceased pets to help with the summer "vacation season" and so forth. Special appeals, such as for a new ambulance, generally met with success. Bequests were regularly announced into the 1930s, including $3,500 in 1920 on condition that the lady's pets be given permanent homes at the shelter when she was gone. The very devoted Mrs. Blumenberg sold most of her furniture and collections to benefit WARL.[59]

Most memorable was a series of high-profile fund-raisers in the organization's first decade. These events were all aimed at and patronized by the most elite Washington society. "Smart society, accompanied by its aristocratic pets, was among the stream of visitors" to the first WARL Bazaar in 1919. Mrs. Warren Harding sent White House flowers to decorate the event. Bridge and maj-jong teas, held at the most fashionable hotels and clubs, saw attendance by the wives of Presidents Taft and Coolidge, and Secretaries of State Hughes and Kellogg, and (as a special ornament) the Baroness de Cartier de Marchianna. Three hundred ladies attended one such event in 1920, all carefully named in the press, including who partnered with whom at the tables. Theatrical (a "musical fantasy" titled "Fairy Lane") and film evenings flowed from the hard-working organizers. These had pretty much died out by the late 1920s.[60]

Appeals to the District government for a line in the city budget met with rejection, and the same response came from Congress.[61] In 1929 WARL became a charter member of the Community Chest, bringing it a more reliable annual income. The League suffered a blow when the shelter lost its tax-exempt status in 1931, entailing a $115 bill to the organization; its status was restored the following year. A similar tax imbroglio occurred in 1941.[62]

Governance of WARL rested with an elected president, an array of vice-presidents,[63] the usual officers, committees and a sizeable (15-20 members) Board of Directors. Throughout this period the League always elected the First Lady as its honorary president. Although the presidents changed frequently, a fair-sized group of dedicated supporters appeared year after year in one position or another; four charter members still served in 1939. Many of these also directly volunteered at the shelter and even kept strays at their own homes.[64] There was a strong crossover between WARL and WHS officers.

Presidents of WARL were: 1914 – Mrs. Peter Goulet Gerry; 1914-17 – Mrs. S. M. (Edith) Ackley; 1917-19 – Martha C. Codman; 1919-20 – Chester A. Snow; 1920-23 – Adm. Sydney A. Staunton; 1923-30 – Mrs. Truman G. Palmer; 1930-35 – Mrs. William F. Ham; 1935-36 – Mrs. Harry C. Moses; 1936-40; Mrs. C. Augustus Simpson; 1940-41 – Mrs. Merton E. (Annella) Twogood; 1941-42 – Mrs. LaVerne Beales.

Evening Star, 29 May 1921, p. 6; WARL Directors minutes, 21 May 1921; 26 Apr 1922; (later) 28 June 1934, p. 37; 5 Aug 1934, p. 24; WARL Exec Comm minutes, 27 June 1934.

[59] (Dues) WARL Ann Rpt, 1924; (bequests) Evening Star, 7 Mar 1920, p. 29; (sale) 18 Apr 1930, p. 17.

[60] A sampling only: Evening Star, 21 Mar 1919, p. 7; 8 Apr 1919, p. 8 (including the names not only of guests but also of their pets); 14 Jan 1920, p. 10; (theatrical) 9 Apr 1919, p. 8. Articles about WARL became much less frequent after 1924.

[61] (Congress) WARL Directors minutes, 14 Dec 1921; 31 May 1922; (District) WARL Directors minutes, 26 Nov 1923; WARL Ann Rpt, 1924; WARL "A Few Facts".

[62] Comm Minutes/Orders, 28 Sept 1932; Director's minutes, 5 Oct 1932; Wash. Post, 1 Aug 1941, p. 5; Memo, Sec of Board of Commissioners, 13 Mar 1945 (in WARL archives). It was one of the earliest members of the Community Chest.

[63] Originally 15, raised to 25 in 1924 (WARL Directors minutes, 30 Apr 1924).

[64] (Volunteering, animals in homes) WARL Ann Rpt 1924; WARL Sec Ann Rpt, 1932.

Paid staff grew to seven by 1940: kennelmen, drivers, matron and office employees. "Capt. Parker" (no source gives his personal name) followed Mary Coursey (after an interval) as manager of the facility from about 1931 to at least '39, and was much loved in that position. "Under his guidance the Washington Animal Rescue League [shelter] has grown to be one of the best administered in the country. . . It is a model for all similar enterprises and could well serve as a model for private kennels and veterinarian hospitals in both cleanliness and arrangement." Preston Thomas served as a very valuable agent from 1932 to at least 1942. Jessie (Mrs. Charles H.) Jones served as the on-site supervisor for most of this period.[65]

No doubt anyone working in an animal shelter has many stories. Here are a few

Tales from the WARL Shelter

- A man claiming to be a League fundraiser called citizens with candy for sale. "We have no one soliciting in any form for the League," said V-P Twogood. Police investigated. (Wash. Post, 14 Jan 1936, p. 5)
- Pranksters took to calling various public institutions on April Fools' Day and asking to speak with non-existent persons (the Zoo: "Mr. Fox" or "Mr. Lion"; the streetcar company: "Miss Car"; St. Elizabeths Mental Hospital: "Lizzie [Borden?]"; WARL: "Kitty"; the pound's character is unrecorded). The phone company said calls that morning ran 10% higher than usual. Threat of police action ended the practice in the early '30s. (Wash. Herald, 26 Apr 1922, p. 4; Evening Star, 1 Apr 1930, p. 17; 1 Apr 1931, p. 17)
- Eleanor Roosevelt once approached a National Park Service officer to ask for assistance with a lost dog. Officer Howell took the stray to the WARL shelter in his motorcycle sidecar. "The job was easy because the dog liked the unexpected ride." (Evening Star, 18 Dec 1933, p. 1)
- A "shabbily-dressed" woman brought a very young baby (presumably her own) to the shelter asking that it be euthanized the same as a cat. "She told me she lived in Anacostia, that she was destitute and that the baby had no milk." In spite of the attendant's offer of help, the woman slipped away, leaving the infant. (Evening Star, 23 Dec 1931, p. 17)
- WARL entered investigations on the surreptitious poisoning of cats (1931) and dogs (1932). (Evening Star, 21 Jan 1931, p. 8; Wash. Post, 12 Aug 1932, p. 16)
- WARL received a "black-hand letter" ("a single sheet of stationery on which was drawn a human hand, painted a dull black with shoe polish"), probably from the same woman who had recently written abusing the League for unspecified policies. At the same time, several women began hanging around the shelter ostentatiously writing in notebooks, telling strangers (incorrectly) that the shelter had their dogs, and annoying people with "other 'crazy conduct'." (Evening Star, 6 Apr 1930, p. 1)
- WARL personnel ("including three of the best monkey chasers this side of Venezuela, one automobile and a snare into which Pluto [the monkey] didn't stick his conceited little neck") failed to retrieve a loose monkey in the Bloomingdale neighborhood. "That monkey can stay up that tree all night if he wants to. I'm going home," declared a defeated Thomas Henry. A neighbor took him five

---

[65] (Staff) Wash. Post, 22 Sept 1940, p. 74; (Parker) Evening Star, 12 July 1937, p. 29; WARL Directors minutes, various dates; (Thomas) WARL Directors minutes; Evening Star, 20 Dec 1942, p. 18. See WARL Exec Comm minutes, 23 Oct 1936 for a curious imbroglio, in which Mr. Jones attempted to get Parker's job through unsigned letters.

night if he wants to. I'm going home," declared a defeated Thomas Henry. A neighbor took him five hours later. The League did once catch a baby alligator from an apartment building lobby and a fox from the Treasury Department building. *(Respectively: Wash. Post, 3 Aug 1936, p. X1; 3 Oct 1938, p. X13; WARL "The Twins . . .")*

- A pet owner brought in a litter of Pekinese pups whose mother had died, looking for a substitute dam. "After much deliberation a satisfactory mother – a tabby cat – was found, and the pups survived." *(Wash. Post, 22 Sept 1940, p. 74)*
- After a botched attempt to shoot an injured horse on the street, WARL distributed a diagram of how to perform the operation to all MPDC officers. *(WARL Sec Rpt, 27 Apr 1932; WARL Exec Comm minutes, 27 Sept 1933)*

In 1932 WARL made the momentous move to its first purpose-built shelter, the building still standing at **71 O Street NW**. The impetus for this project was twofold: (1) an increasing need for space and facility for an increasing number of animals;[66] and (2) the National Capital Park and Planning Commission[67] plan to develop the District's immediate southwest area as a government enclave. Sale of the Maryland Avenue property to the District government (the street was being widened) paid for most of the new land and building; the public was encouraged to donate the expense of specific components in exchange for a name plaque, as was done also at the 1977 facility.[68]

The neighborhood into which WARL moved – near the no-longer-existent Truxton Circle about a mile due north of the Capitol – was a long-established community by 1932, and in fact showing some deterioration as warehouses and workshops (especially garages and auto repair shops) increasingly crowded against the blue-collar residents. Its next-door neighbor to the east, picturesquely called Swampoodle, had already largely succumbed to this trend.

The League's Real Estate and Building Committee had first considered a site at South Capitol and D Streets SW, "an unusually desirable location" near its current shelter and only five blocks north of the pound, and had made a deposit when "a few congressmen" (like all neighbors) objected to such an annoying house close to their offices. The O Street site was the next choice. In fact, even semi-gritty O Street protested; neighbors immediately to the east of the property hired a downtown law firm to protest the shelter as a non-conforming use in violation of zoning regulations. Unfortunately for them the Commissioners disagreed and permitted the "animal hospital" but limited it to 40 animals.[69]

The present lot 110 of square 616 (the shelter and its parking lot) encompasses the consolidated lots 43-48 and originally carried the addresses 67-77 (odd numbers only). Lots 45-48 (71-77 O Street), previously holding houses, were joined as tax lot 811 in 1907 for the construction of a two-story brick warehouse ("waste paper packing plant", F. C. Butt & Co.), enlarged to three stories in 1913, which was

---

[66] No non-profit organization has ever been known to admit that it has enough space, but in this case the complaint was correct.
[67] Now National Capital Planning Commission.
[68] WARL, "A Few Facts"; New shelter dedication brochure.
[69] Comm Minutes/Orders, 2 Sept 1931; WARL Sec Ann Rpt, 1932; letters regarding zoning protest attached to the building permit. The Corporation Counsel reaffirmed its stance (though it is not clear that this opinion arose from a complaint about WARL) in 1936; see above "Early Shelter Movements". Neighbors, as the East Central Civic Association, tried to dislodge the shelter again in 1940 but were rebuffed (Comm Minutes/Orders, 6 Sept 1940).

demolished for the shelter.[70] The 1870s houses on lots 43 and 44 (tax lot 867) were purchased by WARL in 1953 (but only consolidated as lot 110 in 1985) and taken down for today's parking lot sometime afterward. The new shelter was about one block west of the League's first, rented space on Decatur Street.[71]

Architect Ralph W. Berry received the contract to plan (in separate jobs) the street-facing shelter/office and, on the rear alley, a garage. Berry designed nearly 100 houses in the District and others in Montgomery County, Maryland, between 1923 and 1937, almost all brick or stone structures in the wealthy upper-northwest area. This was a rare non-residential building for him.[72] Berry and League officials visited shelters in New York, Baltimore, Philadelphia and New Orleans. The architect submitted his proposal to the federal Commission of Fine Arts (which oversees projects affecting the appearance of the capital city) for an advisory-only opinion. The Commission found the design "a good one" but felt that a stone structure was "more appropriate for a suburban type of building" and recommended instead its then-standard "Georgian type of brick building." Berry ignored this advice.[73]

Of the seven bids for construction, the choice went to Bahen & Wright, a general contractor active in the city 1926-40 and working mostly in the eastern half.[74]

No building project is simple. To quote League Secretary Flora Beales' 1932 report (abridged): "We were beset with difficulties from the very beginning – such as delay in removal of the old warehouse, readjustment of plans, securing permits, and finally when the excavating was started a bad soil condition and water was found, necessitating a different foundation." The last added $6,260 to costs, bringing the project to about $26,000.[75]

The shelter opened with an invitation-only ceremony[76] on 23 June 1932. It had (and still has) "an English façade" of Potomac River gneiss (from "the Bucolstone [sic] Quarry") over a brick structure. Public rooms showed the same fieldstone and glazed tile. A slate roof topped both shelter and the separate double garage, and handsome multi-panel windows (sadly now gone) gave an aristocratic feel to the entry and gables. All of this reflects Berry's work on posh new houses for an upper-class clientele.[77]

---

[70] For an account of a fire that destroyed a later occupant, the Cook and District Waste Paper Company, see Wash. Post, 23 Apr 1927, p. 1. It was "an old brick structure." The place burned again three years later (Wash. Post, 30 Aug 1930, p. 1); its removal must have gratified the neighbors.

[71] Building permits 76/6 July 1907; 77/6 July 1907; 2370/29 Nov 1913. Perhaps a house on lot 48 was demolished in 1907 – the building records are not clear on the exact location of many properties, but see Evening Star, 26 Feb 1900, p. 10, which mentions a house there. The history of the lots is derived from the records of the District Surveyor's Office with the kind assistance of Mr. Neal Isenstein.

[72] DC building permit database, Washingtoniana Div, ML King Library. Perhaps his disappearance as an active architect from 1931 (immediately after designing the shelter) to 1934 tells us that he was the R. W. Berry who held some civil posts in his home of Chevy Chase, Maryland, at that time (Wash. Post, 14 Oct 1931, p. 8; Evening Star, 8 July 1933, p. 26). It is difficult to disentangle him in newspaper accounts from a near exact contemporary and well-known topographer with the U.S. Geological Survey, Ralph Whitely Berry, of nearby Kensington (Evening Star, 24 Feb 1949, p. 21). The "A. Moore Berry, Architect" addressed in the CFA documents was Judge Berry, the architect's father, who lived with him and perhaps handled some of his business matters (see Evening Star, 7 Mar 1939, p. 9). Mrs. Berry frequently attended local society events.

[73] Building permits 146152/28 Aug 1931; 146153/28 Aug 1931; Wash. Post, 25 Oct 1931, p. M22; WARL Sec Ann Rpt, 1932; CFA minutes, 24-26 Sept 1931.

[74] WARL Sec Ann Rpt, 1932; DC building permit database, Washingtoniana Div, ML King Library.

[75] Evening Star, 5 Sept 1931, p. 13; WARL Sec Ann Rpt, 1932.

[76] "With much newspaper and radio fanfare" (WARL, New shelter brochure).

[77] Perhaps some League members knew Berry in this way. (Opening) Wash. Post, 24 June 1932, p. 18; Evening Star, 23 June 1932, p. 17; (building) Evening Star, 25 Oct 1931, p. 14; 19 June 1932, p. 13; WARL Sec Ann Rpt,

Visitors, and reporters, were adequately impressed: "The most modern and well-equipped facilities for the care and shelter of stray and sick beasts," "thoroughly insulated and fireproofed," and "safe, sanitary and comfortable accommodations." With its 50 cages for dogs and a dozen cat cages, separate runs for each, veterinary clinic, two "comfortable" stalls for horses (in the garage), and an upstairs caretaker's apartment, "the new building compares favorably with the best anywhere" – "a credit to the City and to the Directors."[78] Cages carried the names of their donors (including the Washington Cat Club), and a plaque in the main hall commemorated the 1917 donation of the earlier building by Martha Codman and Chester Snow, which later paid for the new one. League members made other special donations: shrubbery, the paved walk, office furniture. The contractor also made unspecified contributions.[79]

With the new building came new staff. The move was a convenient occasion to discard unsatisfactory workers, but another consideration also came into play: should the new matron be white or colored? We don't know this information for earlier staff except for Coursey (white) and the two agents Parker and Smallwood (black) – in fact we know little about the very small staff at all. In this case, after considerable discussion and review of nearly a hundred applications, "it was thought best to hire a white person as matron or house manager."[80]

At its inauguration the building already held 40 dogs and 12 cats. In its new quarters the League increased its clinic service to three veterinarians (later reduced back to one paid doctor but expanding this effort through the Tail-Waggers Club, below).[81] Through an agreement with the District government, city-owned horses retired in favor of trucks went to WARL, which placed the healthy ones in nearby farms. At the same time, routine ambulance runs to take pets from homes dropped back from daily to four days a week, though the truck was available 24 hours a day for injured animals. Educational outreach grew in scope.[82] Generally the League's work at O Street continued smoothly as before, but with a larger staff, more professional operations and continued harmonious governance.[83]

Throughout the study period WARL took in a surprisingly large number of animals: rising from about 6,000/year to 11,000 during its first decade and to 18,000-21,000 in its second. It consistently held about three times the number of waifs as did the pound in the 1920s and '30s.

Before leaving this section we must stop to consider why **WARL** had such a smoother time of it in the 1920s and '30s than its sister organization **WHS**. Both experienced some financial distress, especially during the Depression, but WHS fell into an organizational disarray that did not afflict WARL. Two possible causes of this difference come to mind:

1932; building permits. The two Star articles have good pictures of the facility; Wash. Star, 18 Nov 1974, p. 32, shows the pens and run.

[78] "The runs are covered with a shelter . . . protecting the animals from heat and rain. There are hose connections in the tiled kennels so that they may be kept clean and have plenty of fresh water. There is over-head ventilation and . . . a thermometer in the room so that the temperature may be properly regulated" (Secretary's Ann Rpt, 31 Mar 1933).

[79] Wash. Post, 24 June 1932, p. 18; Evening Star, 19 Jan 1932, p. 13; 23 June 1932, p. 17; WARL Sec Ann Rpt 1932. The plaque is now at the current shelter.

[80] WARL Exec Comm minutes, 9 May 1932; WARL Sec Ann Rpt, 1933.

[81] Perhaps these doctors were donating their time. "A number of veterinarians were antagonized due to not being recognized in any of their work through the League" (WARL Exec Comm minutes, 25 May 1938).

[82] (Animals held) Evening Star, 23 June 1932, p. 17; (clinic, horses) WARL Exec Comm minutes, 25 Aug 1937; WARL, "The Twins . . ."; (ambulance) WARL, "Please! Cooperate . . .". Purchase of a small "pick-up ambulance" in 1938 was intended to eliminate the need for taxi trips (WARL Ann Rpt, 1938).

[83] The Executive Committee minutes of 25 Mar 1936 record with no sense of irony: "It seems that, because of the large amount of publicity we are receiving, Mr. Smith, of the Pound, is worried about his job. Mrs. Moses will see him, to explain that we really do <u>different</u> work from the Pound."

- WARL was from its beginning focused on a specific, concrete task – sheltering lost animals, while WHS remained largely issue-oriented. The constant demand of the shelter operation kept WARL from wandering into diffuse, ancillary issues, while WHS's loss of direction deepened as it held onto its prime concern for horses long after those animals had largely disappeared from the city. Notice the relatively small number of stances taken by WARL (vivisection, pet care) compared to the very long list of concerns adopted by WHS. A secondary benefit of this was that shelter work could much more directly involve WARL officers and members as volunteers than the recurring lobbying- and education-oriented efforts of WHS;
- WARL seems to have fallen much less than WHS under the influence of strong-willed presidents. Over the period of this study WHS had six presidents who served at least seven years; WARL had one. Without the steadying demand of shelter operations, WHS's interest and tone changed with each president (Snow – horses; Smith – vivisection). WARL adopted a more collegial governance.

At the same time, the two organizations showed a common development in the 1920s and '30s which led them both to their current and much healthier condition: they broke out of their upper-class bubbles and incorporated the District's middle class. This is a difficult trend to pin down. We have no way (as far as I know) to analyze the financial or social status of their membership over these years, but a very noticeable change from the 1910s and early '20s is the absence of society events (card parties at the Willard, etc.) as fund-raisers and the gushing over the gilded names of their supporters. By the 1930s both groups were placing pleas for membership and funds in the public papers. Following the lead of their middle-class younger cousins HES and APA (below) they took to parades, adoption days and advice to pet-owners. (WARL, with the never-stopping needs of its shelter, seems to have made this move before the more insular WHS.) Of course, another factor could well have been a shift in the concerns of the wealthy to other, more fashionable causes.[84]

WARL's history before 1940 is completed by descriptions of **three adjunct organizations**, all originating in the 1930s to support its work.

- The **Washington Herald** (later **Times-Herald**) **Animal Rescue Service**[85] was a pick-up service operated only in suburban Maryland and Virginia. Eleanor "Cissy" Patterson, socially prominent owner of the Washington Herald, established and personally financed the operation in November 1935 upon finding a family of starving dogs abandoned in a Virginia farm. "She appealed to the League for assistance and there followed some years of a remarkable association. Until her death [1948] Mrs. Patterson supported the mercy errands of two suburban ambulances while the League in turn faithfully adhered to its agreement to admit and care for the many Maryland and Virginia cases."[86]

    The service started operations with one van – "the most modern vehicle of its kind in the country," with a built-in killing chamber for distressed animals. It must have been large, since the organization promised to take unwanted horses. The service immediately demonstrated its

---

[84] Any reader, thinking back over the past five or so years, can easily make a long list of issues once fervently espoused and now forgotten by the glitterati.
[85] Sometimes, and mistakenly, the Maryland-Virginia Ambulance Rescue Service. The Times and Herald merged in 1939.
[86] Wash. Herald, 18 Nov 1935, sect 2 p. 1; WARL, New shelter dedication brochure.

usefulness; on its first day "more than a score of calls were received at the Herald and the Animal Rescue League before the new animal ambulance . . . started its rounds." Nearly 1,100 animals were brought in over ten days in November 1935. It purchased a reported 150 horses yearly. [87]

- Simultaneously with the start-up of the ambulance service came the organization of the **Maryland-Virginia Animal Rescue League**. This effort was so closely tied to the Herald's ambulance service that contemporary accounts confused them ("the M-V ARL, or the Times-Herald Animal Rescue Service, as it is frequently called"). It used the O Street building for its office, and paid WARL 45 cents for each animal it left at the shelter, WARL being barred from assuming the cost of out-of-town hobos by Community Chest rules.[88]

- WARL began discussion of forming a local chapter of the **Tail-Waggers' Club**[89] in 1936. The organization originated in England and by 1936 had chapters in thirteen American cities and a host of Hollywood patrons.[90] In this regard the Club was different from the other animal-related organization described here in that it was distinctly part of a national system rather than an autonomous group: "Straight from England, its charter was granted after much effort on the part of Mrs. Lawrence Wood Robert."[91]

Tail-Waggers' advertised a laundry list of goals and benefits ("to sponsor legislation beneficial to dogs and their owners, to provide funds for existing dog shelters, to educate children in animal kindness, to advise . . . owners on care and feeding of dogs, to properly handle our stray animal population") but largely sold its $1 memberships on the benefits of: (1) the special identity tag each member-pooch would wear, aiding in recovery of run-aways; and (2) its promise to open a charity dog clinic. The Club became active in 1937, headquartered in the O Street shelter.[92] The tags appeared immediately but it is not clear when the clinic project, as distinct from WARL's established service, started.

In a return to the League's society roots, Club members – four- and two-legged – initially seemed largely upper-crust. One of the earliest canines enlisted was Cretz, "dean of diplomatic dogs" and once owned by Queen Marie of Romania; another was the "refined and disdainful black French poodle" of Lt. Hubert Chandler. Fund-raisers from the late '30s included theatricals, embassy receptions and other events reminiscent of earlier times. The Evening Star's "safety dog", Knee-Hi, was given honorary membership in 1939, and during the war Washington Tail-Waggers sent contributions to their British cousins.[93]

---

[87] (Vehicle, service) Wash. Herald, 18 Nov 1935, sect 2 p. 1 (with photo); 19 Nov 1935, sect 2 p. 1; (statistic) Times-Herald, 27 Apr 1941, p. E2; WARL Exec Comm minutes, 6 Mar 1936.
[88] (Quote) Times-Herald, 27 Apr 1941, p. E2. Nonetheless, see Wash. Herald, 18 Nov 1935, sect 2 p. 1: "The Washington Herald Animal Rescue Service, cooperating with the newly formed M-V ARL." L. C. Probert's will left a large sum to the M-V ARL by that name (Evening Star, 12 Feb 1937, p. 3), but admittedly the relationship is not clear today. (Charge) Wash. Herald, 19 Nov 1935, sect 2 p. 1; WARL Exec Comm minutes, 6 Mar 1936.
[89] This is the correct form of the several variations of the name, taken from the organization's newsletter.
[90] I cannot pass up the names: Bette Davis, Dolores Del Rio, Leslie Howard, Dick Powell, Rupert Hughes, and boxer Jack Dempsey (Wash. Post, 12 Apr 1936, p. R16).
[91] Evening Star, 27 Apr 1938, p. 23.
[92] (Goals) WARL Tail-Waggers' Club Comm minutes, 16 Sept 1936 (the committee considered writing Walt Disney to ask if Mickey Mouse would serve as honorary president; Mickey and Minnie become the first members); (tag) Evening Star, 13 Nov 1937, p. 30.
[93] (Dogs) Evening Star, 4 Feb 1938, p. 23; 11 Feb 1939, p. 7; (events) 4 Feb 1938, p. 23; 27 Apr 1938, p. 23, and others; (Knee-Hi) 26 Oct 1939, p. 24; (contributions) 11 Feb 1939, p. 7.

In 1950 The Club incorporated independent of WARL but stayed at O Street. Dr. Crosby Kelly, who had "been in charge of the clinic since its beginning", treated 8,283 animals ("dogs, cats, horses, pigs and one rabbit") that year, charging only for inoculation.[94]

---

[94] Tail-Waggers' Club Ann Rpt, 1951; The Suburban Spectator (pub by the Woodward & Lothrop Department Store), Sept 1952 (with a photo of Kelly; both at the Washingtoniana Div, file "Animals").

CHAPTER TWENTY-FOUR

Later Humane Organizations

There are in Washington three major associations which are the champions and protectors of poor, hungry and abused animals [WHS, WARL, HES]. Each has the support of the public, works in its special sphere and does much to lessen suffering of animals and to relieve those persons who feel distress that so many animals suffer. (Evening Star, 21 Nov 1923, p. 6)

A few later humane organizations in Washington round out our account. All of them did good work with good intentions, but with few or none of their official publications available now, their histories must be pieced together from news accounts of the time. These organizations tended, for some reason, to take names very similar to existing groups and to each other, so that even contemporary readers became confused, requiring occasional published explanations by knowledgeable persons differentiating one from the other. None of them used acronyms but we will here for convenience.[1]

The Humane Education Society

The Humane Education Society is composed of sincere and earnest people who love animals, and under their auspices [such] a home . . . may become a valuable feature of the District's practical charities. (Evening Star, 10 Aug 1922, p. 6)

Sun and rain stain the battered old sign that hangs at the front gate [of the HES farm]. And, as time gradually blots out the letters, the memory of this haven for homeless beasts fades just as surely. (Wash. Post, 29 Oct 1933, p. SM6)

The Humane Education Society[2] came into being in March 1920 with the aim "to inspire children with the sentiment of kindness for animals" and to crusade for the usual list of causes: vivisection, trapping, performing animals, slaughter house reform and so forth. What led to its formation and what need was felt for an organization largely paralleling WHS we do not know. Among the founders are many of the usual names: Blumenberg, Venable, Sargent, former WHS President Snow and most importantly **James P. Briggs**,[3] also heavily involved in WHS.[4]

---

[1] WHS and WARL also did not use acronyms in our study period but later took up this more modern practice.
[2] Sometimes The Humane Education Society for Homeless Animals
[3] Briggs figured prominently in the earlier discussion of WHS, which see. Briggs was a native of Maine and moved to Washington as a young man (Evening Star, 11 Sept 1945, p. 2). His photo, sporting with homeless dogs at the farm, is in Wash. Post, 9 Nov 1924, p. SM10. A touching if somewhat hagiographic portrait of him is that by his widow, Anna, for which I thank Mr. Jim Taylor, current president of NHES and Briggs' grandson. This book – not widely available – is deposited in the Washingtoniana Division of the ML King Library.
[4] Evening Star, 30 Mar 1920, p. 15.

Briggs served briefly as president until formal adoption of the organization's constitution in May, when Paul Bartsch took the position. The group reiterated its educational interest ("by . . . means such as public lectures, meetings, exhibitions, work with school children") but after "a spirited debate" chose to take no stand on vivisection.[5]

The infant organization started life with a bang, holding the first "Be Kind to Animals Week" parade, an event specifically not intended to raise funds ("There will be absolutely not a cent collected") but to publicize the cause. Banners, speeches, illustrated lectures, hoards of Boy and Girl Scouts and a detachment of cavalry from Ft. Myer enlivened the day. HES covered all expenses, and how such a new society could pull this off is not recorded, but then, it was a group "composed of prominent Washington men and women."[6]

HES's first parade was such a success that the organization constructed a larger event the following year. Local newspapers caught the fever and hyped the coming extravaganza for weeks. "Plans . . . are proceeding swimmingly." The District government formally declared the dedicated week, ministers used the humane theme for their sermons on "Humane Sunday", and preliminary fund-raising film/variety evenings and society card parties filled the What's Happening pages.[7]

The parade itself was a great, splashy affair following the inaugural parade route up Pennsylvania Avenue to the presidential reviewing stand at the White House. But floats, teams of draught horses, the Ft. Myer "Arkansas canaries" (mules), Miss Alice B. Taylor's prize collie Pershing, the Soldiers' Home's celebrated Shropshire sheep "and dozens of other aristocrats of the animal world" all gave way to the President's own Laddie Boy, probably the most ballyhooed dog ("much press-agented") in White House history. More humble pets received prizes from a select committee.[8]

The following year (1923) the Society shifted gears and exchanged elite canines for common dogs – a "Mutt Show", modeled after established events in Baltimore, New York and other cities. The proposal stemmed from the obvious if theretofore overlooked fact "that there are hundreds of plain 'dogs' here which have no pedigrees but which are beloved by their owners." These plebian pooches paraded their stuff at the Coliseum for two days and then down Pennsylvania Avenue; professional judges had the challenge of devising criteria for awards. John Phillip Sousa and Irene Castle donated prizes. In spite of its middle-class nature,[9] "that the show will be a social event seems certain." A second "annual" show was held (belatedly) in 1925 but without the high-society hoopla; it was the last.[10]

By the time of the Mutt Show James Briggs had resumed the HES presidency, a position he held until his death over twenty years later. The Society claimed about 200 members in 1922. Membership dues ranged from $2 to $5.[11]

---

[5] Evening Star, 12 May 1920, p. 7.
[6] Evening Star, 7 Apr 1920, p. 4.
[7] Evening Star, 14 Apr 1921, p. 3; Wash. Times, 1 May 1921, p. 14. One film, "Our Four-Footed Friends", featured "prominent Washingtonians and their animal friends." How interesting it would be to have this footage today!
[8] Many more details will be found in Evening Star, 8 May 1921, p. 6; 14 May 1921, p. 2; Wash. Herald, 14 May 1921, p. 2 (with a photo). The highlight of the parade was Laddie Boy's attempt to jump from his "gorgeously decorated" float into his master's arms; he was thwarted by Wilson Jackson, "the colored master of the hounds at the White House." Other attractions were a three-horned sheep and an 800-pound hog. Several hunt clubs participated, an interesting date for the anti-hunting HES.
[9] "Just as no dog was discriminated against so the owners – male and female, white and black – meet on common ground" (Worden, "A Poorhouse Paradise").
[10] Evening Star, 30 Oct 1923, p. 16; 31 Oct 1923, p. 4; 10 Nov 1925, p. 27.
[11] Evening Star, 4 Aug 1922, p. 22; Wash. Post, 13 Feb 1925, p. 6.

As, in effect, HES's only president and its guiding hand, Briggs deserves notice. A man of some position (he was a lawyer first in the Department of the Interior, and then from 1919 to his death in the legal office of the Bureau of Internal Revenue), he could have lived the standard upper-middle-class man's life of the time – fraternities, hobbies, social functions, dabbling in business and real estate – but gave himself and his estate over entirely to the cause of animals. "Though he worked hard as an attorney during the week, Mr. Briggs . . . devoted every spare moment to [animals'] rescue and care." Following his 1925 marriage to a much-younger neighbor and regular WARL volunteer, Anna C. Reynolds, Briggs moved the family to the caretaker's house in the newly-established farm, where his wife cooked the inmates' food while her husband worked (six days a week) in town. "After his workday was done, Briggsie spent long hours taking care of the animals and repairing the kennels." The couple returned to Washington on the birth of their first child in 1929.[12]

For a period in the early 1920s HES held exactly the sort of society fund-raisers executed in that period by its sister humane organizations. Its "dance and carnival," "silver tea and musicale," "spring kermis" (dance show), and card parties saw attendance from such ladies as the wives of Presidents Theodore Roosevelt, Taft, Harding, Coolidge, of Nicholas Longworth, Henry C. Wallace, Harlan Stone, Peter G. Gerry (of WARL), Henry L. West (of the Cat Club), as well as Alisa Mellon and "Mrs. Edgar Allen Poe" (of Baltimore). Actor George Arliss and his noted colleagues Elsie Janis, Irene Castle and Minnie Maddern Fiske supported the effort. Humane benefactor Mary Peet left a large part of her estate to HES in 1929 (along, it will be remembered, with a smaller bequest to her maid Sarah Beckley).[13]

With wonderful celerity HES grew beyond its originally stated goal of education into the shelter business. In August 1922 the Society announced its plan to raise $25,000 and buy a 150-acre farm about fifteen miles from the District in Brookville, Maryland, and there establish a "rest farm" for all homeless beasts. Two well-placed ladies (one a senator's wife)[14] led this effort but President Briggs was the public face of the project. While waiting for a full subscription HES established "a home for dogs in a small country place."[15]

The Be Kind to Animals Rest Farm (later the Animal Rescue Farm)[16] was visited by a Mr. King in late 1923. He found a well-ordered establishment where, "amid contentment and free from care, were animals, some too old to work, some that had never known a home before and others thrown out on the world for various reasons." Horses, dogs and cats, "under the watchful eyes of a Mr. Warden and his wife," all had comfortable quarters and appropriate food and water. Planned improvements would make the farm "one of the best institutions caring for stray and homeless animals in the entire country." Briggs borrowed $4,800 for this venture by mortgaging his own house.[17]

---

[12] Briggs, For the Love of Animals, pp. 55, 73.
[13] Some examples: Wash. Times, 12 Apr 1922, p. 9; Evening Star, 3 Feb 1924, Society p. 6; 18 May 1924, p. 55; (Arliss) 16 Mar 1928, p. 39; (Janis) 3 Nov 1922, p. 35; (Peet) Evening Star, 13 Mar 1929, p. 3.
[14] Mrs. Duncan U. Fletcher, "wife of the Florida senator," and Miss Edna M. Patton. "The idea had been in the minds of these two women for several years, but obstacles always appeared in the way" (Evening Star, 4 Aug 1922, p. 22).
[15] Ibid.; Evening Star, 9 Nov 1922, p. 6.
[16] This was not the Brookville site originally planned but an 80-acre farm on River Road in "the village" (now a very pricey suburb) of Potomac, Maryland (Evening Star, 8 Nov 1925, p. 6). Detailed driving directions will be found in Evening Star, 4 Dec 1924, p. 6.
[17] (King) Evening Star, 12 Dec 1923, p. 6; see also N. C. Williams' enthusiastic report in Evening Star, 17 Apr 1925, p. 6. (Mortgage) Evening Star, 29 Nov 1925, p. 3. The farm itself cost $3,800 and it was mortgaged in 1924 (Evening Star, 29 June 1924, p. 7).

The HES in its general operations mostly resembled other such efforts in Washington: it took charity strays and cast-offs, gave out animals for adoption to stringently qualified persons, and employed a full-time caretaker.[18] The chief differences with other shelters were that it accommodated any type of animal (though we mostly read of horses, cows, dogs and cats), and most importantly that it did not kill them. Some of the wards "will find good homes through the kind offices of the directors, and others will lead a comfortable life until death calls them." Diseased animals, however, were put down.[19]

The farm was generally described as well thought-out and –run. The first resident caretaker was "William" (Warden?), an African-American who lived there with his family, "selected for his integrity and genuine love of animals";[20] Mrs. P. W. Falconer was manager in 1925. Salaries for a farm manager and the caretaker came to $100 a month. Dogs lived in a purpose-built one-story building with fireproof cages and a central run. Cats shared a roomy common space with wire-enclosed yard, also in a new building.[21] The caretaker's house was probably an existing farmhouse – it had no heat, stove, electricity or plumbing. The farm included a dog cemetery.[22]

The farm held about 120-140 tenants (in one account: 6-8 "rather decrepit" horses, 20-30 cats, 100 dogs; later accounts routinely say 50-60 cats and 150 dogs), and some cows, hogs and ducks. The shelter once housed a turkey but a German shepherd ate it. Original plans called for a receiving station in the city but it was not mentioned afterward. HES members occasionally picked up street animals but the large number were deliveries by uninterested owners or others.[23] Like WARL, the Society sometimes purchased broken-down horses. "Those who can afford it are expected to give something for placing or obtaining a dog there. The requirement, however, is waived for persons without means."[24] Adopted animals could be returned, as at WARL. The Society, wishing to reduce dog/cat populations, eschewed breeding at the farm and of course guarded against "adoption" for experimentation purposes.[25]

A few details round out this portrait of HES's shelter. Dogs ate a "slum-gullion" of meat, corn bread and dog biscuits;[26] cats had milk, salmon and commercial cat food. With grain and forage for horses added,

---

[18] Plans to accommodate paid boarders probably never materialized. HES had a "rescue vehicle" (Briggs, For the Love of Animals, p. 55).

[19] Evening Star, 17 Apr 1925, p. 6; Worden, "The Poorhouse Paradise". Briggs denied that any animals were executed (Evening Star, 29 June 1924, p. 7).

[20] "Even the most ferocious-looking bulldog . . . yelps in friendly delight when he sees William" (Evening Star, 29 June 1924, p. 7).

[21] "The buildings . . . are not palatial but they are well-kept and in good repair. There is an eleven-room house and several barns. Around the entire [area] extends a strong fence" (Worden, "The Poorhouse Paradise"). This article gives a fairly detailed description of the place and some useful photos. Briggs built the pens himself, "learning carpentry as he went along" (Briggs, For the Love of Animals, p. 55).

[22] Evening Star, 29 June 1924, p. 7; 21 June 1925, p. 6; Worden, "The Poorhouse Paradise"; Briggs, For the Love of Animals, pp. 59, 72.

[23] In 1924 HES futilely offered to take in the German shepherd Fritz, ordered destroyed by the Police Court for viciousness. "Fritz attempted to prove his good character in court and permitted strange folk to caress him. Before the trial ended, however, Fritz leaped at an attorney" and as a result was gassed at the pound. (Evening Star, 31 Mar 1924, p. 16)

[24] "The Society has had wonderful success in placing animals in good homes . . . over 300 dogs and 100 cats having been thus placed in the last few years" (Worden, "The Poorhouse Paradise").

[25] Evening Star, 4 Aug 1922, p. 22; 29 June 1924, p. 7; 21 June 1925, p. 6; 10 Nov 1925, p. 27; Wash. Post, 13 Feb 1925, p. 6; 17 Apr 1925, p. 6. Wash. Post, 9 Nov 1924, p. SM10, and 29 Oct 1933, p. SM6 names a few formerly-famous horsed retired there, and some interesting dogs.

[26] "Not salvaged from somebody's trash can or lunchroom, but . . . from one of Washington's leading hotel supply firms and guaranteed fresh" (Evening Star, 29 June 1924, p. 7). The writer could not resist adding (nor can we): "That stew smelled dog-gone good to the reporter, too."

the monthly bill for provisions averaged $400 each month. Early plans to provide "free clinics for pets of the poor" (provided by two of "the leading veterinarians of Washington" – volunteers) did not materialize, but another early idea – making strong horses available to teamsters so that tired animals could take a rest-vacation – was actually advertised in 1927. True to its educational mission, orphans and school children visited the farm. HES placed regular classified notices of its services in local newspapers but only in its heyday period of 1925-26.[27] Aside from routinely joining other groups in protests against vivisection and the other usual causes HES in the 1920s focused on its shelter operation.[28]

In late 1925 HES suffered a public relations disaster: Rose Saffranek ("Miss Rose" to the children at New York Avenue and North Capitol Street), a kind, eccentric lady who had taken in "an even dozen of the lowliest mongrels and alley cats that she could find," tried to mollify annoyed neighbors by turning over the two noisiest dogs to the Animal Rescue Farm, but was refused for lack of available kennel space. Saffranek complained bitterly to the Evening Star ("They seem to be able to take pedigreed dogs from rich people, but my poor mutts don't stand a chance"). In spite of a vigorous defense by member Louise C. Worden ("I have paid several visits . . . The 'pedigreed dogs' . . . mentioned . . . are conspicuous by their absence. Most of them are just plain dogs"), the paper sent a reporter to investigate.[29]

"Animal Rest Farm Inmates Pitiable", with accompanying pitiable photos, completely trashed the HES shelter, bemoaning the conditions of the facility, medical care, and food, describing the suffering of specific animals and – most damning – revealing a nasty war between recently-fired caretaker Sarah Faulkner (who refused to move) and her non-resident replacement Aldrich Butt, each accusing the other of causing the problems. "Whether the condition that exists there today is due to poor management, overlapping authority or lack of funds, . . . the animals themselves have become victims rather than beneficiaries of the kindness."[30]

This fiasco fed the papers for a few weeks ("Following The Star's article . . . complaints have poured [in] alleging that its description [of] the farm was unjust, unfair and erroneous"), including a generous and informed defense of HES by WHS Secretary John Heap. The Society pleaded poverty, hastily arranged care for the sickest animals, and booted out Faulkner, giving resident oversight to its secretary, who quickly had the place cleaned and repaired. Visiting veterinarians declared the Star's depiction unfair.[31]

The 1925 expose did not kill the HES shelter but the group showed a clear decline after that. Publicity and fund-raisers disappeared soon thereafter. Indeed, it is surprising to read in the farm's 1933 obituary that it had continued to operate more-or-less successfully almost to the end. Briggs stated in 1925 that the Society put $10,000 into the place the previous year and in its last years expenses ran $600 a month. "Now [1933] it considers itself fortunate to obtain that amount over a six-month period."[32] Briggs' 1929 arrest for keeping an illegal animal hospital (veterinary clinic) in his home near Gallaudet College (he was, in fact, holding dogs there for transfer to the farm, something he seems to have done regularly), and his 1930 legal problems with WHS for diverting that organization's funds to HES and

---

[27] Evening Star, 4 Aug 1922, p. 22; 7 Oct 1927, p. 8; Worden, "The Poorhouse Paradise". For a heart-warming account of a visit by children (each one named) of the Washington Orphan Asylum, see Evening Star, 21 June 1925, p. 6.

[28] The organization issued a plea for greater safety at racing stables following a well-publicized fire in 1923 (Evening Star, 22 Oct 1923, p. 6).

[29] Evening Star, 8 Nov 1925, p. 6 (a complete account of Saffranek); 16 Nov 1925, p. 6.

[30] Evening Star, 29 Nov 1925, p. 3.

[31] Evening Star, 30 Nov 1925, p. 6; 2 Dec 1925, p. 2; 6 Dec 1925, p. 5.

[32] "Times were hard. Often we found ourselves having to beg or borrow money in order to feed animals at the Farm. How I hated pleading for money!" Mrs. Briggs opened a candy shop to supplement income, without great success (Briggs, For the Love of Animals, pp. 73-74).

other groups both damaged the Society and demonstrated its declining fortunes. Painfully, an anticipated bequest of $100,000 was lost to unanticipated relatives. Neighbors brought suit against the farm as a nuisance. Everything went wrong.[33]

The Animal Rescue Farm (still fronted by "a battered old sign 'Be Kind to Animals Rest Home'") closed in 1933, killed both by lack of funds and of a robust organization to oversee and support it. "Two years ago the turnover of the dog population at the farm was rapid. Stray dogs and injured animals . . . were . . . sent to the farm daily . . . Every pen was full and the lying-in hospital was operated to capacity. . . Now there are almost no visitors. The veterinarian has gone and the . . . animal hospital [has] been locked . . . Weeds fill the long wired-in pens that extend from a central house . . . Two or three decrepit old horses still wander in the woods of the farm." A sad end for such a hopeful and useful venture.[34]

With the end of the farm whatever vitality the Humane Education Society still had evaporated and the organization (such as it was) lived on only as a soapbox for President Briggs, who remained its head to his death. He regularly spoke on humane causes at animal-related events, at commemorative celebrations (National Dog Week, Be Kind to Animals Week) and on radio, many projects still listing HES as a sponsor. He was a vegetarian, a rabies-skeptic (and therefore opposed to compulsory inoculation for that disease), belonged to the Anti-Capital Punishment League, and served as the president of the National Society for Humane Regulation of Vivisection. Briggs died of a heart attack in 1945.[35]

After Briggs' death HES underwent a re-organization (1948) under his widow, Anna, as the National Humane Education Society, which very much "need[ed] more membership and monthly dues funds." It was this group that bought a 146-acre farm in Leesburg, Virginia, in 1950, as will be related in the Afterword.[36]

Animal Protective Association

Unlike most organizations, [APA] asks for nothing but co-operation in taking care of homeless dogs and cats. (Wash. Post, 23 Aug 1936, p. R14)

Virginia W. Sargent as a student at Carberry Elementary School won $5 in a WHS essay contest on the theme of "Humanity to Animals" in 1911. Nearly seventy years later the elderly Sargent reminisced: "I am reminded of my eighth-grade class years ago, where our teacher, a Miss Young, welcomed the formation of a 'Band of Mercy' . . . We had a 'Kindness to Animals' essay contest and I won one of the prizes; also one in high school [Eastern High School]. . . It proves what good influence a kind-hearted teacher can exert upon the sensitive minds of young people toward God's animal creations." In this way was born the most persistent and appealing "promoter of religious-humane education" in twentieth-century Washington, DC.[37]

---

[33] (Finances) Evening Star, 29 Nov 1925, p. 3; Wash. Post, 29 Oct 1933, p. SM6; (arrest) Evening Star, 27 Nov 1929, p. 2; (WHS) Wash. Post, 22 Nov 1930, p. 5; (bequest) 29 Oct 1933, p. SM6; (suit) 10 July 1931, p.2.
[34] Wash. Post, 29 Oct 1933, p. SM6. The animals were taken by a New York shelter (Briggs, For the Love of Animals, p.74).
[35] See his obituary, Evening Star, 11 Sept 1945, p. 2. His death is touchingly described in Briggs, For the Love of Animals, p.76.
[36] (Re-org) Evening Star, 31 Aug 1948, p. 6; (farm) Wash. Post, 30 June 1950, p. B3.
[37] Evening Star, 24 June 1911, p. 6; 5 Apr 1924, p. 31; 11 Oct 1980, p. 12.

Sargent's strong Christian faith shows through clearly in her years of humane work and her many, many short writings. "As a lover of all God's creatures, a God-fearing practical humanitarian, I should like to [say that] animals and birds in our midst . . . should and can be respected as God's creatures. He is their Creator as well as ours, and a Christian respects the works of His hand," reads a typical letter. She described herself as of a Scotch family and daughter of a Presbyterian elder. All her life she strongly supported the First Presbyterian Church and assisted in its Sunday school program. She graduated in the first class of the YMCA's School of Religious Education in 1922.[38]

Sargent and Sarah Beckley were the only prominent humane volunteer workers in Washington before World War II of modest income.[39] She worked for the U.S. Department of Agriculture, though only for fifteen years. She joined WHS at the lowest membership level ($1). She never married and lived with family most of her life.[40] She was "a strict vegetarian" and "a passionate nature lover" (all her own words) who spent her summers (in "what office leave I can spare") at "my little summer suburban home" in nearby Garrett Park, Maryland.[41]

Sargent's intense attachment to the cause of her "animal friends and helpers" is easiest seen today in her near continuous stream of letters published in local newspapers, beginning in 1921 and running to her last years – often four or five a year and we don't know how many others not published. (She also spoke on radio.) None of these lectured readers or wagged a finger at them; all expressed a warm love for her fellow-creatures of God and offered easy, sensible steps how to aid them, from joining one of the several humane organizations (she always included contact information) to feeding birds in winter. Mostly she promoted local efforts, but she also wandered into issues of vivisection, Easter chicks, rodeo animals, circus lions, bull fighting, hunting, animals in markets, validity of rabies scares, nourishing animal food, child labor, and the morality of current movies. She protested wartime scrap drives held on Sundays and in 1957 scolded the Soviet government for "shooting a defenseless little dog into outer space."[42]

She was always practical. She joined the three local humane organizations active in the 1920s and remained faithful to all even after she had started her own. She helped with the 1919 WARL bazaar and the pound's 1930 Thanksgiving doggie dinner. When the government demolished some dormitory buildings near Union Station in 1930 and the old Center Market in 1931 Sargent worked daily "outside my government office hours and between trains to my suburban home" to coax frightened cats from the wreckage. She fed birds in winter but "not . . . where they might accumulate to annoy anyone plying his legitimate business." She was not one of the "sentimentalists" derided by WARL, but saw the need to put down unwanted animals: "To homeless creatures a merciful death is preferable to a miserable existence, and there is no true kindness in the sentiment 'It's a shame to kill them.'"[43]

The obvious confluence of animals/children's moral education/church led Sargent to form her own organization. As early as 1924 she had organized a pet show at the Capitol Hill Boys' Club. In 1931 she

---

[38] (Quote) Evening Star, 8 Jan 1949, p. 6; (background) 2 Apr 1927, p. 11; 26 Oct 1942, p. 9; (graduation) 15 Apr 1922, p. 11.

[39] I say this on the evidence of her regular clerical job and that, unlike the other women described here, she had no husband for support. Her record of financial contributions to her organization clearly indicates that she had some resources, possibly just savings. Her Capitol Hill neighborhood was not fashionable and none of the usual society ladies worked with her. Let us note that James Briggs nearly drove himself and his family to penury with his support of HES.

[40] Her parents died in 1928 and 1932, and her brother Thomas in 1967 (Evening Star, 27 Oct 1946, p. 19; 24 Dec 1967, p. 9). "I've been too busy with suffering dogs to bother with a husband" (Wash. Post, 19 Sept 1939, p. 3). See also Evening Star, 13 Nov 1933, p. 5, and Wash. Post, 13 Nov 1933, p. 13 (with photo) for an account of a family tragedy (the lady died soon afterward).

[41] (Vegetarian) Evening Star, 24 Dec 1921, p. 17; (nature) 19 Sept 1924, p. 6.

[42] The last demands to be documented: Evening Star, 21 Nov 1957, p. 18.

[43] (Bazaar) Evening Star, 30 Mar 1919, p. 44; (dinner) 27 Nov 1930, p. 17; (cats) 18 July 1930, p. 8; 17 April 1931, p. 8; (birds) 8 Jan 1949, p. 6; (killing) 5 June 1925, p. 6.

described herself as leader of the "Animal Protection Band of the **Church Humane Education League**," giving her own address as headquarters. Anyone knowing of needy animals should "notify me . . . and put out your scraps for them until I and my two helpers, who have been working day and night to rescue these poor things from starvation, can get around with our humane equipment to capture them."[44]

By the following year (1932) this organization had morphed into the **Animal Relief and Humane Education League**, still at her house at 322 E Street NE, and had taken over sponsorship of Be Kind to Animals Week from the moribund HES. Perhaps it was the debilitation of that organization that led her to create the League in the first place – she had been a close colleague of Briggs in earlier years. The new ARHEL stated its opposition to vivisection and the customary panoply of complaints, promised to promote humane education and vegetarianism everywhere, and "to do actual rescue work for stray and deserted animals." It quickly organized a children's auxiliary under WHS's name, Bands of Mercy, and sponsored school essay contests.[45] It was the only District humane society in this period that did not originate within the upper class.

The organization began rounding up strays immediately, generally in cooperation with WARL, to which shelter they were sent. Cats (200-300 of them) rescued from demolished government buildings; dogs and cats left off by departing owners; an abused collie purchased from its thoughtless owner; Sargent once euthanized a disabled dog for its master. The League's officers "often spend hours and days of personal effort feeding, coaxing and generally succeeding in rescuing lost, terrorized and stray dogs" – all duplicative of WARL's efforts and often done in conjunction with that organization. The group must have been quite small – it had only six officers in 1933, none of them names familiar from the more rarified milieu of WHS or WARL – and claimed to survive entirely on dues but in fact through the funding of Sargent herself.[46]

Inevitably ARHEL soon moved into sheltering the many animals it collected from streets and countryside. In 1933 the group was offering to house pets and even horses, probably at Sargent's place in Garrett Park. Its few officers included a matron, and there was a "local temporary receiving station." This band of dedicated humanitarians ventured into neighboring Maryland and Virginia on their work. One dedicated volunteer was Anna C. Briggs, whose HES shelter had recently closed. The two lived near each other. Sometimes they found homes for their "waifs" but sometimes had to put them down.[47]

1934 marked an important advance for Sargent and her friends: ARHEL became the **Animal Protective Association**,[48] and the APA opened a (probably more substantial) shelter at 5200 Wisconsin Avenue NW.[49] This facility operated like its established counterparts, with its own telephone number, visiting hours (closed on Sundays, of course) and 24-hour drop-off. It "picks up lost or deserted animals, and tries to restore them to their owners or find good homes for them." Like WARL, it did not place female animals, leaving open the question of what it did with them and with unclaimed animals.[50]

---

[44] (Pet show) Evening Star, 9 Apr 1924, p. 10; (League) 22 Dec 1931, p. 8. She was president of this League (Wash Post, 3 Oct 1931, p. 6). She was not listed as a supporter of the "Crusaders for Kindness" character-training program proposed for DC public schools in 1930 (Evening Star, 23 Apr 1930, p. 23).
[45] (Goals) Evening Star, 17 Apr 1932, p. 28; 20 Apr 1932, p. 11; (Bands) Wash Post, 19 Apr 1932, p. 18 (with photo). Sargent stated in 1932 (Evening Star, 25 Nov 1932, p. 8) that the League had been organized "for over two years," which would take it back to the first notice of the Church HE League.
[46] (Work) Evening Star, 20 Apr 1932, p. 11; 25 Nov 1932, p. 8; 10 Aug 1933, p. 17; 28 Aug 1934, p. 8; (officers) 20 Apr 1933, p. 12.
[47] Evening Star, 1 Aug 1933, p. 8; Wash Post, 26 Dec 1933, p. 6; Briggs, For the Love of Animals, p.75.
[48] There were similarly named organizations in many US cities at the time but, like the Animal Rescue Leagues and Societies for the Prevention of Cruelty to Animals, they were entirely independent of each other, linked only by common goals and methods.
[49] (Building permits) Evening Star, 11 Aug 1934, p. 17; (opening) 9 Dec 1934, p. 13.
[50] Wash. Post, 22 Dec 1934, p. 8: Evening Star, 3 Feb 1935, p. 26.

In the first half of 1933 ARHEL took in 600 animals; the total for three years (1933-35) stood at 5,760. Sargent's accounts of these ladies' tireless and lonely work seeking out and feeding or capturing desperate animals (mostly cats) are undoubtedly accurate: "The Association keeps a watchful eye on areas of government improvement [demolition/building] and its agents [have] been at work feeding and rescuing the waifs . . . Some evenings, with the press of other orders, there is only time to feed; but someone will visit the spot every day until every possible rescue is made." APA also went on the street to distribute Thanksgiving and Christmas dinners to homeless cats, dogs and to horses "stabled in poor areas of the city." During this period APA "specialized on feeding homeless cats . . . Eventually it hopes to capture and destroy humanely the surplus cat population of Washington."[51]

Advertisements from 1936 placed the facility on Bradley Road in Bethesda, Maryland; apparently the facility had been forced to move from Wisconsin Avenue. APA began looking for permanent quarters, settling in the then-outskirts of eastern Washington, at 3900 Wheeler Road SE. The 1½- story house and 2-story "animal rescue home" were occupied in October 1937 (World Animal Day). Sargent covered the estimated $13,500 cost as a memorial to her parents. Her own cat, Fluffy, was the first resident. Along with the dedication, Sargent announced plans to resign the presidency of APA in favor of Anna Briggs so that she could concentrate on children's humane education but this did not happen, and she continued to head the organization to its end.[52]

The new shelter lived a financially precarious life. With the move, staff was reduced to one, meaning that APA could not pick up pets from houses, and telephone service cut off just the following year. The phone was off once more in 1943, and APA again reduced its efforts (and phone service) in 1948, when it "need[ed] more membership and monthly donor funds from the public." The organization was not a member of the Community Chest funding system.[53] Sometimes bright spots lighted the routine, as when 40 members of the Junior Animal Protection Association gathered at the shelter for Bobby Briggs' seventh birthday; and we read of a branch of APA in neighboring Prince George's County, Maryland, in 1946. The Wheeler Road shelter closed in 1953 "because of the increasing number of apartment units in the area." Hopes of establishing a new facility in upper Montgomery County, Maryland, were thwarted by zoning restrictions. APA then continued simply as an education and advocacy organization, operating from Sargent's home back in Garrett Park, where it had started.[54]

Virginia Sargent moved permanently from her E Street home to Garrett Park in 1953. About fifteen years later she joined Anna Briggs' family in a specially built addition to their house and lived there until retiring to a nursing home, where she died in 1984, still president of the Animal Protective Association.[55]

News articles of 1936 reported on the recently opened **Times Free Animal Clinic**, organized by the Washington Times. Dr. Milton A. Bosley, president of the D.C. Veterinary Medical Association, treated

---

[51] (Statistics) Evening Star, 1 Aug 1933, p. 8; Wash. Post, 9 Dec 1935, p. 17 ("More than 300 animals were rescued from deserted buildings along Pennsylvania Avenue when the government started its razing activities"); (efforts) Wash. Post, 23 Aug 1936, p. R14 (including its work in re-developing southwest Washington); (dinners) Evening Star, 17 Dec 1935, p. 7; 26 Nov 1937, p. 31; 30 Dec 1945, p. 19. The Association fed 200 cats in 1937; the article gives the menu, which included salmon laced with catnip. (Cats) Evening Star, 3 Feb 1935, p. 26.
[52] Rossel E. Mitchell was the architect and Lacy H. Smith the builder. (Bethesda) Evening Star, 5 Oct 1937, p. 2; (buildings) 12 June 1937, p. 25; 10 July 1937, p. 25; Wash. Post, 11 July 1937, p. R1; (financing, presidency) 5 Oct 1937, p. 2. There is a photo of the dedication (perhaps an additional building) in Wash. Post, 25 Sept 1938, p. 6. Animals were buried on the grounds (Evening Star, 16 Oct 1937, p. 22).
[53] Evening Star, 14 Oct 1938, p. 14; 21 Nov 1943, p. 3; 31 Aug 1948, p. 6.
[54] (Children) Evening Star, 1 May 1938, p. 2; (branch) Wash. Post, 6 Aug 1946, p. 6; (close) Evening Star, 6 May 1953, p. 56; (later) Wash. Post, 6 Mar 1955, p. B4; letter, Sargent to District Commissioners, 8 July 1964 (National Archives, RG 351, Entry 17 "Register of Letters Received").
[55] After 1957 the Animal Protective Association, Inc. (Briggs) Information supplied by Jim Taylor; (death) Wash. Post, 30 Mar 1984, p. B16. She is buried in Rock Creek Cemetery in Washington.

pets gratis at his own animal hospital (311 6th Street NW) two afternoons each week, underwritten by the newspaper. In its first three weeks' operation the clinic handled 235 dogs and cats. "Its fame has spread ... as far north as New York City." Without searchable access to back issues of the Times, however, we cannot know how long this good service continued.[56]

The **Animal Defense Society** appeared very occasionally in newspapers of the late 1930s and early '40s, always in association with Elizabeth B. Howry, a well-connected lady of the city (she had been presented to the Court of St. James) whose other, and very active, interests included opera and Democratic politics. The Society aimed "to abolish all cruelty to dumb creatures," worked often with the Anti-Vivisection Society (a 1938 article confuses them as "The Animal Defense and Anti-Vivisectional Society"), and held a few society-packed events (a play is mentioned) of the sort familiar from the earlier organizations. In fact, the Society seems to have been a personal effort of Howry, rather as the HES became a personal platform for Briggs, who cooperated with her.[57]

Other Organizations

A letter writer of 1922 outlined the variety of humane organizations in the District for the guidance of Evening Star readers – WHS, HES, WARL – "There may be others."[58] In fact, in the first half of the century a fair number of **other groups** in the Washington area concerned themselves with animal welfare. These fell into three types:

- **Suburban organizations:** A comprehensive directory of humane agencies published by the American Humane Association in 1949 listed seven in nearby Maryland and two in Virginia.[59] Virginia Sargent knew of two shelters in Maryland and three in Virginia in 1953 (Evening Star, 19 July 1953, p. 23). The *Washingtonian* magazine in 1971 found seven and five respectively.
- **Coordinating bodies:** A 1947 memo in WHS archives discussed the then-active "Federated Animal Welfare League of Maryland-D.C.-Va. and West Va."; the 1971 *Washingtonian* article named state-wide coordinating humane organizations in both Maryland and Virginia.
- **Ancillary organizations:** A good number of groups concerned themselves with specific aspects of animal welfare, sometimes working with one of the larger organizations on projects. Some of these were branches of national bodies. Among those mentioned in press articles were: Audubon Society (issues related to birds), Izaak Walton League (fish), Jack London Club (circus and performing animals), Dog Lovers Protective Society (dogs, probably very short-lived), Washington Aquarium Society (pet fish – they disapproved of square tanks), Anti-Steel-Trap League (fur-bearing animals), League to Conserve Food Animals (western cattle and sheep herds), and American Red Star (army animals).[60] There were also local conservation groups, such as the Fish and Game Protective Association.

---

[56] Wash. Times, 6 Jan 1936, p. 11; Jan 1936 (date unclear), file clipping Wash. Div.

[57] Evening Star, 9 Jan 1936, p. 12; 25 Apr 1938, p. 20; 28 Apr 1938, p. 24; 13 June 1943, p. 22 (ADS joins Civil Defense effort to protect animals; see Appendix D13); 9 Aug 1964, p. 39 (Howry's obituary, with photo). Hearings . . . 1939 (Senate), 8 Feb 1938, pp. 79-82, includes an extract of the Society's letter in support of raising Poundmaster Marks' salary. It was last heard from in 1945, testifying against a vivisection proposal (Evening Star, 15 May 1945, p. 10).

[58] Evening Star, 21 Nov 1923, p. 6, and other similar references.

[59] Excluding those concerned only with children. This document is in the WHS archives.

[60] Sources for the smaller or defunct organizations are: (London) Evening Star, 23 Mar 1922, p. 14; (Dog Lovers) Wash. Post, 10 Apr 1945, p. 9; (Aquarium) Wash. Post, 17 Jan 1916, p. 4; (Steel-Trap) Evening Star, 5 June 1925, p.32 (organizers included Briggs, Smith, Hutchins, Palmer, all familiar from discussions above); (Food Animals) Wash. Times, 12 Apr 1922, p. 9; (Red Star) Evening Star, 25 Mar 1917, p. 13; see Appendix D13.

CHAPTER TWENTY-FIVE

Summary

This last period of our study – 1912-1940 – saw the culmination of trends noted in the earlier Summary: the near-complete disappearance of farms and of individually kept farm animals from the District accompanied at a slightly slower pace by disappearance of draft horses, guard dogs and other work animals, and packs of stray dogs, leaving the city's human populations knowing animals only as treasured pets. Add to this the abatement of rabies scares, which by 1940 continued more in memory than experience, and we see a very different social environment regarding animals than at the beginning of the century.

In this period the general attitude toward homeless animals changed from control/elimination to rescue – the Shelter model over the Pound model. No longer would anyone declare that "a stout club will do" to solve the stray dog problem as happened at the 1854 meeting. Three indicators can be cited to demonstrate this trend:

- After 1912 the Congress and Commissioners enacted a number of laws and regulations addressing animal welfare (e.g., requiring vaccinations) while the only acts regarding farm animals addressed the minor nuisance of chickens;
- The pound itself moved both in practice and image closer and closer to the Shelter model, with a program of dog-adoption days, pet safety programs and avuncular poundmasters;
- The major local humane organizations (WHS and WARL) gradually broadened their membership and with it their center of gravity from the upper to the middle class, indicating an increasing acceptance of their humane goals.

These trends have only increased into the present time – a victory for our good impulses when favored by broad social and economic trends and supported by an enlightened and energetic citizenry.

CHAPTER TWENTY-SIX

Dead Animals

Mann's business passed to Patsy's son Charlie, who closed his rendering plant and now only collected carcasses for a flat yearly payment of $3,000, delivering the bodies to soap manufacturer Norton and Comp., which kept the innards and returned the hides to him ("It was nothing . . . to receive 10 to 15 dead horses per day.").[1] He continued this work through successive contracts until 1923, when the District took it over.[2] Over time the District had undertaken the collection and disposal of garbage, ashes and other refuse as a direct function of the city government.[3] By 1920 only the collection of dead animals and night soil was still contracted out, and the 1923 annual District appropriation required that **city crews collect dead animals** in the coming fiscal year, under the City Refuse Division of the Engineer Department. Three men were assigned to this duty. Two trucks and one horse-drawn wagon supported the work in 1931. Their duties must have been well-performed: "Maryland residents . . . haul carcasses over the District line and leave them by the roadside, knowing the District authorities will remove such material promptly."[4]

A useful 1926 article on District street-cleaning procedures states that of the 43,609 carcasses collected in 1925 about 30,000 were cats and 12,000 dogs, the rest being "rodents, horses, mules, cows, sheep, goats, poultry and miscellaneous pets. Generally about 500 miscellaneous animals are removed from pet stores and express [transport] company headquarters. These include animals [in transit] which die from accidents or diseases . . . Canaries, parrots, guinea pigs, trained mice and rats, and a great variety of other pets are delivered to the rendering establishment."[5]

---

[1] Norton, "History", pp. 5-6.
[2] Comm Minutes/Orders, 1 Dec 1891; 4 June 1900; 18 June 1902; 6 June 1905; 1 Apr 1910. This is the last such contract mentioned in the minutes but the story can be followed through the annual reports of the Street Cleaning/City Refuse Divisions. By 1920 Mann's plant had moved to Four Mile Run, Virginia (Wash. Times, 2 July 1920, p. 13). See also: Wash. Post, 30 Mar 1900, p. 10; 8 Nov 1902, p. 2, in which the body of Admiral Dewey's dog, shot as rabid, was removed by the Washington Sanitary company after the Street Cleaning Department had been notified.
[3] As recommended by the Commissioners in their 1898 annual report.
[4] (Responsibility) City Refuse Div Ann Rpts, 1924, 1931; (Maryland) Evening Star, 26 Dec 1926, p. 69.

Not all animals were left on the street; here is a charming story from 1926: "'In dear remembrance of my dead child, Fannie. She leaves to mourn her mother, Bessie Brown, her father, Shack, a host of good friends and Cousin Lon.' Finding this note on a freshly packed grave on Buzzards Point [sic; in Southwest Washington] yesterday Policeman Davis settled down to unravel what appeared to be an unauthorized burial of a baby or young child. After confiding to his superiors the details of his serious mission Policeman Davis went back and ordered the body exhumed. It was found to be the body of a dog" (Evening Star, 17 Sept 1926, p. 1).

[5] Among the express company pick-ups were eight deceased Alaskan reindeer intended for Christmas displays and then the Zoo (Evening Star, 26 Dec 1926, p. 69). Possums, rabbits and rats also figure in official Department reports. One must wonder about larger game animals such as deer, which today figure regularly in the crew's work there is no mention of them in earlier reports.

The city continued the practice of selling the hides, rendered at a private plant in Rosslyn, Virginia, into soap. Hides of larger animals were sold separately, the resulting revenue totaling $3,000 in 1926. In 1918 the city purchased the old Washington Fertilizer plant in Cherry Hill, Virginia, for the incineration of garbage, and by 1935 all carcasses were destroyed there. The nearby city of Alexandria also brought its animal bodies there after 1933 (Appendix C9).[6] Later information on this service is lost to the increasingly slim reports of the Commissioners, but we can express some surprise at the steady – indeed, increasing – number of animal corpses taken from city streets. This undoubtedly is due to large numbers of minor pests and wildlife such as rats and squirrels, which were not picked up earlier but now figured in the count.

---

[6] Evening Star, 26 Dec 1926, p. 69; Schmeckebier, The District of Columbia, p. 387; City Refuse Div Ann Rpts, 1935, 1937. The arrangement with Alexandria was formalized by the Commissioners (Minutes/Orders) on 20 Oct 1933 and makes no mention of a charge levied.

Cat Shelters

The Barber Refuge for Animals
Wash Times Magazine, 13 April 1902, Magazine p. 8

Mrs. Beckley's Cat Shelter
Wash Post, 18 October 1908, p. SM3

"The Difference Between Catching Dogs and Cats"
Wash Post, 16 June 1912, p. 17

WARL in the News

Washington Animal Rescue League Bazaar

The Washington Animal Rescue League invites your patronage of its First Bazaar, to be held next MONDAY and TUESDAY, April 7 and 8, at RAUSCHER'S, 1034 Connecticut ave., day and evening. Scores of attractions for young and old. Bridge a feature; tables, $8 each. Open evenings at 8:30. ADMISSION FREE.

Evening Star, 7 Apr 1919, p. 24

"Fairy Lane"

A Musical Fantasy, followed by a series of Fancy and Character Dancing.
Under the Direction of MISS HAWKE.
For the Benefit of the Animal Rescue League.
BELASCO THEATER, TUESDAY MATINEE
APRIL 29, AT 2:15 O'CLOCK.
Tickets, 50c to $2.50. Seats now on sale

Wash. Post, 29 Apr 1919, p. 14

Evening Star, 9 Oct 1921, p. 59

FOUND.

BRINDLE BULL, male; all white head and odd eyes, clipped ears, short tail, four white feet. Owner will please claim. Apply Washington Animal Rescue League, 349 Maryland ave. s.w.

SPITZ and poodle, white; small size; male; wearing tag No. 2955. Apply Washington Animal Rescue League, 349 Maryland ave. s.w.

TERRIER—Smooth hair, black with white markings; short tail; female; one upstanding ear. Apply Washington Animal Rescue League, 349 Maryland ave. s.w.

Evening Star, 24 May 1925, p. 5

FOUND.

German police dog, male, about one-year-old, light tan in color. Will the owner of this dog kindly claim at once as it is grieving. Apply The Washington Animal Rescue League, 349 Maryland ave. s.w.

Evening Star, 2 Feb 1926, p. 9

WASHINGTON ANIMAL RESCUE LEAGUE offers free of charge for the Summer to poor, disabled horses and mules, good pasture on a farm near Silver Spring, with running water. Inquire 349 Md. ave. s.w. Main 8088.

Evening Star, 3 July 1927, p. 3

The new O Street shelter
Evening Star, 25 Oct 1931, p. 14

Home of Rest for Horses Is Plan Of Washington's New Rescue League

Social Leaders Take Initiative in Forming Organization to Prevent Cruelty to Animals.

Boston Woman Explains Operation of Society—Hospital to Be Operated by Officers of League.

A horse falls on a slippery pavement. The usual crowd gathers. The horse is picked up and tries to limp along. A policeman interferes, goes to the nearest telephone, and in five minutes there comes speeding up an ambulance. The horse is hurried away to a horse hospital.

Even after his lameness is cured it may be found that the animal is run down, is tired out, is nervous, and then he is taken away to the Home for Rest. There he gets fresh air, plenty of food, and later is returned to his owner, a new horse.

All that may happen in Washington, if the Animal Rescue League carries out the plans made at its meeting to organize yesterday afternoon.

By J. R. HILDEBRAND.

Unless plans miscarry, Washington may have, in the near future, the following humane provisions for its animals:

A horse ambulance and a dog ambulance.
A motor car for the collection of stray cats.
A special bicycle for carrying injured cats.
A home of rest for run down horses.

Except at a White House function or a charity ball, there has not been assembled in the Capital such a representative gathering of society women as that at the Woodward & Society is expected, with its few inspectors, to do something it never set out to do. It is not our aim to attend to all the cases that arise, any more than it would be for a society for the prevention of burglary to take over the work of the police force in that direction.

"We have laws in Washington, but they are not enforced. Policemen fail to enforce them, because the Commissioners' orders in this respect do not breath the order of command.

"When a new group of Commissioners come into office we go before them and point out that certain laws exist for the protection of animals. They always look pleased and surprised, and agree that it might be a good idea to enforce them. Then they have an order issued through the superintendent asking policemen should be as mandatory as they are for the apprehension of burglars."

About $2,000 is the minimum for which an animal hospital in this city can be started, according to horses, dogs and cats, but to provide a boarding place for these animals when their owners are out of town.

"Rest Cure" for Horses.

Mrs. Smith spoke highly of the success of the "rest cure" for horses. These animals are nearly human enough, she said, to get tired and run down just as a man. It is not only a humane act, but a stroke of good business to let them recuperate. She gave instances in which owners were highly grateful for such service in Boston.

Interesting stories of "cabbies" who sent their horses to the home during the summer months, and went regularly on Sunday to visit them, were related by Mrs. Smith. After her address Mr. Hutchins extolled her work and called her the "most useful woman in America."

"The men of Washington, I found, could not bring this matter to a successful conclusion," Mr. Hutchins said. "So I put the matter up to the women. This afternoon you see the result."

A Needed Work.

"We must make it clear that we are not engaged in a sentimental affair," Mrs. Smith warned. "But we must show the community that

"a small group of meddlesome rich persons"
– the press joined in on a common view
Wash Times, 1 Apr 1914, p. 3

The WARL Shelter

The Maryland Ave shelter
Wash. Post, 30 Mar 1919, p. S13

WARL's first ambulance
WARL Archives

The O St shelter
WARL Archives

The Christmas Horse Banquet
Drawing by Laura Friend Smythe;
Evening Star, 5 January 1933, p. 17

Thanks to Mr. Kent Boese;
WARL Archives

Personages

T. Edward Clark
Association of Oldest Inhabitants Archives (HSW)

Cecil French
Evening Star, 7 Oct 1904, p. 20

Sarah Beckley
Drawing by Laura Friend Smythe;
Wash. Post, 18 Oct 1908, p. 2

Mary Coursey
Evening Star, 20 June 1914, p. 9

Personages (2)

James P. Briggs
Kindly provided by Mr. Jim Taylor (Nat. Humane Education Society)

Virginia Sargent
Kindly provided by Mr. Jim Taylor (Nat. Humane Education Society)

Secondary Shelters

Mr. and Mrs. Frank J. Buckley
Drawing by Laura Friend Smythe;
Wash. Times Magazine, 3 Aug 1902, p. 4

Humane Sunday
Evening Star, 13 Apr 1940, p. 14

Society for Friendless Dogs shelter
Wash. Times, 13 Nov 1905, p. 11

Tail-Waggers Club
Evening Star, 19 July 1942, p. 3

Animal Protective Assn
Evening Star, 21 Nov 1943, p. 3

Humane Education Soc shelter
Both illustrations: Evening Star, 29 June 1924, p. 7

Afterword: What Happened to Them All

After taking this story rather thoroughly up to 1940, it would be a shame not to at least outline the later lives of these several efforts. The pound, not surprisingly, gets the longest treatment; for a good account of the local shelter scene, see Free, "No Room". Each section ends with a brief portrait of the organization today (late 2014) supplied by the group itself.

The Pound

Subsequent to the 1945 revision of dog laws District pound **procedures** continued much as before under the dedicated and irascible Poundmaster Frank Marks. **Legalities** saw some change: the Commissioners transferred oversight from their office to the Metropolitan Police in 1953, much to Marks' vocal annoyance. It left Police jurisdiction for the Health Department in 1958, and in 1973 to the Community Health and Hospital Administration of that Department's replacement, the Human Resources Department.[1] None of this came easily because of the continued confusion over what the authorizing federal acts actually allowed the Commissioners to do.[2] Congress finally relinquished control over dogs to the Commissioners on 13 Sept 1961.

Handling of the dog tax – now called licenses – moved from the Collector of Taxes to the Superintendent of Licenses in 1952. A special study committee had reported to the Commissioners the year previous what had long been true (if not from the very earliest laws, as is my contention): "The licensing and registration of dogs is primarily a regulatory action . . . rather than a revenue-producing action." In 1969 that office was absorbed into the new Department of Economic Development. The cost of retrieving an animal from the pound rose from $4 to $8 in 1980.[3]

One distinct change of procedure was that the pound began to sell cats (for $1) by order of the Commissioners in 1954.[4] The same order allowed "institutions" to buy animals (dogs for $3, cats for $2), contemporaneous with the creation of the **Animal Allocation Board**. This controversial body, established

---

[1] (Police) Reorganization Order 52, 30 June 1953 (National Archives, RG 351, Entry 21 "District General Files", folder 1-100 "Internal Audit Reports"). In fact, the pound and all its positions were abolished and re-constituted as MPDC functions, probably bringing it under greater control than Marks liked. (Health) Wash. Post, 27 June 1958, p. A3 (Human Services) Star-News, 29 Mar 1973, p. B3, which describes the move as "recent".

[2] This problem was brought up by the Commissioners in a letter to the House District Committee (3 Dec 1959; National Archives, RG 351, Entry 21 "District General Files", folder 1-104 "Dogs"), as the question of leashing came up once again.

[3] Special Committee report, 28 Aug 1951 (National Archives, RG 351, Entry 21 "District General Files", folder 1-105 "DC Dog Pound"); Reorganization Order 20, 20 Nov 1952 (National Archives, RG 351, Entry 21 "District General Files", folder 1-100 "Internal Audit Reports"); Wash. Post, 15 Mar 1969, p. A19; 28 Aug 1980, p. A1. "Licensing" in reference to paying the dog tax was used in occasional discussions as early as 1838 and officially in the 1875 Bd of Health report advocating for the tax's re-institution, but fairly seldom; early discussions of cats, however, regularly used the word.

[4] Commissioners Order 54-398, 13 Feb 1954.

by a Commissioners Order of 23 Feb 1954, met to allocate unclaimed pound animals to local university laboratories. Marks ran – unsuccessfully – for vice-president from the anti-vivisection faction.[5]

And we should note that in 1960 the pound's killing chamber had apparently become dysfunctional, since it was reported taking victims to WARL for dispatch in their Euthanaire ("a device that removed oxygen from a chamber"). The pound installed its own Euthanaire soon after this; dogs were sedated by injection before being put into the box. It switched to injection of barbiturates in 1973, the method also then used by WARL. The innovation of "lethal injection has resulted in a hardship and requires far more time to put animals to sleep," complained Poundmaster King.[6]

One last legal innovation seems to have originated with a letter from the Progressive Citizens Association of Georgetown to the Commissioners in 1960, which urged regulation regarding dogs which "commit a nuisance" (i.e., poop on the sidewalk), a cause quickly picked up by other groups. A defecation-control order was on the books by 1965.[7] The Commissioners repeated their vaccination requirement in 1959 (21 Apr).

Marks' successor and former assistant, **John R. King, Jr.**,[8] "a merry big man" of 38 from Baltimore, distinguished himself from his predecessor by stating that although he was a dog-lover (now a requirement for the job) he was no fanatic on the question of vivisection.[9] Longtime poundman Matthew C. Norman took the assistant post, becoming the first African-American to hold a supervisory position at the pound. The staff and salaries had increased (to 12 men!), but in general the routine remained familiar – "the actual dog-catching is done by men with nets." There continued to be no cat laws, to King's great relief.[10]

---

[5] Wash. Post, 26 Jan 1954, p. 21; Evening Star, 11 Dec 1954, p. 27; National Archives, RG 351, Entry 21 "District General Files", folder 1-105 "Animal Allocation Board". For those interested in this issue, definitely see the thorough report of Dr. Alan M. Chesney, Dean of the Medical Faculty at Johns Hopkins University (4 Dec 1953), summarizing various states' laws on animal experimentation and giving multitudinous statistics on the use and origin of experimental animals by institutions in Washington and Baltimore (National Archives, RG 351, Entry 21 "District General Files", folder 1-105 "Medical Testing"). The pound sold 60-70 dogs monthly to laboratories in 1971, the only local jurisdiction to do so (Evening Star, 13 Apr 1971, p. 1; Wash. Post, 10 June 1974, p. C1, with statistics).

Marks spoke of persons purchasing pound dogs for re-sale to laboratories – "dog pirates" he called them (Evening Star, 9 May 1957, p. 68).

[6] Wash. Post, 2 May 1960, p. B1; 9 May 1973, p. C1; Evening Star, 13 Apr 1971, p. 1. This device is described unfavorably in Free, "No Room". Documents relating to stray dogs before the City Council in 1973 (8 May 1973, at National Archives, RG 351, Entry 45 "Hearing Files, 1967-1974", "Dogs, Stray", including King's testimony) include a list of every city in the US using this machine. The number of animals put down could not have been great if the poundmen transported them across town for the procedure.

The pound experimented with injection (sodium pentobarbital) in 1958 also (Wash. Post, 25 Dec 1958, p. A16).

[7] Letters, 23 Apr 1960; 11 Apr 1965 (National Archives, RG 351, Entry 21 "District General Files", folder 1-104 "Dogs"). The latter refers to Comm Order 61-1734 and Police Reg 18, sect 2. Dr. Alan Beck, a university scientist, estimated that dogs deposited 25 tons of feces daily in Washington in 1973 – a seemingly incredible number (Wash. Post, 9 May 1973, p. C1).

[8] Photos of King are in Evening Star, 23 Nov 1959, p. 18; 3 Aug 1960, p. 21; 16 Nov 1969, Sunday Magazine p. 22; 13 Apr 1971, p. 1. King entered District government service in the late 1940s.

[9] "Mr. Marks fought a constant and rear guard action to keep these quotas [of animals for experimentation] to a base minimum" (Evening Star, 26 June 1958, p. 24).

[10] Evening Star, 15 June 1958, p. 17; 26 June 1958, p. 24; 7 Dec 1962, p. 20; 13 Apr 1971, p. 1. For Norman's 1968 retirement, with a good photo, see Evening Star, 3 Mar 1968, p. B3, including some interesting information on pound operations in his day; and his death notice, Evening Star, 27 Jan 1977, p. B4. The pound crew was called to the White House in 1980 to retrieve an errant wild turkey (Evening Star, 23 Apr 1980, p. 58).

In keeping with its more sedate routine, the pound increasingly offered what would now be called community outreach activities – hosting regular dog vaccination days and Dog Week events, and advertising lovable pups for redemption.[11]

The Randall Community Center, attached to nearby Randall Junior High School, had been established adjacent to the pound in 1936[12] and the city's park department ever eyed the pound for expansion space. The city's DDOT plans archives (holding blueprints for all city buildings) contains plans to build tennis courts over the pound site from both 1946 and 1951.[13] "District Recreation Board Chairman Harry S. Wendeer said his agency has repeatedly requested removal of the pound because of the smell and noise, but has been turned down because of the cost," reported the Washington Post in 1950, after another rebuff.[14] The facility's proximity to a school brought a steady stream of protests from parents and community groups.[15]

Efforts to **move the pound** continued through the 1950s ("the present facility . . . long has been a source of annoyance in the neighborhood"): to Mt. Olivet Road NE (taking a piece of the National Arboretum); to Burnham Barrier Island ("just below Benning Rd., NE," then used "as a dump fill"); a site just north of Gallaudet University; exile to distant Blue Plains; further south to long-suffering Buzzard Point; to "the Gun Factory area" apparently near the Zoo ("This should bring a howl from Dr. Carmichael [the Zoo director]"). The planned Southwest Freeway, just to the north, furthered the need to find a new location.[16]

In 1965 the city contracted with the Weiss Construction Company to construct a new pound at its current 1201 New York Avenue NE address for $138,000. The blueprints for this project were prepared by W. A. MacLaurie and dated the same year.[17] The pound moved in July 1966, to the relief of the nearby Skyline Inn, whose manager "had a huge file of barking complaints from . . . tenants." Since then the old pound building has been used by the Randall Recreation Center.[18] The building received landmark protection from the District government in 2014.

---

[11] For examples, see: (vaccination) Wash. Post, 7 July 1948, p. B2; (Dog Week) 19 Sept 1939, p. 3; (puppies) 19 Dec 1949, p. B1.

[12] This information thanks to Tony Simon of the Commission on Fine Arts. The city at that time was given use of the land but the formal transfer of title from the Federal government occurred in 2008. Before the rec center the land had been used as a storage site by the Highway Department (Wash. Post, 10 May 1941, p. 13).

[13] Cabinet 11/drawer 13. See also Wash. Post, 10 May 1941, p. 13 for expansion plans of the rec center.

[14] Op. cit., 30 Apr 1950, p. M15.

[15] See a number of letters from 1945-46 on this question in National Archives, RG 351, Entry 21 "District General Files", folder 1-105 "DC Dog Pound"; Evening Star, 5 Nov 1951, p. 21, has an arresting photo of dogs and kids staring at each other through the fence. "The annual debate of just which is more annoying to whom – the pups in the dog pound or the students in [the] school – is under way again." Marks had plenty to say about the latter! The poundmaster consistently opposed moving his operations.

[16] (Mt. Olivet, island, Gallaudet, Blue Plains) Wash. Post, 2 Sept 1956, p. A15; 3 July 1959, p. B1; National Archives, RG 351, Entry 21 "District General Files", folder 1-105 "DC Dog Pound"; (Buzzard Pt, Zoo) memo, R. L. Plavnick to C. H. Conrad, 8 Apr 1959 (National Archives, RG 328, Entry 7 "Planning Files 1924-67", Box 51, 545: 27-30 "Buzzard Point"); testimony, John R. King, 8 May 1973 (at National Archives, RG 351, Entry 45 "Hearing Files, 1967-1974", "Dogs, Stray").

[17] Wash. Post, 24 Sept 1965, p. B3; DDOT plans archives, Cabinet 18/drawer 1, which also contains 1981 expansion plans. See also drawings in Cabinet 21/drawers 7 and 11.

[18] Evening Star, 7 July 1966, p. 21; Wash. Post, 17 July 1966, p. L4. The institution immediately met the same noise complaints at its new, forlorn location: "They've been barking ever since they moved in there. It got so bad . . . I couldn't sleep." A 1966 proposed re-design of the rec center by Chlothiel Woodard Smith (or at least her company), found in Cabinet 11/drawer 13, eliminated the pound building in favor of a swimming facility.

The pound came under its first real period of **public criticism** in the early 1960s. It certainly is possible that either attention or facilities had deteriorated, but a major factor must have been heightened expectations of a public which no longer remembered packs of mangy curs in the parks and instead compared the pound to private shelters (which had the luxury of limiting their intake). One predictable element was the condition of the now-fifty-year-old pound itself. An inspector's report of 1963 found the facility in considerable disrepair. And ticks infested the pound, something that could (and should) have been controlled.[19]

Other complaints related to policy and were of the more fastidious sort: "It does not check lost dog ads; it does not provide resting boards in kennels; it does require spaying of females" and so forth. "Inspection of the pound can leave you with the impression that philosophically it has not changed since the days of President Grant" – an unkind and unfair charge.[20]

Poundmaster King retired in 1974 and for four years the shop was managed by an absentee acting supervisor, the Department's Chief of Animal Disease Control, veterinarian George Banks. With no firm oversight and strong union protection the poundmen – once Einstein's polished gem – came more to resemble Wheelock's slovenly crew; one ran a trash business on the side, another farmed out guard dogs.[21] Facing a deluge of complaints, the District government turned to the humane organizations for assistance.

A decade earlier the city had been approached by the Humane Society of the United States, a group that split from the American Humane Association in 1954 specifically to lobby for humane legislation rather than engage in direct street work. HSUS in 1962 proposed (illogically, given its stated mission) to take over pound operations in the District of Columbia, building its own facility and using government funding for operations. Indeed, the management of local animal control services was increasingly taken over by such organizations: by 1971 the pounds in Arlington and Fairfax Counties and Alexandria, Virginia, and in Montgomery County, Maryland, had been contracted to private shelter operators. Nonetheless, HSUS got a turn-down from the city government. Now – 1978 -- the District hired a WHS-recommended candidate to take over pound operations.

Ingrid E. Newkirk[22] had trained in law enforcement and served in the Montgomery (MD) County pound (until she was forced out for publicizing deplorable conditions there) and as the county's Director of Humane Investigation. In Washington, the strong-willed and deeply committed Newkirk began a thorough house- and pen-cleaning campaign, scrubbing floors, ridding the freezing unit of "four inches of maggots" (the facility had become "a cafeteria for rats"), tightening adoption screening, and establishing the pound's neuter/spay clinic. To gain more control over staff and procedures she recommended the District turn over operations to a private concern. The District **contracted the service to WHS** in 1980, keeping it at the New York Avenue location, but changing its name to Animal Care and Control Facility.[23] Newkirk stayed on as

---

[19] (Inspector) Report, 22 Nov 1963 (National Archives, RG 351, Entry 21 "District General Files", folder 1-105 "DC Dog Pound"); (ticks) Wash. Post, 2 May 1960, p. B1.

[20] Free, "No Room"; see also letter, Marie L. King to Winifred A. Hunter, 4 Nov 1963, and others in the same file (National Archives, RG 351, Entry 21 "District General Files", folder 1-105 "DC Dog Pound"), which give much more of the same.

[21] Information from here to the dog-population statistics paragraph comes from cited sources and from Ms. Ingrid Newkirk via email interviews. Evening Star, 8 Sept 1978, p. D2, describes pound operations as "defunct" and cites a recent Congressional report describing pound employees as "the rudest and most impolite in the government." The year of King's retirement is calculated from this article, and it has a fetching photo of Newkirk. The poundmen numbered nine in 1977, with two trucks (Evening Star, 12 Aug 1977, p. B1, which gives statistics for neighboring jurisdictions also, and good photos of poundmen Lonnie Whitted and J. C. Johnson).

[22] A good photo will be found in Evening Star, 8 Sept 1978, p. D2.

acting director (in her capacity as the District's Chief of Animal Disease Control, succeeding Banks) until WHS's manager, Willy Swenholt,[24] assumed the responsibility. Soon afterward she retired from government service to found the national animal-rights organization People for the Ethical Treatment of Animals. Ingrid Newkirk was the last District poundmaster, and Washington the last local jurisdiction to use the time-honored name Pound.[25]

In 1970 the greater Washington area held an estimated half-million dogs and cats; 110,000 of them had been housed (and some euthanized) in the communities' pounds and animal shelters that year; 60,000 were put down throughout the region in 1973. King in 1973 guessed the District housed 100,000 stray dogs, up from 50,000 ten years earlier. Newkirk, in 1979, returned the figure to 50,000.[26]

Supervision of the three-year contract for animal control and sheltering (invariably awarded to WHS, although there are occasional other bidders) and also issuance of dog licenses were both under the Animal Services Program of the District's Department of Health, Health Regulations and Licensing Administration in 2014. Three employees handle these responsibilities along with other duties. (Extermination of rats and other health hazards fall under the same Department's Rodent Control Program.) At the time of writing, the Department is considering a major revision of animal-related regulations as well as such currently-discussed issues as care of injured wildlife, urban farming (bees, chickens), use of animals in schools for educational programs, safety of animals in emergencies, and plans for a new shelter facility to replace the New York Avenue buildings.

Although the District estimates the city alone to hold 140,000 dogs, only 4,157 are licensed. (The estimated 180,000 cats remain unregulated, although that is also being reconsidered.) Tags cost $15, of which $2 supports WHS's spay/neuter program. Replacement tags are issued at no charge. Total income (including the $2 program donation) was $84,945 in 2014.[27]

In 2014 the WHS shelters (New York Avenue and a satellite storefront on Georgia Avenue NW), on behalf of the District, took in a total of 9,521 animals (of which: dogs – 2,807; cats – 4,764; birds, small mammals, reptiles – 1,924, livestock – 26), half brought in to the shelter and half taken from the streets. Pick-up from homes was stopped in 2011. About 10% were returned to their owners, 60% adopted, and

---

[23] Often referred to by WHS as The New York Avenue Adoption Center. See Evening Star, 38 Mar 1979, p. 71, for a discussion of the Animal Control Act of 1979. (Adoption) Evening Star, 9 Feb 1979, p. 65; Wash. Post, 2 Oct 1980, p. C2 (monks from the Franciscan Monastery are grilled). The staff had risen to 20 by this time (Wash. Times, 21 July 1980, p. 14). The actual transfer occurred in October of 1980.

[24] Swenholt was, at least, the manager in 1985 (Wash. Post, 19 July 1985, p. C2).

[25] Letter, 13 Aug 1962 (National Archives, RG 351, Entry 21 "District General Files", folder 1-101 "Humane Society"), letter, 7 Dec 1962 (National Archives, RG 351, Entry 21 "District General Files", folder 1-105 "DC Dog Pound"); Free, "No Room". For a fine comparison of the services and charges of the various area pounds, see Free, "No Room". Evening Star, 14 Aug 1962, p. B5 discusses dogs in Rockville MD.

Anyone wanting to extend this study should review the documents from the District of Columbia Council hearings on stray dogs in 1967-74 referenced in the Bibliography, which give much specific information of the city's pound service, dog population/problem, and interesting comparative tables of pound operations in US cities and the DC area. Some of the testimony sounds wonderfully familiar: "Due to dogs seized from militant owners the Pound began to suffer from illegal break-ins and dogs were being stolen or released from the . . . enclosure" – something T. Zell Hoover would have recognized! (testimony, John R. King, 8 May 1973.)

[26] Free, "No Room"; Wash. Post, 10 June 1974, p. C1, with statistics and interesting background on the methods used and disposal of carcasses; testimony, John R. King, 8 May 1973 (at National Archives, RG 351, Entry 45 "Hearing Files, 1967-1974", "Dogs, Stray"); Evening Star, 28 Mar 1979, p. 71. WHS estimated 400,000 dogs and about the same for cats in 1972 (Wash. Post, 22 Mar 1972, p. C1). King noted that in the 1960s strays tended to be smaller breeds, but at that time had moved toward German shepherds.

[27] My thanks to Mr. Edward Rich, Senior Assistant General Counsel of the Department of Health, for help in learning these figures.

10% euthanized (by injection) due to medical or behavioral issues (the other 20% holding in the shelter). Carcasses are incinerated by a contractor weekly; cremation at one of two private crematories can be arranged at an owner's request.

Fees collected (adoption, vaccination shots, sales of leashes and collars, gift certificates and so forth) at the shelter totaled $767,278 (not including license-money turned over directly to the District) in FY 2014. Wildlife called in as a nuisance are taken to a separate humane organization (City Wildlife, located next to the WARL shelter) or simply released, depending on medical need.[28]

Washington Humane Society

The Washington Humane Society gradually recovered from its existential crisis of the early 1930s, re-orienting its work toward pets and abused animals of all sorts. The comprehensive 1971 article by Ann Cottrell Free noted that the Society had been "relatively unaggressive for many years, [but] has become more active since 1969." In 1971 it had three paid agents. The Society had begun taking rescued animals to the city pound where they required boarding for long periods while legal questions were sorted out, swamping the pound's capacity.[29] Sister organizations existed in all neighboring suburban jurisdictions and several of them had taken over local pound operations on a contract basis.[30] WHS assumed these duties for the District in 1980 on contract and has continued them since. (In one year, as a result of the inevitable criticism that engulfs any organization working with animals, another group got the work but had to turn it back to WHS soon afterward.)

As of this writing WHS has a paid full- and part-time staff of 109, 1,677 volunteers (!) and an annual budget of over $8.2 million, derived from the above-mentioned shelter fees and also investments, donations, and "contract revenue". Besides the two shelter locations, the organization operates a spay/neuter clinic near the Navy Yard, a vaccine center, and two administrative locations, the main office being on MacArthur Avenue NW. WHS hopes to amalgamate all of these functions at one new location in the next few years.

WHS provided a total of 32,151 individual services in 2014. The breakdown is this: 2,799 adoptions; 691 animals returned to owners; 5,459 lost/found reports processed; 16,193 field service requests responded to; 5,200 low/no-cost vaccinations; 4,000 spay/neuter operations; 1,809 cruelty investigations – a wonderful record of service.

In 2016 WHS and WARL formally merged under the name Humane Rescue Alliance.[31]

Washington Animal Rescue League

The Animal Rescue League continued its efficient operations at O Street, supplemented by the animal clinic in the co-located but organizationally distinct (since 1950) Tail-Waggers' Club. When that organization disbanded in the mid-1990s WARL established its own medical center (1996).

---

[28] Further detailed information regarding WHS's current operations and its relationship with the District government, kindly supplied by Ms. Alison Putnam of WHS, is with the other material deposited in the Washingtoniana Division.

[29] Testimony, John R. King, 8 May 1973 (at National Archives, RG 351, Entry 45 "Hearing Files, 1967-1974", "Dogs, Stray").

[30] Free, "No Room". All information from this point on was provided by WHS.

[31] Wash. Post, 24 Oct 2016, p. B5.

By the mid-1960s the facility clearly required updating and its neighborhood had greatly deteriorated. The District government proved uncooperative in the renovation project and then announced that it planned to take the property for a school playground. Although this last threat receded, the organization began a five-year search for larger quarters, taking it to a spacious and striking building at 71 Oglethorpe Street NW (at the very edge of the District) in 1977. The new shelter received a state-of-the-art renovation in 2005. Like the old pound, the WARL shelter received historic protection in 2018.[32]

In 2014 the WARL shelter took in 1,904 animals total (dogs – 1,244; cats – 660; about ¼ brought in by the public, ¾ from other humane organizations). Of these 1,563 were adopted, 37 returned to their owners, 54 transferred to other shelters, and 205 put down for health reasons. WARL had a paid staff of 53 (plus hundreds of volunteers) and annual budget of $5.4 million.[33]

Humane Education Society and the National Humane Education Society

Following the death of founder James Briggs in 1945 his widow Anna kept the Humane Education Society going but in a virtually non-existent way. During this time her great friends and supporters were her children and Virginia Sargent of the equally small APA. In the course of her humane work Briggs made the acquaintance of Alice Morgan Wright, "an heiress, an animal rights activist, an organizer of UNESCO, and a sculptress" who proposed that they reinvigorate the organization on a national basis – the National Humane Education Society, announced in 1948. As Sargent's APA shelter faced closure, Wright funded purchase of a 145-acre farm in Sterling, Virginia, (1950) to take over the work, named Peace Plantation Animal Sanctuary. After a move to Lucketts, Virginia, (1965) the facility settled in Walton, New York, (about 1982); it closed in 2014. NHES continues its work at the Briggs Animal Adoption Center in Charles Town, West Virginia, inaugurated in 2000. Anna Briggs died in 2011 at the age of 101, leaving behind an extensive family also dedicated to the welfare of animals. The organization has definitely taken on a broader geographic scope of activities than the old HES and no longer functions as a specifically Washington DC group.[34]

---

[32] WARL New shelter dedication brochure; Monahan, Such Courage, Such Heart. Both buildings were nominated for landmark status on the basis of research by this writer.
[33] Information provided by Ms. Susan Strange of WARL, to whom I extend my thanks.
[34] Briggs, For the Love of Animals, and information supplied by NHES. Anna Briggs remained spunky and dedicated to her cause to the end – for an account of her rescue of homeless cats from New York City subway tunnels see Wash. Post, 9 Sept 1984, p. A15. Her obituary, with photo, appeared in Wash. Post, 18 Feb 2011.

Other Humane Organizations

Two authoritative directories of 2014 (for a broad geographical area, including Baltimore) listed: shelter/adoption organizations – about 140; rescue/adoption groups specializing in one breed of dog – about 100; pet enthusiast clubs, all specialized to some degree – 33 (including the Aquarium Society).[35]

Dead Animals

Responsibility for dead animal removal from public spaces had passed from the Engineer Department to the Environmental Services Department by 1973.[36]

In 2014 this work was handled by the Department of Public Works, Solid Waste Collections Division. The crew consists of two full-time men working six days a week and with two refrigerated vehicles in east/west territories. Carcasses are stored at a Department facility on Benning Road NE until picked up biweekly by a private contractor, which incinerates them at its plant in Virginia. Although the bulk of animals found are dogs and cats, smaller rodents (including rats) and minor wildlife (raccoons, opossums) also figure in the work; deer are common in the winter. The work is now recorded by poundage rather than count;[37] unfortunately the District government cannot report the amount taken in the last year.

---

[35] *Pet Lovers Companion*; the website: petfinder.com. There is probably a fair amount of duplication here, but the point is to show the explosion of such efforts since our study period.

[36] Wash. Post, 1 Apr 1973, p. A1; Star-News, 29 Mar 1973, p. B3; later information from the District Department of Public Works, Solid Waste Collections Division.

[37] Norton & Comp.'s (Alexandria VA) president reported receiving 400,000 pounds of dog carcasses in 1971 but it is not clear if this is only from the pound or District-wide collection (Wash. Post, 10 June 1974, p.C1).

The Facilities Today

Former pound on South Capitol St
Photo by author

Former WARL shelter on O St
Photo by author

Current facility on New York Ave
Photo by author

Super-modern pens at the Oglethorpe St shelter
Photo by author

Current HRA shelter on Oglethorpe St
Photo by author

Staff at the New York Ave facility
HRA

Staff at the Oglethorpe St shelter
WARL archives

APPENDIX A

BASICS OF DISTRICT OF COLUMBIA HISTORY

A1: Chronology of District Governance

1791: Congress approves the specific site for the new capital and donation of land from the states of Virginia and Maryland; the already-established towns of Alexandria (Virginia, 1749) and Georgetown (Maryland, 1751) are incorporated into the new District; a new capital city, Washington, is laid out; areas outside these three "corporations" are "counties" (of Alexandria and of Washington); three presidentially-appointed Commissioners administer the District.

1800: Federal Government moves to Washington from Philadelphia.

1801: Congressional act ("The Organic Act") lays out governance of the corporations and counties, and specifies that any legal matter not covered by an act of Congress or derivative order of the Commissioners continues to be subject to the earlier Maryland or Virginia laws; this arrangement continues through the following Corporation, Territorial and Commissioner governments until a comprehensive code for the District is adopted in 1901 (with later amendments).

1802: The new City of Washington is incorporated, governed by a Mayor and Council; the specifics of terms, powers and electoral procedures are revised from time to time, most notably in 1812 and 1820.

1846: Alexandria City and County are retroceded to Virginia; the District now lies only on the northern (Maryland) side of the Potomac River.

1871: The separate governments of Washington, Georgetown and the County are abolished in favor of a unified government similar to those of U.S. territories, with a presidentially-appointed Governor and elected Council; practical administration continues divided along the earlier jurisdictional lines for the next few decades.

1874: Congress abolishes the Territorial-form of government and appoints three Temporary Commissioners to govern the District.

1878: The Commissioner-form of government is made permanent.

1967: The Commissioner government abolished and replaced with a Mayor-Council government ("Home Rule"), at first appointed and later elected (1973), which continues today, though still under the ultimate jurisdiction of Congress.

A2: Maps of the District, 1854 and 1891

1854

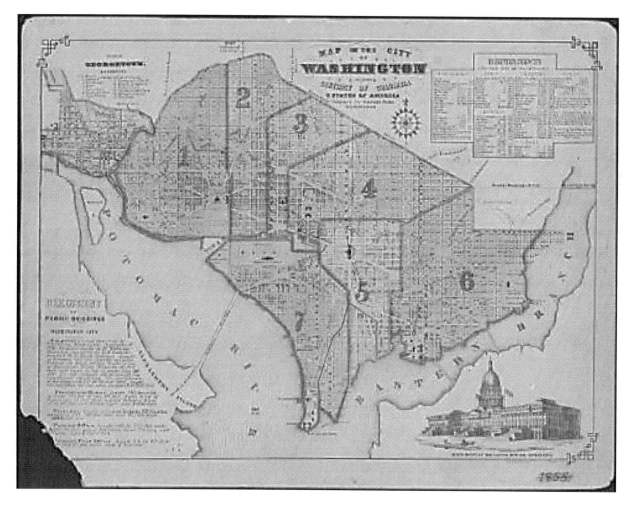

Georgetown is the unnumbered area to the left, Washington the larger area to the right broken into seven wards. As the population grew the number of wards increased.

ML King Library, Washingtoniana Div

APPENDIX A - Basics of District of Columbia History 243

1891

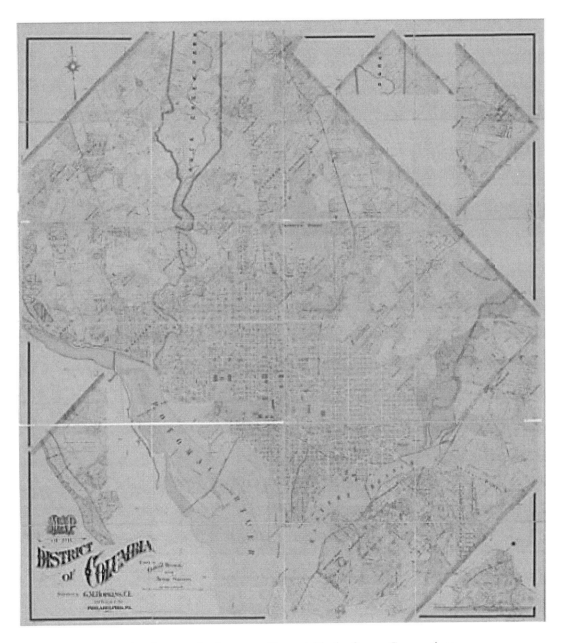

Notice the growth of communities outside the former Corporations.

Library of Congress

A3: Population of the District

Washington DC Population by Decade

Year	Population
1800*	14,093
1810*	24,023
1820*	33,039
1830*	39,834
1840*	43,711
1850	51,687
1860	75,080
1870	131,700
1880	177,624
1890	230,392
1900	278,718
1910	331,069
1920	437,571
1930	486,869
1940	663,091

* Inc Alexandria City and County, returned to Virginia in 1846.

Gilmore, "Washington DC History Resources"

APPENDIX B

LAWS RELATING TO ANIMAL CONTROL

Notes

- Laws/regulations are **cited from official compilations** unless noted otherwise. See Notes on Sources for a full discussion.

- **Minor laws/regulations** before 1940 and important ones after that date are **only cited in the text**.

- Entries in *italics* either were **not passed** or were soon repealed.

- **Federal bills** not passed are cited by date of first introduction; listed HR bills also include text of any related S bills.

- Only **significant Board of Health and Commissioners orders** are listed; **minor administrative orders** mentioned in the text are cited there by full date.

- **Text Codes** match the law/regulation to a corresponding number (in red) on the copy of that text deposited at the Washingtoniana Div. Information on **"No text available"** should be searched in the cited newspaper article or other source.

Appendix B1

The Corporations of Washington and Georgetown (1791-1871)

Nuisances/Board of Health -- Washington

Date approved	Resume	Source/Notes	Text code
20 Sept 1803	Supt of Police established, given responsibility for nuisances	Acts of Washington	Cp 1
14 Aug 1819	Health Officer established, given vague responsibility for nuisances	Acts of Wash	Cp 2
30 Mar 1822	Bd of Health established, assumes responsibility for nuisances	Acts of Wash; slightly revised 22 May 1822; 26 July 1837	Cp 3
26 May 1823	Bd of Health removes untended nuisances	Acts of Wash	Cp 4
17 Aug 1832	Strengthens powers of Bd of Health re nuisances, institutes fines	Acts of Wash	Cp 5
20 May 1848	Omnibus BoH act; Bd of Health responsibilities, powers re nuisances specified	Acts of Wash	Cp 6
20 May 1853	Omnibus BoH act, as above	Sheahan, pp. 266-273; modest revision of 1848 act	Cp 7
17 Jan 1856	Omnibus BoH act, as above; Commissioner of Health appointed	Acts of Wash; substantive revision of 1853 act; slightly revised 24 Mar 1862	Cp 8
10 Jan 1870	Strengthens powers of Bd of Health	Daily Nat Republican, 28 Feb 1870, p. 3; repealed 21 Jan 1871	Cp 9

Farm Animals -- Georgetown

Date approved	Resume	Source/Notes	Text code
20 Nov 1791	Stray geese/swine prohibited, kept by finder	G'town Code 1811	Cp 10
4 Aug 1795	Stray swine prohibited, taken by police to market	G'town Code 1811	Cp 11
27 July 1796	Stray goats prohibited, taken by police to market	G'town Code 1811	Cp 12
10 Oct 1796	Fines for strays, taken by police	G'town Code 1811	Cp 13
18 May 1799	Stray stallions prohibited, owner fined	G'town Code 1811	Cp 14
14 June 1814	Stray horses prohibited	G'town Code 1821	Cp 15
28 Apr 1827	Swine-raising restrictions	Ordinances of G'town	Cp 16
11 Nov 1837	Swine/geese/goats regs tightened, fines to Poor House	Ordinances of G'town; refers to 1827 statute as "swine/geese/goats"	Cp 17
19 July 1845	Poor House pays fee to police for swine delivered	Ordinances of G'town	Cp 18
13 Mar 1858	Swine-raising restrictions, police remittance raised	Ordinances of G'town	Cp 19
23 Nov 1859	Poor House must return swine	Ordinances of G'town; repealed 24 May 1867	Cp 20
7 June 1862	Swine-raising limited to one, police remittance raised again	Ordinances of G'town	Cp 21
22 Apr 1865	Cow-raising restrictions	Ordinances of G'town	Cp 22
9 Aug 1867	Stray swine prohibited	Ordinances of G'town	Cp 23

Farm Animals -- Washington

Date approved	Resume	Source/Notes	Text code
28 Mar 1809	Stray swine prohibited, finder shares procedes with Almshouse	Acts of Wash	Cp 24
27 Oct 1809	Swine-raising restrictions, stray swine prohibited, finder shares with city	Acts of Wash	Cp 25
26 July 1815	Stray geese prohibited, taken to Almshouse	Acts of Wash	Cp 26
21 Mar 1817	Stray swine prohibited, finder shares with Almshouse; constables fined if shirking duty	Acts of Wash	Cp 27
by 1819	Regs re fences; all strays prohibited; fines prescribed; Justice of Peace responsible for strays	Corp act; Cranch, Code, pp. 223-229	Cp 28
11 May 1819	Stray goats prohibited, killed	Acts of Wash	Cp 29
1 Apr 1820	Stray swine prohibited, finder shares with city	Acts of Wash	Cp 30
2 Aug 1828	Stray debilitated horses prohibited, killed	Acts of Wash	Cp 31
by 1833	Expenses for keeping strays set	Corp act; System of Civil . . ., ch. XXIII, sect. 17	Cp 32
28 May 1835	Stray stallions over 16 months prohibited	Acts of Wash	Cp 33
8 Apr 1836	Swine-raising restrictions; stray swine prohibited, sold at market; police fined for shirking duties	Acts of Wash	Cp 34
17 Jan 1838	Swine-raising restrictions; stray swine prohibited, taken to Asylum; police fined for shirking duties	Acts of Wash; stray-swine provision repealed 26 Sept 1838	Cp 35
20 Jan 1841	Stray swine prohibited, taken to Asylum	Acts of Wash	Cp 36
28 Apr 1841	Police reminded of duty; interfering prohibited	Acts of Wash	Cp 37
20 May 1848	Diseased animals at large prohibited	Acts of Wash; repeated 20 May 1853; BoH act, 17 Jan 1856	Cp 6

Farm Animals -- Washington (cont'd)

Date approved	Resume	Source/Notes	Text code
10 Sept 1849	*Would have imposed swine-raising restrictions; stray swine, goats prohibited, taken to Asylum; police fined for shirking duties*	*Corp act; Daily Nat Intelligencer, 12 Sept 1849, p. 1; not passed*	*Cp 38*
Sept 1851	Diseased horses at large declared nuisance	BoH ordinance; Daily Nat Intelligencer, 29 Sept 1851; repeated 27 Mar 1856, p. 14; possibly annual	Cp 100
26 Aug 1852	Restrictions on animals held for slaughter; police fined for shirking duties	Acts of Wash	Cp 39
3 June 1853	Omnibus nuisance act; restrictions on diseased and stray horses, geese, goats	Acts of Wash	Cp 40
17 Jan 1856	Restrictions on diseased and stray horses, geese, goats repeated	Corp act; Sheahan, pp. 164-166	Cp 41
by 1857	Justice of Peace responsible for strays, mad dogs	Acts of Wash	Cp 8
1 Aug 1863	Cow-raising restrictions	Corp act; Ould and Cross, pp. 162-164	Cp 42
5 May 1868	Revived 1853 prohibition on stray hogs, goats, geese	Acts of Wash; slightly revised 24 May 1866, Webb, pp. 119-120	Cp 43
9 Nov 1868	Almshouse must return hogs, geese if requested	Corp act; Daily Nat Intelligencer, 6 May 1868, p. 1	Cp 44

Dogs -- Georgetown

Date approved	Resume	Source/Notes	Text code
2 June 1792	Tax on dogs	Text not available; G'town Code 1811	Cp 46
17 Feb 1798	"Diminish number of dogs"	Text not available; G'town Code 1811	Cp 46
4 May 1798	Further to "Diminish"	Text not available; G'town Code 1811	Cp 46
29 Aug 1803	Further to "Diminish"	Text not available; G'town Code 1811	Cp 46
4 Sept 1804	Dogs prohibited in market	Ordinances of G'town	Cp 47
5 July 1805	Tax on dogs	Text not available; G'town Code 1811	Cp 46
21 July 1807	Tax on dogs; strays prohibited	Ordinances of G'town; slightly revised 9 June 1808	Cp 48
29 June 1808	Restrictions for rabies	Corp act; Wash Federalist, 29 June 1808, p. 3; temporary	Cp 49
18 May 1811	Police to kill all strays	Corp act; Spirit of Seventy-Six, 21 May 1811, p. 4	Cp 50
6 Oct 1815	Tax on dogs increased	Ordinances of G'town; slightly revised 10 Oct 1818	Cp 51
24 July 1819	Stray dogs prohibited	Ordinances of G'town	Cp 52
29 Mar 1822	Tax on dogs increased	Ordinances of G'town	Cp 53
3 Aug 1824	Tax on dogs decreased; constables to check each household	Ordinances of G'town	Cp 54
3 May 1828	Defines "owners" of dogs	Ordinances of G'town	Cp 55
18 Feb 1829	Revives prohibition on dogs in market	Ordinances of G'town	Cp 56
12 Sept 1829	Unlicensed dogs killed	Ordinances of G'town	Cp 57
25 June 1836	Revives prohibition on stray dogs	Ordinances of G'town	Cp 58
28 July 1855	Muzzled dogs not to be killed	Corp act; Evening Star, 27 June 1857, p. 2	Cp 59
14 Feb 1857	All dog ordinances to be harmonized	Ordinances of G'town	Cp 60
25 June 1859	Comprehensive ordinance: tax, rabies emergency, dogs in market	Ordinances of G'town	Cp 61

Dogs -- Georgetown (cont'd)

Date approved	Resume	Source/Notes	Text code
1 Aug 1860	Dog tags instituted; dangerous dogs killed	Ordinances of G'town	Cp 62
10 May 1867	Comprehensive ordinance as above, some charges raised; spayed females taxed as males	Ordinances of G'town	Cp 63

Dogs -- Washington

Date approved	Resume	Source/Notes	Text code
12 Sept 1803	Tax on dogs	Acts of Wash	Cp 64
30 May 1804	Repeals fine for non-payment	Acts of Wash	Cp 65
5 Sept 1804	Registration of dogs, fine re-imposed	Acts of Wash	Cp 66
4 Nov 1807	Tax on dogs; strays prohibited	Acts of Wash	Cp 67
4 Aug 1809	Tax on dogs increased, bounty on strays increased	Acts of Wash; tax on females increased by 1818, Hewitt, pp. 75-76.	Cp 68
9 Oct 1817	Restrictions for rabies	Acts of Wash	*Cp 69*
29 July 1819	*Would have prohibited stray dogs, and in market; dogs on street leashed*	*Corp act; City of Wash Gazette, 3 Aug 1819, p. 2; replaced 14 Aug 1819*	*Cp 70*
14 Aug 1819	Stray dogs prohibited, and in market; dogs on street leashed	Acts of Wash; sight variation on 29 July 1819	Cp 71
1 Apr 1820	Comprehensive act: tax, tags, strays, market, rabies; constables fined for shirking duty	Acts of Wash	Cp 72
11 Nov 1824	Dogs prohibited in market	Acts of Wash	Cp 73
8 June 1826	Vicious dogs prohibited	Acts of Wash	Cp 74
23 Aug 1827	Police must enforce law	Mayor's directive; United States Telegraph, 28 Aug 1827, p. 4	Cp 75
25 July 1829	Comprehensive act as above; constables fined if shirking duty	Acts of Wash; slightly revised 27 Apr 1838	Cp 76
12 Mar 1838	Free blacks allowed to keep dogs	Acts of Wash	Cp 77
22 May 1844	Dogs prohibited in market	Acts of Wash	Cp 78

Dogs -- Washington (cont'd)

Date approved	Resume	Source/Notes	Text code
24 May 1853	Omnibus market act; dogs prohibited in market	Corp act; Sheahan, p. 195; almost identical to 22 May 1844	Cp 79
3 June 1853	Dog fights prohibited; dogs must be controlled on street	Corp act; Sheahan, p. 150; slightly revised 7 Nov 1867, Webb, p. 465	Cp 80
25 July 1853	*Would have required muzzling of dogs*	*Corp act; Daily Nat Intelligencer, 27 July 1853, p. 1; not passed*	*Cp 81*
by 1857	Justice of Peace to kill mad dogs, owners fined	Corp act; Ould and Cross, pp. 162-163	Cp 42
27 May 1857	Omnibus market act; dogs prohibited in market	Acts of Wash	Cp 82
14 Jan 1858	Comprehensive act as above; constables fined if shirking duty	Acts of Wash	Cp 83

Dogs -- County

Date approved	Resume	Source/Notes	Text code
25 July 1864	Unlicensed dogs killed by police	US Statutes; inc in statute of 1 Dec 1873, sect. 189	Cp 84
spring? 1867	Specifics of dog licensing procedure	Levy Ct; Callan, pp. 15-16	Cp 85

Pound -- Washington

Date approved	Resume	Source/Notes	Text code
16 July 1862	Charge of animals given to Police Property Clerk	US Statutes	Cp 86
23 Mar 1863	Contractor pound for farm animals, dogs	Not published in Acts; Daily Nat Intelligencer, 27 Mar 1963, p. 1; initial text Daily Nat Intelligencer, 28 Aug 1862, p. 1; repealed 14 Apr 1866	Cp 87
23 July 1866	Police holding procedures refined	US Statutes	Cp 88
22 Aug 1867	*Would have established dog pound*	*Acts of Wash; appropriation 4 Oct 1867; not acted upon*	*Cp 89*

APPENDIX B - Laws Relating to Animal Control 253

Cruelty -- Georgetown

Date approved	Resume	Source/Notes	Text code
7 Mar 1868	Animals at markets protected	Ordinances of G'town	Cp 90
5 Nov 1869	Horses and others protected	Ordinances of G'town	Cp 91

Cruelty -- Washington

Date approved	Resume	Source/Notes	Text code
by 1819	Animal fights, dog attacks, cruelty in general prohibited; draught animals protected	Corp act; Cranch, Code, pp. 278-289	Cp 92
12 July 1821	Horses protected	Acts of Wash	Cp 93
3 June 1853	Horses protected	Corp act; Sheahan, p. 152; slightly revised 7 Nov 1867, Webb, p. 465	Cp 80
28 Sept 1860	Calves ungagged	Acts of Wash	Cp 94
12 July 1862	Animals at markets protected	Acts of Wash	Cp 95

Cruelty -- District-wide

Date approved	Resume	Source/Notes	Text code
21 June 1870	SPCA established, works with police	US Statutes	Cp 96

Dead Animals -- Georgetown

Date approved	Resume	Source/Notes	Text code
4 Aug 1795	Prohibited on private property	G'town Code 1811	Cp 97

Dead Animals -- Washington

Date approved	Resume	Source/Notes	Text code
27 Oct 1809	Owners to bury if on streets	Acts of Wash	Cp 25
8 July 1820	Scavengers remove carcasses	Acts of Wash	Cp 98
11 July 1820	Negligent owners fined, city removes	Corp act; Rothwell, p. 117	Cp 99
3 July 1843	Carcasses declared nuisances	BoH minutes; repeated annually	Cp 100
20 May 1848	Bd of Health responsibilities, powers re carcasses specified; diseased animals must be destroyed, buried by owners; Bd has responsibility	Acts of Wash; repeated 20 May 1853; BoH act, 17 Jan 1856	Cp 6

Dead Animals -- County

Date approved	Resume	Source/Notes	Text code
4 May 1863	Leaving carcasses on public road prohibited	Levy Ct; Callan, p. 1	Cp 101

Appendix B2

The Territorial Government (1871 to 1874)

Nuisances/Board of Health

Date approved	Resume	Source/Notes	Text code
21 Feb 1871	Terr Govt established; Bd of Health retains animal control; nuisances	US Statutes	T 102

Farm Animals

Date approved	Resume	Source/Notes	Text code
May 1871	Strays prohibited	BoH ordinance; summarized Daily Nat Republican, 3 May 1871, p. 4	T 103
Nov 1872	Stray goats prohibited	BoH ordinance; text not available; Evening Star, 16 Nov 1872, p. 2	--
26 June 1873	Animals prohibited from public parks	Acts of Territory; restated, extended nationwide by Cong act, 3 Mar 1875	T 104

Dogs

Date approved	Resume	Source/Notes	Text code
May 1871	Muzzling in summer; not allowed loose at night; rabid dogs to be killed	BoH ordinance; summarized Daily Nat Republican, 3 May 1871, p. 4; extract (dogs) Evening Star, 14 June 1872, p. 2	T 103
19 Jan 1872	Dogs treated as property, may be redeemed	Acts of Territory	T 105
Apr 1873	Licensing act for dogs voided	DC Supreme Ct "Mayor of Wash v Meigs"; MacArthur, pp. 53-60	T 106
Sept 1873	Citizens can defend themselves against vicious dogs	Police Ct; text not available; Evening Star, 3 Sept 1873, p. 2; affirmed by DC Supreme Ct "Murphy v. Preston" 1887; Mackey, pp. 514-521	T 106A
spring? 1874	Muzzling in summer increased	BoH ordinance; text not available; Nat Republican, 18 June 1874, p. 4	--

Pound

Date approved	Resume	Source/Notes	Text code
19 May 1871	Contractor pound re-established; restrictions on animals re-stated; proceeds used for Sanitary Fund	BoH ordinance; text not available; Evening Star, 12 May 1871, p. 4; 7 June 1871, p. 1; Snty Fund finally approved by Treasury 25 June 1895	--
Mar 1872	District-operated pound established, with elaboration of earlier provisions	BoH ordinance; revision of 1871 ordinance; Comm Ann Rpt, 1900 (HO Ann Rpt, pp. 80-81)	T 107
spring? 1874	*Would have prohibited stray farm animals in County; established county pound*	*County Acts of Wash; not signed into law*	*T 108*

Cruelty

Date approved	Resume	Source/Notes	Text code
23 Aug 1871	Omnibus cruelty act; violations, penalties specified; SPCA role outlined, with police cooperation	US Statutes	T 109

Dead Animals

Date approved	Resume	Source/Notes	Text code
May 1871	Bd of Health assumes responsibility for nuisances; procedures, penalties established	BoH ordinance; summarized Daily Nat Republican, 3 May 1871, p. 4; further text Evening Star, 24 May 1871, p. 4	T 102
9 Sept 1873	Dead animals must be reported	BoH ordinance; Evening Star, 22 Sept 1873, p. 2	T 110

Appendix B3

The Commissioner Period (1874-1945)

Nuisances/Board of Health

Date approved	Resume	Source/Notes	Text code
? 1874-78	Stray animals in county to be impounded	Text not available; listed in index of Comm Minutes/Orders as pp. 351, 502, but that volume of minutes missing	--
22 July 1874	Responsibility for garbage assigned to Bd of Health	Comm order; BoH Ann Rpt, 1874; Garbagemaster abolished, 23 Mar 1875	Cm 111
19 Nov 1875	Omnibus nuisance ordinance; Bd of Health has supervision of nuisances; violations, penalties specified	BoH ordinance, incorporating earlier ordinances; Comm Ann Rpt, 1900 (HO Ann Rpt, pp. 77-80)	Cm 112
27 June 1879	Commissioners given control of animals thruout District	US Statutes	Cm 113
4 Aug 1879	Animal regs extended to some parts of county	Comm Minutes/Orders	Cm 114
26 Jan 1887	Commissioners given control of police regs about animals and dogs	US Statutes	Cm 115
Jan 1891	Animal regs extended further to all "improved subdivisions"	Text not available; Comm order; Evening Star, 9 Jan 1891, p. 3	--
16 Aug 1893	Stray animals thruout District to be impounded	Comm Minutes/Orders	Cm 116
27-Jan-1905	Commissioners given control over all garbage collection	US Statutes (Jt Res)	Cm 117
23-Dec-1907	Would have prohibited animals (inc dogs) in public parks	Comm Minutes/Orders; rescinded 1 Feb 1908	Cm 118

Farm Animals

Date approved	Resume	Source/Notes	Text code
19 Nov 1875	Swine, diseased animals prohibited from municipalities and dense suburbs; restrictions on keeping animals	BoH ordinance, incorporating earlier ordinances; Comm Ann Rpt, 1900 (HO Ann Rpt, pp. 77-80)	Cm 112
16 Aug 1893	Strays prohibited throughout District	Comm Minutes/Orders	Cm 119
28 Aug 1897	Restrictions on cow pens/stables	Comm order; Comm Ann Rpt, 1898, pp. 4-5	Cm 120
24 May-1902	Further restrictions on cow pens/stables	Comm order; HO Ann Rpt, 1903	Cm 121
22 Jul 1908	Further restrictions on animal pens/stables	Comm order; HO Ann Rpt, 1909	Cm 122

Cattle in the Streets

Date approved	Resume	Source/Notes	Text code
13 May 1875	Driving cattle thru city streets prohibited	Comm Minutes/Orders, text taken from 30 Nov 1881 restatement	Cm 123
10 June 1887	Further, specific restrictions	Police reg; Comm Ann Rpt, 1887, pp. 169-170	Cm 124
2 Dec 1891	Driving cattle thru suburbs prohibited, other specifics	Comm Minutes/Orders	Cm 125
5 Jul 1910	Lame, diseased animals prohibited from roads	Comm Minutes/Orders	Cm 126

Chickens/Pigeons

Date approved	Resume	Source/Notes	Text code
10 June 1887	Stray, noisy fowl prohibited in Wash/G'town; owners fined	Police regs, 1887	Cm 124
10 June 1887	*Would have impounded stray, noisy fowl*	*Police regs, 1887; part of above; not enforced*	Cm 124
by 1896	Stray, noisy fowls prohibited thruout District; owners fined	Police regs, 1896	Cm 127
1896	*Pigeons not regulated as "fowls"*	*Text not available; Police Ct; cited in Corp Counsel opinion, 3 Oct 1896; not observed in practice*	--
by 1906	Restrictions on stray fowl tightened	Police regs, 1906	Cm 128
3 Dec 1906	Raising fowl prohibited in most parts of the city	Comm order; HO Ann Rpt, 1908; voided by Police Ct decision "D.C. v Keen" June 1907 (Nat Arch, RG351/21, file 1-113a)	Cm 129
10 Sep 1908	Restrictions on fowl tightened	Comm Minutes/Orders	Cm 130
7 Jul 1909	Restrictions on fowl tightened, conditions of raising them specified	Comm Minutes/Orders	Cm 131
24 Feb 1939	Restrictions on fowl tightened	Comm Minutes/Orders	Cm 132

Dogs

Date approved	Resume	Source/Notes	Text code
19 Nov 1875	Muzzling in summer increased, and during rabies emergency	BoH ordinance, possibly incorporating earlier ordinances; Comm Ann Rpt, 1900 (HO Ann Rpt, pp. 77-80)	Cm 112
22 Apr 1878	*Would have prohibited spitz dogs*	*HR 4539; LOC Law Library; not passed*	*Cm 133*
19 June 1878	Omnibus dog act; licensing required, unlicensed dogs impounded, rabies emergencies outlined, dogs are property	US Statutes	Cm 134
10 June 1887	Dangerous or noisy dogs prohibited; dangerous dogs leashed on street	Police regs, 1887	Cm 124
29 July 1892	Restrictions on dangerous dogs	US Statutes	Cm 135
19 Dec 1899	Rabies emergency, temporary muzzling	Comm Minutes/Orders	Cm 136
31 Mar 1902	*Would have given Commissioners control of dogs in public streets*	*S 4792; LOC Law Library; not passed*	*Cm 137*
30 Jun 1902	Females in heat controlled, fines revised	US Statutes	Cm 138
3 Dec 1906	Barking dogs prohibited; dangerous dogs to be leashed; owners of unlicensed dogs fined	Comm order; HO Ann Rpt, 1908	Cm 129
23 Dec 1907	*Would have prohibited dogs in public parks*	*Comm Minutes/Orders; rescinded 1 Feb 1908*	*Cm 118*
16-Jun-1908	Rabies emergency, temporary muzzling	Comm Minutes/Orders; reissued 25 June 1908; also 4 Aug 1910, revised text Wash Herald, 8 Aug 1910, p. 7; and following years	Cm 139
27-Sep-1911	Police court hears licensing complaints	Comm Minutes/Orders	Cm 140
May 1912	*Leashed dogs do not require license*	*Text not available; Police Ct; apparently not effectuated, perhaps overturned on appeal; Evening Star, 18 May 1912, p. 6*	--
27 Jun 1912	Dogs at large prohibited in Rock Creek Park	Comm Minutes/Orders	Cm 141
12 Jun 1923	Leashing an alternative to muzzling during rabies emergency	Comm Minutes/Orders	Cm 142
24 Feb 1939	Drivers not liable for injury to chasing dogs	Comm Minutes/Orders	Cm 143
24 Feb 1939	Leashing required on streets; dogs prohibited on private property without permission	Comm Minutes/Orders	Cm 132
5 Jul 1945	Raises dog tax; leashing, vaccination, quarantining for rabies allowed	US Statutes	Cm 144

Cats

Date approved	Resume	Source/Notes	Text code
11 Jun 1912	Cats at large prohibited	Comm Minutes/Orders	Cm 145
by 1915	Would have impounded stray cats from streets	Police regs, 1915; not enforced	Cm 146

Miscellaneous Animals

Date approved	Resume	Source/Notes	Text code
24 Feb 1939	Wild-animal pets need permit; beekeeping restrictions	Comm Minutes/Orders	Cm 132

Pound

Date approved	Resume	Source/Notes	Text code
16 Dec 1899	Fee required to claim untagged dogs	Comm Minutes/Orders	Cm 147
16 Apr 1900	Would have given pound operations to WHS	S 4232; LOC Law Library; not passed	Cm 148
28 Feb 1901	Proceeds to Police/Fire retirement funds	US Statutes	Cm 149
2 Mar 1911	DC budget funds new pound/stable	US Statutes	Cm 150
6 Jun 1930	Poundmaster salary raised; reinstated as MPDC special officer	US Statutes	Cm 151
23 Jun 1936	Transferred to jurisdiction of Commissioners	Comm Minutes/Orders	Cm 152

Shelters

Date approved	Resume	Source/Notes	Text code
20 Apr 1908	Commissioners given authority to regulate hospitals/asylums	US Statutes	Cm 159
19 May 1909	Requires licensing of animal hospitals/shelters	Comm Minutes/Orders; slight modifications 7 Oct 1909, 16 Feb 1910	Cm 160
15 Jan 1937	Animal shelters allowed in residential districts	Comm Minutes/Orders	Cm 161

Cruelty/SCPC/WHS

Date approved	Resume	Source/Notes	Text code
24 Mar 1876	*Would have strengthened powers of SPCA (to seize and sell abused animals)*	*S 647; LOC Law Library; not passed*	Cm 153
Oct 1880	Fines paid to SPCA directly rather than govt	Comm order; Nat Republican, 28 Oct 1880 p. 4	Cm 154
13 Feb 1885	SPCA becomes WHS; cruelty to children prohibited	US Statutes	Cm 155
13 Dec 1886	*Would have raised fines for abuse*	*HR 10139; LOC Law Library; not passed*	Cm 156
12 Mar 1888	*Would have revised procedures; defined further abuse*	*HR 8344; see 1892 bill; LOC Law Library; not passed*	*Cm 157*
25 June 1892	Revisions to earlier procedures; docking, animal fights prohibited	US Statutes	Cm 158
29 July 1892	Further to dog fights, dangerous dogs	US Statutes	Cm 135

Dead Animals

Date approved	Resume	Source/Notes	Text code
19 Nov 1875	Dead animals must be removed; penalties specified	BoH ordinance, possibly incorporating earlier ordinances; Comm Ann Rpt, 1900 (HO Ann Rpt, pp. 77-80)	Cm 112
10 June 1887	Dead animals cannot be left on public land	Police regs, 1887	Cm 124
16 Aug 1893	Dead animals must be transported in sealed wagons	Comm Minutes/Orders	Cm 119
2 Mar 1895	Commissioners can contract out removal of dead animals for 5 years	US Statutes; preliminary act, 7 Aug 1894; repeated periodically	Cm 162
19 May 1896	Dead animals cannot be left on docks or in river	US Statutes	Cm 163
by 1902	Dead animals cannot be left in any open area	Police regs, 1902	Cm 164
28 Feb 1923	District govt to take dead animals rather than contractor	US Statutes	Cm 165

APPENDIX C

STATISTICAL COMPILATIONS

Notes

- **Statistics before 1872** refer only to the City of Washington unless indicated otherwise, and represent fiscal years (Oct-Sept or July-June) or calendar years as noted.

- In some cases **official historical compilation tables** give different figures from those reported in the earlier annual reports; in these cases I have used the later numbers, thinking that they represent some correction. I have also occasionally rounded figures, and selected between two close but differing numbers.

Source abbreviations:

Aud	Auditor
Tax	Collector of Taxes
MPCD	Metropolitan Police
Atty*	Attorney for DC
BoH	Board of Health
HO*	Health Officer
PM	Poundmaster
Str Cl*	Street Cleaning Dept

*Later names:
-- Atty: After 1902 the Corporation Counsel (Corp Cnsl).
-- HO: After 1903 the Health Department (HD).
-- Str Cl: After 1912 the Division of Street Cleaning (Str Cl), and after 1920 the City Refuse Division (City Ref), both of the Engineer Department.

For further information on sources, see Notes on Sources.

C1: Farm Animal Population Statistics

Farms in the District of Columbia

CY	No. of Farms	Total Acres	Av. Acres	No. of Workers
1850	267	27,454	102	
1860	238	34,263	144	
1870	209	11,677	55	1,350
1880	435	18,146	41	1,445
1890	382	11,745	30	1,668
1900	269	8,489	31	1,431
1910	217	6,063	27	
1920	204	5,668	27	804
1930	104	3,071	29	435
1945 (sic)	40	1,854	46	70 (1949)

US Census reports, "Agriculture" (Much more detailed statistics, 1850-80, will be found in the original census sheets at the National Archives: "Nonpopulation Census Schedule for the District of Columbia", RG 29, microfilm roll M 1793.)

Farm Animals in the District of Columbia*

CY	Dairy Cows	Other Cattle	Horses	Mules	Sheep	Swine	Chickens
1860	639	267	641	122	40	1,099	6,482 (1880)
1890	1,251	142	838	81		802	8,004
1930	451	438	173		6	1,353	12,529

* These figures probably don't represent all farm animals kept in the District, many being owned singly and informally by families for private use or small-scale sales.

US Census reports, "Agriculture"

"In 1853 there were perhaps two or three thousand porkers within the city [Washington] limits. . . Now there are probably twenty or thirty thousand hogs at large." (*Evening Star, 10 Mar 1868, p. 2*)

"The number of cows kept for dairy purposes in the District, as shown by the applications for permits to keep dairy farms, was 1,356. No estimate of the number of other domestic animals can be made." (*PM Ann Rpt, 1897*)

"The District [government] now has on hand 150 horses and mules, five herd of dairy cattle and no less than 1,200 hogs." (Many of the cattle, at least, were kept in suburban Maryland.) (*Evening Star, 10 Sept 1933, p. 2; Board of Examiners in Veterinary Medicine Ann Rpt, in Comm Ann Rpt, 1933, lists all dairy herds held by DC government agencies.*)

Animal Enclosures in 1881

	Hog-pens	Cow Stables/Yards
Washington	11	314
Georgetown		55

HO Ann Rpt (Sanitary Survey), 1881

Fowl/Pigeon Houses Registered

FY	Houses
1915	1,232
1916	1,377
1917	1,488
1918	1,621
1919	1,758
1920	1,936
1921	2,145
1922	2,293
1923	2,424

HO/HD Ann Rpt

C2: Complaints Regarding Hogs, Cows and Fowl

Complaints* Regarding Hogs

Year	"Hog Pens in Filthy Conditions"	Illegal Hog Pens	Filthy/Illegal Combined	Year	"Hog Pens in Filthy Conditions"	Illegal Hog Pens	Filthy/Illegal Combined
1867 CY†			80	1887	15		
1868			105	1888	3		
1869	102	53		1889	17		
1870	108	46		1890	44		
1871	62	49		1891	57		
1872	41 (MPDC) 219 (HO; FY)	4 --		1892	48		
1873 FY	211			1893	40		
1874	61			1894	79		
1875	45			1895	26		
1876	68			1896	14		
1874	61			1897	10		
1875	45			1898	9		
1876	68			1899	17		
1877	57			1900	4		
1878	50			1901	8		
1879	49			1902	7		
1880	119			1903	5		
1881	94			1904	5		
1882	40			1905	13		
1883	26			1906	10		
1884	26			1907	44		
1885	40			1908	1		
1886	14						

* Corresponding numbers for cases prosecuted by the Atty are the same or very slightly lower.
† 1867-72: Reported to MPDC Sanitary Company,

1867-72: MPDC Ann Rpt; 1872-1908: BoH/HO/HD Ann Rpt

Complaints Regarding Cows

FY	Filthy/Illegal Cow Yards Complaints	Cow Stables Complaints	Keeping Cow Yard Prosecutions	FY	Filthy/Illegal Cow Yards Complaints	Cow Stables Complaints	Keeping Cow Yard Prosecutions
1872	35			1888	14	53	
1873	92			1889	33	83	
1874	84			1890	14	26	5
1875	90			1891	5	22	
1876	437 (sic)			1892	19	32	
1877	151			1893	9	13	
1878	193			1894	1	28	
1879	23		3	1895	11	20	
1880	23	119	17	1896	23	21	
1881	45	148	79	1897	1	2	
1882	73	124	16	1898	11	5	
1883	35	117	1	1899	33	2	
1884	18	227	37	1900	32		
1885	17	101		1901	1		
1886	12	52	4				
1887	13	48	17	1905	1		

Complaints: BoH/HO/HD Ann Rpt; Prosecutions: Atty Ann Rpt

Unregistered Fowl and Pigeon Houses

FY	Violations	Prosecutions
1911	545	
1912	771	35
1913	650	10
1914	453	19
1915	445	
1916	325	
1917	342	
1918	290	
1919	485	
1920	613	
1921	615	

HO/HD Ann Rpt

C3: Animal Capture Statistics

Expenditures for Killing Dogs

Year	Georgetown	Washington
1818 FY		$22
1819		22
1820		33
1837		16
1838		2
1839		17
1841*		100
1842		121
1845 CY	$163	
1846	139	
1847	138	
1848	154	
1849	163	
1850	142	
1851	107	
1852	62	
1853	126	

* 1841-42: "Killing dogs, burying dead animals".

Corporation Register's reports (1818-20 from local newspapers; 1845-53 included in annual Georgetown Acts)

Income and Expenditures Related to the Sale of Farm Animals

Hogs and geese were, by law, turned over to the Asylum (poorhouse) when captured by the police. Since the annual reports of the Asylum Intendent give no indication that the institution raised its own animals (as opposed to vegetables, from which it gained a fair income) the figures below might give some idea of the trend in captures. The source of the horses and cows is uncertain.

We have no information on the rate paid contractors for transport of the animals.

FY	Income of the Wash Asylum from Sale of Animals				Expenditure (from Gen Funds) for "Carrying Hogs to the Almshouse"
	Hogs	Geese	Horses	Cows & Calves	
1842					$434 (sic)
1843					64
1844					120
1845					85
1846					15 / 53*
1847	$17				
1850	246	$24	$20	$20	150
1852	82				
1854	407		71		190
1855					199
1856					222
1857					33 (sic)
1858					238
1860					120
1861	311				282
1863	74†		12		132

* Two figures reported.
† Separately: $18 for "farm-fed hogs."

Income: Asylum Intendent Ann Rpt; Expense: Register's Ann Rpt

Stray Animals Reported by MPDC

Year	Animals "Found Estray"*	Animals "and Vehicles Restored to Owner" †
1864 CY	80	37
1865	78	34
1866	69	33
1867	65	18
1868	92	80
1869	170	172
1870	121	230
1871	185	211
1872 FY		315
1873	234	307
1874	240	251
1878		285

* Lost/strayed/stolen horses and cattle; in some years "restored to owners."
† Meaning "[animal] hitched to vehicle"? Horses/cattle/mules.

MPDC Ann Rpt

Animals "Found Estray" by MPDC

FY	To Poundmaster Number	To Poundmaster Estimated Value*	To Property Clerk	Total	FY	To Poundmaster Number	To Poundmaster Estimated Value*	To Property Clerk	Total
1882	14			123	1907	22		47	379
1883	17			153	1908	31		30	368
1884	21			225	1909	35		12	276
1885	34			238	1910	70	85	37	251
1886	76		11	296	1911	162	70	22	294
1887	62		43	322	1912	166		11	194
1888	56		42	398	1913†	186	30	7	144
1889	35	$681	53	446	1914	257	40	8	106
1890	48		67	447	1915	108	35	18	168
1891	62		84	481	1916	83	20	9	77
1892	30		59	495	1917	81		8	58
1893	60		130	539	1918	87	125	13	133
1894	57		56	458	1919	58		14	68
1895	44		65	477	1920	36	19	6	59
1896	42		39	421	1921	158	440	7	55
1897	42	824	29	366	1922	150		4	34
1898	58		16	349	1923	118	75	1	36
1899	38		12	317	1924	56	475	1	57
1900	34		8	228	1925	106	1,200	4	42
1901	31		17	268	1926	56	230	1	62
1902	50		25	288	1927	54	215		156
1903	26		33	300	1928	132	475	4	39
1904	110		43	395	1929	90		1	34
1905	130		23	357	1930	134		2	61
1906	75	105	19	355	1931				48

* It is hard to know what to make of these fantastic figures; they are given here as reported.
† Note that from this year onwards a number of entries show the total taken as smaller than the two constituent columns.

MPDC Ann Rpt

Animals Impounded*

Tables in the PM Annual Reports also give key figures by month.

In Einstein's earliest years (1872-78) dogs were only taken during the summer months and only if at large but unmuzzled. After 1878 the muzzling requirement lapsed but was replaced by the need to be tagged year round. After 1900 muzzling was intermittently if increasingly required also.

FY	Horses	Mules	Cows/Calves‡	Hogs	Geese	Sheep	Goats	Dogs§	Cats	Total
1872†	88		225	40	210	124	152	375		1,214
1873	128	36	359	93	165	38	186	1,081		2,086
1874	60	22	169	57	64	4	129	2,290		2,795
1875	36	15	118	23	111		142	2,246		2,691
1876	36	5	60	3	93		162	2,309		2,668
1877	30	10	75	17	128		168	2,456		2,884
1878	44	2	109	17	119		162	2,828		3,281
1879	29	10	112	30	144	2	114	4,956		5,397
1880	32	1	255	12	483	8	106	1,728		2,625
1881	37	7	188	7	109	5	121	3,177		3,651
1882	39	3	161	3	252	8	90	3,884		4,440
1883	15	2	204	2	80		66	3,007		3,376
1884	31	2	120	2	75		29	2,699		2,958
1885	15	4	52	2	48	3	64	3,190		3,378
1886	22	2	66	1	89	1	52	2,968		3,201
1887	21		87	2	16	2	50	2,880		3,058
1888	25	4	85	3	26		36	2,572		2,751
1889	27	3	64		14		17	2,581		2,706
1890	54	2	110		19		25	2,834		3,044
1891	60	5	132	2	78		26	2,523		2,826
1892	62	20	109	2	28	1	20	3,077		3,319
1893	76	2	38	2	3		33	2,963		3,120
1894	88	12	26			7	21	3,408		3,562
1895	80	6	26	1	18		11	3,601		3,743
1896	64	3	18		17		3	3,226		3,331
1897	60	12	13	1	7		9	2,962		3,064
1898	54	7	7				5	2,889		2,962
1899	40	8	15		2		6	2,274		2,345

Animals Impounded* (Cont'd)

FY	Horses	Mules	Cows/Calves‡	Hogs	Geese	Sheep	Goats	Dogs§	Cats	Total
1900	38	7	17	1	32		19	6,266		6,374
1901	58	2	29		15		2	2,902		3,008
1902	34	4	17	2	4	1	2	2,728		2,792
1903	26	1	7				2	3,369		3,405
1904	18	1	1	2			3	2,656	547	3,228
1905	12		4				1	3,139	1,095	4,251
1906	15		10					3,716	2,764	6,505
1907	20	2	2					3,985	3,378	7,391
1908	29	6	3					6,694	4,038	10,770
1909	22	1		1	3			6,498	4,517	11,042
1910	12	4	4		7		8	4,929	1,429	6,393
1911	11	1	9				5	5,531	1,275	6,833
1912	17	1	6					4,703	1,252	5,976
1913	6				1			3,599	6,132	9,738
1914	6		6				1	3,768	4,994	8,775
1915	8							3,210	4,430	7,648
1916	5							2,974	3,913	6,892
1917	3		1					3,029	3,984	7,013
1918	7	1	2					3,257	2,555	5,822
1919	13	1						2,747	2,149	4,910
1920	24	3						2,854	1,746	4,627
1921	30	14	1			1	3	3,607	1,988	5,644
1922	30	3	3				1	3,104	2,316	5,487
1923	29	1		1			2	3,338	2,080	5,451
1924	48	3	2				3	3,794	1,861	5,701
1925	59	6	1					4,080	1,614	6,127
1926	28	2					1	3,988	1,302	5,740
1928	22	1					2	4,528	1,459	6,012
1929	15	1		1			1	5,112	1,637	6,678

Animals Impounded* (Cont'd)

FY	Horses	Mules	Cows/ Calves‡	Hogs	Geese	Sheep	Goats	Dogs§	Cats	Total
1930	17							5,068	1,215	6,301
1931	3							5,267	1,228	6,498
1933	5							5,105	1,395	6,504
1934	2							5,132	1,327	6,461
1935	4							5,377	1,558	6,940
1936	1							4,769	1,292	6,062
1937	3							3,818	869	4,690
1938	3				Ducks	Rabbits	3	5,122	1,776	6,904
1939	2				2	2	1	5,013	1,284	6,304
1940	4					3		6,381	1,670	8,058

* 1872-1906: Statistics taken from periodic cumulative tables, which sometimes differ from figures reported earlier in specific years.
† Partial year.
‡ Calves extremely few.
§ Figures for dogs in late 1930s adjusted to show only animals brought into the pound, and do not include those held from the previous year.

PM Ann Rpt

Sources of Pound Dogs (Selected Years)

FY	Captured	Surrendered
1910	4,929	1,868
1915	1,733	1,477
1920	1,718	1,122
1925	3,002	1,078
1935	3,190	2,187
1940	3,745	2,441

PM Ann Rpt

Rep. Collins: "You say 3,190 [dogs] were captured and 5,377 were cared for [in 1935]. How did you happen to get that extra number [1,187]? Did the people bring them there?"
Poundmaster Marks: "Yes, sir; . . . people call us and we collect the dogs, and a lot of them bring them there." *(Hearings . . . 1938 (House), 9 Feb 1937, pp. 88-91)*

Requests for Animal Pickup*

FY	No. of Requests
1905	1,662
1906	2,680
1907	3,130
1908	3,828
1909	3,521
1910	1,868
1911	2,199
1912	2,015
1914	4,573
1915	4,874

"Calls Made"†

FY	No. of Calls
1937	4,534
1938	5,067
1940	5,012

* Almost entirely for collection of unwanted cats.
† Not specified what these were for; probably same as above.

PM Ann Rpt

Disposition of All Pound Animals (Selected Years)

FY	Redeemed	Sold	Died	Returned	Killed	Dogs Killed
1875	766	8	3	22	2,092	
1880	894	42	1	21	1,667	1,610
1885	220	45			3,082	3,052
1890	255	25			2,750	2,740
1895	218	66			3,449	3,445
1900	999	144		174*	5,057	5,054
1905	314	114		5	3,818†	2,722
1910	448	107		4	5,834	4,403

Disposition of Dogs Only (Selected Years)

FY	Redeemed	Sold	Died	Returned	Killed	Other
1915	394	130		26	2,668	
1920‡	611	378		30	1,834	Escaped – 1
1925	651	1,288		348	2,115	
1930	456	760		160	3,617	
1935	318	1,191		254	3,541	
1940	337	640		74	5,287	Transferred to other departments – 18

* Animals held in quarantine for rabies observation then returned to owners, and in later years.
† Beginning of impounding and putting down cats.
‡ Separately: Horses/mules redeemed/sold – 27.

PM Ann Rpt

C4: Dog Tax Receipts, Pound Income ("Pound Fees"), and Pound Expenses

Dog Tax Receipts - Georgetown

CY	Tax
1808	$35*

* "Amount remaining at end of year".

Corporation Register's report (from local newspaper)

Dog Tax Receipts*

Charges for dog tax: 1803-78 – $1; 1879-1945 – $2.

FY	Receipts	FY	Receipts	FY	Receipts	FY	Receipts	FY	Receipts	FY	Receipts
1816	$101	1841	1,114	1862	594	1887	11,923	1906	18,411	1925	27,714
		1842	1,074	1863	637	1888	11,540	1907	20,093	1926	30,966
1819	173	1843	1,392			1889	6,975	1908	21,452	1927	32,099
1820	300	1844	1,160	1865	618	1890	13,701	1909	21,489	1928	34,785
1821	374			1866	5,850†	1891	12,171	1910	21,921	1929	34,450
1822	462	1847	1,250	1867	4,471	1892	13,833	1911	22,115	1930	38,482
1823	387			1868	4,843	1893	15,388	1912	20,026	1931	37,519
1824	524	1850	1,459	1869	7,418	1894	17,357	1913	17,589		
1825	620			1870	5,395	1895	15,416	1914	16,759	1933	42,732
		1852	1,447	1871	2,140	1896	14,108	1915	15,901	1934	43,552
1829	610	1853	1,325			1897	14,469	1916	16,637	1935	45,411
1830	855	1854	1,173	1879	10,505	1898	15,974	1917	14,414	1936	48,129
		1855	934	1880	8,579	1899	14,696	1918	14,973	1937	50,204
1834	711	1856	857	1881	3,336	1900	16,234	1919	16,031	1938	47,525
		1857	1,011	1882	2,997‡	1901	17,709	1920	16,925	1939	48,831
1837	755	1858	818	1883	3,176	1902	16,996	1921	22,356	1940	49,398
1838	975			1884	8,094	1903	16,698	1922	24,439		
1839	981	1860	956	1885	12,786	1904	16,773	1923	25,858		
1840	1,098	1861	479	1886	14,124	1905	17,819	1924	25,957		

* Amounts probably include charges for duplicate tags (see below).
† I can find no explanation for this dramatic increase.
‡ Reported as $3,008 in PM Ann Rpt.

Sources: 1819-71: Corporation Register's reports (before 1834 from local newspapers); 1879-1940: Tax Ann Rpt (repeated in Aud Ann Rpt); PM Ann Rpt

Licenses Issued

FY	Licenses Issued	Duplicates Issued
1879	5,281	
1897	7,345	
1909	10,998	3,500
1910	11,215	1,172
1911	11,313	1,250
1912	10,250	450
1913	9,061	431
1914	8,659	316

1879-97: PM Ann Rpt; 1910-14: Tax Ann Rpt

Fees Collected for Duplicate Dog Tags

FY	Fee	FY	Fee
1925	$304		
1926	140	1934	188
1927	183	1935	181
1928	135	1936	346
1929	258	1937	207
1930	191	1938	161
1931	209	1939	171
		1940	168

Tax Ann Rpt

Pound Fees

FY	Reported by PM Rpt	Reported by Tax Report	FY	Reported by PM Rpt	Reported by Tax Report
1876	$832		1888	397	391
1877	780		1889	484	503
1878	846		1890	548	501
1879	960		1891	765	696
1880	1,010 / 1,054*		1892	778	835
1881	1,338		1893	623	577
1882	1,140		1894	619	507
1883	1,021	$919	1895	586	698
1884	673	689	1896	527	550
1885	436	454	1897	526	501
1886	406	419	1898	401	366
1887	383	367			

Pound Fees (Expanded Reporting)

FY	Reported By PM Report "From Fees"	Reported By PM Report "From Sales"	Reported By PM Report "From Food"†	Reported By PM Report Total	Tax Report Total
1899	$259	$125		$384	$362
1900‡	1,978	231		2,209	1,874
1901	990	249		1,239	1,427
1902	759	265		1,024	964
1903	853	335	$4	1,192	1,301
1904	690	242	11	943	951
1905	630	226	5	861	853
1906	620	168	4	792	790
1907	508	211	17	736	694
1908	1,566	248	13	1,827§	1,764
1909	2,537	74	3	2,614	2,627
1910	884	216	5	1,105	1,085
1911	1,710	268	1	1,969 (sic)	1,975
1912	1,604	214	10	1,828	1,805
1913	784	143	1	928	462

Pound Fees (Expanded Reporting: cont'd)

FY	PM Report "From Fees"	PM Report "From Sales"	PM Report "From Food"†	PM Report Total	Tax Report Total
1914	1,017	235	8	1,260	640
1915	795	202	5	1,002	501
1916	732	210	9	951	475
1917	688	251	2	941	468
1918	594	273	3	870	436
1919	732	572	7	1,311	651
1920	1,292	689	15	1,996	967
1921	2,167	761	16	2,944	1,472
1922					1,299
1923					1,148
1924					1,415
1925	1,302	1,365	80	2,747	2,690
1926	1,048	1,014	422 (sic)	2,484	2,076
1927					2,456
1928				2,384	2,346
1929				2,653	2,611
1930				2,262	2,245
1931				2,735	2.711
1933				2,534	
1934				2,384	2,384
1935				2,109	2,742
1936	553	1,989	7	2,549	2,530
1937	278	1,245	35	1,558	1,523
1938	510	1,418	31	1,959	1,928
1939	510	1,142	25	1,687	1,652
1940	668	1,275	28	1,971	1,971

* Two figures reported.
† "Sales of bones from food for animals" (PM Ann Rpt, 1937).
‡ This remarkable increase reflects the new muzzling requirement.
§ Of which $56 from sale of horses.

PM Ann Rpt; Tax Ann Rpt (repeated in Aud Ann Rpt)

"The pound fees average $500/year" (*Evening Star*, 10 July 1910, pt. 2 p. 6)

MPDC Revenue From:

FY	"Forage/Keep of Estrays"	Sale of Estrays
1892	$9	
1895		$60
1914	45*	
1916	12	7
1921	25	

* Distribution roughly divided between the Policemen's Relief Fund and the contingent fund.

MPCD Ann Rpt

Pound Expenses

	Reported By			
	Poundmaster			Auditor
FY	"Service" [labor]	"Incidentals"	Total	Salaries, Supplies, Routine Maintenance†
1876			$2,000*	
1880			1,054*	
1881			1,338*	
1882			1,141*	
1900			5,349	
1908	$4,464	$1,744	6,208	
1909	5,851	2,618	8,469	$4,571
1910	5,175	1,902	7,077	6,632
1911	5,100	1,116	6,216	6,375
1912	4,400	1,343	5,743	5,825
1913	3,200	1,316	4,516	4,402
1914	3,200	1,225	4,425	4,122
1915	3,200	1,264	4,464	4,630
1916	3,200	1,269	4,469	4,891

Pound Expenses (Cont'd)

	Reported By			
	Poundmaster			Auditor
FY	"Service" [labor]	"Incidentals"	Total	Salaries, Supplies, Routine Maintenance†
1917	4,300	1,079	5,379	5,107
1918	4,900	1,891	6,791	5,504
1919	5,620	1,147	6,767	4,769
1920	6,100	1,219	7,319	
1922				7,281
1923				7,016
1924				7,802
1925				6,854
				Not inc salaries
1926				1,226
1927				1,113
1928				1,558
1929				906
1930				946
1931				1,450
1934				839
1935				1,962

* Not including poundmaster's salary ($1,200).
† Maintenance of building and vehicle but not new construction.

1876: BoH Ann Rpt; 1880-1920: PM Ann Rpt; 1909-40: Aud Ann Rpt

C5: Animal-Related Arrests/Prosecutions

Arrests Reported by MPD

FY	"Violating Dog Law"	"Keeping Dangerous Dog"	"Violating Muzzling Regs"	FY	"Violating Dog Law"	"Keeping Dangerous Dog"	"Violating Muzzling Regs"
1885	2,524			1910	43	15	
1886	1,025			1911	23	10	234
1887	1,102			1912	40	1	273
1888	394			1913	51	2	313
1889	52			1914	45		388
1890	272	4		1915	12		239
1891	46	9		1916	41	2	282
1892	48	3		1917	33		141
1893	78	8		1918	53	1	317
1894	90	11		1919	36	2	212
1895	55	6		1920	69	3	319
				1921	59	2	384
1897	128	23		1922			128
1898	48	20		1923	56		47
1899	66	11		1924	28	3	25
1900	105	11		1925	64	17	64
1901	87	15		1926	155	6	74
1902	78	25		1927	112	3	124
1903	41	30		1928	145	4	127
1904	46	22		1929	161	4	194
1905	45	18		1930	152	4	130
1906	39	19		1931	233	3	123
1907	73	21					
1908	62	17		1940	131		
1909	246	16					

1886-1930: MPDC Ann Rpt; 1931-40: Corp Cnsl Ann Rpt.

Prosecutions Reported by Attorney of DC* (Part 1)

FY	"Obstructing Poundmaster"	"[Violating] Pound/Dog Law"/ Unmuzzled Dog	"Biting/ Dangerous Dog"	"Female Dog at Large in Heat"	"Unlicensed Dog"	"Larceny of Dog"
1876		50				
1877			56			
1878			19			
1879	4					
1882	2					
1883	3					
1884		30				
1885						
1887				1		
1888	1			1		
1889				2		
1890						
1895				3		
1896				5		
1898				2		
1899				1		
1900				3		
1901				5		
1902			16	11		
1903			52	7	27	2
1904			40	6	40	9
1905			45	5		
1915			3		4	
1916			6	2	38	

Prosecutions Reported by Attorney of DC* (Part 2)

FY	"Barking Dog"	"Goat Running at Large"	"Cow in Yard"	"Chickens at Large"	"Driving Cattle thru Streets"
1876					
1877					
1878		1			
1879					
1882					
1883					
1884					
1885			5		
1887					
1888	1		2	5	10
1889	2				2
1890	3				

* Other regular entries record "Dog fighting" and "Horse tied to tree", both very small numbers.

Atty/Corp Cnsl Ann Rpt

C6: Rabies* and Rabid Animals

* Before 1900 "hydrophobia".

Persons Bitten by Dogs*

In spite of the District's intent to carefully track instances of rabies, official statistics show a degree of confusion and inconsistency. The figures given here are, as far as possible, taken from standardized tables in the Commissioners Annual Reports.

Year	Persons	Year	Persons	Year	Persons
1905 FY	20	1920	182	1931 CY	869
		1921	259	1932	885
1911†	157	1922	270	1933	967
1912	177	1923	297	1934	1,008
1913	163	1924	337	1935	1,205
1914	180	1925	441	1936	1,238
1915	159	1926	540	1937	1,301
1916	130	1927	531	1938	1,658
1917	136	1928 FY/CY‡	489 / 690	1939	1,391
1918	202	1929	619 / 844	1940	1,747
1919	195	1930	666 / 818		

* HD (1928-40) also reported a very small number of bites by cats, squirrels, parakeets, monkeys and others.
† 1911-31: Cases divided between serious and minor, but almost entirely the latter.
‡ 1928-40 CY: Number of dogs inspected by District veterinarian after biting people.

To help clarify the 1928-40 statistics:

- *1938: number of dog biting incidents reported to Health Dept: 1,658; number of dogs inspected by District veterinarian: 1,332 (because the other 300 could not be caught); total number of examinations required for these inspections: 3,417; other animals inspected: 7 cats, 2 squirrels;*
- *1935: number of dogs inspected because of biting incidents: 1,032; number inspected on suspicion of rabies but without biting: 24.*

Source: 1905: PM Ann Rpt; 1911-31 (FY): MPDC Ann Rpt; 1928-40 (CY): HD Ann Rpt; cf. C6 "Instances of Rabid Animals" below, which gives the number of bite cases requiring lab examination for rabies as opposed to simple bite incidents reported here.

Rabies in Humans – Reported Cases

CY	Number of Cases
1906	2
1907	10
1908	84
1909	43
1910*	29

* 7 months

HO special report, quoted in Wash. Times, 2 Aug 1910, p. 1.

Rabies in Humans – Deaths*

Year	Deaths	Year	Deaths
1878 FY	1	1903	1
1881	1	1911 CY	1
1896	1	1913	1
1898	1	1914	1
1902	1	1915	1

* Only years reporting deaths given. Board of Health annual reports began in 1849.

HO/HD Ann Rpt

"Within the last twenty years this disease has appeared in this city . . . in only six instances." (*Evening Star*, 24 Dec 1877, p. 2)

"There have been but two cases [deaths] of hydrophobia during the period covered by these tables [1874-80]; both cases were of white males, one aged 17 years, and the other 4; both from dog bites." (*HO Ann Rpt, 1880*)

"Speaking of the matter today, Dr. Wm. C. Woodward, the health officer, stated that since 1874 seven persons have died from hydrophobia. Previous to that year the records of the health department are not complete. The first of these seven persons died in 1877, being a young white man, seventeen years of age. A white boy, aged eight years, died from the disease in 1888. A young white man, twenty-seven years of age, died in 1892, and a white boy, twelve years of age, in 1894. The same year a little white girl, three years of age, died from the disease, and the following year a white woman, fifty-four years of age. The last person to die from the disease was young Springman, who died three years ago, aged eighteen years." (*"Deaths from Rabies", Evening Star, 28 April 1900, p. 15*)

"According to the Health Department, . . . during all of last year [1944] 128 persons were bitten and there were three deaths." (*Evening Star, 13 July 1945, p. 1*)

Instances of Rabid Animals Examined by the Bur of Animal Industry

Year	Dogs Taken for Observation		Other Animals Taken for Observation*		People Bitten†		Animals Bitten
	Suspected	Confirmed	Suspected	Confirmed	Suspected	Confirmed	
1899 FY				12‡			
1900	62	41				15	
1901						11	
1902		13					
1903	21	18		4			
1904		10			6		
1905	23	9			6		
1906		2					
1907		9					
1908	99	68					
1909	160	67		4		37	12
1910	82	47		4			
1911	105	54	7	4	66	52	30
1912	62	32	17	12	61	32	14
1913	58	38	5	3	53	31	35
1914 CY	21	8			18	3	1
1915	19	8	5	1	17	9	5
1916	21	3§	4	§	14	2	
1917	25	2	2		26	2	4
1918	46	24	2		38	27	16
1919	29	15	3		30	16	11
1920	24	9	3		18	5	4
1921	20	13	3		14	10	4
1922	48	23	8		38	16	50
1923	57	39	4		29	24	
1924	67	20	7		33	22	13
1925	102	91	5		71	67	89
1926		117			123£		
1927		67			47		
1928		21				24	
1929		51				36	

Instances of Rabid Animals Examined by the Bur of Animal Industry (Cont'd)

Year	Dogs Taken for Observation		Other Animals Taken for Observation*		People Bitten†		Animals Bitten
	Suspected	Confirmed	Suspected	Confirmed	Suspected	Confirmed	
1930		45				47	
1931		6				8	
1934						1	
1937	32	1	10				
1938	19	1	6		25		

* Cats, cows, horses.
† Inc in some years a small number bitten by cats and squirrels.
‡ "Livestock".
§ 1916-38: All confirmed cases of bites by any animal reported as one figure.
£ 1926-27: Not clear if bitten by suspected or confirmed rabid.

HD Ann Rpt; cf. "Bitten by Dogs" above, which gives total number of bite cases as opposed to those requiring lab examination for rabies, as here.

Persons Taking the Pasteur Treatment

Year	DC Residents	Non-DC Residents	Total
1911 FY	63	38	101
1912	57	31	88
1913	55	56	111
1914 CY	16	23	39
1915	9	13	22
1916	7	28	35
1917	14	15	29
1918	31	39	70

HD Ann Rpt

C7: Animal Cruelty Statistics

"Cruelty to Animals" Cases Handled by MPDC

Year	Arrests*	Prosecutions	Convictions	Year	Arrests*	Prosecutions	Convictions
1862 CY	21			**1896**	527	438	
1863	19			**1897**	429	490	
1864	11			**1898‡**	493	494	
1865	18			**1899**	719	799	
1866	6						
1867	29			**1904**	1,141	1,200	
1868	20			**1905**	1,422	1,325	
1869	23			**1906**	1,868		
1870	33			**1907**	2,055		
1871	41			**1908**	1,233		
1872 FY	18			**1909**	674		
1873	71			**1910 CY**	974		
1874	39			**1911**	1,960	274	
				1912	2,260	222	202
1876		3		**1913**	1,747	92	87
1877		9		**1914**	1,236	128	113
1878	19	11		**1915**	865	105	94
1879	13	9		**1916**	746	73	67
1880	15	7		**1917**	636	71	
1881†	21	18		**1918**	417	34	
1882	104	96		**1919**	190	31	
1883	93	22		**1920**	116	24	
1884	241	116		**1921**	111	24	
1885	268	257		**1922**	98	20	
1886	225	218		**1923**	85		
1887‡	246	275		**1924**	61		
1888	351	348		**1925**	26		
1889	239	225		**1926**	28		
1890‡	251	262		**1927**	18		
1891	272			**1928**	20		
1892	409			**1929**	18		
1893	312	303		**1930**	31		
1894	317	306		**1931**	27		
1895	417	412					

* Reports of the 1870-80s show these to be almost exclusively men.
† SPCA Ann Rpt: 1881 – 14 arrests, 13 convictions; 1882 – 32 arrests.
‡ Note that the MPDC reports 1898-1903 show fewer arrests than the Atty reported prosecutions.

Sources: Arrests: MPDC Ann Rpt; Prosecutions/Convictions:
1876-1905: Atty/Corp Cnsl Ann Rpt; 1911-22: WHS Ann Rpt

"Violation of Humane Laws" Cases Handled by MPDC*

FY	Cases	FY	Cases
1890	2	1899	10
1891	6	1900	21
1892	6	1901	2
1893	1	1902	27
1894	4	1903	39
1895	5	1904	18
		1905	6
1897	6	1906	25
1898	10		

* Shown separate from Cruelty cases above; not clear what these are.

MPDC Ann Rpt

Cases Handled by SPCA/WHS

CY	Animals Examined*	Prosecutions	Convictions	CY	Animals Examined	Prosecutions	Convictions
1881	ca 2,000	48	19†	1904	21,190	1,234	1,223
1882	ca 3,000	67	20	1905	22,733	1,560	1,535
1883	667	46	39	1906	28,778	1,977	1,942
1884	2,361	263	238	1907	26,331	1,720	1,668
1885	2,084	186	166	1908	14,865	645	624
1886	1,854	184	166	1909	9,740	537	514
1887	1,839	273	258	1910	12,045	1,231	1,168
1888	1,877	255	229	1911	16,134	2,017	1,929
1889		215	198	1912	16,148	1,824	1,718
1890		158	136	1913	15,108	1,352	1,286
1891	2,289	313	291	1914	11,610	909	875
1892	4,041	233	194	1915	8,945	712	692
1893	8,854	350	320	1916	6,940	655	633
1894	8,067	298	275	1917	6,241	490	475
1895	9,052	387	363	1918	4,152	233	230
1896	9,804	471	429	1919	2,965	117	116
1897	10,257	398	371	1920	2,605	102	98
1898	15,233	664	607	1921	2,426	99	92
1899	18,503	880	834	1922	1,795	66	63
1900	13,373	631	617	1923	1,400	57	54
1901	12,378	643	629	1924	300	31	31
1902	9,889	815	809	1925	703	20	18
1903	19,491	959	940				

* To 1900 titled "Cases Examined", "Animals Examined" thereafter.
† Per the cumulative table in WHS Ann Rpt, 1919; cf. the detailed list of 1881 reproduced in Appendix D9.

SPCA/WHS Ann Rpt

C8: Animals in Shelters

Animals Held at the Bertha Langdon Barber Refuge

CY	Cats				Cat Boarders	Dogs
	Brought in	Killed	Adopted	Died		
1897 (4 mth)	460	273	65	85*		
1898	1,976	1,633	98		45	
1899	2,128	2,128	87			19†

* "Principally kittens."
† All destroyed.

WHS Ann Rpt

Animals Held at the WARL Shelter

CY	Cats *		Kittens		Dogs *		Puppies		Horses		Others †		Total ‡	
	Taken In	Adopted/ Returned	TI	A/R	TI	A/R	TI	A/R	TI	A/R	TI	A/R	TI	A/R
5/14-12/18					4,052				154				24,771 / 25,593§	
1915 (10 m)	2,500				200				21					
1915 CY													4,198	
1916									32				6,000-7,000	
1917	1,958		3,465		950				37				6,413	
1918 FY	1,708		3,590		1,329				38				6,664	
1919					1,100								6,743	
1920									42		110		11,391	388/
1921	2,789	185/	7,179		1,268	188/15			19		39		11,391	
1922	3,383	214/2	7,379		1,369	317/44			11		70		12,190	
1923	3,086	58/2	7,482	123/	1,525	287/71			22		35		12,178	
1924	4,362	88/10	9,100	107/4	2,515	343/102	392						16,426	
1925													16,400	
1928							1,928						18,564	

Animals Held at the WARL Shelter (Cont'd)

CY	Cats * Taken In	Cats * Adopted/Returned	Kittens TI	Kittens A/R	Dogs * TI	Dogs * A/R	Puppies TI	Puppies A/R	Horses TI	Horses A/R	Others † TI	Others † A/R	Total ‡ TI	Total ‡ A/R
1932	4,442		9,037		3,448		1,572	1,932			121		18,620	235 / 167
1933	3,928	198/	8,218		3,373	198/167	1,484	1,933	7/		135		18,620	296/
1934	4,383	124 / 3	8,932		3,629	111/182	1,211	1,934			217		18,372	
1935	4,443	84 / 4	8,855		3,892	135/212	1,490	1,935			156	9	18,836	
1936	5,044	/6	9,844	107/	4,279	172/239	1,914	1,936	52	/1	179	6	21,260	
1937	4,791	27 / 5	10,215	298 / 3	4,350	445/281	2,309	1,937			177	3	21,842	
1938	4,676	/6	9,954	198 / 10	4,494	272/286	2,152	1,938			192	45	21,468	
1939	4,541	/9	8,607	/223	4,000	238/251	1,762	1,939			221		19,131	

* Inc kittens/puppies if no specific number is shown for them.
† Perhaps inc horses 1932-39.
‡ Totals do not always match sum of individual figures due to discrepancy in sources.
§ Two numbers reported.

WARL Sec Ann Rpt, from WARL Archives or reported in newspapers.

"Through the doors of the O Street building go between 19,000 and 20,000 animals a year. About 10 per cent of this huge number . . . are adopted. There's never any trouble finding a home for a kitten, but the League's rules are strict, and the majority of dogs never find new masters." (*Times-Herald*, 27 Apr 1941, p. E2)

Animals Brought to WARL Shelter by the Times Herald Rescue Service on Behalf of the Maryland and Virginia ARLs

These animals came from the Washington suburbs of Maryland and Virginia, and give an idea of the ratio of suburban to city animals at the WARL shelter.

CY	Cats	Kittens	Dogs	Puppies	Others, inc Horses	Total
1937	1,325	1,527	1,320	645	214	5,031

Memo, MVARL, 1938?

C9: Collection of Dead Animals

Expenditure for Dead Animal Removal

FY	Expenditure	Notes
1830	$15	
1837	3	
1840	1	"Removing a dead horse"
1841	100	"Killing dogs, burying dead animals"
1842	121	same
1843	56	
1844	77	
1845	58	
1846	70	
1847	72	
1850	165	
1852	231	
1853	375	
1854	607	
1855	680	
1856	730	
1857	783	
1858	847	

Corporation Register's reports

Reported by MPDC

Year	Rptd by Sanitary Comp	Rptd by Public to Telegraph Off	Rptd by Public and Officers, Forwarded by Telegraph Off to HO
1864 CY	285		
1865	517		
1866	447		
1867	861 / 786*		
1868	1,955		
1869	1,781	542	
1870	1,264 / 1,534†	595	
1871		577	
1872 FY	1,660‡	1,134	204 (sic; 1,204?)
1873		2,003	2,219
1874		1,397	1,467

* "Horses, cows, etc"/"Hogs, dogs, etc"
† Two numbers reported.
‡ 7 months; last year the Sanitary Company did this work.

MPDC Ann Rpt

Removed by City Trash Hauler

"Reported" are those called into the crew by police as found by MPDC or the public; "Removed" represent total taken up.

FY	Rptd by MPDC	Removed by Contractor/ City Crew*	FY	Rptd by MPDC	Removed by Contractor/ City Crew*
1874		4,410	**1886**	4,684	8,808
1875		4,614	**1887**	3,907	9,120
1876		4,555†	**1888**	3,498	7,863
1877		4,509	**1889**	3,395	7,954
1878		4,825	**1890‡**	3,978	8,344
1879		6,415	**1891**	5,165	9,910
1880		4,338	**1892**	5,439	10,528
1881	1,829	5,957	**1893**	5,326	9,649
1882	1,921	7,276	**1894**	5,576	10,340
1883	1,743	6,560	**1895**	5,015	7,512
1884	3,025	6,433	**1896**	5,374	8,419
1885	5,009	8,870	**1897**	5,776	7,161

Removed by City Trash Hauler (Cont'd)

FY	Rptd by MPDC	Removed by Contractor/City Crew*	FY	Rptd by MPDC	Removed by Contractor/City Crew*
1898	5,683	10,129	1920	5,825	19,995
1899	5,448	8,162	1921	5,717	24,704
1900	5,238	12,170	1922	6,042	28,675
1901	5,284	8,636	1923	5,377	30,120
1902	5,761	9,088	1924	5,637	34,764§
1903	5,204	9,955	1925	5,552	43,609
1904	5,072	9,432	1926	5,547	43,624
1905	4,763	9,593	1927	4,839	47,064
1906	4,942	11,975	1928	4,972	44,976
1907	5,894	14,892	1929	4,850	47,309
1908	5,836	19,181	1930	3,836	49,000
1909	5,930	17,993	1931	3,819	50,460
1910	6,094	18,675	1932		57,475
1911	5,575	16,720	1933		62,157
1912	5,174	17,492	1934		86,844£
1913	5,610	21,287		From Virginia#	
1914	4,651	19,148	1936	247	88,845
1915	4,772	20,570	1937	123	106,108
1916	4,691	22,724	1938	136	105,189
1917	4,887	24,562	1939	91	54,320
1918	4,774	22,891	1940		65,193
1919	4,665	19,974			

* At some point in the early twentieth century the crew began to pick up squirrels, rats and other minor rodents, affecting the count.
† Of which 1,092 were horses, cows and other "large animals".
‡ "The increase in dead animals [collected] is almost entirely attributable to the number of dogs killed at the pound" (HO Ann Rpt, 1890).
§ Inc 154 "large animals."
£ Inc 35,000 rats from a special extermination campaign.
"Large animals" brought to the incinerator by the City of Alexandria, Virginia.

Sources: 1864-74, 1885-89: MPDC Ann Rpt; 1872: Anon, "Affairs in the District . . ."; 1874-99: BoH/HO Ann Rpt; 1900-40: Str Cl/City Ref Ann Rpt*

* These reports also give the annual cost of dead-animal removal, and number and amount of fines levied on the contractor for poor performance.

Dead Animals Collected by Type (Part 1)

FY	Horses	Mules	Cows	Goats	Dogs	Cats
1901	689	28	38	25	3,302	3,402
1902	669	25	58	17	3,519	4,016
1903	320	18	40	12	4,195	4,083
1904	314		34		3,688	4,145
1906	417		42		4,471	5,783
1907	649		54		4,899	7,574
1908	614		67		7,666	9,058
1909	672					
1910	662					
1911	589				5,773	7,251
1912	688				5,704	10,150
1913	584				5,239	14,791
1914	554		14		4,907	12,932
1915	614				4,715*	13,339*

Dead Animals Collected by Type (Part 2)

FY	Rabbits	Rats	Poultry/Chickens	Misc	Total
1901	80	522	417	133	8,636
1902	96	660	486	142	9,688
1903	190	519	430	139	9,955
1904		573	337	341	9,432
1906		775	367	120	11,975
1907		1,065	488	163	14,892
1908		1,209	380	187	19,181
1909					17,993
1910					18,675
1911		475	166	228	16,720
1912		432	260	258	17,492
1913		337	160	176	21,287
1914		356	179	209	19,151†
1915		339	196	141	19,344

* Of which 1,976 dogs and 4,608 cats came from the pound.
† 1914-15: Totals differ from annual Str Cl Ann Rpt statistics above.

1901-07: Str Cl Ann Rpt; 1908-15: Osborn, "Disposal of Garbage".

"Thirty-nine tons of cats met violent deaths [died on the streets] during the eleven months of the past fiscal year [1920]. . . The average cat weighs six pounds. Figure it out for yourself." (*Wash. Times, 2 July 1920, p. 13*)

"Approximately forty tons of cats passed away on the District streets during the year [FY1921], in addition to the tabbies who were ushered into a more peaceful world by the arm of the poundmaster." (*Wash. Times, 4 Sept 1921, p. 10*)

DC Government Revenue from Sale of "Dead Animal Hides"

FY	Revenue
1924	$1,975
1925	2,610
1926	2,137
1927	1,868
1928	2,012
1930	1,253
1931	825
1933	276

Refuse Div Ann Rpt

APPENDIX D

TEXTUAL AND OTHER MATERIALS

D1: Board of Health Minutes Regarding Animals and the Pound, 1822-78

Below is a resume, taken from the manuscript minutes of Board meetings, of all recorded significant minutes of the Board regarding animals and the District pound.

17 Aug 1832: Proposal to loosen regulations regarding hog sties; 24 Aug: preceding is rescinded; 29 Sept 1835: proposal to tighten hog regulations; 30 Sept 1854: "to abolish hog pens and prevent all female hogs to run at large"; 21 Oct 1869, 18 May 1870: stray hogs and cows proposed added to nuisance list. *These various proposals either did not pass or were recommendations to the Corporation, which did not adopt them as law.*

3 July 1843 and later years: Dead animals declared nuisances and subject to legal action.

19 Oct 1866: Board reads a Police report on hog slaughtering/pens; discussed again, 9 Apr.

17 Aug 1870: Complaints about dead animals left on wharf by contractor, and "parties" carrying dead horses over Long Bridge "in a very offensive condition."

13 Sept 1870: Hog-raising restrictions delayed to next January; Mayor asked to remove "the large hogpen on New Jersey Ave."; latter problem still not resolved, 4 Oct .

5 May 1876: The Board's muzzling order to be published; and again, 8 May 1877, 10 May 1878.

30 June 1876: All Board employees except the Poundmaster and his staff are immediately discharged [!], and the PM's and poundmen's salary reduced; the order was rescinded the following day. *The impetus for this extreme measure is not given but at this time the Board was locked in a financial dispute with Congress, and it might have been a negotiating ploy. At the same time, we must admit that the Board minutes from this period are spangled with complaints about its staff and with actual firings (e.g., 13 Apr 1877).*

4 Aug 1876: A committee will plan a reorganization of pound operations and the salary of "employees selected" be raised to $1.50/day. The committee's report was delivered at the 8 August meeting but then failed approval, 11 August; it was tabled again four days later and not reported on further. *The minutes vaguely refer to financial considerations in regard to this.*

2 Apr 1878: Wayman Brooks wrote the Board regarding "existing appointment on the Pound force." No further information is given on his concern. *Brooks made regular appearances in newspapers of the time, usually in connection with some crime.*

D2: Newspaper Profiles

Good Newspaper Profiles of the Pound and Its Operations

Critic-Record, 24 July 1873, p. 1 "The Dog-Catchers – A Visit to the Pound – The Slaughter of the Innocents"

Nat. Republican, 18 June 1874, p. 4 "About Unmuzzled Dogs – A Tour with Poundmaster Einstein Yesterday"

Nat. Republican, 25 June 1877, p. 4 "Doomed Canines"

Nat. Republican, 23 May 1881, p. 4 "Raiding the Goats"

Evening Star, 19 Sept 1885, p. 2 "Hunting the Dog – An Early Morning Chase Through the Streets of the City"

Evening Star, 30 Aug 1890, p. 12 "With the Pound Man – The Adventures of the Bold Hunters of Stray Animals" (with drawings)

Wash. Post, 30 Aug 1891, p. 9 "With the Dog-Catcher" (with drawings)

Morning Times, 28 July 1895, pt. 2, p. 9 "Washington's Dog-Catcher Will Soon Be Around"

Morning Times, 19 Oct 1895, pt. 2 p. 10 "Killing the Canines"

Wash. Post, 9 May 1897, p. 21 "Chasing the Growler"

Wash. Times, 11 Aug 1897, p. 8 "Einstein's Pound Party"*

Wash. Post, 18 Dec 1899, p. 12 "War on Stray Canines"

Evening Star, 29 June 1901, p. 28 "Meeting of the Ways" (with drawings of staff)

Wash. Times, 13 Apr 1902, p. 17 "Campaigning with 'Gen.' Einstein" (with photos)

Wash. Times, 26 July 1903, Magazine p. 5 "The Fate of Convict Dogs at the Washington Pound" (with photos)*

Wash. Post, 10 Apr 1904, p. B6 "Tramp-Dog Lodgings"

Wash. Times, 7 Aug 1904, p. 4 "It's the Day of the Dog-Catcher and How He Does it" (with photos)

Evening Star, 16 July 1905, pt. 4 p. 1 "Dog Calaboose of the National Capital" (with photos)

Evening Star, 20 Sept 1908, pt. 4 p. 4 "The Gehenna of the City's Dogs" (with photos)

Evening Star, 10 July 1910, pt. 2 p. 6 "Sidelights on the Pound and the Dog-Catcher's Life"

Evening Star, 27 Aug 1911, pt. 4 p. 3 "Spending a Busy Day with the Dog-Catcher" (with photos)

Evening Star, 29 Mar 1920, p. 2 "2,747 Dogs Handled at Pound; Sales May Reach $1,400"

Wash. Post, 25 Sept 1921, p. 10 "Dogs of Low and High Degree on Equal Footing at the Pound"

Evening Star, 3 Aug 1924, p. 11 "Day's Trip with Dog-Catchers Gives Food for Philosophers"

Evening Star, 6 July 1947, p. 92 "Refuge for Dogs" (with photos)

Evening Star, 16 Nov 1969, Sunday Magazine p. 22 "The Cat Man"

Evening Star, 13 Apr 1971, p. 1 "We Cover the Sins of Their Owners"

Evening Star, 12 Aug 1977, p. B1 "The Men Who Catch Dogs" (with photos)

* These two articles share almost exactly the same text.

Footnotes at the first substantive mention of the successive buildings, poundmasters, staff and other features specify newspaper sources of drawings and photos.

Good Newspaper Profiles of WHS Operations

Wash. Critic, 16 Dec 1886, p. 3 "The Humane Society's Work"

Wash. Post, 24 July 1898, p. 10 "Shelter for Animals" (Barber Shelter)

Wash. Times, 7 Apr 1901, pt. 2 p. 17 "Boarding House for Cats" (later shelter)

Wash. Times, 4 May 1902, p. 7 "The Washington Humane Society"

Wash. Times, 1 Nov 1903, Magazine p. 2 "The Humane Society and Its Work in Washington"

Wash. Times, 30 July 1905, Magazine p. 6 "A Hot Day with the Humane Society"

Evening Star, 8 Jan 1911, p. 52 "School Children Form Bands of Mercy" (youth program)

Evening Star, 24 Mar 1912, p. 26 "The Washington Humane Society"

Evening Star, 15 Sept 1912, p 55 "With the Humane Society on the Streets of the City"

Good Newspaper Profiles of the WARL Shelter

Evening Star, 20 June 1914, p. 9 "Cats Cared for During Vacation"

Evening Star, 6 Apr 1916, p. 5 "Little Gray Cat Saved from Death"

Wash. Post, 30 Mar 1919, p. S13 "Dumb Friends' Refuge"

Evening Star, 9 Oct 1921, p. 59 "The Animals' Poor House"

Wash. Times, 29 Oct 1922, p. 7 "Washington Has Reason to Be Proud of Comfortable Haven for Outcast Beasts at Animal Rescue League" (with photos; some errors of fact; inc info on Pound)

Evening Star, 25 Oct 1931, p. 14 "Pets to Have New Free Clinic" (with drawing)

Good Newspaper Profiles of the HES Shelter

Evening Star, 4 Aug 1922, p. 22 "Farm Home for Stray Animals Is Aim of D.C. Organization"

Evening Star, 29 June 1924, p. 7 "'Animal Poor Farm' for Capitol Derelicts Makes 'Dog's Life' Something to Be Envied" (with photos)

Wash. Post, 9 Nov 1924, p. SM10 "Famous Old Steeplechaser Ending Days on Rest Farm" (with photos)

Wash. Post, 29 Oct 1933, p. SM6 "Animals' Poorhouse 'Broke'" (with photos)

D3: Pictures of the Dog Hunt

The Epic of the Raid

A representative of The Republican secured a seat with General Einstein and accompanied the raiders. The poundmen are recognized afar and soon after striking North Capitol Street the warning cry was rung out by half a hundred throats, the sounds of alarm mingling strangely with the bells of St. Aloysius, and across the open lots and commons in every direction could be seen the flying forms of men, women and urchins rushing to secure their goats, cows or horses. If the animals were all secured and safe before the enemy arrived, as was the case in most instances, we were greeted with jeers and derisive laughter as we passed. So far nothing had been captured and General Einstein had received a full measure of abuse from the Irish women and curses from the men and boys.

We had got beyond the crowd and cries of Swampoodle when a herd of cows without keepers were espied about three squares ahead. The men, accustomed to such work, were out in a jiffy and had the cows in charge. Looking to the right we saw two boys lying stretched under a large oak, one forming a pillow for the other. When they realized the situation the corners of their mouths dropped and big tears were soon streaming down their cheeks. As they happened to be only a short distance from where the animals had strayed the General lectured them for their carelessness, exacted promises of better things in future, and changed their grief to joy by returning the cows.

A crowd formed at this point, of course, and we had to dash off lively to get away from it. Turning in suddenly above Freedmen's Hospital, we get into a lot of horses, goats and cows. No time must be lost. The hoodlums' "yodel" of "Hog catchers!" had again gone up and was resounding far and near.

We occupy a commanding position, and the scene which ensued almost beggars description. From every hut and house in the valley below and on the hillside beyond pour out men, women and children. They rush in every direction as though the Millennium was at hand. Whipped and frightened goats go bounding into doors and gates; flocks of geese with wings spread are hurried into yards and pens. Boys rush up and grasp the horned tethers [of cows] and hold them [tight]; while the war cry of "Hog catchers! Hot catchers!", resounding in every direction, and mingled with the cries of children, threats of women and coarse epithets of men and boys, made the pandemonium complete. Attempts at rescue of impounded animals, even with police officers present, were not uncommon.

We followed quietly and are amused at the abuse which the women heap upon the poundmaster. The men are silent and sullen – we have the laugh on them now; but the women cudgel their brains for epithets to hurl at us. "Thieves!" "Robbers!" "Hog stealers!" come from every side, and the colored poundmen laugh and sometimes "guy" them in return.

We pass down Seventh Street into the city again, the cows are taken to the pound, and General Einstein remarks: "I haven't caught much, but I guess it's a good Sunday lesson." The Republican man trudges off to write up his trip, firmly convinced that "a poundman's life is not a happy one." *(Nat. Republican, 23 May 1881, p. 4; abridged)*

Boys vs. Dog-Catchers

Neighborhood boys were a constant if bothersome auxiliary to the dog hunt. Here are a few accounts, abridged:

As the morning wore on the work of the dog-catchers became somewhat complicated by the fact that the streets were becoming filled with people. The small boy was emerging from his home. He appeared everywhere. Whenever a dog was sighted generally half a-dozen small boys appeared about the same time. The small boy, through his ignorance of the good accomplished by the pound service, and his sympathy with a dog, naturally arrays himself on the side of the dog. By yells and hoots and kicks, he manages often to get a dog out of the way, just as the dog-hunter thinks he has secured it. Then he runs ahead of the wagon yelling: "Dog-catcher! Dog-catcher!" in a high key and thus puts all the other small boys within several squares on the alert. *(Evening Star, 19 Sept 1885, p. 2)*

In hot weather an early start is made, for the troublesome small boys are not out in such large numbers to chase away the dogs and annoy the men so as to seriously interfere with their business. The appearance of the wagon on the street, no matter how early in the morning, soon attracts a number of boys, and the horses have to be driven fast to escape them. When the wagon reaches the neighborhood of a school building about recess time it is an amusing spectacle to see two of the poundman's colored assistants trying to make a catch. If the dog has good use of its legs it can give the boys and the men a long chase. *(Evening Star, 30 Aug 1890, p. 12)*

The dog wagon has a special charm for the average school boy, white and colored, and when it appears on the streets it is followed around by dozens of boys who delight to join in the chase. The small boys organize themselves into an advance guard and inadvertently warn the populace that the dog-catcher is coming. *(Wash. Post, 30 Aug 1891, p. 9)*

Adults also joined the chorus:

A subtle flash runs from house to house before the wagon comes in sight, often: "The dog-catcher's coming," it says, and Mrs. So-and-so waits on her front stoop with a tea kettle when the wagon drives up, and: "After my little Fido, ar-re ye, ye murdherin's thafe av' th' worruld, bekase he have no muzzle? Well, if ye shtep a fut in me yar-rd I'll scald th' black-shkin off yez." And then a shout to the neighbor across the street: "Oh! Mrs. Schmidt, 'tis th' dog-catcher; hurry and get Bismark into th' house." *(Evening Star, 27 Aug 1911, pt. 4 p. 3)*

Sometimes the boys were not so lovable:

Now over to Florida Avenue near North Capitol Street. Boys are playing baseball on a vacant lot. They don't think much of dog-catchers. A juvenile anvil chorus is striking up. The boys crowd around. "You ain't going to take that dog. G'wan away from here with your old dirty wagon!" The dog is led out [to the wagon]. His appearance starts a young riot. "Aw, don't let 'em take that dog, Mrs. Jones." "I'll wrap this hat aroun' your trowsy ole dome, you_." Three quick steps does [Poundmaster] Smith make toward the gang. He is intrepid in the face of threats. The boys retire to second-line trenches. And Prince goes to the pound. *(Evening Star, 3 Aug 1924, p. 11)*

Chatter Among the Poundmen

A few articles attempted to record the talk among the poundmaster and the dog-catchers during their duties, and this gives some idea of the relationship among them:

Finally some ill-starred dog rashly jumps through a hole in a fence and in his fatal ignorance yelps saucily at the chuckling and wily dog-catcher. The dog-catcher stops and says: "Doggy, doggy, doggy." The dog comes up another foot and yelps and prances about. "Come hyar, doggy," softly pleads the dog-catcher, and the dog prances another foot nearer. "Whop, whop, doggy, doggy, doggy, come, come," continues the dog-catcher seductively, and holding his hand as if he had a piece of meat. The yelping dog takes the fatal step and the next moment he is bagged.

"Got him, 'Lijah?" asks another of the colored men, who has been watching the operation from the other side of the street.

"Yah, yah, you bet. When I drops this yer net over him he ain't gwine to get away," and Elijah carefully lifts up one corner of the net, and catching hold of the dog behind the ears, swings him up into the wagon and locks the gate. *(Nat. Republican, 25 June 1877, p. 4)*

At the corner of First and B Streets NE the first unlicensed animal was seen by "Lynx-Eyed" Burrell. He immediately passed the tip to John Wells, who reached for the net.

"Watch him close, Buck," exclaimed General Einstein in a stentorian stage whisper.

"I got my eye on him," replies Buck.

Without an instant's hesitation the black-and-tan turned tail and scooted across the street.

"It's no use," said General Einistein in tones of disgust. "I've either got to disguise John Wells or fire him. It's got so that every unlicensed dog in town knows him a block away."

"I'll git him yet," cried Wells, as he leaped upon the wagon and touched his spirited horse with the lash.

"Go after him, John," shouted General Einstein in an encouraging voice.

(The dog got away. *Wash. Times, 13 Apr 1902, Ed/Drama p. 17*)

D4: The District Pound Compared with Those of Other Cities

Einstein was proud of his operation and loved to compare it to pounds in other large East Coast cities, especially in his early years when he was anxious to establish it on a sound footing with the District government.

I am convinced that our pound system is the most effective of any in this country, certainly far superior to that of any of the large Eastern cities with which I have become acquainted *(PM Ann Rpt, 1878)*; There are fewer stray dogs in the District of Columbia than at any previous time; and from my observations in other cities I believe that local conditions compare favorably with those elsewhere *(PM Ann Rpt, 1905)*.

Here are some more specific comparisons (abridged):

The system of capturing dogs in this city is perhaps the best and most economical in vogue. In New York and other cities a stipulated price is paid by the poundmaster for every dog delivered at the pound. In New York the price paid is 50 cents each. This is a costly policy, as well as being an incentive to dishonesty. To take 2,456 dogs by this method would entail an expense of $1,228, whereas we have captured that number and 246 other animals at an expenditure of $671, nearly 50 percent less." *(PM Ann Rpt, 1877)*

From reports and correspondence with some of our larger cities I am satisfied that better results are accomplished by our system than any other in vogue in this country. In Brooklyn, N.Y., with ten men employed, the number of dogs captured from July 1 to September 15, 1878, was between 1,200 and 1,300; while in this city, with four men and one wagon, there were over 2,000 taken during the same period. There they had some 4,200 licensed, the amount received from license, redemption, &c., footing up $4,800; their expenses from July 1 to September 15, were $2,300. Our expenses, including everything, for the same period did not reach quite $575, or about one-fourth of that city. *(PM Ann Rpt, 1878)*

Methods of execution, from newspaper articles:

Mr. Einstein favors killing dogs by electricity, and will try to get an appropriation to be used in perfecting a system. Baltimore drowns dogs and Philadelphia puts them in a close room and turns on the gas, but Mr. Einstein says frequently a canine will come back to life. *(Wash. Post, 30 Aug 1891, p. 9)* – [Quoting Einstein:] "Compared with the methods adopted in other cities for disposing of outlaw dogs, that practiced here has the advantage both in dispatch and from a humane standpoint. In Jersey City, for instance, the killing is effected by drowning, which, to say the least, in not more humane, to say nothing of the accidents that are liable to occur. Why, not long ago in Jersey City a cage containing thirty dogs was being lowered into the dock, and in their struggles for freedom the dogs broke some of the bars and escaped. The Philadelphia plan, suffocation by asphyxiation, is a decided improvement on drowning, but then even this could be greatly improved on." *(Morning Times, 28 July 1895, pt. 2 p. 9)* – [SPCA, in its annual report of 1883, tells us that Boston poisoned its dogs with cyanide.]

D5: Citizens Write MPDC About Dogs

MPDC Annual Reports of the 1900s included letters (always laudatory) from District citizens. Below are two regarding dogs (from the MPDC Ann Rpt of those years, abridged):

February 23, 1909

Sir: Your favor of the 20th instant, relative to the report I made to you of having been bitten by a dog in front of the synagogue, with which you have honored me, is received. Please accept my most grateful thanks for the kind and prompt manner in which you have taken the matter up. I went from the station house to the place where I was bit to see if I could locate the dog. I saw the dog and believe I can locate the house where the owner lives. The boys are too young to take into court, but I want the dog killed. I am advised by my attending physician, Dr. Thomas Martin, to have that done as soon as I can learn the owner of the dog. I will report the fact to you, together with the number of the house in which he lives.

    Thanking you again, Major, for you kind promptness in the matter,
    I am, sir, most respectfully,
    Theo. C. Ray

April 6, 1903

Dear sir: It affords me great pleasure to extend to your department my appreciation of the kind attention one of your officers displayed in taking in my dog "Bob", a valuable pointer who strayed away from my residence yesterday evening. Aside from being valuable for hunting, he is a great prize as an intelligent family pet and companion to my children.

    You can hardly realize how welcome [was] a ring at our doorbell, followed by the information from one of your officers of the Mount Pleasant precinct that my dog was being held as found property and could be recovered by proving ownership.

    I earnestly congratulate you on the efficiency and complete system of your department, [and] the close supervision your men exercise in saving of property from loss and destruction, as well as the prevention of crime.

    Very respectfully,
    Geo. F. Zeh

D6: The Mythical Origin of Washington's Stray Animals

Excerpted from "The Runic Inscription at Great Falls", a satirical article recounting a band of wandering Vikings who visited the Nation's Capital. "The Northmen came over five centuries before Columbus. They heard he had taken passage by the Cunard line, and [echoed?] him by chartering the yacht Henrietta, beating him 500 years by the dodge." Among other achievements they left a rune prophesying that the Evening Star would "eclipse all other papers."

They left one sick old man, with two hogs and two dogs for company. He was very old and very feeble, but lived about three hundred years in the salubrious climate of South Washington. Getting discouraged about dying in South Washington he took the street cars for the city, got the typhoid fever and died directly. His hogs and dogs begat other hogs and dogs, and dogs and hogs, and hogs and dogs, propagating in such prolific style that there are now 486,387 hogs in the Seventh Ward, and 9,826,942 more dogs than hogs in that part of the city. They are held in the greatest reverence on account of their distinguished descent. It is held to be a sin to kill or molest them, and the policemen treat them with the greatest consideration. *(Evening Star, 20 July 1867, p. 1)*

D7: Mark Twain Lampoons the Animal Problem in Washington

On New Year's morning, while Mr. George Worley's front door was standing open, a cow marched into the house – a cow that was out making her annual calls, I suppose – and before she was discovered had eaten up everything on the New Year's table in the parlor! Mr. Worley was not acquainted with the cow, never saw her before, and is at a loss to account for the honor of her visit. What do you think of a town when cows make New Year's calls? It may be the correct thing, but it has not been so regarded in the circles in which I have been accustomed to move. Morals are at a low stage in Washington, beyond question. *("More Washington Morals", 19 February 1868, Daily Alta California; quoted in Muller, Mark Twain in Washington, D.C., p. 68.)*

This is a pure spoof by Twain – there was no George Worley in the city at that time. My thanks to Mr. Muller for pointing out this anecdote to me.

D8: Washington Cats Immortalized (?) in Poetry

To the Editor of The Evening Star *[9 Aug 1897, p. 9]*:

[I wish to call attention] to what has become another nuisance to the civilized portion of the city. I refer to the hundreds of cats that prowl our alleys and make night hideous. They mount the woodsheds, then with powerful voices sing:

> Come forth, my love, let's bay the silvery moon
> > Nor care we for the golden orb of light:
> The poundman runs the mongrel dog: the coon
> > Is chased by coppers every night.
>
> But we, my love, may howl and squall
> > Till weary by the way.
> And those who do not like our ball
> > Can only curse or pray.
>
> No rooster dares his clarion voice unfold.
> > Or wabbling duck his quacking love express.
> Or goose give warning as of old.
> > Or pig with grunting words caress.
>
> But we, my love, may howl and squall
> > Till weary by the way.
> And those who do not like our ball
> > Can only curse or pray.

There is much more of this, but as I am not a cat I might be punished if I kept it up. . . I. N. Hammer

Poundmaster Emil Kuhn published this cheeky little doggerel in Wash. Herald, 22 June 1912, p. 6, parodying Kipling's famous model; cat impoundment was a third-rail for all District poundmasters.

> When the oldest Tom Cat has been drowned
> And the youngest scared out of its hide;
> When the Cat Club has been long a 'dead one'
> And the youngest cat-catcher has died;
> Then the District of Columbia Commissioners
> Will be silent for an aeon or two,
> Until anxious to get to the limelight
> They will find something to do that is new.

This gem quite likely was not written specifically with Washington cat-catchers in mind but nonetheless deserves re-publication. It appeared in Wash. Times, 20 June 1912, p. 12, attributed: "From the unpublished songs of the Village Dogcatcher by M. E. T."

> Put on the kettle, mother,
>   And make me a cup of tea.
> All day I've been on the wagon,
>   And I'm tired as I can be.
> We turned down into an alley,
>   Where a blear-eyed tabby sat,
> At half past five in the morning.
>   And till night we chased that cat.
> I've climbed full fifty fences
>   And crawled under stables too.
> I've shinned up trees and barked my knees,
>   Dear wife. I'm black and blue.
> I've gone through yards on my hands and feet.
>   I've cursed 'till the air was thick.
> But never a'near that pussy cat
>   Did get – it makes me sick.
> I've made up my mind about something.
>   I can stand their yowls at night.
> I can stuff my ears with cotton
>   And shut my windows tight.
> But since I am not a monkey,
>   Nor an acrobat, nor a flea,
> Either I must resign my position,
>   Or the law must rescinded be.
> So put on the kettle, mother, etc. etc.

D9: Samples of Cases Handled by the SPCA/WHS Agents

Table of Cases Prosecuted by the Society

Date		Complainant	Offence	Disposition of Case
1881				
March	7	J.H. King	Beating horse with large stick	Fined $3
"	29	A member	Working lame mule	Fined $5
April	25	R. Ball	Overworking horse	Fined $5
"	28	"	Overloading and overworking horse	Fined $10; appealed
"	29	J.H. King	Beating horse	Fined $5
May	16	"	Working diseased horse	Fined $5
June	1	J.H. King	Tying calves	Fined $5
"	8	"	Muzzling calves	Dismissed
"	15	"	" "	Fined $10
"	15	"	" "	Fined $10
"	17	"	Overworking diseased hill-horse	Fined $5
"	21	J.H. King	Working galled mule	Fined $5
"	24	"	Abandoning glandered horse	Judgment suspended
July	7	"	Overdriving cart-horse	Dism. with reprimand
"	7	"	" "	" " "
"	7	"	" "	" " "
"	20	"	Muzzling calf	Fined $1
"	20	"	Beating mule on the head	Fined $1
"	21	"	Overloading ice-cart horse	Dism. with reprimand
August	2	"	Beating horse with stick	Fined $5, or 10 days in workhouse
"	3	R. Ball	Starving and neglecting horse	Dism. with reprimand
"	6	J.H. King	Working horse with sore back	Fined $50; appealed
"	11	"	Abandoning glandered horse	Horse shot
"	12	R. Ball	Beating horse with whip and stick continuously for an hour and a half	Fined $50; appealed
"	12	J.H. King	Working horse with sore back	Charge withdrawn
"	12	"	" "	" "
"	13	"	Working mule with sore back	Fined $15
"	19	"	Working horse with " severe case	Charge withdrawn
"	19	"	" " " "	Fined $20; appealed
"	19	"	" " " "	Jury disagreed; new trial
"	19	"	" " " "	Fined $10; pardoned
"	19	"	" " " "	Fined $20; appealed
"	19	"	" " " "	Fined $25; "
"	23	"	Working injured horse	Dism. with reprimand
"	24	"	Working lame horse	Fined $10
"	25	"	Setting dogs on cat and leaving cat to die	Dism. with reprimand
"	27	R. Ball	Beating horse	Fined $10

Sept.	3	J.H. King	Overworking and abandoning back horse	Fined $10; appealed
"	13	"	Overloading Herdic [taxi] coach	Fined $1
"	16	"	Tying cow head and foot	Fined $5
"	17	"	Working horse with sore back	Fined $25; or 60 days in workhouse
"	20	"	Starving dogs	Dismissed
"	30	R. Ball	Cutting and torturing horse	Fined $25; or 60 days in workhouse
Oct.	1	"	Overloading horse	Fined $10
"	6	"	Overworking glandered horse	Fined $5; or 30 days in workhouse
"	19	J.H. King	Working mule with sore back	Fined $5
"	20	"	Working horse with eye knocked out	Fined $1
"	20	"	Working horse with sore back	Fined $10
"	22	"	Overdriving sheep	Dism. with reprimand
"	22	"	" "	" " "
"	24	"	Working horse with sore back	Fined $5
"	24	"	Working horse with broken shoe	Forfeited collateral
"	25	"	Working mule with sore back	Fined $10
"	26	"	Working horse with sore back	Fined $10
Nov.	14	R. Ball	Breaking dog's leg	Fined $25, or 60 days in workhouse
"	18	J.H. King	Working horse with sore back	Forfeited collateral
"	28	"	Whipping horse	Dism. with reprimand
"	29	"	Whipping mule	" " "
Dec.	3	"	Working two mules with sore backs	Judgment suspended
"	5	R. Ball	Working crippled horse	Fined $5
"	6	J.H. King	Working horse with sore back	Dismissed
"	6	"	Working two mules with sore backs	Gave per. bond
"	8	"	Working horse with sore back	Fined $25; appealed
"	8	"	Working mule with sore back & shoulders	" "
"	17	"	Working horse with " " "	Fined $50; "
"	22	"	Running into and killing Herdic horse	Dismissed
"	26	"	Working horse with sore back	Forfeited $5 collateral

In addition to the foregoing, 14 cases were prosecuted by the Police and convictions obtained in 13, with fines amounting to $100.95, which was paid to the District.

SPCA Ann Rpt, 1881

Summary of work by Agents of the Society for the Prevention of Cruelty to Animals for the Year ending December 31, 1898

	Agent Rabbitt	Agent Reiplinger	Agent Haynes (7 Months)	Agent King (5 Months, 25 Days)	Total
Number of cases investigated	5,063	4,666	3,279	2,225	15,233
Remedied without prosecution	4,821	4,454	3,133	2,161	14,569
Prosecuted	242	212	146	64	664
Convicted	227	206	141	35	607
Acquitted	15	6	5	29	55
Cases of animals unfit to work	242	212	146	0	500
Cases of animals abandoned to die	3	1	0	6	10
Animals killed by the Agent	58	121	81	33	294
Cases of beating or whipping	27	20	9	11	67
Cases of overloading	16	19	6	7	48
Cases of overdriving	5	23	2	7	37
Driving when galled	59	77	62	15	213
Driving when lame	95	63	61	6	225
Lack of food or shelter	38	9	6	2	55
Amount collected in Police Court	$1081.69	$947.01	$597.00	$275.30	$2,900.04

SPCA Ann Rpt, 1898

Synopsis of Work for the Years 1915 and 1916

	1915	1916
Number of animals examined	8,945	6,940
Number of cases prosecuted	712	655
Number of convictions	692	633
Number of acquittals	20	22
Number of personal bonds taken	25	21
Cases in which collateral was forfeited	607	538
Cases in which fines were imposed	52	57
Cases in which workhouse sentences were imposed	8	17
Animals killed by the agent	179	229
Collateral forfeited	$3,192	$2,779
Fines imposed	$448	$506

Fines uncollected	$120	$203
Amount collected in Police Court for Society	$3,520	$3,082
Days of jail or workhouse sentences	285	570
The prosecutions were for the following offenses:		
Cases of animals unfit for service	54	39
Cases of animals abandoned to die	2	5
Cases of beating or whipping	45	49
Cases of overloading	9	11
Cases of overdriving	5	3
Cases of overworking	-----	2
Working animals with sore necks or shoulders	151	140
Working animals while lame	428	391
Failure to provide food and shelter	6	3
Working horses with Cuban Itch	5	2
Working sick horses	-----	1
Neglecting sick horses	-----	3
Shooting dog	-----	1
Cutting and beating dogs	2	-----
Branding horse with hot iron	1	-----
Beating goat	1	-----
Abandoning young pigeon to starve	1	-----
Kicking horse in stomach	-----	1
Cutting horse with knife	1	-----
Working horse with bit cutting mouth	1	1
Beating cow	-----	1
Locking cat in house two weeks without food	-----	1
Working mule with chain bit	-----	1

SPCA Ann Rpt, 1916

D10: Mrs. Beckley and Her Cat Shelter

Two contrasting accounts of Sarah Beckley, both probably accurate (abridged).

A representative of The Post found Mrs. Beckley sitting with a cat on each shoulder and a couple of cats in her lap. Cats occupied the sofa and rubbed against the legs of the center table. In each corner was a comfortable cat, and in the bedroom cats curled cozily on the cushioned pillows and spread themselves along the coverlet. One big maltese occupied a statue-like position on the small stand at the head of Mrs. Beckley's bed.

Cats are proverbially fastidious in their choice of food, but even the daintiest could not complain of Mrs. Beckley's daily bill of fare. "I give them the best that a cat can possibly desire in the way of food," she said.

[For breakfast, at 7:30] "I give them a saucer of milk each, following it with fried liver chopped up with whole wheat bread. I never feed white bread to my boarders. It does not agree with them. At noon I give them a light luncheon of salmon and brown bread, and at 5:30 comes their main meal. I give them for this meal chopped beef, potatoes and string beans. No, my charity cats do not fare as well as boarders."

On a remote corner of the stove sat a saucepan with contents stewing in a depressing sort of way. "Oh, that's our dinner," said Mrs. Beckley. "It's just bacon and beans – I wouldn't feed my cats on that – but it is good enough for us." *(Wash. Post, 18 Oct 1908, p. SM3)*

[This] is she who has dedicated her life to the rescue of suffering creatures, Mrs. Sarah Berkley [sic] of 126 D Street SW. She – what does she get in return for her immeasurable services in a hallowed course? Love and esteem? Not by the multitude. To her many other difficulties is added the difficulty in an age of vulgar prejudice that the African race can boast of her as partially theirs.

Mrs. Beckley has often told me of the insensate ridicule to which she is exposed. But she has the strength to ignore it, for she is mature enough, sympathetic enough, to realize the real tragedy of the situation. She told me of how she once rescued a cat from a sewer while a mob stood around laughing. Amid hardships unimaginable, she kept a whole winter a horse whom she had rescued from cruel hands. She tended him and healed him; he grew in strength as she declined. For while she gave to the horse, she faced starvation herself. She came home loaded with food for him, and even the seller cursed her for feeding a "worthless" horse.

She, poor and worn-out, did the deed of rescue which the comfortably situated of the world, though cheerfully accepting the services of the outraged, have shamelessly neglected to do, and still shamelessly neglect. Her life is one of continual sacrifice; she gives not money, she gives herself. Here is a rare and worthy worker in the cause of true humanity, one with a heart bleeding for the suffering of the oppressed, yet willing and able to face the horrors and go into their midst to give the aid she can. Another Mrs. Beckley is not easy to find, search the continent through and through. *(Wash. Bee, 6 Feb 1909, p. 5)*

D11: The WARL Shelter Compared with the Pound

The differences between the District pound and the private WARL shelter are well presented in the League's 1950 application for continued funding from the Community Chest. Note that the pound operations reported here are somewhat more limited than those of an earlier time.

There is no other agency, public or private, promoting the same type of program as the Washington Animal Rescue League. The pound is open only from 8:30 AM until 3:30 PM five days a week or about forty hours a week. We are open to receive ambulance calls and animals 24 hours a day every day in the year, or a total of 168 hours a week. We have an emergency pick-up service for injured animals, on call 24 hours every day. The pound has no emergency pick-up service. The pound calls only for dogs. The League shelters all types of animals – as an example, the League receives approximately 11,000 cats each year. The League has veterinarian service which the pound does not have. In comparing the operation of the pound with that of the League, we wish to call attention to the fact that the League received approximately $7,200 from the Chest. The pound received approximately $34,000 from the District. From this comparison of cost, it can be seen that it would be enormously expensive for the tax-payer if the pound extended their services to meet those of the League. It is doubtful in the extreme if the pound would ever be allowed that much money. Until the pound extends its service to meet that of the League, the League is not duplicating the work of the pound, simply supplementing it. *(WARL, Community Chest funding application, 1950; WARL archives)*

D12: U.S. Capitol Police Deal with Critters (and Humans)

From the Architect of the U.S. Capitol archives (File "Animals"; abridged):

Dec 13, 1901
[To] Capt. J. P. Megrew

Dear sir:

I respectfully submit the following report of the boy Charles Ferguson, age 10, white, #302 C St NW.

 At 1:30 this afternoon I caught the above-named boy in the act of chasing squirrels in the NE part of the Capitol Grounds. He said he thought they were wild, and he was at liberty to catch or kill them if he could. I took him to the Guard-Room, where he spent ¾ of an hour crying and promising "not to do it again" and to tell all the other boys the squirrels were to be left alone.

 Officer A. W. Swenson knew the boy's parents. He went home with him and the parents gave the boy a severe chastising, which I think ought to keep him from troubling the squirrels any more.

 Yours Respectfully,
 A. F. Barrett

[To] Mrs. J. T. Bodfish
The Congressional, Washington, D.C.
June 6th, 1918

My dear Madam:

I have made diligent inquiry as to the fate of your poor cat but have not been able to find out a single thing about it.

 None of the officers appear to have killed such a cat and it seems to me that they would have known it from your description. I am also informed that the officers have been killing cats in the Capitol Grounds when they found them pursuing any squirrels but the officers tell me that most of the animals have been of mongrel and very wild type and that they are careful about animals that appear to be very domestic. I really sympathize with you in this matter and I am very sorry that I can give you no information. If any comes before me I will be glad to send it to you.

 Very respectfully,
 E. W. [Elliott Woods]
 Superintendent, U.S. Capitol Building and Grounds

D13: Tangential Notes on Animals in the District

These brief reports record various aspects of animal life in the city uncovered during my research that seem useful to preserve but which do not fit comfortably in the main narrative. None claim to be comprehensive but all have interest.

Dog Names and Breeds (Common and Presidential)

A reporter's visit to the Tax Collector's office in 1893 resulted in the preservation of an odd bit of trivia: the most common dog names in the late 19th century. We will let his words carry this tale: "Quite a story could be written of the names of the dogs as they appear in the license book. There are at least a dozen Grovers and, strange to say, that name is always given to big dogs. Then there are Harrisons, Blaines, Shermans and one Tom Platt.[1] There are the usual number of Tootseys Jacks, Fidos and the like."

Three articles of the 1930s catch us up on the then-current trends in canines' names. By 1931 "an examination of the . . . dog tags issued last year shows not a single Towser, . . . but a single Fido, and nary a Rover." Popular names had shifted to Pat, Mike, Jack, Buddy, Peggy and Sport. "Hundreds of dogs have been called Lindy since the famous 1927 . . . flight. Scotch terrier owners usually whip their imaginations no further than Scottie, and lots of dogs are named after Zero, beloved comic strip hound. . . Pop-Eye and Texas belong in the Smith and Jones class." An article concentrating on society dogs flatly states: "None of the debutantes-to-be . . . has a dog named Fido. . . High-sounding Oriental titles are usually bestowed upon snub-nosed Poms and plume-tailed Pekes. And the most fashionable names for other breeds . . . today sound like a page from the Almanac de Gotha. Even dogs of uncertain ancestry have risen out of the Towser and Rover class. . . A dog today can have as many spots as a leopard and still escape the name Spot."

As for White House pets: presidents from this period seem to have preferred fairly unpretentious names, perhaps to demonstrate their common touch. President Harding's dog Laddie Boy was a favorite of the humane movement, whose photo appeared in both the WHS and WARL annual reports. Coolidge had Peter Pan (fox terrier), Laddie Buck (Airedale), Oshkosh, Rob Roy, Prudence Prim (collies); Hoover had Weeja (Norwegian elkhound). Of the latter's earlier pets, a wag reporter wrote: "The White House dogs, which one might expect to find with names such as Moratorium, Depression, Farm Relief and the like, have on the contrary, very democratic names. Patrick, Big Boy, Mark and Gillette make up the first kennels of the land."

In regard to popular breeds, a veterinarian noted in 1885: "Newfoundlands, setters, terriers, pugs [are common], but not many fox terriers as yet. They are the coming pets for ladies' dogs." Reports about the licensing office did not list breeds but the largest number were noted as brown; Hattie Small, director of the dog-license division, commented in 1936 that "pugs and fox terriers have given way to Scotch terriers, police dogs and Boston bulls." The 1934 society-oriented article quoted above gave this run-down for the upper-class: *out* – German shepherds ("as outmoded as horsehair sofas and fainting spells"), Airedales ("as

---

[1] Grover, naturally, after the large-sized president; the others were contemporary political figures, including Platt, who was more of a political operative than actual politician.

out of style as high-top, button shoes"), poodles, bulldogs, Russian wolfhounds; *in* – Great Danes, sealyhams, scotties, Pekingese, Pomeranians.

Daily Critic, 8 July 1885, p. 3; Evening Star, 9 Oct 1893, p. 8; 14 Dec 1923, p. 6; 12 July 1931, p. 1; 15 Aug 1936, p. 7; Wash. Post, 28 Apr 1929, p. SM4; 8 Aug 1934, p. 12; the 1923, '29, '31 and '36 articles have more information on presidential pooches and some amusing anecdotes (Theodore Roosevelt's dog once treed the French ambassador at a White House garden party).

Buying Pets

Washingtonians brought their pets mostly from small-scale breeders and families with litters to sell; their ads appeared in the classified sections regularly from the late 19th century onward, often with no name but just an address. (Of course, you could always buy a used dog at Gen. Einstein's establishment.) The first regular commercial outlets for pets sold birds: Schmid's Bird Store at 712 12th Street NW began to advertise in 1886, joined soon after by Hastbrecht's (1880-90s) and Lee's (1900s), both also downtown. The more suburban Norris Bird and Pet Store operated in the Brightwood neighborhood in the 1910s, while Fairchild's located downtown in the 1920s. Over time Schmid's began to offer other live products – goats, puppies, cats, rabbits, mice, rats, queen bees – so that owner Edward S. changed its name to Schmid's Pet Emporium in 1892. Although Washington newspapers referred routinely to "pet stores" in the pet-advice columns, Schmid's was the only such business listed under that heading when the City Directory initiated the category in 1935. The store closed in 1964.[2]

Only one identifiable large-scale local dog breeder could be found in this research: the Iowa Pet Farm of Rosslyn, Virginia, advertising in 1922. But of catteries ("or 'kat kennel[s]', as these colonies of pussies are now called") the area was better stocked. The first was opened by Mary Cornish Bond in 1902 specializing in Persians, the only such establishment south of Philadelphia.[3] Her friend Miss Burrett opened the Columbia Cattery soon after. To give an idea of the size of these operations, Bond held 11 cats and Burrett 19 in 1902, many or most of them seemingly their own prize babies and not for sale; five years later they held 125 between them: some boarders, some charity cases, some for sale, some pets of the owners. The Algonquin Cattery advertised in the 1900s also (specializing in Persians – a name for Bond's establishment?). In the next decade we find the Chevy Chase and the Bostwick Catteries, and the College Park and the Calvert Catteries in the 1920s. Only the Columbia Cattery was downtown, and some of the later ones in the Maryland suburbs. Newspapers regularly carried ads for catteries throughout the Mid-Atlantic states. All of these establishments bred, sold and boarded felines.

An unnamed local dealer in 1891 discussed with an Evening Star reporter where he obtained his stock, and I record this unlooked-for information for a curious posterity:

- Turtles, frogs, snakes, common pigeons – Local boys "from their rural explorations"
- Cats, guinea pigs, ferrets – Ohio (but Angoras only from Maine)
- Chickens, peacocks, fine pigeons – Local breeders

---

[2] For anecdote-filled profiles, see Evening Star, 31 May 1936, p. 50; Times-Herald, 23 Jan 1944, p. C5. Lee's also offered puppies and monkeys.

[3] "From this inclosure no pussy cat has ever gone forth to a cat show but to win; none return but covered with honors." Mrs. Bond owned the renowned Persian Menlik III.

- Monkeys – "Brought from tropical climes by sailors" or from New York dealers
- Mocking birds – Texas
- Common goldfish – Local breeders
- Fancy goldfish – Japan

(Pet stores) classified ads, various dates; (catteries) classifieds; Wash. Times, 13 Apr 1902, Magazine p. 8; Evening Star, 6 Jan 1903, p. 15; Wash. Herald, 25 Feb 1908, p. 7; (stock) Evening Star, 16 May 1891, p. 7. See also the DC General Files 1-107 "Pet Shops" at NARA.

U.S. Government Cats

Cats inhabiting federal buildings occasionally made the news. A Washington Post article of 1911 described the keeping of mousers in army depots, post offices, "most other large governmental buildings," and even "the immense cold-storage depot in Manila," which used exclusively a special breed from Pittsburgh that "do not thrive when transferred to an ordinary atmosphere." The main Treasury building introduced a few cats in the late 1800s (after an unsuccessful experiment with ferrets) to control a burgeoning rat population only to find it then had a growing cat population also. The Department's cleaning crew twice (1895, 1905) took matters in hand "by means not particularly humane." Three were kept to resume their duties.

In 1918 the Post Office Department published its interest in acquiring mousers for its facilities. (Unfortunately I could not find the original announcement.) As a result, Victoria Emmanuel – a cat abandoned by the Italian embassy and living at the WARL shelter – became the "special pet and protégé" of District Postmaster M. O. Chance in 1919. "Now Victor [sic] Emmanuel spends his [sic] daytimes, when he is off duty, curled up on the postmaster's official desk." Soon thereafter Victoria Emmanuel gave birth to a litter of five "victory kittens"; over one thousand people put in bids for the little ones, which the Postmaster decided would be awarded to the clerks selling the most victory bonds. "Victoria is now the favorite of the whole post office."

Up the street, at the office of the Provost Marshal General at 8th and E Streets, NW, Thomas (the mascot of the earlier occupant, the Land Office) became "the pet of soldiers and stenographers alike," disdainfully accepting their attention. "He . . . cares little whether it be Gen. Crowder or little Sally King from Podunk, Ill., who pets him. As far as he is concerned, he prefers to be let alone. 'Off my neck, general,' he seems to say."

The most curious incident, however, occurred in 1929, when the Director of Public Buildings decided to move against a colony of strays settled in the foundations of government temporary offices across the street from the Center Market. "Had [the cats] been orderly beings they probably never would have stirred up any undue notoriety, but they developed a propensity for exploring about the buildings during the night hours, leaving a wake of havoc in their prowling." To make matters worse, they had a protector in clerk Mary E. Woodward, who surreptitiously fed them every morning. When government cat-catchers failed to take the lot (the few captives were turned over to WARL), Director Grant threatened to gas (chloroform) the whole colony or perhaps simply wall them in so that the structures could be weather-proofed before winter. Miss Woodward brought in WHS, which extracted an agreement from Grant to not seal the animals up but to turn them over to WHS rather than its less-conscientious colleague, WARL.

(An unexpectedly comprehensive report of 1893 explains the need for cats in government buildings: "Rats, Mice and Bugs – Vermin Give the Government a Great Deal of Annoyance", Evening Star, 5 Aug 1893, p. 11).

Wash. Post, 29 July 1895, p. 2; 24 Nov 1905, p. 12; 5 Feb 1911, p. MS6; 13 Oct 1929, p. M4; Evening Star, 30 June 1918, p. 20; 6 Apr 1919, p. 13; 8 May 1919, p. 23; Wash. Herald, 19 Jan 1919, p. 3. All these articles are well worth reading. For further sketches of DC and federal mascot animals, see Times-Herald, 3 Sept 1944, p. B8.

Rats and Cats Flee Center Market

The 1931 demolition of the old Center Market in downtown Washington for construction of the National Archives led to an unlooked-for exodus of both resident rats and cats, and an even less-expected outcry over government plans to deal with the pests. The "large number of stray cats . . . made homeless" were collected "by gentle coaxing" by agents of WHS and WARL and (reportedly) sent to foster homes.

Homeless rats presented a more unusual problem. Mr. W. G. Gentry, "the most celebrated of all prairie-dog catchers" in Wyoming ("where men are men and rats are prairie-dogs") and a recent immigrant to Washington, took the extermination contract, only to find his poison-gas plans shot down by the District Health Officer. Gentry then proposed an array of traps but a member of WHS protested the possibility that the rats would be sent to scientific labs for test use. (In fact, they were drowned.) We do not know the conclusion of this episode.

Evening Star, 15 Apr 1931, p. 17; 17 April 1931, p. 8 (a first-hand account); 24 Apr 1931, p. 17 (with a photo of Gentry); 26 Apr 1931, p. 17.

Starlings! Pigeons! Squirrels!

Starlings, famously introduced into North America in 1890 so that every bird mentioned in Shakespeare would live in Central Park, migrated to the mid-Atlantic states in the late 1920s. From 1928 to about 1934 letters complaining about "these annual visitors" (the majority of the letters) and defending them (the minority) filled columns of local newspapers and the Commissioners' in-box. Starlings ate valuable grain crops, destroyed song birds and other native species, made lots of noise and, of course, though not explicitly stated, pooped everywhere.

The Commissioners, besieged by merchants' and civic associations, "tried everything they could think of": hanging wires with bits of tin near building ledges, spraying water from fire hoses, letting off fireworks, trimming trees, tying pieces of glass to branches, setting out noisemakers, garish lighting, cat dolls (for their fright value), live owls (brought from the Zoo to protect the Smithsonian), smudge pots and "an inflated rubber tiger and a few toy balloons" (on the District Building), and once setting loose a mob of WPA workers waving "pebble-filled cans, poles and old telephone books." The balloon trick showed promise but the problem persisted. Shooting, poisoning and encasing trees in wire gauze were ruled too extreme.

The Commissioners appealed to the Department of Agriculture, which only offered the helpful advice that these birds probably were not (as posited by some conservation clubs) protected as a migratory species. In 1933 they appointed a Starling Nuisance Abatement Committee headed by Clifford Lanham. "It's taken me more than three years to learn how little I know about starlings," he admitted. "Generalissimo" Lanham was still at the job in 1940. Letters were sent to other cities asking their advice, and similar inquiries were received from Toronto, Lansing and Hamilton, Ohio. No one had a good idea.

The starling dilemma returned furiously in the mid-1940s. The District (now represented by its Committee on Cleanliness and Sanitation) experimented with an obnoxious "dusting powder" and considered loosening its bird-hunting restrictions. The public flooded the Commissioners with rather far-fetched suggestions, ranging from the tongue-in-cheek (starling pie) to silly ("tossing moth balls into the nests"). Someone remembered that a former Superintendent of Parks had built shelters for pigeons in Rock Creek Park and then had an assistant remove the residents' eggs and return them boiled solid; reportedly, the birds supinely sat on these useless artifacts for the rest of the season (something that is difficult to credit), eliminating the pigeon nuisance.

The last spasm of starling-panic occurred before the 1956 presidential inauguration, when residents of Flushing and Rome, New York; Cincinnati, Ohio; Great Bend, Kansas; and La Crescenta, California all sent not-very-useful advice on the matter to President Eisenhower. The Treasury installed an electronic wire system on its headquarters in 1954 (replacing earlier nails) and the White House followed (a signal/noise system) in 1962.

Complaints about **common pigeons** date at least to 1897, when the birds appeared in the MPDC annual report: "There is no law existing . . . whereby the citizen may be protected from . . . pigeons alighting upon residential property . . . which might be despoiled by their temporary occupancy . . . Several elegant residences, put up at great expense, with delicate ornamentation, have suffered from this nuisance." To put this in perspective, the complaint referred to privately-owned birds (which did not come under the same restrictions as "fowls") rather than vagabonds, and a householder shooting them could be charged their value. The MPDC Superintendent recommended the Commissioners consider "a regulation concerning this evil."

The late 1950s-early '60s also saw considerable discussion of wild pigeons, with (of course) no resolution. "The pigeons are causing hysteria around our house," wrote a correspondent to the Evening Star. The Manor Park Citizens' Association asked the city to spray trees "to scare away birds." A lady living near Dupont Circle attached a fringe of "76-cent feather dusters" atop her house – with success. A Minnesota company supplied traps that captured many on downtown buildings, where they mostly starved. A man from Austin, Texas offered to buy all the District's pigeons, but did not say how he would take them or what he wanted them for.

A report of 1916 (stating that 294 species inhabited the capital) commented on another offending bird: "Grackles stroll about the parks and Capitol grounds with a dignity suggesting that they are successfully imitating the senatorial gait."

Squirrels fared much better in public opinion. Their chief human enemies were not irate citizens but hunters and couturiers, the latter instigating a squirrel-fur craze in the 1920s. Another natural foe had apparently quit the scene by that time: "A few years ago it was thought impossible for the small boy to resist stoning birds or squirrels in the public parks, but no one disturbs them now [1925]."[4]

Public fondness for "our dear little squirrels" is wonderfully illustrated (unexpectedly) in the regular correspondence between public and the U.S. Capitol's Superintendent of Grounds regarding their comfort and welfare (along with an occasional inquiry about birds), dating from the beginning of the century into the 1960s: offers to donate them to the Capitol, requests for Capitol squirrels from other institutions (the

---

[4] Perhaps; Times-Herald, 28 July 1940, p. C12 cites as hazards to the little furry creatures "rifles and slingshots in the hands of boys, and adults as well." See the dangerous boy cited in Appendix D12. For a contrasting attitude (in agricultural California) see Wash. Post, 16 Apr 2017, p. C3.

Soldiers' Home in Washington, for example; only the Altoona (PA) Hospital seems to have been accommodated), a small number of complaints ("they drive away the birds," send them to Rock Creek Park), and most consistently concern about their housing and alimentary needs. The Capitol put out squirrel boxes until the 1950s (at first purchased from the Schmid Emporium, later made in its own shop). Growers sent offers (and advertisements) of bulk nuts for their winter feeding; a man from Indiana supplied ten barrels in 1912 and had to be politely turned down for many years thereafter.

A new Superintendent in 1944 audaciously declared squirrels a nuisance and a danger to young trees, but confessed "that any war to the death against the critters would have repercussions from the thousand sightseers who annually feed and fondle them."

Squirrels were so lovable that they appeared prominently in ads for new, bucolic suburban divisions. Dogs were prohibited from the Capitol grounds and Lafayette Park to protect them (and songbirds); when the city heavily trimmed downtown trees in 1934 the Park Service put out 132 wooden boxes as emergency housing for them; the same Park Service scattered peanuts (2,000 quarts) for them in winter, as did citizens and the Boy Scouts, encouraged to do so by the Humane Society. This sentiment was not confined to Washington – when squirrels died in numbers at the Virginia state capitol the groundskeeper attributed this to overeating. "They have been waxing fatter and lazier, sometimes refusing to give the public sitting room on the park benches."[5] In the deepening Depression Clarence Gale willed $100 to WHS "for the care of the squirrels, . . . in appreciation of the pleasure given his mother by [their] antics [in] the park." The National Zoo proposed a program to protect "homeless squirrels."

Starlings/pigeons*: Evening Star, 2 Feb 1928, p. 8 (the earliest newspaper letter); 5 Nov 1931, p. 8; 26 Nov 1933, p. 15; 2 May 1956, p. 52; 22 May 1960, p. H12; Wash. Post, 9 Dec 1928, p. M28; 26 Nov 1929, p. 1 (in which the Post offers $50 for the most effective suggested solution and $10 for the most humorous); 28 Nov 1933, p. 13; 3 Dec 1933, p. M24; 28 Jan 1935, p. 6; 6 Jan 1937, p. 1 (owls); Evening Star, 7 Nov 1947, p. 41; Wash. Post, 5 Feb 1949, p. B1; 3 May 1949, p. B1; 6 Apr 1957, p. B1; 10 Nov 1962, p. A1; citizens' letters and some other material from National Archives, NCPC files, RG 351, Entry 21 "General Files", file 1-100 "Animals, Fowl & Wildlife (General)", file 1- 113 "Birds (General)"; WARL Exec Comm minutes, 27 Jan 1937; National Archives, RG 351, Entry 17 "Register of Letters Received" (letter, Sargent, 1964); (grackles) quoted in Evening Star, 17 July 1966, p. C6.* ***Squirrels****: Evening Star, (boys) 20 Apr 1925, p. 6; (Capitol) AOC archives, "animals"; (sightseers) Wash. Post, 25 Sept 1944, clipping, AOC archives; (boxes, with picture) Times-Herald, 28 July 1940, p. C12; (Virginia) Evening Star, 15 Aug 1925, p. 5; (Allen) 21 Aug 1930, p. 17; (Park Service) 31 Oct 1926, pt. 2 p. 8; 10 Jan 1930, p. 8; undated 1934 (file clipping Wash Div); Wash. Daily News, 17 Dec 1937 (file clipping Wash Div); (Zoo)Wash. Times, 10 Aug 1938, p. 5; Times Herald, 28 July 1940, p. C12. For a sketch of squirrels at the White House, see Jonathan Pliska's article in White House History, cited below in "Sources for Further Research," and Wash. Post, 15 Apr 2018, p. C3.*

In-Town Hunting

What recourse did the average Washingtonian have when irritated by feathered and furry pests? The District government several times emphasized to citizens that it had no provision for routing such nuisances as wild birds or squirrels, but that police regulation 302 "Taking of depredating wildlife" – one of the city's

---

[5] As times change so do attitudes – the Park Service removed the boxes in 1985 and undertook a major squirrel relocation effort. Official complaints included the "overeating" cavil. (Wash. Post, 11 Apr 2016, p. B3, with thanks to the doughty John Kelly)

Hunting regulations – allowed private citizens to protect their own property "by humane means . . . as may be reasonably necessary."

Apparently these restrictions had some effect: (1908) "No game . . . is being shot in the District except rabbits, [which] damage . . . young fruit trees, and then . . . only . . . on the property where the damage is done. No restriction is placed upon the killing of hawks, crows or owls of the larger variety." The District's great advocate for animal welfare, Virginia Sargent, wrote the Commissioners in 1964 urging that these laws require "humane disposal" of captured beasts.

Small animals had long been protected on the grounds of the Capitol and in federal parks of the District.

Evening Star, 15 Dec 1908, p. 9; Congressional acts "For the Protection of Birds, Game . . .", 3 Mar 1899, and 3 Mar 1901; National Archives, RG 351, Entry 17 "Register of Letters Received". A Congressional revision of District hunting and fishing laws was passed on 23 Aug 1958, followed by Comm Order 59-392 of 12 Mar 1959.

Protecting Animals in Wartime

An unexpected discovery of this research was the regular concern of the U.S. Government for animals in war situations. In 1916 the Department of War requested the American Humane Association to organize care of military animals – horses and mules – on the European front, resulting in formation of the American Red Star Animal Relief program.[6] WHS became early involved, raising funds. AHA framed this work (modeled after a British program) as having both humanitarian (for the animals) and economic (for the army) benefits.[7]

By the Second World War the Red Star had become "a civil defense organization for animals." With no animals employed in battle, its efforts turned to their protection during air raids, an event which of course did not occur in the U.S. The organization distributed pamphlets advising owners how to properly tag their pets, shelter them during air raids, and treat them for panic ("sodium bromide, or aspirin, from 2 to 10 grams, according to size, makes a good bromide for a fear-stricken animal") and injury. After the war, the project was renamed Red Star Animal Emergency Services and remains an active AHA effort.

The federal government, through the District Civilian Defense Department, organized an Animal Rescue Service "to provide care for dogs, cats, horses or cattle during possible enemy attack." The program was planned in conjunction with the local pound, humane organizations, animal hospitals and veterinarians. Its stated goals deserve to be copied in their entirety: "To protect human beings from panic-stricken or gas-contaminated animals during or after air raids; To prevent and alleviate suffering of animals resulting from air raids; To relieve air-raid wardens and other protective services of additional duties and responsibilities; To conserve the economic value of living or injured animals; and To give information and advice to animal owners on procedure during and after air raids."

The Service claimed ten animal ambulances, two pound wagons, 17 animal hospitals and 27 veterinarians at its call, and was headquartered at the WARL shelter. As fear of enemy attack subsided these well-laid plans became unnecessary and the project made inactive in December 1943.

---

[6] It will be remembered that WHS had expressed its concern for horses sent from the U.S. for use in the Boer War and the World War.

[7] A plaque placed on the east wall of the old State, War and Navy Building (now the Eisenhower Office Building) in 1921 states that 243,135 horses and mules served the American armed forces in the war, of which 68,682 died in battle (Evening Star, 14 Oct 1921, p. 17).

The final such effort uncovered survives in a series of 1950-51 memos in the WHS archives, in which an impressive collection of Washington-area humane organizations (WHS, WARL, APA, plus Arlington, Alexandria, Montgomery and Prince George's Counties' groups) met under the leadership of the AHA to plan protection of animals in the event of a nuclear attack. The resulting organization, "The Animal Relief in Atomic Emergency for the Metropolitan Area of Washington", mercifully was never needed.

(WW 1) Evening Star, 25 Mar 1917, p. 13; 10 June 1917, p. 15 (a substantial account); (WW 2)11 Jan 1942, p. 57; 10 June 1943, p. 33; 13 June 1943, p. 22; 11 Dec 1943, p. 4; (Atomic) Memo, organizing comm., 31 Jan 1951 et al. (in WHS archives). This last was modeled on a Massachusetts SPCA project. The ML King Library, Washingtoniana Division's vertical file "Animals" holds a brochure "The Handling of Animals Under Wartime Conditions" published by the American Red Star Animal Relief in 1942.

D14: Sources for Further Research

Here are some sources of information on ancillary topics uncovered during the research:

Archival Material

- *Extermination of rats and insects:* This was the responsibility of the Health Department. Note that the Board of Health considered the nuisance of flies at its August 1872 meeting and again in 1922, including distribution of a film "The Fearful Fly" *(Daily Critic, 14 Aug 1872, p. 3; Wash. Times, 2 Aug 1921, p. 15)* and rats in 1909 and 1922 *(Evening Star, 12 July 1909, p. 2; 14 Apr 1922, p. 1)*.
- *Police dogs:* See CFA approval of a new facility at Blue Plains, May 1980 at CFA (thanks to Mr. Tony Simon for pointing this out to me).
- *Hunting with dogs:* See Congressional Acts of 3 Mar 1899, and 30 June 1906; and a memo in DC General Files 1-106 "Dogs" at NARA
- *DC Government animals:* See the Veterinarian's Ann Rpt; each department also generally reported on the animals under its control, usually under the heading "Horses".
- *Dairies:* Reported annually in the Health Officer Ann Rpt.
- *Inspection of animals intended for slaughter:* Also reported in the Health Officer Ann Rpt.
- *Slaughterhouses, rendering plants:* The annual MPDC reports of the Sanitary Company, in its earliest years, discuss rendering plants and slaughterhouses in the District in some detail; after that the Sanitary Inspector of the Health Department oversaw these activities. The 1881 Sanitary Inspection found 17 in Washington (and none in Georgetown). "Slaughtering has practically ceased in all places in the District of Columbia save at the Benning abattoir . . . A few calves and sheep are killed at small houses in the city and suburbs" (HO Ann Rpt, 1904).
- *Efforts to protect birds, game animals and (less frequently) fish in parks:* Many Congressional proposals regarding this issue appear in the Congressional Record in the late 19th and early 20th centuries; see also "Game" in Webb.
- *"Dog and Pony Shows":* Also appears with some regularity in the Congressional Register.
- *Dog fights* were a standard item in the MPDC Annual Reports into the 20th century.

Many of these issues are conveniently addressed in Webb.

Further reading

This list of selected sources was compiled by Dr. Bernard Unti of the Humane Society of the United States.

Animal Abuse and Cruelty

Cottesloe, Gloria, <u>Lost, Stolen, or Strayed: The Story of the Battersea Lost Dog's Home</u>. London: David and Charles, 1971.

Lockwood, Randall, and Frank Ascione, eds., Cruelty to Animals and Interpersonal Violence. West Lafayette, Indiana: Purdue University Press, 1998.

Mechem, Kirke, "The Bullfight at Dodge", Kansas Historical Quarterly 3 (Aug. 1933): 294-308.

Thurston, Mary Elizabeth, The Lost History of the Canine Race. New York: Avon Books, 1996.

Animal Research and Experimentation

Buettinger, Craig, "Antivivisection and the Charge of Zoophile Psychosis in the Early Twentieth Century", The Historian 55 (Winter 1993): 277-88.

Buettinger, Craig, "Sarah Cleghorn, Antivivisection, and Victorian Sensitivity About Pain and Cruelty", Vermont History, 62 (Spring 1994): 89-100.

Buettinger, Craig, "Women and Anti-Vivisection in Late Nineteenth-Century America", Journal of Social History 30 (June 1997): 857-72.

French, Richard D., "Animal Experimentation: Historical Aspects", in Warren T. Reich, ed., Encyclopedia of Bioethics. New York: Free Press, 1978. Volume 1, 75-79.

Gossel, Patricia P., "William Henry Welch and the Anti-Vivisection Legislation in the District of Columbia, 1896-1900", Journal of the History of Medicine 40 (1985): 404-7.

Human Vivisection: Foundlings Cheaper than Animals. Washington, D.C.: Humane Society, 1901.

Lederer, Susan E., "Political Animals: The Shaping of Biomedical Research Literature in Twentieth-Century America", Isis 83 (1992): 61-79.

Lederer, Susan E., Subjected to Science: Human Experimentation in America Before the Second World War. Baltimore: The Johns Hopkins University Press, 1995.

Leffingwell, Albert, M.D., The Vivisection Question. New Haven: Tuttle, Morehouse, and Taylor, 1901.

Leffingwell, Albert, M.D., An Ethical Problem, or Sidelights Upon Scientific Experimentation on Man and Animals. New York: C.P. Farrell, 1914.

Parascandola, J., "Physiology, Propaganda, and Pound Animals: Medical Research and Animal Welfare in Mid-Twentieth Century America. Journal of the History of Medicine and Allied Sciences, 62 (2007): 277-315.

Proceedings of the International Anti-Vivisection and Animal Protection Congress, Held at Washington, DC, Dec. 8th-11th, 1913. New York: The Tudor Press, 1913.

Unti, Bernard, "'The doctors are so sure that they only are right': The Rockefeller Institute and the Defeat of Vivisection Reform in New York, 1908-1914", in Darwin H. Stapleton, ed., Creating a Tradition of Biomedical Research. New York, 2004, 175-89.

Westermann-Cicio, Mary L., "Of Mice and Medical Men: The Medical Profession's Response to the Vivisection Controversy in Turn of the Century America", Ph.D., diss., State University of New York, Stony Brook, 2001.

Animals in American Society

Biehler, Dawn Day, Pests in the City – Flies, Bedbugs, Cockroaches, and Rats. Seattle WA: University of Washington, 2013.

Brandow, Michael, New York's Poop Scoop Law: Dogs, Dirt, and Due Process. West Lafayette IN: Purdue University Press, 2008.

Brown, Frederick, "Cows in the Commons, Dogs on the Lawn: A History of Animals in Seattle", Ph.D., diss., University of Washington, 2010.

Dickey, Bronwen, Pit Bull: The Battle Over an American Icon. New York: Vintage Books, 2017.

Greene, Ann N., Horses at Work: Harnessing Power in Industrial America. Cambridge: Harvard University Press, 2008.

Grier, Katherine C., Pets in America. Chapel Hill: University of North Carolina Press, 2006.

Lindsay, Samuel, ed., Legislation for the Protection of Animals and Children. New York: Columbia University Press, 1914.

Mason, Jennifer, Civilized Creatures: Urban Animals, Sentimental Culture, and American Literature, 1850-1900. Baltimore: Johns Hopkins University Press, 2005.

Mighetto, Lisa, Wild Animals and American Environmental Ethics. Tucson: University of Arizona Press, 1991.

Pearson, Susan J., The Rights of the Defenseless: Animals, Children and Sentimental Liberalism in Nineteenth-Century America. Chicago: University of Chicago Press, 2010.

Schaffer, Michael Curie, One Nation under Dog: America's Love Affair with Our Dogs. New York: Holt, 2010.

Tarr, Joel, "A Note on the Horse as an Urban Power Source," Journal of Urban History 25 (March 1999): 434-48.

The Humane Movement

Blaisdell, John, "170 Years of Caring: The Animal Welfare Movement in Bangor, Maine", Maine History 39, 3 (2000): 186-203.

Carson, Gerald, Men, Beasts, and Gods: A History of Cruelty and Kindness to Animals. New York: Charles Scribner's Sons, 1972.

Daitch, Vicki M., "The Transformation of the Animal Welfare Movement in the United States 1950-1975". Ph.D. diss., University of Illinois at Chicago, 2000.

Davis, Janet, The Gospel of Kindness: Animal Welfare and the Making of Modern America. New York: Oxford University Press, 2016.

Finsen, Lawrence, and Finsen, Susan, The Animal Rights Movement in America. New York: Twayne Publishers, 1994.

Hubbard, Floyd Morse, Prevention of Cruelty to Animals in the States of Illinois, Colorado, and California. New York: Columbia University Press, 1916.

Hubbard, Floyd Morse, Prevention of Cruelty to Animals in the States of New York. New York: Columbia University Press, 1916.

Krows, Marion Soteman, The Hounds of Hastings: The Welfare of Animals in a Small Town. With a foreword by Sydney Haines Coleman. New York: Columbia University Press, 1938.

McCrea, Roswell, The Humane Movement: A Descriptive Survey. New York: Columbia University Press, 1910.

McShane, Clay, "Gelded-Age Boston", New England Quarterly 74 (June 2001): 274-302.

Shultz, William J., The Humane Movement in the United States. New York: Columbia University Press, 1924.

Slade, D. D., Killing Animals Humanely. Boston: MSPCA, 1872.

Stillman, William O., "The Prevention of Cruelty to Animals", in "Organization for Social Work", Proceedings of the Academy of Political Science. New York: Columbia University Press, 1912.

Swallow, William A., Quality of Mercy: A History of the Humane Movement in the United States. Boston: MSPCA, 1963.

Turner, James, Reckoning with the Beast: Animals, Pain, and Humanity in the Victorian Mind. Baltimore: The Johns Hopkins University Press, 1980.

Rowan, Andrew, "The Development of the Animal Protection Movement," Journal of NIH Research 1 (Nov.-Dec. 1989): 97-100.

Unti, Bernard, [with William DeRosa], "Trends in Humane Education, Past, Present and Future", State of the Animals 2003. Washington DC: Humane Society Press, 2003.

Unti, Bernard, [with Andrew Rowan, D. Phil.], "A Social History of Animal Protection in the Post-World War Two Period", State of the Animals 2001. Washington DC: Humane Society Press, 2001.

Unti, Bernard, "The Quality of Mercy: Organized Animal Protection in the United States 1865-1930," Ph.D. diss., American University, 2002.

Unti, Bernard, "Cruelty Indivisible: Historical Perspectives on the Link between Cruelty to Animals and Interpersonal Violence", in Frank N. Ascione, ed., International Handbook of Theory, Research, and Application on Animal Abuse and Cruelty. West Lafayette, IN: Purdue University Press, 2008.

Wang, Jessica, "Dogs and the Making of the American State: Voluntary Association, State Power, and the Politics of Animal Control in New York City, 1850-1920", The Journal of American History, March 2012: 998-1024.

Individuals and Organizations

Angell, George T., Autobiographical Sketches and Personal Recollections. Boston: AHES, n.d.

Barnes, Joseph, "Friend of Every Friendless Beast", Rochester History 35 (Oct. 1973): 1-24.

Bridges, Lamar W., "An Editor's Views on Anti-Cruelty: Eliza Jane Nicholson of the Picayune", Journal of Mississippi History 39, 4 (1977): 303-16.

Coleman, Sydney, Humane Society Leaders in America, With a Sketch of the Early History of the Humane Movement in England. Albany: AHA, 1924.

Covotsos, John, et al., The Illinois Humane Society, 1869-1979. River Forest, IL: Rosary College Graduate School of Library Science, 1981.

Freeberg, Ernest Frithiof, A Traitor to His Species: Henry Bergh and the Birth of the Animal Rights Movement. New York: Basic Books, 2020.

Heap, John P., "History of the Washington Humane Society", Records of the Columbia Historical Society 25 (1923): 57-61.

Kaufman, Martin, and Herbert J. Kaufman, "Henry Bergh, Kit Burns, and the Sportsmen of New York", New York Folklore Quarterly 28 (March 1972): 15-29.

[Monahan, Linda], Such Courage, Such Heart: A Centennial History of the Washington Animal Rescue League. Washington, DC: WARL, 2014.

Morris, Elizabeth, Origin and History of the Morris Animal Refuge Association for Homeless and Suffering Animals. Philadelphia: The Association, 1903.

Ohio State Society for the Prevention of Cruelty to Children and Animals, The Ohio State SPCCA: Its Work and Its Needs, 1886.

Palmer, Virginia A., "Lenore H. Cawker, The Animals' Friend", Milwaukee History 2, 2 (1979): 43-48.

Silver Festival of the Women's Branch of the Pennsylvania Society for the Prevention of Cruelty to Animals. Philadelphia: 1893.

Steele, Zulma, Angel in Top Hat: A Biography of Henry Bergh. New York: Harper and Brothers, 1942.

Unti, Bernard, Protecting All Animals: A Fifty-Year History of The Humane Society of the United States 1954-2004. Washington DC: Humane Society Press, 2004.

Women's Branch, PSPCA, A Few Concise Rules for the Management of Dogs. Philadelphia: Women's Branch, PSPCA,1878.

WSPCA, Outline of the History of the Women's SPCA. Philadelphia: WSPCA, 1908.

Legislation and Court Rulings

Animal Welfare Institute, Animals and Their Legal Rights: A Survey of American Laws from 1641-1990. Washington, DC: Animal Welfare Institute, 1990.

Favre, David, and Vivian Tsang, "The Development of Anti-Cruelty Laws During the 1800s," Detroit Law Review (Spring 1993): 1-35.

Kelch, Thomas G., "A Short History of (Mostly) Western Animal Law: Part I." *Animal L.*, 19 (2012), 23.

Kelch, Thomas G., "A Short History of (Mostly) Western Animal Law: Part II." *Animal L.*, 19 (2012), 347.

Michigan State University, Animal Legal and Historical Center: https://www.animallaw.info

Lindsay, Samuel, ed., Legislation for the Protection of Animals and Children. New York: Columbia University Press, 1914.

United States Congress, Senate Committee on Agriculture and Forestry, Hearings Before the Committee on Agriculture and Forestry of the Senate of the United States on S. 5566, Amending an Act to Prevent

Cruelty to Animals While in Transit by Railroad or Other Means of Transportation. Washington DC: Government Printing Office, 1908.

Williams, Frank Backus, Legislation for the Protection of Animals and Children. New York: Columbia University Press, 1914.

Presidential Pets and Other Mascots

Algeo, Matthew, Abe & Fido: Lincoln's Love of Animals and the Touching Story of his Favorite Canine Companion. Chicago: Chicago Review Press, 2015.

Bausum, A., Sergeant Stubby: How a Stray Dog and His Best Friend Helped Win World War I and Stole the Heart of a Nation. Washington DC: National Geographic Books, 2014.

Brun, James, Owney of the Railway Mail Service. Washington DC: National Postal Museum, 1990.

Janis, Brooke, and Rowan, R., First Dogs: American Presidents & Their Best Friends. Chapel Hill NC: Algonquin Books, 1997.

Kelly, Niall, Presidential Pets. New York: Abbeville Press, 1992.

Pickens, Jennifer B., Pets at the White House. Dallas: Fife & Drum Press, 2012.

Schank, Katie Marages, "White House Pets". Washington DC: White House Historical Association, 2007.

"Nature and Wildlife in the President's Park," White House History, The Quarterly Journal of the White House Historical Association, No. 43 (Fall 2016).

Veterinary History

Jones, Susan D., Valuing Animals: Veterinarians and their Patients in Modern America. Baltimore: Johns Hopkins University Press, 2003.

Sharrar, G. Terry, "The Great Glanders Epizootic, 1861-1866: A Civil War Legacy", Agricultural History 69 (Winter 1995): 79-97.

Swabe, Joanna, Animals, Disease and Human Society: Human-Animal Relations and the Rise of Veterinary Medicine. London: Routledge, 1999.

Teigen, Philip, "Nineteenth-Century Veterinary Medicine as an Urban Profession", Veterinary Heritage 23 (2000): 1-5.

Teigen, Philip, "Reading and Writing Veterinary History", Veterinary Heritage 24 (2001): 3-7.

BIBLIOGRAPHY

See Notes on Sources for a further discussion of these materials

Laws

For **texts of individual laws**:

- **Colonial and early Maryland State** laws are mostly taken from Kilty's compilation.
- **Corporation of the City of Washington, and of Georgetown** acts will be found in annual volumes titled "Acts of the Corporation of Washington", and "Ordinances of the Corporation of Georgetown". Those of the **County of Washington** survive in codes.
- Periodic compilations of Corporation laws ("**Codes**") in force at the time of the publication include laws otherwise not available, as do local newspapers, particularly the Daily National Intelligencer.
- Laws ("Acts") passed by the **Territorial Government** of 1871-74 were compiled chronologically in volumes.
- **Congressional laws** relating to Washington DC will be found in the volumes of "United States Statutes at Large", arranged chronologically.
- Orders of the **Temporary Commissioners** are found in the National Archives in volumes titled "Minutes, including Orders [of the Temporary Commissioners . . .]".
- Orders of the **Permanent Commissioners** from 1878 onward are likewise bound in a long series of volumes titled "Minutes, including Orders [of the Commsioners . . .]".

Books/compilations of laws and court rulings cited individually in the narrative footnotes and/or appendix:

Abert, William Stone, and Lovejoy, Benjamin G., <u>The Compiled Statutes in Force in the District of Columbia . . . 1887-'89</u>. Government Printing Office, Washington DC. 1894.

Callan, Nicholas, <u>Ordinances Passed by the Levy Court of the County of Washington, District of Columbia, from May 4, 1863, to May 4, 1868</u>. [Washington DC. 1868]

[Cranch, William], <u>Code of Laws for the District of Columbia: Prepared under the Authority of the Act of Congress</u>.........Davis & Force, Washington DC. 1819.

Cranch, William, <u>Reports of Cases Civil and Criminal in the United States Circuit Court of the District of Columbia From 1801 to 1841</u>. Little, Brown and Co., Boston MA. 1853.

Davis, William A, <u>The Acts of Congress in Relation to the District of Columbia, from July 16th, 1790 to March 4th, 1831, Inclusive</u>.........William A. Davis, Washington DC. 1831.

[D.C. Assembly Commission], Laws of the District of Columbia, Prepared by the commissioners appointed . . .. Government Printing Office, Washington DC. 1873.

District of Columbia Digest. Thomson West, St. Paul MN. c. 2006.

Hewitt, William, Digest of the General Acts of the Corporation of the City of Washington, to the First of January, 1818:.........Jacob Gideon, Jr., Washington DC. 1818.

Kilty, William, The Laws of Maryland. Frederick Green, Annapolis MD. 1799.

MacArthur, Arthur, Reports of Cases Argued and Determined in the Supreme Court of the District of Columbia, 1873-74. W.H. & O.H. Morrison, Washington DC. 1875-77.

Mackey, Franklin H., The Supreme Court of the District of Columbia, Sitting in General Term, from April 1, 1886, to July 11, 1887 (Mackey, Vol. V). Law Reporter Print, Washington DC. 1887.

Ould, Robert and Cross, William B. R., The Revised Code of the District of Columbia. A. O. P. Nicholson, Washington DC. 1857.

Rothwell, Andrew, Laws of the Corporation of the City of Washington to the End of the Thirtieth Council, June 1833 . . .. F. W. de Krafft, Washington DC. 1833

Sheahan, James W., Corporation Laws of the City of Washington, to the End of the Fiftieth Council . . . to which are added the laws enacted from June 3, 1853 to June 1, 1860. Robert A. Waters, Washington DC. 1860.

Thompson, M., An Analytical Digest of the Laws of the District of Columbia. W. M. Morrison, Washington DC. 1855.

Thompson, M., An Analytical Digest of the Laws of the District of Columbia. W. H. & O. H. Morrison, Washington DC. 1863.

[U. S. Government], Laws and Regulations Relating to Public Health in the District of Columbia in Force July 1, 1930. Government Printing Office, Washington DC. 1930.

U. S. Senate, A System of Civil and Criminal Law for the District of Columbia. (22nd Congress, 2nd Session, Doc. No. 85.) Duff Green, Washington DC. 1833.

Webb, William B., The Laws of the Corporation of the City of Washington. R. A. Waters, Washington DC. 1868.

Newspapers

Alexandria Gazette
Capital
City of Washington Gazette
Critic-Record (sometimes Daily Critic)
Daily National Intelligencer (sometimes National Intelligencer)
Daily National Republican (sometimes National Republican)
Daily Union
Evening Critic (later Washington Critic)
Evening Star (later Washington Star)
Evening Union
Federal Republican (Georgetown)
Georgetown Advocate
National Messenger (Georgetown)
National Tribune
Roll Call
Semi-Weekly Union
Spirit of Seventy-Six (Georgetown)
Star-News
Suburban Citizen
Washington Critic (also Evening Critic)
Washington Daily News
Washington Herald
Washington Post
Washington Star (later Star-News)
Washington Times (sometimes The Times, or the Morning and the Evening Times; also the later Wash Times)
Washington Times-Herald

Newspapers from other cities are cited individually in the footnotes.

Government Documents

For convenience, listings of materials only available as manuscripts at the National or District Archives include the Record Group and Entry numbers.

Corporations of Washington and Georgetown Assembly journals
Corporations of Washington and Georgetown Register annual reports

Territorial Legislature journal

Annual reports of:

> Commissioners
> Board of Health/Health Officer/Health Dept
> Metropolitan Police Dept
> Auditor
> Collector of Taxes
> Attorney for the District/Corporation Counsel
> Poundmaster
> Street Cleaning Dept/Engineer Dept: Division of Street Cleaning/City Refuse Division

District Board of Health minutes, 1822-78 (DC Archives, Record Group 165, Vols 1-3)
Metropolitan Police regulations
District tax assessments
District building permits
District Surveyor records
District of Columbia Supreme Court records (NARA, Record Group 21, Entry 60 "Law Case Files, 1863-1938"; Entry 69 "Equity Case Files, 1863-1938")
District of Columbia General Files (NARA, Record Group 351, Entry 21 "General Files", boxes 73-75)
Letters Received by the District Commissioners (NARA, Record Group 351, Entry 15 "Subject Indexes to Letters Received, 1874-1897"; Entry 17, "Register of Letters Received, 1874-1897")
Opinions of the Attorney for the District/Corporation Counsel (NARA, Record Group 351, Entry 25 "Index to Opinions of the Office of Corporation Counsel, 1874-1953"; Entry 26 "Opinions of the Office of Corporation Counsel, 1874-1953")
District of Columbia Council Hearings (NARA, Record Group 351, Entry 45 "Hearing Files, 1967-1974", "Dogs, Stray")

U.S. Senate and House of Representatives, testimony regarding the budget of the District of Columbia (cited here in this way: <u>Hearings on the District of Columbia Appropriations Bill for 1907 (House)</u>, 7 Mar 1906, pp. 734-739)
U.S. Capitol, Architect of the Capitol files (AOC archives, "Animals")
U.S. Census records

Commission of Fine Arts minutes
National Capital Planning Commission records (NARA, Record Group 328, Entry 7 "Planning Files 1924-67")

Other Documents

"Affairs in the District of Columbia" (42nd Cong/2nd session, HR Rpt 72). Government Printing Office, Washington DC. 1872.

Association of Oldest Inhabitants archive (at WHS)

Bryan, Wilhelmus B., "Bibliography of the District of Columbia to 1898" for the Columbia Historical Society. Government Printing Office, Washington DC. 1900.

Norton, George H., "A History of Four Generations of Norton & Company". ms, Washington DC. 1970. (Deposited with other material at Washingtoniana Div)

[Osborn, Irwin S.,] "Disposal of Garbage in the District of Columbia" (64th Cong/1st session, HR Doc 661). Government Printing Office, Washington DC. 1916.

Senate Committee on the District of Columbia, "Giving Police Power To and Increasing Salary of Poundmaster of the District of Columbia" (71th Cong/2nd session, S Rpt 723). Government Printing Office, Washington DC. 1930.

Senate Committee on the District of Columbia, "Prevention of Cruelty to Animals" (61th Cong/2nd session, S Rpt 425). Government Printing Office, Washington DC. 1910.

Society for the Prevention of Cruelty to Animals (Washington DC)/Washington Humane Society annual reports; WHS Executive Committee minutes, misc materials

Washington Animal Rescue League annual reports; WARL Secretary annual reports (always in April); Directors/Executive Committee minutes; by-laws

Washington Animal Rescue League pamphlets: "A Few Facts", 1931?; "A Day at the Washington Rescue League", by 1941; "Please! Cooperate with the Washington Animal Rescue League to Save Strays", ca. 1942; "The Twins Begin to Learn the Happiness of Owning a Pet", 1950?; Community Chest funding application, 1950; New shelter dedication brochure, 1977; other, miscellaneous documents cited in text.

Worden, Louise C., "A Poorhouse Paradise for Animals: A place worth visiting in the nation's capital", in Outdoors Pictorial, Washington DC. Late 1920s. (From NHES archives)

Einstein family graves, Washington Hebrew Cemetery, Washington DC.

Repositories

All of the above-listed documents can be found at:

National Archives (NARA)
District of Columbia Archives
Historical Society of Washington, Kipplinger Library
Library of Congress (Manuscript Division, Law Library)
ML King Library (Washington DC), Washingtoniana Division

The George Washington University, Gelman Library (Special Collections)
The George Washington University, Burns Law Library (Special Collections)
Washington Humane Society archives*
Washington Animal Rescue League archives*
National Humane Education Society archives
U.S. Capitol, Architect of the Capitol archives
Commission of Fine Arts archives

* Now merged at the Oglethorpe Street facility.

DC building permits are summarized on a comprehensive database accessible at the Washingtoniana Division of the ML King Library.

Useful **websites for these documents** are:

- Corporation acts/ordinances, codes and court reporters:
  Hathi Trust: http://www.hathitrust.org/
  Google Books: http://books.google.com/
- US Statutes at Large: http://www.constitution.org/uslaw/sal/sal.htm
- Congressional documents:
  http://memory.loc.gov/ammem/amlaw/lawhome.html
- Census reports:
  http://www.census.gov/prod/www/decennial.html
- Commissioners annual reports on the ProQuest databank, "U.S. Serial Set" (accessible in Washington DC at the National Archives, and the Law Library of the LOC), and (accessible generally, but a less complete set) on the Washingtoniana Division's site:
  http://digdc.dclibrary.org/cdm/

Newspapers can be accessed (and searched) through these **websites**:

Genealogy Bank: http://www.genealogybank.com/gbnk

Library of Congress/Chronicling America:
http://chroniclingamerica.loc.gov

ProQuest: http://dclibrary.org/node/214

A small number of newspaper articles are taken from dated clippings in the vertical files of the Washingtoniana Division of the ML King Library: "Animals" (for example, those relating to Squirrels in the appendix) or "Soc. & Clubs – Animal Rescue League", and marked as such.

Published Sources

American Humane Association, "Humane Directory". American Humane Association, Albany NY. 1949.

Briggs, Anna C., For the Love of Animals: The story of the National Humane Education Society. National Humane Education Society, n.p. c. 1990.

City directories

Dickens, Charles, American Notes for General Circulation. Chapman and Hall, London. 1842.

Free, Ann Cottrell, "No Room, Save in the Heart", in *Washingtonian* (April 1971). Washington DC.

Gilmore, Matthew B., "Washington DC History Resources: District of Columbia Population History". https://matthewbgilmore.wordpress.com/district-of-columbia-population-history.

Heap, John P., "History of the Washington Humane Society", in *Records of the Columbia Historical Society*, vol. 25. CHS, Washington DC. 1923.

Kelly, Joseph T., "Memories of a Lifetime in Washington", in *Records of the Columbia Historical Society,*
vol. 31/32. CHS, Washington DC. 1930.

[Monahan, Linda], Such Courage, Such Heart: A Centennial History of the Washington Animal Rescue League. Privately printed, WARL. 2014.

Muller, John, Mark Twain in Washington, D.C. – The Adventures of a Capital Correspondent. The History Press, Charleston SC. c. 2013.

Pet Lovers Companion. P.O. Box 239, Mount Vernon VA 22121. 2013-14 edition.

Schmeckebier, Laurence F., The District of Columbia – Its Government and Administration. The Johns Hopkins Press, Baltimore MD. c. 1928.

Townsend, George Alfred "Gath", Washington, Outside and Inside. James Betts & Co., Hartford CN. c. 1873.

Websites

Pet Finders (shelter/adoption, related resources):
https://www.petfinder.com/

Washington Humane Society:
http://support.washhumane.org/

Interviews/Private Communications

All interviewed and/or visited in early 2015

Mr. Jim Taylor, President, National Humane Education Society
Ms. Stephanie Shain, Chief Operating Officer, Washington Humane Society
Ms. Alexandra Feldt, Executive Affairs Manager, Washington Humane Society
Ms. Alison Putman, Director, Office of the CEO, Washington Humane Society
Ms. Susan Strange, Volunteer and Archivist, Washington Animal Rescue League

District government officials:

Mr. Johnny L. Gaither, Asst Assc Administrator, Solid Waste Collections Division, Dept of Public Works
Ms. Linda Grant, Public Information Specialist, Dept of Public Works
Dr. Vito R. DelVento, Program Manager, Animal Services Program, Dept of Health

Ms. Ingrid Newkirk, former Poundmaster (by email, January 2018)

NOTES ON SOURCES

Laws

The bibliography gives titles, etc. on sources of laws throughout the District's history. Some further notes will help researchers:

- The best collections of the annual **"Acts"** and **"Ordinances"** of the Corporations of **Washington and Georgetown** respectively (passed by their elected assemblies) are found on microfilm rolls in the Historical Society of Washington, the Washingtoniana Division of the city's ML King Library, and from the two websites cited below. Some annual books are in the Special Collections Division of the George Washington University's Gelman Library and Burns Law Library, the Library of Congress's Law Library, and in the National Archives (Record Group 351). Laws are given chronologically, and generally at the back of each volume is either a list of titles or a subject index. Ordinances of Georgetown begin with 1822 and run to 1871. Laws relating to the **County of Washington** (made by an appointed Levy Court) must, in effect, be found wherever they are found.
- Laws from missing years can generally be filled in from the periodic **Codes**, compiled both by order of the local government and as private ventures, although in some codes the date of passage is not always given, and so we know that the law was active as of a certain year but not when it passed. Early ordinances of Georgetown can be taken only from the Codes of 1811 and 1821. Washingtoniana, LOC, the Historical Society of Washington, and the two websites have good holdings of these legal compilations. Local **newspapers**, particularly the Daily National Intelligencer, published laws of the City of Washington, including some that were later withdrawn and so not published in official sources.

The **Journals** of the two Councils (complete on microfilm at Washingtoniana; original journals in the Manuscript Division of the Library of Congress for Georgetown, MSS 88088, only duplicates this) do not include texts of laws, only compressed accounts of discussions and actions day-by-day.

Many of the early codes and digests can be found at the very useful sites:

Hathi Trust: http://www.hathitrust.org/
Google Books: http://books.google.com/

- **Acts** (and journals) of the **Territorial Government** are kept on microfilm at Washingtoniana (1871-72) and LOC Law Library (1871-73). Acts of the full 1871-74 period can be consulted in two large and impressive volumes of the official copies at the National Archives (RG 351, Entry 4 "Laws of the Legislative Assembly").
- **Laws** of the **U.S. Congress** relating to Washington DC (and any other topic) are printed for each successive Congress in volumes titled "United States Statutes at Large" and are easily consulted in the Archives or online (http://www.constitution.org/uslaw/sal/sal.htm). Also useful for federal laws of the period are the Congressional Record, journals and hearings, kept on shelves in the Legislative Study Reading Room just off of the main reading room. Texts of laws proposed but not passed and related Congressional documents and reports can easily be consulted at the Library of Congress' Law Library.

- **Orders** of the **Temporary Commissioners** from 1874 to 1878 are kept in the National Archives (RG 351, Entry 12 "Minutes, including Orders [of the Temporary Commissioners . . .]"), indexed – one volume for minutes and two for orders. Unfortunately the second of the two volumes of orders is missing.
- **Orders** of the **Commissioners** from 1878 to 1952 are found in 73 large volumes at the National Archives (RG 351, Entry 14 "Minutes, including Orders [of the Commissioners . . .]"). Each volume includes a subject index. The annual Commissioners reports also include (for some years) their orders of the previous year but only those of broad import and with no index.
- **Court Decisions** will be found in the various court reporters collected by Cranch, MacArthur, Mackey and others, all listed in the bibliography if specifically used here; The District of Columbia Digest seems comprehensive and takes these cases into the early 21st century. The original pleadings (for cases cited here) can be found in the DC Equity Court holdings at the National Archives.
- **Ordinances** of the **Board of Health** (to 1878) and the later **Health Officer** (after 1903 **Department**) are not available in any systematic collection, but can often be found in the Health Officer Annual Reports, or reprinted or summarized in the local newspapers. The ms. **Minutes of the Board of Health** (1822-78) in the DC Archives are not much help in this regard.
- **Regulations** of the **Police Department** were compiled at irregular intervals and available in the LOC Law Library. **Police orders** (internal bulletins), issued at the rate of several a week and announcing new administrative and legal procedures, were collected (in very brief format) in the MPDC annual reports for about ten years from the mid-1900s.
- Good compilations of **all District laws and regulations relating to health issues** will be found in the various codes referenced in the bibliography, particularly that by Webb and the 1930 publication Laws and Regulations. The annual reports of the Health Officer include such compilations in 1897, 1900, 1903, 1908 and 1912; some other annual reports give the health-related laws and ordinances passed in the preceding year (the first such is 1896).

Annual Reports and Other Materials

Most annual reports (Poundmaster, Health Officer, Police, SPCA/WHS) are relatively short and in consistent format, and are cited here only by year, the specific page being unnecessary.

For the convenience of later researchers, the following table gives the page number of the Commissioners Annual Reports in which the **Poundmaster Reports** will be found.

Page numbers for 1874-77 refer to the annual Board of Health reports, which were generally issued in a fuller form separately from the summary published in these early Commissioners Report. Pages after 1878 refer to the annual Commissioners Reports, which before 1897 were paginated sequentially throughout but after then separately by volume; page numbers from 1897 on refer to Volume III, the Health Officer/Department Report. After 1933 the Commissioners Reports returned to one, sequentially-paginated volume. In 1937 the pound became an independent agency and was given the last place in the Commissioners Reports.

	In BoH Rpts		
1872	Evening Star, 18 Dec 1872, p. 1	1900	28-29
1873	Nat. Republican, 15 June 1874, p. 4	1901	25-26
1874	287	1902	24
1875	79-80	1903	23
1876	243 (also 10, 13-14)	1904	32-33, 83-84
1877	65-68	1905	26-27, 61-63
	In Comm Rpts	1906	44-47
1878	105-10 (also 89-90)	1911	36, 83-84, 86
1879	157-59	1912	34-35, 91, 93
1880	320-21	1913	60-61, 117-18, 120
1881	384-87	1914	30-31, 76, 79
1882	387-89	1915	31-32, 84-85, 88
1883	436-3	1916	31, 75, 78, 83
1884	305-06	1917	29, 66-67, 70, 75
1885	317-18	1918	23, 60-61, 67, 73
1886	466-67	1919	29, 78, 86
1887	736	1920	28, 60, 65, 72
1888	654	1921	22
1889	619-20	1922	22
1890	649-50	1923	18
1891	502-03	1924	15
1892	663-64	1925	16
1893	802	1926	14
1894	655	1927	None
1895	1083-84	1928	12
1896	978-79	1929	17
	In HO/HD Rpt (Comm Rpt, Vol. III)	1930	18
1897	40-42	1931	18
1898	29	1932	None
1899	35		**In HD Rpt (Single-Vol. Comm Rpt)**
1907	32, 91	1933	112
1908	29, 79	1934	143
1909	17-18, 65-67	1935	112-13
1910	24-25, 77-79	1936	157-58
		1937-40	Last page of Comm Rpts

Before 1875 there was no separate Poundmaster Report but merely a description of pound operations in the BoH Report; thereafter the BoH/HO Report included a specific PM Report, often written by the Poundmaster.

A full set of these reports has been deposited with the Washingtoniana Division of the ML King Library here in Washington DC. Complete Commissioners Reports are conveniently available on the ProQuest web site cited above. After 1923 the ProQuest reports become incomplete and one must use the Washingtoniana Division's set (available on-line; see the Bibliography), which ends with 1929. For those after 1930 I used the original copies at the National Archives.

Financial reports of the Corporation Registers of Washington and of Georgetown were sometimes bound at the end of the annual compilations of Acts and Ordinances of the two cities.

MPDC annual reports before 1878 were included with the annual reports of the Secretary of the Interior (1861-72) and the Attorney-General (1873-77) and can be read on the ProQuest database (US Serial Set); they are in the Commissioners Reports (Vol. I) thereafter.

Attorney of DC/Corporation Counsel; Auditor; Collector of Taxes; Board of Health/Health Officer/Health Department; Street Cleaning Dept/Engineer Dept (Div of Street Cleaning/City Refuse Div) all wrote annual reports included in the Commissioners Annual Reports.

The ms. minutes of the District **Board of Health** must be consulted at the DC Archives. They are not indexed and I have summarized those relating to animals and the pound in Appendix C1 to save future researchers the trouble of reading through them entirely, as I had to do.

Information from the **SPCA/WHS reports** is generally taken from the President's Report or the minutes of the Executive Committee. These are available on microfilm (and in the original volumes) at the Washingtoniana Division. The Society's Executive Committee reports (1910-27, 1936-40), with much valuable related material are available at the WHS archives and summarized for other years in the annual reports. **WARL reports/minutes** are found in the archives of that organization.

Most historical **newspapers** are now available on-line and searchable – a boon for serious researchers and a temptation for lazy ones. In some cases the on-line citation includes "page" which reflects the page number shown on the original publication; others show "image" which means the number of the page (image) counting from the paper's first page. Printed newspapers number each section separately, but an on-line newspaper article cited by image counts each page (image) simply from page one onward to the end as one sequence. In this study all articles are cited as "page" but in many cases are in fact "image" numbers. To further complicate matters, some databases show "Page" as one number higher than that of the original newspaper – that is, the database says p. 4 but the page number on the reproduced paper is clearly p. 3; I used that of the original whenever I could.

Plaque in the HRA shelter lobby
Photo by author

Made in the USA
Lexington, KY
19 December 2019